DISEASE AND HEALING IN THE NEW TESTAMENT

An analysis and interpretation

J. Keir Howard

University Press of America,® Inc.
Lanham · New York · Oxford

Library of Congress Cataloging-in-Publication Data

Howard, J. Keir (James Keir)
Disease and healing in the New Testament : an analysis and
interpretation / J. Keir Howard.
p.   cm
Includes bibliographical references and index.
1. Spiritual healing—Biblical teaching. 2. Bible. N.T.—Criticism,
interpretation, etc. I. Title.
BS2417.H37 H68   2001   234'.131'09015—dc21   2001027036 CIP

ISBN 0-7618-1979-7 (hardcover : alk. paper)

CONTENTS

iii

PREFACE

This study of disease and healing in the New Testament arises out of my concerns as a practising specialist physician, and also an ordained Anglican priest, with regard to the claims of the modern healing movement in the Christian Church. 'Healing' services, ranging from sacramental anointing to charismatic 'signs and wonders', are now to be found as regular features of the worship in most communions of the Church. Those involved in the healing movement claim that 'healing', a term rarely given adequate definition, was central to the early Christian mission and should be an essential part of today's proclamation of the gospel.

It is essential to ask, however, whether the New Testament documents actually provide the level of support for the Church's 'healing ministry' that is generally assumed. Many books have been written about Christian healing and even on healing in the biblical texts, but none, to my knowledge, has attempted a comprehensive and critical examination of the New Testament data from scientific and medical perspectives as well as theological. This book is an attempt to provide such an in-depth critical analysis and scientific interpretation of those passages in the New Testament which relate to disease and healing. Particular attention is given to the recorded healings by Jesus in the Gospels and by the apostles in Acts, attempting to relate them to modern medical concepts, particularly modern diagnostic categories. The curative/healing techniques that appear to have been used are also critically examined. The aim is thus to answer a number of key questions about the cure or healing of illness in the New Testament. Is there a consistent and coherent pattern in these healings? Does the evidence suggest that they are intrinsically credible events from the point of view of modern pathological understandings, allowing them to be classified as possible or probable happenings?   Further, by setting them into the socio-historical context of the time, is it possible to gain some idea of how the contemporaries of Jesus and his followers saw and interpreted their actions?   The New Testament letters are also examined in order to provide a complete picture and gain some idea of the place of 'healing' within ordinary Christian congregations in the first century of the Christian era.   There are immense difficulties in attempting to relate the technical concepts of modern medicine to the illnesses met in the New Testament which are generally defined solely on a symptomatic basis.   Nonetheless, no historical study of the New Testament can afford to omit this component and it is essential for any critical evaluation of the work of Jesus and his followers.   The completion of this task allows the final question to be answered, namely, of whether the New Testament documents genuinely provide the theological support for the modern healing movement that is so often claimed for it.

Inevitably, technical and medical terms are used in the book. Most, if not all, have been explained at some point in the text and it is hoped that this book will be sufficiently readable to be of value to all who study the New Testament.   There are particular groups who should find these pages helpful in gaining greater insight into the Gospel healing narratives as well as other passages dealing with disease and healing. These include students and their teachers in an academic setting, commentators on the New Testament, researchers in medical history and those engaged in New Testament research, as well as doctors and others with an interest in the medical aspects of the Bible.   It is also hoped that ministers who are looking for background to assist in sermon and study preparation will find much that is useful and stimulating in this study. Above all, it is hoped that this book will be of particular help to the many Christian folk who are asking questions about the claims of the modern healing and charismatic movements by providing a balanced exegesis of the relevant passages in the New Testament.

The debt to those who have previously explored the field of health and healing in the Bible is immense and I have attempted to record in the footnotes and references the extent of my indebtedness to those who have researched this area before me. I may frequently disagree with their conclusions, but I gratefully acknowledge my debt to their stimulus. My interest in the area of this study has extended over many years and I am grateful to the many friends, colleagues and students with whom I have debated these issues from time to time. I owe a particular debt of gratitude to the Revd Professor Clyde Curry Smith, of the University of Wisconsin, who supervised my PhD thesis for Fairfax University on which this book is based. He has given most generously of his time, talents and wisdom. He has continuously directed me towards fresh understandings and new ideas and I have valued immensely his scholarship, his critical mind and, above all, the friendship that this study has engendered. I also take this opportunity of expressing my thanks to the librarians at Victoria University of Wellington, St John's College, Auckland, the Royal Society of Medicine, London and the Hutt Hospital for their help and patience at various times. Many friends and colleagues have read and criticised all or part of the study at different stages of its development. In particular, I thank the Right Revd Dr Tom Brown, Bishop of Wellington, as well as the Revd Ray Oppenheim and the Revd Canon Colin Wright, in whose parishes I have had the privilege of ministering. Dr Stuart Mossman, Dr Chris Roy and Dr J.D.G. Worst have provided many useful ideas and comments and Mr Gavin Drew of the New Zealand Bible Society has brought his logical mind to bear on critical and philosophical issues. I also express my gratitude to Mr John Mabon who provided invaluable help with proof reading and pointed out numerous infelicities in the text as well as technical terms that needed explanation. I also thank Ms Beverley Baum, Production Editor of University Press of America, as well as her predessor, Ms Helen Hudson, and the editorial team for their help in manuscript preparation. Last, but certainly not least, it is my particular pleasure to record my thanks to my wife, Dorothy, for her patience and forbearance, true Christian virtues indeed, as well as her encouragement when often tempted to give up in the midst of a busy professional life.

J Keir Howard
Wellington, New Zealand
The Feast of St Luke, 2000

Note: Standard abbreviations have been used throughout this study for books of the Bible. As this is a study that attempts to link the 'sciences' of medicine and theology, journal titles have been given in full to prevent misunderstanding and confusion for readers not familiar with another area of literature. The first time that a reference is cited in each chapter, it is given in full and thereafter in a shortened form. In line with a growing trend, I have omitted accents in the Greek text, although I realise that this will offend purists.

Chapter 1

SETTING THE SCENE

Spiritual healing ... is being promoted in Christian circles as never before. ... We can no longer be interested in divine healing simply out of personal curiosity

Peter Masters

The period since the end of the Second World War in the western world has been marked by improvements in general health and well being that are probably unparalleled in any previous era of human history. At the same time, however, it has been a period of an almost morbidly neurotic preoccupation with personal health, safety and longevity. This is reflected at all levels of society, from governmental legislation, attempting to make life 'healthier' and 'safer', to the individual pursuit of health and so-called healthy living styles, reflected in the continuing flow of books about health and fitness, about living longer and personal fulfilment. The lack of familiarity with death and genuine sickness on the part of many in the developed nations, particularly when compared with previous generations, has led to a greater unwillingness to accept them and to increased and frequently unrealistic expectations of what normal medical services can provide. From the point of view of the medical profession, these preoccupations have been reflected, on the one hand, in the increased rates of litigation against doctors and other health professionals when their level of practice is believed to have fallen short of expectations and on the other, in the marked growth of interest in 'alternative' forms of treatment which are thought to offer better and 'safer' relief from symptoms than normal medical practice with its use of powerful drugs and technology [1].

The Christian Church has not been immune from this preoccupation with healing and the quotation at the head of this chapter underlines the quite extraordinary emphasis given to the subject in recent years. This has been associated with a variety of practices, ranging from sacramental healing with prayer and anointing at one end of the spectrum, to extreme forms of faith healing among charismatic and pentecostal groups at the other. Such a remarkable growth in religious healing practice cannot be ignored and this study of disease and healing in the New Testament is set against the background of a burgeoning healing movement in the Christian Church, particularly the remarkable claims and assumptions of the charismatic and related faith healers. These practitioners claim to base their actions on the evidence of the New Testament, expressing a belief that the apostolic church, as pictured in the Acts of the Apostles, experienced healing as an everyday event and this experience should be the obligatory model for church life and practice today. This conviction is coupled with an interpretation of certain New Testament texts that is designed to provide a basis for all Christians to claim a right to healing. There is no attempt to relate the New Testament to its cultural milieu: rather it is viewed as being literally applicable to the twentieth century in every respect [2].

In addition, these groups demonstrate a strong predilection towards irrational concepts of disease and healing, disease being frequently understood as the specific result of sin. Such concepts have shown a tendency to surface from time to time throughout recent history, but in real terms they belong to a period before there was any genuine understanding of pathological processes. The writer has remarked elsewhere, 'Until there was any proper understanding of the causative factors in disease and the actual disease processes themselves, there was a tendency to see sickness as the result of divine visitations and punishment for wrongdoing' [3]. In the absence of any other viable theory, disease was understood to be the result of failure to meet one's religious and moral obligations. The modern charismatic healing movement couples these ideas with assertions that certain disease entities are the direct and quite specific result of demonic possession, a return to understandings of disease causation that seem little removed from those in the witch hunting manuals of the sixteenth and seventeenth centuries. It is this selective fundamentalism, together with the emphasis on what is termed 'exorcism' or 'deliverance', that represent what are perhaps the most sinister aspects of the charismatic approach to healing [4].

At this point it is worth digressing to give some consideration to what actually is meant by the term 'healing'. It is common experience that ideas and concepts are often forced into the Procrustean beds of rigid preconceptions and prejudices [5]. The modern use of the word 'healing', either in the context of modern healing movements or in relation to the wide variety of forms of alternative medicine, seems very much to have followed this pattern. The word has been used in a very loose fashion and has become to all intents and purposes a portmanteau word carrying almost any meaning that may be given it at any particular time, somewhat after the fashion of Lewis Carroll's Humpty Dumpty: ' "When I use a word," Humpty Dumpty said in a rather scornful tone, "it means just what I choose it to mean - neither more nor less" ' [6].

Consequently, any consideration of healing as a concept, as well as any study of the claims and counter claims of those who practice the varying forms of 'healing', need to recognise that the word itself has become one of the many so-called 'weasel' words of modern society. From the standpoint of orthodox scientific medicine, at least, the word 'healing' tends to be found in what might be seen as 'bad company'. John Wilkinson has underlined the point that 'healing' is not a word that is much used in normal medical practice and remarks that, 'we shall find chapters on healing in books about alternative medicine and references to healing in articles by doctors whose medical orthodoxy is often in doubt. So much so, that for many doctors healing is synonymous with quackery. In other words healing is to be distinguished from the orthodox practice of medicine and the word is not used in polite circles' [7].

Medical practitioners, who tend to think in terms of discrete pathological processes, would, in general, prefer to use words such as, 'cure', 'recovery' or 'remission', depending on the specific context. Kleinman has suggested that healing represents a socio-cultural process that is associated with the management of illness rather than the treatment of disease [8]. Illness is essentially a construct that denotes the level of psychosocial distress that has been caused by a disease or as a result of other factors. In these terms, 'healing' does not relate to the cure of overt pathology, but rather the alleviation of inner distress. In this sense, as will be demonstrated in the study of the healing stories of the Gospels and Acts, the term healing is well suited to these narratives. The problem is, however, that in popular usage 'healing' essentially means that people have got better and this usually means that the disease process itself has been 'cured' or at least alleviated. Consequently, although this study adopts the term 'healing', it does so in relation to the concept of recovery from a disease, whether this is genuine cure or simply relief of symptoms to the extent that a person is able to resume a normal life. Further, as used, it does not necessarily imply permanent cure.

Somewhere Karl Popper remarked that, 'in politics and in medicine, he who promises too much is likely to be a quack' and it is this issue which requires to be to be faced squarely and addressed in an objective fashion. Attention needs to be given to two important questions. Firstly, it has to be asked whether the claims of modern charismatic, pentecostal and related faith healing groups that their practices are based on the theology and practice of the first century Church can be sustained. Such claims are based on the assumption that the New Testament documents present a unitary picture of early Christianity: a doubtful assumption in itself. Secondly, the subsidiary question has to be asked, whether the remarkable claims that are being made by the modern healing movement may be validated by proper objective and critical examination.

The latter issue, although of major importance, lies outside the purpose and scope of this study, the emphasis of which is upon an analysis and exegesis of the relevant passages of the New Testament. The major question to be investigated is simply whether the biblical accounts of healing and the general tenor of the New Testament documents and their references to disease and healing, will support the interpretations given to them by the charismatic and other healers. A second issue to be addressed is whether the Church of the first century, as reflected in the New Testament, pursued 'miraculous' healing with the same obsession as charismatic and related churches today. The study is deliberately limited to the New Testament, as this constitutes the fundamental documents of history and interpretation on which the Christian Church depends for its primary witness to the words and work of Jesus and the witness to him of the first Christians. It is also the base on which the claims for modern 'spiritual healing' are made. Later developments in thought and practice strictly lie outside the boundaries of this study which concentrates on the earliest documents of the Christian faith that provide the primary witness on which the modern 'healing movement', whether charismatic or non-charismatic, claims to base its practice. Nonetheless, some attention will be paid to the later growing emphasis on the place of the 'miraculous' in the experience of the expanding Church as this has had a marked effect on its thought and practice in subsequent centuries [9].

The approach will not be primarily theological, although of necessity theological issues will require to be discussed simply because the context will need examination, but the main task will be to examine reported events in both the Gospels and Acts and seek to apply modern diagnostic and therapeutic categories to them. The study will also look at passages in the New Testament letters that have a bearing on the theme of disease and healing from the same point of view. The examination of the data is thus conducted primarily from a medical standpoint. The study accepts that Jesus healed - the evidence is far too strong to dispute this and the issue will be discussed in more detail in the course of the study. It further accepts that there is no good reason to doubt that the apostles also healed, although probably to a lesser extent. The questions that it seeks to answer are, in the first place, 'What conditions did Jesus and the apostles heal?' and, secondly, 'How did Jesus and his apostles heal?' In addition, consideration is given to the supplementary question, 'Is there evidence that the early Church actively pursued a healing ministry that was an essential part of its evangelistic proclamation and a continuance of the ministry of Jesus?' The attempt is made, therefore, to look behind the explanations and theological interpretations offered in the texts and to investigate whether it is possible to uncover the nature of the various disease entities themselves as far as these are described together with the methods used to bring about cure or at least alleviation.

An attempt is made to distinguish carefully between recorded event and the interpretation given in the texts. Interpretations and explanations are inevitably culturally conditioned, but the event itself exists independently of its explanation. One may therefore accept the truth of the events recorded without necessarily accepting the interpretations given to them. All too often, because the text provides a 'supernatural' explanation, the event itself has been dismissed as fiction. As Stevan Davies has put it, 'historical scholarship has taken a supernatural explanation to be all there is to an historical fact when, rather, the fact was first and the explanation followed' [10]. To put this in another way, it is important to distinguish, and to distinguish clearly, between the reported event and the reported explanation. They are not the same. This study, therefore, will try to uncover the nature of the events and place them, as far as possible, within the context of modern medical diagnostic categories and look at the means that appear to have been used to effect cures and/or the alleviation of symptoms to the extent that people felt well once again and were able to resume a normal life. The other New Testament documents will also be examined to see what evidence they provide for a significant level of interest in, and also the practice of, the healing of diseases within the early Church, the life of which these documents reflect. It is, after all, only possible to make the claim that one's practice is based on that of the earliest Christian communities if it can be shown that these communities actually did what it is claimed they did.

Notes and references

[1] The rapid growth of 'alternative' medicine over the past twenty years or so has been extensively documented. Some representative studies are (in order of publication): Smith, T. (1983). Alternative medicine. *British Medical Journal.* 287.307; Fulder, S.J. and Munro, R.E. (1985). Complementary medicine in the United Kingdom: patients, practitioners and consultations. *Lancet.* ii. 542-545; Murray, J. and Shepherd, S. (1988). Alternative or additional medicine: a new dilemma for the doctor. *Journal of the Royal College of General Practitioners.* 38. 511-514; Knipschild, P., Kleijnen, J. and Riet, ter G. (1990). Belief in the efficacy of alternative medicine among general practitioners in the Netherlands. *Social Science and Medicine.* 31. 625-626; Marshall, R.J., Gee, R., Israel, M., *et al.* (1990). The use of alternative therapies by Auckland general practitioners. *New Zealand Medical Journal.* 103. 213-215; Thomas, K.J., Carr, J., Westlake, L. and Williams, B.T. (1991). Use of non-orthodox and conventional health care in Great Britain. *British Medical Journal.* 302. 207-210; MacLennan, A.H., Wilson, D.H. and Taylor, A.W. (1996). Prevalence and cost of alternative medicine in Australia. *Lancet.* 347. 569-573 and Eisenburg, D.M., Kessler, R.C., Foster, C. *et al.* (1998). Unconventional medicine use in the United States. *Journal of the American Medical Association.* 280. 1569-1575; Harris, P. and Rees, R. (2000). The prevalence of complementary and alternative medicine use among the general population: a systematic review of the literature. *Complementary Therapy and Medicine.* 8. 88-96

[2] For a brief overview see Richards, J. (1984). The Church's healing ministry and charismatic renewal. In: Martin, D. and Mullen, P. (eds). *Strange Gifts: A Guide to Charismatic Renewal.* Blackwell, Oxford. pp 151-158. For an extensive analysis of the movement to the mid-1970s see Harrell, D.E. (1975). *All Things are Possible: The Healing and Charismatic Revival in Modern America.* University of Indiana Press, Bloomington. The charismatic case is set out in detail in Williams, J.R. (1990). *Renewal Theology 2: Salvation, The Holy Spirit and Christian Living.* Academie Books, Grand Rapids. pp 367-375. See also Wimber, J. and Springer, K.N. (1987). *Power Healing.* Hodder

& Stoughton, London and Greig, G.S. and Springer, K.N. (eds), (1993). *The Kingdom and the Power.* Regal Books, Ventura, CA.

[3] Howard, J. Keir. (1993). Medicine and the Bible. In: Metzger, B.M. and Coogan, M. (eds). *The Oxford Companion to the Bible.* Oxford University Press, New York. p 509. The propitiatory inscriptions from temple sites in Lydia and Phrygia from the second and third centuries give clear evidence of the ancient belief that sickness is a divine punishment for sin and cure can be effected through rites of expiation (see Chaniotis, A. (1995). Illness and cures in the Greek propitiatory inscriptions and dedications of Lydia and Phrygia. *Clio Medica.* 28. 323-344).

[4] The list of books dealing with exorcism and 'deliverance' is endless. The following is but a sample: Subritsky, Bill. (1986). *Demons Defeated.* Sovereign World, Chichester; Prince, D. (no date). *Expelling Demons.* Derek Prince Ministries, Fort Lauderdale; Peterson, R. and Peterson, M. (1989). *Roaring Lion.* OMF, Singapore; Maxwell, W.H.A. (1989). *Demons and Deliverance.* Whitaker House, Springdale, PA. It should be noted, however, that exorcism is not confined to charismatic circles and both the Anglican and Roman Catholic churches, for example, still employ 'official' exorcists!

[5] In Greek mythology, Procrustes, it will be remembered, was the robber, who made all his victims, whether short or tall, fit into the same bed by a variety of unpleasant means.

[6] Carroll, Lewis. (1939=1872). *Through the Looking Glass,* In: *The Complete Works of Lewis Carroll.* Nonesuch Press. London. p 196. A good example of loose and confusing use of the word 'healing' will be found in the Church of England Report, (2000) *A Time to Heal: A Contribution to the Ministry of Healing.* (Church House, London).

[7] Wilkinson, J. (1986). Healing in semantics, creation and redemption. *Scottish Bulletin of Evangelical Theology.* 4: 17-37.

[8] Kleinman, A. (1980). *Patients and Healers in the Context of Culture.* University of Califormia Press, Berkeley, CA. See also, Pilch, J.J. (2000). *Healing in the New Testament: Insights from Medical and Mediterranean Anthropology.* Fortress Press, Philadelphia. He totally rejects any biomedical model and defines 'healing' as 'restoration of meaning to life' (p 141), thinking of it solely in social terms. He misses the point that reintegration of sick people into society (particularly Jewish society) requires some element of 'cure' of the underlying pathology.

[9] The later development of the Church's healing practice has been examined in some detail in Barrett-Lennard, R.J.S. (1994). *Christian Healing after the New Testament.* University Press of America, Lanham, MD.

[10] Davies, S.L. (1995). *Jesus the Healer: Possession, Trance and the Origins of Christianity.* Continuum, New York. p 19.

Chapter 2

THE HISTORICAL AND CULTURAL CONTEXT OF HEALING IN THE NEW TESTAMENT

The task of medicine is to promote health, to prevent disease, to treat sickness and to minimise disability

John Wilkinson

Introductory comments

It is unlikely that practitioners of the healing art at any time in history would be in disagreement with the broad thrust of John Wilkinson's statement at the head of this chapter. Differences would arise, however, about the ways in which these admirable ideals should be expressed in practical terms. The reason for such disagreement arises from the fact that concepts of health, disease and healing within any society are culturally dependent since they are held within the accepted frameworks of meaning which are part of that culture; that is to say, the way people understand the world and their place in it. An animistic world view, which sees everything peopled with spirits and every rock and tree having a life force of some sort within it, will tend to view the ills of life as being the result of spiritual forces in some way or another.

The person believed to be able to manipulate such spiritual forces becomes the 'healer'. At the other end of the conceptual spectrum is that approach which sees sickness and healing as being due to 'natural' causes alone, however the term 'natural' might be defined, whether in the form of a post-Enlightenment reductionism or such earlier ideas as illness being due to an imbalance of the 'humours' which made up the person.

Most societies are complex and will present with a mixture of views and attitudes in which concepts based on preconceived theoretical ideas (whether magical or not) and understandings of therapy based on empirical experience are held together. Modern western society, for example, contains a multitude of differing world views from the scientific to the mystical and, in parallel, a multitude of 'healing' practices ranging from high technology medicine at one end of the spectrum to the use of crystals and astrological manipulations at the other. The problem, however, is that although it is possible for people to hold mutually exclusive views without apparent difficulty, the simple fact is that both cannot be correct. Bacterial meningitis, for example, cannot be caused by both a bacterium and an evil spirit: one or other of these postulates has to be wrong.

The similar holding of mutually exclusive ideas was also very much the situation in the Graeco-Roman world in which people embraced differing attitudes to, and understandings of, disease and healing. It is necessary, therefore, to give some attention to these matters and consider the general concepts of health and healing within their original social and religious contexts in the New Testament world at large, particularly as they have a bearing on the work of Jesus and the later attitudes of the early Church to healing. This section is intended to be no more than a brief introduction to broad concepts and ideas without extensive detail. Several studies of medicine in the biblical and particularly New Testament period exist, both in general works on the history of medicine as well as more specialised studies of Greek and Roman medicine and medicine in the Bible and Jewish thought of the period [1].

Colin Hemer has noted that the 'cultural world of the New Testament was extraordinarily complex, and divers concepts of medicine and the nature of disease coexisted within it. Even within the Greek perspective, popular superstition and magic persisted in a civilisation which developed a scientific and rationalistic approach to medicine, and there was a continuing link between the rational and the religious in a relationship that is not easy for us to enter into' [2]. In some senses, however, this is not so very different from the way in which rational concepts of disease, diagnosis and treatment are held side by side with quite irrational and indeed, magical ideas in modern society. This is the case not only among religious fundamentalist groups who attribute various illnesses and behaviours to the influence of demons, but also to secular 'New Age' practitioners who have resurrected old magical ideas in their practice.

The first century of the Christian era was a time when 'under the influence of Platonists and Neoplatonists, absolute credulity came into vogue' [3]. People were as concerned then with living as long and healthy a life as possible, as they are today. The Roman world, however, in terms of health was probably more akin to a Third World situation than it was to modern western society, in spite of its sophistication. This is hardly surprising, as the great scourge of infection remained the major influence on demographic structures until the twentieth century. It has been calculated that life expectancy at birth in the Roman world was probably less than 25 years and with little more than 8 per cent of the population living beyond 60 years [4]. Both infant and maternal mortality were also probably very high [5]. Accurate estimates are impossible and those that have been made rely on comparisons between the first century world and modern Third World situations that may, in fact, not be strictly comparable at all, although both malaria and tuberculosis would be common to both societies as major killers.

It is only when these matters are given proper consideration and understood in relation to the ideas of the time that it becomes possible to reach some appreciation of what the contemporaries of Jesus understood his ministry to be, not simply in respect of the developing christology of the Church, but perhaps more importantly from the standpoint of this study, with regard to the way in which the indifferent, the uncommitted or the opposition may have understood what was going on. In the same way it becomes possible to relate the general views on healing presented in other New Testament documents, as they reflect the developments in the life and thought of the early Church, to the broad concepts of the time. Lambourne has drawn attention to the danger of ignoring this historico-cultural setting, noting that, 'modern discussion of the healing miracles has only too often unconsciously imported into the Palestinian drama quite anachronistic viewpoints and problems' [6]. It is thus necessary to consider the approaches to health and healing and the parallel issues of magic and exorcism as they were understood in the first century. Jesus and his followers in the early

Christian community shared the common cultural background of first century Palestine: his conceptual framework was that of his time and to make Jesus anything other than a man of his time is to make him an anachronism.

First century Palestinian Judaism was the matrix from which Christianity arose. It was not only heir to the Old Testament traditions, but had also been strongly influenced by the thought systems of the dominant cultures around, especially the all-pervading Hellenism that had deeply affected the whole system of thought of the Mediterranean world of the time. The Judaism of Jesus and his contemporaries was not a closed system of thought, nor was the society of Palestine a closed society. Palestine had always been a crossroads between east and west in the ancient world; it was among other things a regular battlefield. As N.T. Wright has remarked, 'Every forty-four years out of the last four thousand, on average, an army has marched through it, whether to conquer it, to rescue it from someone else, to use it as a neutral battleground on which to fight a different enemy, or to take advantage of it as the natural route for getting somewhere else to fight there instead' [7]. Such a situation leaves its mark on the life of the region and at the time of Jesus, it was strongly influenced, on the one hand, by the world of Greece and Rome and, on the other, it was also exposed to Iranian and other eastern ideas. It was thus a complex and diverse cultural situation and this would appear to have been the case particularly in Galilee.

Some caution needs to be exercised about the racial and cultural mix in Galilee, however, and although it has been argued that the province in Roman times was predominantly gentile in make-up [8], there is good evidence to suggest that the population was largely made up of Jewish, rather than non-Jewish stock [9]. It would appear that so-called sectarian Judaism, the Judaism of the Essenes, the Qumran community and other less than strictly 'orthodox' groups was in particular much more open to Hellenistic and other ideas than has often been suspected in the past. It has to be said, however, that the existence of 'orthodoxy' in first century Judaism has been disputed [10] and Hengel has argued that no distinction can be made between a Hellenistic and Jewish milieu in this period [11]. On Judaism as a whole at this time, Ferguson has commented that the 'variety of expression goes beyond the traditional distinction between Palestinian Judaism and Hellenistic Diaspora Judaism. In fact, this distinction is only a geographical one, for there were Diaspora Jews who maintained the Hebrew language and, like Paul, received a strict Pharisaic upbringing, and there were strong

Hellenistic influences in Palestine, even in conservative Rabbinic circles' [12].

It will hardly be surprising if the ministry of Jesus demonstrated the influence of these various cultural forces, not only in his teaching, but also in respect of his approach to disease and healing. Similarly, the ongoing mission of the post-Easter community became more and more a Gentile mission and thus more and more rooted in Hellenistic cultural ideas which came increasingly to influence the expression of the message of the gospel and the formulations of theology. At the same, time, however, it must be emphasised that all the evidence points to Jesus as seeing himself as the heir to the Old Testament promises and thus thoroughly grounded in the religion of Israel, something that will be discussed in more detail later.

It has been noted that there are two broad approaches to health and healing, both of which were much in evidence in the first century. On the one hand there was what might be termed an empirico-rational approach that was at the heart of the great Greek medical tradition, the archetypical representative of which was Hippocrates. On the other hand there were those concepts and practices that belonged to a magico-religious understanding of disease and health [13]. One side of the coin was thus represented by the physicians who used prescriptions and mainly (although not always) rational treatment for disease and injury. Their approach was essentially empirical, based on trial and error, but the treatment often worked even though founded on what today would be regarded as false theories and concepts. Closely related to this was simple folk medicine, the use of 'practical' home remedies which quite often worked to some degree, and which was also founded on empiricism. Empiricism has always been the basis of folk medicine, irrespective of the culture. The discoveries that certain herbs, for example, will relieve certain symptoms or perhaps even effect cures for some diseases, have all come about as a result of observation and experiment.

The absence of a rational theoretical basis for such forms of treatment does not necessarily mean that they were useless or that no advances could be made in practice. After all, many modern drugs are derived from the earlier observations of folk medicine. Similarly, although any genuinely functional understanding of human anatomy was almost totally lacking, Roman surgery made great strides in the years of the early Christian era, from the period of Celsus, who was roughly contemporary with Jesus, through to Galen, a hundred years later. The great barriers were the lack of effective anaesthesia and the very high risks of post-operative infection that could well be fatal. Nonetheless, the treatment of fractures and dislocations was well advanced and some of the surgical methods used continued well into the nineteenth century, such as the use of jolting techniques to deal with spinal dislocations. A variety of other surgical techniques was also in use, including the removal of bladder stones and the use of cautery for haemorrhoids.

The other extreme of the spectrum of medical treatment was represented by the magician, priest or exorcist who protected people with charms and amulets and healed through a variety of rites, ceremonies and exorcisms. The emphasis of the priest was on the activities of the gods (or God) and it was wedded to a desire to know the will and to seek the beneficence of the divine through prayer and sacrifices. The magician, on the other hand, tended to be involved in occult forces, as also did the exorcist, and was concerned in coercing the deity through the use of formulae and various acts to bring about the desired result. Magic, as Kee has put it, 'is a technique, through word or act, by which a desired end is achieved, whether that end lies in the solution to the seeker's problem or in damage to the enemy who has caused the problem' [14]. It is thus closely allied to what may be called witchcraft. One may readily understand the reasons behind the questionings about the source of Jesus' authority (Mark 3:22-30). It was not immediately apparent from his activity whether Jesus was a magician or a genuine prophet and the consideration of what is essentially the same evidence has led to different conclusions being drawn about him even today. In the Hellenistic world, there were frequently practitioners of the healing art who utilised both empirical medicine as well as magico-religious forms of treatment in varying degrees: it may be argued that the activity of Jesus combined both approaches, although this study will attempt to show that he used mainly empirical methods in his healing ministry.

Empirical medicine

Greek influence was dominant in empirical medicine in the first century and the name most strongly associated with the Greek school of medicine is that of Hippocrates, the influence of whose school of thought was still strong in the first century. His approach, and that of his followers, was to see disease as an internal battle between 'morbid matter', a concrete cause, and the natural self-healing power of the body. Longrigg noted that, for Hippocrates, disease was 'a natural process, a disturbance of the equilibrium of the constituents of the body' [15]. The later Roman physician Celsus was of the opinion (not entirely correctly) that Hippocrates was the first to separate medicine from the study of philosophy [16]. Certainly, it is generally accepted that the Hippocratic school rejected 'supernatural' causes and was pre-eminently rational in its approach, standing over against popular superstition and magic. This development of natural modes of explanation about the causation and character of disease is the hallmark of the remarkable originality of Greek medicine.

The Hippocratic tradition was founded on knowledge and experience, even though these were coloured, to some extent, by the accepted ideas of the time, such as planetary and similar influences [17]. Nonetheless, as Colin Hemer has noted, the 'treatment of disease seemed indissolubly linked with an understanding of the nature of Man and his world' [18] and it was thus limited by an inadequate grasp of the nature of the physiological and pathological processes of health and disease. It is reasonable to suggest that the essential weakness of Greek medicine was that its 'scientific' empiricism was never able to free itself from the controlling influence of deduction from axiomatic philosophical systems and their innate presuppositions. While this meant liberation from 'supernaturalism' on the one hand, it also left Greek and Roman medicine under the influence of speculative ideas [19]. Thus, the elaborate doctrine of the four humours (phlegm, blood, black bile and yellow bile) and the related four basic temperaments (phlegmatic, sanguine, melancholic and choleric) was central to the Hippocratic corpus and was grounded in the Empedoclean principle of the four elements (earth, air, fire and water). While largely worthless as a theory, it nonetheless remained the fundamental prop for European medicine for over two millennia. At the same time, however, although such theories were speculative, they were open to empirical verification and could be modified or discarded over time as their deficiencies became apparent in the light of new knowledge.

The Hippocratic school, therefore, must be given the credit for establishing a rational basis for medicine and thus, as Sherwin-White was to put it, 'launching a firm tradition of secular medicine which was never lost in antiquity thereafter' [20]. This attitude is particularly well illustrated by the approach to epilepsy, the so-called 'sacred disease'. Hippocrates devoted an entire treatise to this condition which, in the ancient world, was generally regarded as being the result of a visitation from some agent from the unseen world (in Palestinian Judaism this was likely to be a demon as in Mark 9:14-29). Hippocrates, however, could write, 'It is not, in my opinion, any more divine or more sacred than other diseases, but has a natural cause like other infection. Men regard its nature and cause as divine from ignorance and wonder, because it is not at all like other diseases. This notion of divinity is kept up by their inability to comprehend it ... fevers, tertians and quartans, seem to me to be no less sacred and divine than this disease, but nobody wonders at them' [21]. In other words, there is no reason to distinguish between divine and non-divine causes, all are ultimately manifestations of the divine wisdom at work throughout the universe.

In Hippocratic medicine, health represented a balance between the person and the environment and there was thus a genuine attempt to approach disease rationally. Sickness was regarded as the result of an effort by the body to restore a disturbed equilibrium and the duty of the physician was to co-operate with nature to secure a readjustment and restoration. The approach to treatment might be described as strictly 'noninterventionist'; the physician was expected to refrain from meddlesome interference and allow the body to do its own recuperative work, as Guthrie put it, 'he watched the course of the disease and did not interfere with nature' [22]. In some senses, it might be said that he had little choice. The therapeutic armamentarium was thin to say the least. Poppy and mandragora existed as sedatives and aperients such as castor oil were used. Local applications for skin infections, ulcers and wounds were better known from trial and error and included a number of essential oils obtained from plants, but the overall range of genuine therapeutic materials was very limited, as it was to remain for many centuries to come [23]. Nonetheless, the Greek physicians accepted the place of the activity of the divine and, because they were not opposed to 'religious' cures through the direct intervention of the gods through prayer and other means, they were able to escape blame in terminal or hopelessly chronic disease, by referring such to the temple for prayer and absolving themselves of responsibility. As Kee points out, only later 'does a split develop between rational medicine in a religious framework and avowed skepticism (sic)' [24] and it may be assumed that throughout the period, prayer for healing was a normal part of the total therapeutic process.

It becomes apparent, however, that although the approach of the Hippocratic school was enlightened, humane and comprehensive, it was a medical practice designed for the upper class patient. In the various treatises, such as *Concerning Air, Waters, Places; The Regimen in Acute Diseases; Prognostics and Epidemics,* the various discussions of diet, living conditions, exercise, bathing, massage and sleeping all relate to situations very far removed from the humble village dweller of rural Palestine or the artisan in a crowded town anywhere in the Empire. Such differences of practice were to be seen for example in the practice of midwifery. The descriptions which were given by Pliny the Elder of the folk medicine practices of his time [25] stand in marked contrast to the much more enlightened methods of obstetrical care recommended by the medical profession [26]. The vast majority of women in the Graeco-Roman world would have been subjected to the traditions of folk medicine and only the wealthy elite would have been able to afford the sort of care recommended by the physicians. The fact is that the rural communities, which takes in the sort of society in which Jesus worked, could not afford to sustain specialist healers or full time drug sellers.

The Hippocratic school was only one of many in evidence in the period of the Roman Empire. Asklepiades and Erasistratus had made their influence felt, especially with the concept of the *pneuma* as a subtle life-giving force that pervaded all nature and caused life to be evidenced. Imbalances of the *pneuma* were considered by this school to be the cause of disease. Graeco-Roman medicine at this period has been aptly described as a 'welter of theorising' [27], yet it was at heart rational in that it tried to produce a reasonable basis rather than see disease as simply the result of the whim of the gods or occult forces that required to be placated or coerced. Within the Hippocratic tradition, however, the two greatest contributors to Roman medicine in the period covered by the life of Jesus and the growth of the New Testament documents were probably Celsus, who was roughly contemporaneous with Jesus (he is known to have worked in Rome from AD 14-37), and Galen (approximately AD 130-200). Galen, in particular, was to have an incalculable influence upon medicine that would last for the next 1200 years.

Celsus was a member of the noble family of the Cornelii and he produced a major encyclopaedic work that covered aspects of philosophy, law, agriculture and medicine. The work on medicine (*De medicina*) covers eight volumes and deals with diet, fevers, mental illness, various internal disorders and specific subjects such as skin, eyes, ears and sexually transmitted diseases, as well as giving a history of medicine from the days of the Homeric epics to his own time in the proem to book 1. Celsus also covers drug and herbal therapies and the treatment of wounds as well as surgery. He is the first to mention the four cardinal signs of inflammation, *calor, rubor, tumor, dolor* (heat, redness, swelling and pain) that remain familiar to all medical students and practitioners to this day. Many of his methods have an almost modern ring to them and there is no doubt that he was essentially a pragmatist - whatever worked, whether a simple folk medicine or something more sophisticated, was to be used. The surgical instruments that he advocates in books 7 and 8 correspond to those found in the house of the surgeon in Pompeii and are currently to be seen in the Naples Museum [28]. There is no mention in his writing of the action of a healing god nor any emphasis on the activity of other spiritual forces. In contrast to the magico-religious approach, Celsus provides a straightforward statement of the facts as he understood them, dedicates himself to results and wisely refrains from indulging in theory or argument. His approach was thus very different from the forceful, argumentative and self-opinionated Galen.

Galen came originally from the important city of Pergamum in Asia Minor and his first medical appointment was as 'medical officer' to the gladiators. His training was eclectic and he was as much renowned as a philosopher and philologist as a physician, but he became the chief guide of the physician from the late Roman Empire until the mediaeval period when his ideas and practices were eventually superseded through the work of Paracelsus, Vesalius and Paré and the other great practitioners of the Renaissance period. His monumental work was to become the standard for all medical practice from which no one dared to differ and there can be no doubt that his achievement was the high water mark of Graeco-Roman medicine [29]. His major contributions, however, lay not so much in his medicine as such, but in his anatomical and physiological observations and investigations. He recognised the value of anatomy as the basis for proper practice in medicine and surgery and, indeed, regarded a physician without a knowledge of anatomy as being like an architect without a plan. His approach to treatment was based very much on the Greek school that saw the role of the physician as simply to assist nature in restoring the body to its proper equilibrium and the harmony of its 'humours'. Consequently, he was caustic about the money grubbing quacks of his time who, he said, did no more than to 'enter the sickroom, bleed the patient, lay on a plaster and give an enema' [30]. Much of Galen's work, however, was based on studies of apes and pigs that he unhesitatingly transferred to the human body, thus perpetuating significant errors that were to last until the great anatomist Vesalius and others corrected them in the sixteenth century. In spite of his mistakes and misconceptions, the wealth of accurate detail in his writings is remarkable.

These two intellectual giants encompass the period of the New Testament. It is extremely unlikely that they had any direct effect on the actual writers, but, nonetheless, they represented the ways in which the best physicians of the time thought and acted and provided a climate of opinion which would have coloured much of the medical thinking of this period. The gentile mission of the Church moved out into a world in which the best medical thought and practice followed the empirical (and, let it be said, 'scientific') approaches of these two great giants.

The continuing growth of the influence of Greek culture throughout the Roman Empire meant that physicians rose in social standing, even though there were still many charlatans at work. The Roman authorities attempted to bring some measure of control to medical practice. Thus, for example, by the time of Tiberius (reigned AD 14-37) a system of flourishing *collegia* or societies devoted to medical practice and teaching, had sprung up and auditoria were built for teaching purposes. Vespasian (reigned AD 70-79) went to the extent of ensuring that in Rome the teacher of medicine was provided with a salary at public expense. There are references in the Oxyrrhyncus Papyri (ca AD 200) to 'public' doctors in Egypt, paid by the state to undertake embalming and forensic work [31]. It is unlikely that such sophisticated medicine was a normal part of everyday life for artisans and the lower classes, 'for the ordinary folk of the lower classes, the neighbourhood barber dispensed the most accessible and affordable medical care' [32].

Greek and Roman medicine as practised by the professional physicians, was largely for the benefit of the more wealthy, something made clear by Celsus in his advice to people at a time of plague that they should undertake a sea voyage [33]. The services of physicians, therefore, would have been used, in most cases, by only the upper classes of society. In a church community such as that of Corinth, for example, it would seem likely, therefore, that certainly some of the members - people such as Gaius and Erastus - would have had sufficient wealth to have been able to call upon a physician when necessary. Indeed, it was the sociological problems arising from conflicts between the 'haves' and the 'have-nots' within the community that seems to have been at the root of many of this church's troubles [34].

In Roman Palestine, on the other hand, those with the wealth to afford the fees of a physician would have been a relatively smaller group. It would have included the Herodian court and the priestly aristocracy as well as the Roman administrators themselves. It is stated by Josephus, for example, that Herod had his own personal court physicians [35] and it is a reasonable assumption that they were of the Greek schools, judging from their use of oil baths and similar forms of therapy, rather than more vigorous forms of treatment. Even in these circles, however, magic and magical practices apparently had their influence (note Acts 13:6-8).

In Jewish thinking, physicians appeared to have been classed as manual workers [36] and the physician's work was considered a trade. Talmudic sources suggest that there were physicians and surgeons in most cities of any size and there is first century evidence for their presence in Lydda and Pegae.   Josephus himself received medical attention after falling from his horse, possibly at Capernaum [37].   He wrote, 'I was bruised on my wrist and carried into a village called Capharnome ... I sent for the physicians and while I was under their hands, I continued in a fever all that day'. The physicians did not appear to have done very much for him, any more than they did for the woman in Mark's story from the same area who, 'suffered many things from many doctors' (Mark 5.26).

The existence of the Temple physician is of particular interest. He was called upon whenever the priests were injured in the course of their duties and also provided a general 'health service' for them and their families. The health of the Temple priests does not appear to have been particularly good, a fact which, in part, might be explained by their diet which was rich in red meats from the sacrifices and, at the same time, low on vegetables [38].   In view of the continuing importance of the priest, particularly in respect of the control of those diseases which produced ceremonial uncleanness, the use of a physician in the Temple suggests a marked shift away from earlier thinking which considered healing as God's monopoly.

There are few New Testament references to physicians.   Jesus occasionally referred to the work of a physician, using what appear to be common proverbial sayings (Mark 2:17, Luke 4:23), but if the comments of Mark 5:26 represent popular feeling rather than editorial spleen, the Galilean populace at any rate did not hold them in generally high esteem.   On the other hand, Paul (though not a Palestinian Jew) seems to have had the general services of Luke as his own personal physician for at least some of the time, both on the basis of early traditions (see Col 4:14 and 2 Tim 4:11) and his own testimony (Philemon 24).   While neither Colossians nor 2 Timothy may be authentically Pauline, it is clear from these references that there were strong traditions linking Paul and Luke, reflected also in Acts. The presence of a personal physician among the group of persons accompanying Paul on his journeys indicates the acceptance of both the physician and his art in the earliest Christian circles.   It may also have something to say about Paul's social status particularly if the relationship between Paul and Luke was that of patron and client on the Roman model. Hemer comments that if Luke was a physician and a highly educated Greek gentile 'was he also a slave, or perhaps a freedman dependant who stood legally in a formalised "client" relationship with his "patron" Paul ?' [39] In general terms, however, the Pauline correspondence has little to say about healing and the presence of a physician may well be an indication of a ministry that was more geared to 'sophisticated' city dwellers than to country folk. Indeed, it would seem that the rural communities were largely ignored in the early Christian mission and it is perhaps significant that the earliest name associated with a consistent rural mission was that of Gregory the Wonder Worker [40].

The high reputation of the medical school at Laodicea for eye treatments is behind the reference of the writer of Revelation to the provision of an eye ointment that would cure spiritual blindness and which could not be matched by the money-making nostrums of the local apothecaries (Rev 3:18). The later rabbinical sources, like the New Testament, also tend to show a somewhat ambivalent attitude to the physicians of the time. They appear to have been one of the 'despised trades', being included among the 'crafts of robbers', a classification which would have carried with it a certain degree of social stigma. A comment, attributed to Rabbi Judah, illustrates this attitude: 'the best physician is destined for Gehenna and the most seemly among butchers is a partner of Amalek' [41]. The rabbinical sayings, however, tend to be rather like most proverbial sayings in that one may always find a completely opposing statement. On the one hand, for example, the rabbis advised people to stay away from a town in which the chief citizen was a physician and on the other, it was advised that 'the disciple of a wise man should not live in a town without a physician' [42]. It is probable that much of the rabbinical feeling against the physicians of the time arose from the fact that they tended to treat the rich and ignore the needs of the poor.

Most references to the healing and cures of diseases are to be found in the Gospels. The pictures derived from the traditions underlying these documents paint a very different attitude to health and healing from that represented by the schools of Graeco-Roman medicine. The people with whom Jesus mixed were largely the ordinary folk of Galilee, the 'people of the land', who were very far removed from the Jerusalem aristocracy, even though many would have been self-sufficient and reasonably prosperous businessmen. The emphasis that comes across in the Gospels is much more that of the popular world, the medicine of a world still inhabited by demons and spirits whose power could bring sickness and other disasters upon a household and in which sickness might also be a direct punishment from God for some real or imagined offence. Such views may be held in the cities as much as in the villages, but the picture of the ministry of Jesus in the Gospels is of a ministry that is predominantly to the rural society rather than to the urban populations of Jerusalem or other larger centres. Rural Palestine was not the place for sophisticated medicine in the first century any more than such communities are today. It is, therefore, to the magico-religious concepts underlying the popular understandings of disease causation, as well as treatment, that attention should now be paid as an important background for the ministry of Jesus and the early disciples.

Magico-religious medicine

The importance of magical ideas in general, and demonology in particular, in Jewish thought in the New Testament period has been well documented [43]. In fact there has probably been an over-emphasis on these issues with parallels being drawn with other practices where they may not, nor possibly do not, exist. This is particularly marked in the studies of both Hull (1974) and Smith (1978) which seriously overstate their respective cases by drawing inappropriate parallels, particularly with the much later (third century) pagan Greek magical papyri as will be discussed later. Nonetheless, it seems clear that throughout the period from the return from the Babylonian exile to the time of Christ, there were marked shifts in thought, especially in respect of spiritual beings, whether angels or demons. The result was that, as Rendle Short remarked, 'the Jews developed views on demon possession not unlike those of the Egyptians and peoples of Mesopotamia and certainly far removed from the sober opinions of Hippocrates and his followers' [44]. To some extent, the Synoptic Gospels appear to reflect these general beliefs in malign spiritual influences. They stand in marked contrast, in this respect, to the Fourth Gospel and the rest of the New Testament, with the exception of Acts, in which demons do not appear as agents of disease and misfortune and in which healing itself has a much lower profile.

The general background of the Synoptic Gospels, however, suggests the world of the 'common people', the world of 'the man on the Clapham omnibus' as G. K. Chesterton put it. It is not the world of the wealthy aristocracy, even though it may be the world of the comparatively wealthy, for it seems clear, for example, that the immediate disciples of Jesus were themselves most likely men of moderate substance who had run their own businesses and presumably prospered.   In addition, it also seems clear that among the many women who followed Jesus there were those with substantial means who were able to fund his mission (note especially Luke 8:1-3 and Mark 15:40-41).   There is no suggestion anywhere that Jesus and his friends begged for their food in the manner of Buddhist monks, yet the mission cannot have proceeded for at least three years without substantial funding.   On the other hand, the wealthy Establishment is portrayed generally as either antagonistic to Jesus or else merely indifferent.   Nonetheless, it would seem that much of the work of Jesus was among the genuinely indigent, as well as 'the sick, the blind the lame and the lepers, who play so important a part in the Gospel accounts of Jesus' ministry' [45].   It should be noted, however, that there are only six specific references to demonic possession in the Synoptic Gospels and they lack totally the extravagant magical approach that is to be found in rabbinical and other writings [46].

The division between rich and poor, however, was much more than a merely social cleavage.   There had grown up an approach that made this distinction virtually a religious one, so that 'poor' and 'pious' became almost synonymous.   This relationship should not be pressed too far, but it seems clear that when used of the upright, the word 'poor' did not necessarily mean poor in terms of material wealth.   The background is surely that of the Old Testament where the 'poor' (πτωχοι in LXX = Heb *'anî*) are those who are oppressed by tyrants and are in special need of God's help and whose trust is in God for deliverance.   They had no resources of themselves, their only resource was God - 'This poor man cried and the Lord heard him and delivered him from all his troubles' (Psa 34:6).   It is likely that Matthew catches something of the current nuance of the term in his reporting of the Beatitudes - 'Blessed are the poor (όι πτωχοι) in spirit' (Matt 5:3) [47].   Jesus and his disciples who, as indicated earlier, seem to have been drawn largely from the ranks of the reasonably prosperous, self-employed small business owner (Luke 8:2,3, etc) could not in any sense be described as 'poor' with the meaning of genuinely indigent.

It was, however, the common people, who included among them an increasing number of the destitute, dispossessed, unemployed and landless 'peasants', who heard Jesus gladly.   They were people who certainly would not have been able to afford the services of a physician.   They were, however, very likely to have been ready to interpret the activity of Jesus in a 'Messianic' way, seeing him as a divinely endowed agent of God, who was, at the very least, a prophet. The statement that Luke (24:19-21) puts into the mouths of the two on the road to Emmaus was probably very close to the reality: they had hoped that this Jesus would have been the eschatological Redeemer of Israel who was to bring in God's final redemption for the deliverance of his people from all forms of oppression [48].

The Synoptic Gospels portray a homespun world, a world of folk medicine and, in particular, a world in which the misfortunes of life, its sudden ills, its death and disease, were often seen to be the result of the activity of malevolent spirits. By and large, it was a situation in which simple folk remedies were used for uncomplicated conditions and 'magical' practices (or at least exorcisms) were called in for those cases which appeared to be inexplicable. Many of these folk remedies are to be found in the Mishnah and Talmud and, although these are much later than the New Testament in their final form, it seems likely that the Mishnah, in particular, reflects some of the ideas and practices that would have been current in the time of Jesus. As in all folk medicine, including that of today, the practices were a mixture of superstition coupled with simple empirical remedies, many of which may well have been effective in varying degrees.

The general practices of folk medicine tend to remain static from one generation to the next with relatively minor variations and the various recipes of the Mishnah are likely to be much older than the actual period of compilation. The sort of 'cures' that were recommended are similar to those used in Europe and North America until relatively recent times, as noted earlier, and which are still in use in many undeveloped parts of the world and in unsophisticated cultures. The Mishnah tractate *Shabbath*, for example, mentions the use of a silver coin for bunions, a nail from a cross for festering wounds, locust's eggs for earache, honey for sores and vinegar for toothache among numerous other folk remedies [49]. Similarly, the Roman writer Pliny the Elder mentions numerous folk remedies in his *Historia Naturalis* such as the use of a drink sprinkled with powdered sow's dung or sow's milk mixed with mead to relieve labour pains, as well as the use of hyena's feet, snake sloughs, vulture feathers and earthworms in raisin wine [50].

Herbs were regularly used, such as infusions of vervain (*Verbena* spp) root for the 'lying in' period after childbirth, in addition to its regular use for convulsions, fevers and nervous disorders. Mercury or dog's mercury (*Mercurialis annualis/perennis*) were thought to induce menstrual bleeding and other plants such as feverfew (*Tanacetum parthenium*), marjoram (*Origanum* spp) and wood sage (*Tencrium scorodonia*) were in regular use. The latter was believed to have antiseptic properties and was used for inflammatory conditions [51]. Such remedies would have had their place in any *Materia Medica* in Europe at least to the seventeenth century if not beyond. Indeed, herbal remedies are becoming popular again today among many people and occasionally they work because they have been founded on observation that certain plants have certain properties. The glycosides from foxglove (*Digitalis* spp), for example, are still the basis of an important group of cardiac drugs and there has been a marked growth of interest in recent years in the pharmacologically active principles that may be obtained from plant sources.

The present writer has observed in another context that 'there is always a tendency to "fear the worst" whenever the real extent of risk in any situation is not fully understood' [52]. This fear, at heart irrational, is converted into attempts to rationalise a situation of misfortune such as a serious illness, a miscarriage, or a deformed baby. The answer to the question, 'why me?' when calamity strikes, is, nearly always, to blame an external agency. At the same time, fear of ill-understood or imagined external agencies may give rise to a set of psychosocial illnesses with remarkably consistent symptom patterns. In the world of the first century, people tended to display the more bizarre features of 'hysterical' illness, the major conversion/somatiform disorders, as may still be seen in third world countries today [53]. In modern western society, however, the features of such illnesses differ and tend to follow a consistent pattern of general ill health, with a variety of totally non-specific symptoms and equivalent lack of clear physical pathology [54].

In the world of the New Testament, the causative external agencies of bizarre and inexplicable illnesses were largely the hosts of spiritual forces that surrounded everyone, and in particular, the evil forces in the form of demons or unclean spirits. The modern equivalents in western society would probably be pesticides or radiation. Those forms of sickness that were understood as demonic in origin, could be combated only by exorcism, or different forms of magical practice, and not the use of the prescriptions of folk medicine. The way in which such conditions were interpreted depended on the context of the event and on the way that people thought about the world in which they lived. In much the same way, in modern society, one may observe the tendency for people to consult with the various practitioners of 'alternative' healing methods, particularly when struck down with some form of vague illness arising out of a fear of the effects of an outside agency or as the unconscious response to some form of intolerable situation.

Something that is outside, or apparently outside, the normal range of conditions that would be dealt with by the standard medical practices of the time is met by the range of alternative practices, whether this is the exorcist of the first century or the naturopath, faith healer or other 'alternative' practitioner of the twentieth.

The Jewish exorcists were often regarded as the experts in the ancient world and Jewish magic was of major importance. There are echoes of this in the New Testament (see for example Acts 6:9, 11; 13:6,8; 19:13ff). The Rabbinic literature, however, provides an immense amount of detail about contemporary beliefs and practices with regard to demons. Most diseases appeared to have been ascribed to the power of demons, particularly conditions such as leprosy, rabies, croup, asthma and various heart conditions, as well as nervous disorders, such as epilepsy [55]. They were also believed to cause people to commit rash or unlawful acts - a useful way of shifting responsibility for one's own behaviour, a reaction not unknown today. It is important to note that such universal and all-embracing effects of the demonic powers are totally lacking from the New Testament. Indeed, it needs to be emphasised that the forces of evil have a very limited role, being called in only to explain those diseases that presented with markedly abnormal and bizarre behaviour patterns and that were outside the ability of simple medicines to have any curative or relieving effect. Again, it also needs to be emphasised that such demonic forces are to be found only in the synoptic traditions (in which Acts is included) and nowhere else in the New Testament.

If Josephus is to be believed, it was those who came from sectarian Judaism who seem to have been most involved in these practices. It was also among these groups that apocalyptic ideas were most apparent. The apocalyptists had developed the dualistic ideas probably derived originally from Iran and the east. This resulted in a remarkable development in Jewish thought about the world of spirits and angelic beings and demons particularly. The demons were believed to be those angels who had rebelled against God and formed a kingdom of Satan (sometimes also called Belial). The Satan was no longer considered as a member of the heavenly court, acting as the prosecutor/accuser, but was now characterised as God's enemy. In the War Scroll of Qumran he commands the army of the 'sons of darkness' and at 2 Cor 6:14, 15 he appears as the Antichrist. He and his demons are also thought to be able to manipulate people's minds and bodies and live in them.

Such developments of thought require to be placed alongside the distinctive Hebrew view of history as linear which was associated with a concept of an end time when God would finally triumph over the current age of evil and bring in a transformation of creation in a new Messianic age. Both apocalyptic and Rabbinic thought represented a modified dualism in which the linearity of time was divided into the two ages. The present age was in the hands of evil 'principalities and powers', but in the future age these would be defeated and the rule of God would be established, not merely in human affairs, but throughout the universe. The new age would share in God's perfection: it would be nothing less than an eschatological new creation [56]. In the meantime, however, the world became a battleground with armies of demons fighting against God's angels to gain control. As D. S. Russell has put it, the picture is 'of a great angelic host and an innumerable company of evil spirits and demons of every kind marshalled under the leadership of the demon prince. They are arrayed like a great army, just as on God's side, the hosts of heaven are drawn up under the control of the Lord of Hosts' [57]. The return to such a 'remystifying' of the universe is one of the more interesting phenomena of certain aspects of modern Christianity, particularly in the charismatic movement. This form of fundamentalism exhibits 'a paranoid world view which militates against rational and common-sense interpretations of reality' [58].

Sickness was part of this demonic malevolent activity and the task of the exorcists was to control and expel such forces, using incantations, charms and various rituals to assert their authority over the demons. Josephus wrote of the Essenes: 'They take great pains in studying the writings of the ancients and choose out of them what is most to the advantage of their soul and body and therefore for the cure of distempers they seek out such roots as may be effective and enquire into the (presumed occult) properties of stones' [59]. Here there appears to be a blend of that timeless folk medicine that is to be found in all cultures which culls its simples from the hedgerows, married to occult practices of a magical sort. This is well illustrated by the description of exorcisms Josephus himself claimed to have witnessed performed by a fellow Jew called Eliazar in the presence of the emperor Vespasian [60]. This Eleazar used the name of Solomon (a prominent name among the 'magicians' as Solomon was considered to be one of the great magical practitioners of ancient days) together with a variety of incantations as well as the inhalation of a plant root to effect his exorcisms. His success appears to have been ascribed to his techniques rather than to any special powers that he possessed.

It is possible to provide a great number of examples of magical activity and exorcism from this period in the works of Philo, Lucian of

Samosata and Philostratus as well as the immense amount of material which has come to light in the so-called magical papyri, dating from the third century [61]. These documents frequently have been quoted as being of relevance to the New Testament situation, particularly in respect of the healing and exorcisms of Jesus [62]. However, the extent to which these various writings really relate to the conditions of first century Palestine is very far from certain. Morton Smith, for example, has been severely criticised for lumping together too much disparate material from these later sources without due consideration either to its historical reliability or its dating [63]. This *caveat* must also be applied to the wealth of rabbinical literature, particularly that from the Talmud, which is often cited as illustrative of thought and practice in the Jewish community of New Testament times, but most of which was not edited in written form until the fifth century. Admittedly, later documents may, and often do, preserve earlier traditions and practices which may pass on over generations with little alteration, but, although these tractates contain a great many references to magic and exorcism, it is very uncertain whether any of this material actually derives from the first century or is even related to the Palestinian situation. Most, if not all, of this material comes from the same period as the wealth of pagan references to similar ideas already mentioned, that is from the period of so-called 'late antiquity', from the third to the seventh centuries, what has been called the 'Age of Uncertainty' [64].

While simple folk remedies tend to remain the same from one period to the next, the growth of what might be termed 'occultism' seems to be more a feature of this later post-New Testament period. The matter remains far from resolved, but it is worth quoting the comments of H. C. Kee at length on this problem. He writes:

> In current and traditional practice among historians of religion, the identification of a roughly analogous phenomenon in a culture contemporary with, prior to, or even later than the first and early second century is seized upon as providing the historical explanation of what was occurring in the nascent Christian movement. The strategy is evident in popular works on miracle, in which the Greek Magical Papyri, dating mostly from the third and fourth centuries of our era, are appealed to as explanation for "what really happened" in the New Testament accounts of Jesus and the Apostles. ... The warning of Weber about mistaking ideal-types for reality and his plea for making clear "the unique individual character of cultural phenomena" have both been ignored' [65].

Kee has also remarked with some acerbity that, until recently, 'our picture of conditions in first century Palestine had to be derived from the anachronistic, idealised records written down in the second and subsequent centuries by the one Jewish group that survived the Roman destruction of Jerusalem in AD 70 (the Pharisees) and from the apologetic, self-serving account of that literarily prolific turncoat, Flavius Josephus' [66]. Nonetheless, it is reasonable to think that these documents do provide some background to what appear to the broad ideas that were common in the Graeco-Roman world.

It would thus seem apparent, both from the New Testament evidence, as well as from the general literature of the period, that the dominant influence, certainly among the ordinary people, was the magico-religious approach to healing. In view of this, it is not surprising that there were many healers and exorcists using the various methods of the time in order to bring relief to those who were considered to be under the influence of such evil forces. It is against this background of popular healing that the work of Jesus is to be considered rather than in relation to the work of the physician. Later Christianity was to turn Jesus into the ideal physician, but this was largely a rhetorical device that used a therapeutic model for the moral deliverance offered through him, a description that occurs as early as Ignatius [67]. In his lifetime and in the earliest documents of the Church this title is not used. Rather he was seen in relation to his immediate culture and those who viewed his work with favour saw him as a prophet in the tradition of the healing prophets such as Elisha whose activities displayed the power of God. On the other hand, his detractors saw his exorcisms as a control over the demons brought about through being in league with the prince of the demons himself.

That Jesus undertook such activities cannot be doubted, the problem is to interpret them. This problem will be returned to at a later stage of the study, but it is worth stating at this stage that there is good evidence that the methods used by Jesus were those of the popular healer. Kee,[68] for example, is quite wrong in arguing that 'there is in none of these healing stories any trace of medical techniques' since these are, in fact, clearly demonstrated in such stories as that of the blind man of Bethsaida (Mark 8:21-26) which will be discussed in detail later. Further, in the accounts of the exorcisms, although there is none of the repetition of nonsense syllables, long lists of divine names and the use of amulets, charms and various bits of paraphernalia which were used by the peripatetic exorcists of the time [59], there is the characteristic authoritative command in a situation of raised emotional tension which seemed to be a constant feature of other exorcists and was associated with a highly emotional response on the part of the person being exorcised with cries, screams and shouts, a lack of behavioural control and no memory of the actual process [70]. These features are clearly seen in many of the exorcisms of Jesus as will be noted at the appropriate points in the later discussion. Further, it should be noted that this technique is a well recognised form of treatment in many forms of religious healing to the present day and is essentially a form of abreaction which very often leads to a marked, if generally only temporary, relief of symptoms [71].

The question, however, that has to be addressed at this stage is where the idea of 'miracle' fits into this pattern of thinking. It has been argued, particularly by Kee [72], that 'miracle' should be seen as a separate concept. In his view, miracle relates to a divine act of grace as a result of supplication or intercession and differs totally from magic which is based on the coercion of unseen Powers as a result of the use of specialised techniques designed to exploit these Powers for personal benefit and gain. This distinction is certainly valid and is important, for behind the miracle stories in the biblical accounts there is always the essential ingredient of God's gracious activity, but it also has to be emphasised that underlying both concepts is a world view which sees such unseen forces, whether divine or occult, as *explanations* of events, they are concepts that explain the 'how' of an event. They belong to the world of magico-religious medicine and to a world view which sees hidden powers, whether divine and beneficent, or demonic and threateningly evil, controlling the human condition, especially in such matters as health and disease. In the end what is seen as miracle by one person is seen as magic by another within this common framework of understanding. Furthermore, there are no very clear criteria for making the judgment about which is which, a point that will occupy the discussion at a later point in considering the work of Jesus.

In the New Testament, the term 'signs and wonders' essentially refers to events that have been generally classified as 'miraculous'. It was a formula specifically applied to the work of Jesus and the apostles and is a particular favourite of the author of Acts (nine out of the ten occurrences of the phrase). It was also used of the activities of false Messiahs and this use makes it difficult to maintain any clear distinction between what was considered to be a divinely ordered event and something that may be better described as 'magic': for Mark, at least, the difference in the inherent nature of 'signs and wonders' was determined by faith alone. The terminology seems to be used about

Jesus for two specific reasons. Firstly, it asserts that the activity of Jesus was derived from God who was the source of the power and authority which allowed him to undertake these actions (note John 3:2). Secondly, it establishes a firm link with other periods in Israel's history when 'signs and wonders' took place, most notably the period of the Exodus from Egypt and particularly in the way this event was reinterpreted by such prophets as Deutero-Isaiah in relation to the situations of their own time. The ministry of Jesus may thus be interpreted as a proclamation of the final and complete return from exile and the inauguration of the time of restoration [73].

In these traditions and in others in the Old Testament 'signs and wonders' were seen as evidence of the gracious, saving activity of God for his people delivering them from the bondage of their enemies. There is little room for doubt that the early Church wished to emphasise that the activity of Jesus was similarly to be identified with the saving activity of God on behalf of his people in such a way as to make it effectively a new Exodus or a new return from Exile. The dominance of the Passover/Exodus motif throughout the New Testament hardly needs emphasis. The New Testament thus sets out the role of Jesus as God's agent in bringing in a new era of deliverance associated with the revelation of God's rule and authority. In fact the modern concept of 'miracle' is anachronistic in terms of the world view prevailing in the Palestine of Jesus and his disciples of the first century in which the activity of God (or his spiritual opponents) was to be seen in everything. The works of Jesus are better referred to as 'signs' in the Johannine sense of pointers to what was going on. They are not productive of faith nor are they explicitly proofs, but they help people to see the activity of God in this person Jesus and reveal his programme in relation to the kingdom of God [74].

One other matter needs to be mentioned at this stage. Although the 'nature miracles' are not strictly the concern of this study, it has been argued [75] that there was a tendency in the Gospels to assimilate all miracles into exorcisms, but such a statement is misleading. Such a tendency would appear to be apparent in the way that Luke deals with the healings, but it is much less marked in the other evangelists. It is possible, however, that some of the nature miracles are to be considered as exorcisms, for example, the stilling of the storm (Mark 6:45-52). Fawcett has commented that the 'mythological apprehension of the world which the evangelists seem to have shared would have led them to think of the wind and sea as agencies of a personal power. No part of creation would have been for them impersonal ... It would be

perfectly natural, therefore, for them to understand Jesus' conflict with
the wind and the sea as being as much a confrontation with demonic
personality as when he was dealing with men and women possessed of
demons' [76]. The boundaries between the natural world and spiritual
powers were not drawn in popular thinking and there was no reason
why demonic powers should not be able to influence weather patterns
or other events in this world view.

Messianic Expectation and Healing

One further issue needs some consideration. It has been argued
frequently that the activity of Jesus was a declaration of his Messianic
role and his healings and exorcisms were to be seen as evidence that
God's kingdom was in the process of arriving (or indeed had already
arrived) [77]. Care has to be exercised, however, about trying to read into
the stories of the Jesus-event interpretations that fit the preconceived
ideas of a developed Christian dogmatic. Whatever else may be said
about Jesus, it is unquestionable that all his actions and all his words
derive from his utter Jewishness and moreover, a specific Jewishness
within the Galilean world of the first century. 'Whatever it is that Jesus
is up to, it is as a Jew *within his particular world of Judaism* (italics
original). His sense of himself, his vocation, his destiny, even his
identity, all exist without remainder within the ferment of his Jewish
understandings of God and the world and history' [78]. In this specific
context, it is not at all clear to what extent healing and exorcism were
understood to be an essential part of Messianic leadership. It may
reasonably be argued that the character and the activity of Jesus
proclaimed him as a 'holy man', as Vermes has put it, 'curing physical
ills and disabilities and "exorcising" sick spirits, ministering to the
diseased in the name of God, his place was in that stream of Judaism
inherited from the prophets and exemplified by such figures as Elijah
and Elisha' [79].

However, the mere fact of healing and exorcising was certainly not
seen by itself as being evidence of the impending arrival of the kingdom
of God - such activity was going on all the time and it was only in a
disclosure situation that people saw in Jesus someone other than a
wandering exorcist or prophet/healer as the confession of Peter and the
response of Jesus to it makes clear (Mark 8:27-30). E. P. Sanders has
strongly criticised the view that the contemporaries of Jesus were
looking for a miracle-working Messiah. He comments, 'the few
references to a coming Messiah in Jewish literature do not depict him as

a miracle-worker. There was no expectation of a coming Son of God at all. Like other ancient people, Jews believed in miracles but did not think that the ability to perform them proved exalted status'[80]. On the other hand, the early ministry of Jesus, especially as presented in the Fourth Gospel, appeared to conform in some degree with the picture that John the Baptist had drawn of a national charismatic leader who would usher in the fires of God's judgment and redeem his people. This is not the place to argue this issue, but it would seem that there was enough general evidence for the national leadership, even if they did not altogether believe it, to use the charge of Messianic pretence in order to ensure the execution of Jesus[81].

The question arises, therefore, whether Jesus, as one who, in some degree, accepted Messianic status, would have been expected to perform 'wonders'. This is not quite the same as the previous question. The existence of exorcists and other 'wonder workers' would seem to make it clear that such activities did not provide 'proof' of Messianic status, but on the other hand, it might have been expected that the Messiah would perform 'wonders' when he came, although this is not entirely clear. It is much more likely that such activity pointed to him as being a 'man sent from God' (John 3:2), a prophetic figure, even the eschatological prophet. As E P Sanders comments, 'whether or not Jesus offered his miracles as signs that he spoke for God, they convinced some that he did so, and they considered him a special figure in God's plan'[82].

On the other hand, it may be argued that the Messiah would be expected to perform 'wonders' as part of his restoration of all things. In the past God had performed great wonders for the deliverance of his people and they demonstrated his power and majesty (note Exodus 4:5, 21, Psalm 77:14, etc). When the Future Age was being ushered in, it was expected that such 'signs' would be in evidence again. Such concepts had their origin in the later prophetic writings and it was an idea that would profoundly influence not only sectarian Judaism, but also early Christianity, particularly using the analogy of the signs and wonders of the Exodus tradition[83]. Theologically, however, these ideas are not to be confused with magic. As was noted earlier, magic is an attempt to coerce power and manipulate it to gain one's own ends. The expectation of Messianic 'miracle' was thoroughly religious: it was the hope of the expression of God's glory and the fulfilment of his will in a new creative activity.

It is within this context that attention needs to be paid to the way in which Jesus himself understood his actions. As will be discussed in more detail later, the healings of Jesus were not in any sense random events. There was very clearly a programmatic element that meant that certain conditions were 'healed' and others were ignored. The activity of Jesus was not simply a matter of compassion; it was a direct, but nonetheless parabolic, statement of the restoration of Israel. If scholars such as N. T. Wright [84] and others are correct in seeing the ministry of Jesus as a prophetic, but subversive, announcement of the rule or kingdom (βασιλεια) of God with an agenda which cut across the presuppositions of both the revolutionaries and the establishment, then the picture of divine restoration was symbolically presented in the restoration of broken and damaged people. The important point to note, however, is that it is certain groups and certain groups only, which formed the prophetic vision and the fulfilment of that vision in the work of Jesus. As N.T. Wright has put it, 'Jesus' healings, which formed a central and vital part of his whole symbolic praxis are ... the symbolic expression of Jesus' reconstitution of Israel' [85]. The forms of illness or disability that were healed were specifically those forms of sickness and disability that excluded a person from full membership of the people of God. The restoration of all things meant that the blind would see, the deaf would hear, the lame would leap and the dumb would sing. In addition, Jesus also deals with such conditions as leprosy or ceremonial uncleanness (as in the menorrhagic woman) that also separated the sufferer from the fellowship of God's people.

It is pertinent to note in this context that the approach of the Qumran community, generally assumed to be Essenes and certainly to be considered as another radical group looking for the revelation of God's kingdom, was very different. The 'Messianic rule' (1QSa) excluded the blind, the lame, the deaf and the dumb from membership of the eschatological community in much the same way as they had been excluded from Israel's priesthood (Lev 21:16-21). The relevant section is worth quoting in full:

> no man smitten with any human uncleanness shall enter the assembly of God· no man smitten with any of them shall be confirmed in his office in the congregation. No man smitten in his flesh, or paralysed in his feet or hands, or lame, or blind, or deaf, or dumb or smitten in his flesh by a visible blemish; no old or tottery man unable to stay still in the midst of the congregation; none of these shall come to hold office among the congregation of the men of renown' [86].

Where Qumran attempted to create a restored community by keeping people out, by taking the sectarian approach to maintaining the purity of God's people, Jesus deliberately created his new community by bringing such people within its fold. All his work pointed to the reality that God was fulfilling his ancient promises that in Abraham all nations of the earth would be blessed and his healing activity was one sign that the kingdom of God was present in and through his own ministry.

The healing activity of Jesus has to be considered, therefore, within the context of his understanding of his mission and its relationship to the fulfilment of the Old Testament prophecies. There seems to be little doubt that the Old Testament hope of restoration contained within it the hope of the removal of sickness, seen as a consequence of the sinfulness of humanity, either in direct personal terms or as a broad result of the Fall. The prophetic hope was for a radical and universal change for the better. The wicked would be destroyed (Mal 4:1), there would be renewal and transformation of the whole earth (Isa 35:1,2; 65:17) and the righteous would flourish (Zeph 3:11-20). Within this framework of divine transformation and the establishment of God's rule of righteousness and peace there would be the eschatological healing of the people of God as the inevitable concomitant of the removal of the effects of human sin as these were understood (Isa 35:6; 42:6-7; 61:1, etc) [87]. There is a reasonable basis, therefore, as has been underlined previously in this discussion, for understanding the healing of sickness as central to the establishment of God's rule [88]. The healings are thus to be seen, not so much as 'evidence', but as a symbolic representation of the universal welcome of God for all who have been previously excluded from the blessings of God - including ultimately the gentiles. The coming of Jesus in a Messianic role is a demonstration of the universal nature of God's welcome - there is table fellowship for all and sundry, irrespective of their background, their social status, their racial antecedents and their 'cleanness' or 'uncleanness' in terms of Jewish ritual purity. The healings were thus not simply acts of compassion and they were not indiscriminate or even universal, rather they were carefully delimited to emphasise a specific theological point in terms of the universality of the divine blessing associated with his person as the one through whom God's rule was to be known and experienced.

This understanding was clearly part of the post-Easter faith of the Church which was able to construct an understanding of the work of Jesus in healing and exorcising which could constitute a 'sign' of his status as Lord and Messiah. The healings and other 'works of power and wonders' were construed by the Church as evidence that in Jesus the apocalyptic 'age to come' had already arrived, the forces of evil were in retreat. Yet it should also be recognised that these actions did not, in themselves, 'prove' that Jesus was the Messiah and it is probably correct to assess them as demonstrating no more than that he was a man of God, albeit the one through whom God was at work in restoration and in bringing in his rule. Judging from Acts 2:22, this was the assessment of the primitive Church. At this verse Peter is reported as saying that Jesus was, 'attested (ἀποδεδειγμενον) by God with works of power, wonders and signs'. These are all favourite Lukan words and in this context they indicate that, for Luke, the acts of Jesus formed his attestation (ἀποδειχνυμι) as a man of God (compare the words of Nicodemus, 'no one can do the signs that you do unless God was with him' John 3:2). The early work of Jesus may have been a pointer for the one with eyes to see or ears to hear, but it was only the Easter Event, the reality of resurrection, the new creative activity of God, that affirmed the greater truth that God had made this same Jesus both Lord and Messiah (Acts 2:36 and note also Rom 1:3,4 where very similar views are expressed).

These hopes persisted through the first century and if Josephus correctly reflects the general views of the time, then it would appear that 'the coming deliverer was expected as an eschatological, wonder-working prophet, for which Moses was the major prototype' [89] and, in consequence, 'the accepted evidence of Messianic leadership was the ability to work miracles or the claim to be able to work them at some crucial moment' [90]. This also seems to be reflected in the response of Jesus to John the Baptist's request at Matt 11:2-5. Jesus was not alone with respect to his range of activities and making such claims as even the New Testament makes clear (see Acts 5:36,37). Josephus was, not surprisingly, somewhat scathing about these 'pretenders' and he talks about the country being full of brigands and imposters who deceived the people [91]. The term, however, was used of wizards, enchanters and the like and suggests that these Messianic pretenders acquired a reputation for supernatural powers, possibly by curing the sick and insane, and these were regarded as signs of their divine authority. Brandon comments that this 'means that Messianic pretenders were regarded as *goetes* by the unsympathetic, such as Josephus, because they were popularly reputed to be wonder-workers' [92]. Thus, as in the 'miracle-mania' of the medieval world in Europe, theology can rapidly degenerate into superstition.

If this view is correct, then it would appear that some at least expected the Messiah to be able to perform 'miracles' or at least to bring healing as the fulfilment of the ancient prophecies. There is a sense, therefore, in which it is possible to argue that the activity of Jesus attested his Messianic role. However, the issue is not one of attestation, but rather one of prophetic symbolism, as far as Jesus himself seems to have viewed his ministry. The healings were undertaken as acted parables, pointing to the welcome that God was to give to all, and especially to those who had been the excluded and marginalised. Such a view would possibly lie behind the use of 'sign' (σεμειον) by John. The issue remains open and will remain a matter of debate. It is clear, however, that there was considerable controversy over this issue from such passages as Mark 8:11-12; Matt 12:38-42; 16:1-4 and Luke 11:29-32. The Beelzebub controversy suggests strongly that whatever views there my have been about the expected activity of the Messiah, it was always possible to controvert the testimony of the 'miraculous', something that Paul was to find some years later in his controversies with the Corinthians [93].

It has to be recognised that what is written about Jesus derives from those who accepted him as Lord and Messiah. The early Christian proclamation contained the clearest assertions that the last days, the ultimate *eschaton* of the Future Age, the age of the new creation to be ushered in by the Messiah, had already dawned in Jesus. This conviction, which has been shared by the Church through all centuries, will have inevitably determined to some extent the picture of the work of Jesus that the four evangelists present and will also have determined the symbolic framework into which they set his ministry. In other words, those who were, from other reasons, already convinced of the Messianic nature of the work of Jesus and had come to know in him the reality of God's new creation, his renewal and transformation of human existence, saw his activity in healing as a 'sign' of his status. This seems very much the standpoint of the writer of the Fourth Gospel for example. Such an understanding, however, seems to be one of disclosure rather than one which the work of Jesus demanded unequivocally. The fact is, as Sanders points out, 'according to the Gospels, the miracles show that Jesus spoke and acted with divine authority, and some saw it that way, though others doubted. They depict Jesus himself as not appealing to the miracles as establishing his authority' [94]. Nonetheless, they do depict Jesus as using the healings as signs of the inclusiveness of the rule of God and the openness of God to all who would come to him, in other words, their function is essentially parabolic.   The healings function in deed in the same way as the parables function in word.   In either case, there was an element of hiddenness and true understanding of the underlying meaning of event or word was dependent on disclosure.

It is also worth commenting that the gospels do not portray Jesus as a Hellenistic 'divine man' who was able to undertake miraculous actions by virtue of his status.   There was nothing in the ministry of Jesus which made him into some God-like miracle worker - he does not stride across the pages of the gospels like a demi-god, but rather as a thoroughly God-dependent and humble man.   The emphasis as has been noted was on Jesus as a prophet and especially the long-promised prophet 'like Moses' and, as has been argued [95], the emphasis was not on the ability to perform miracles for such a person, but on the possession of such characteristics as wisdom and kingliness.   Jesus, in fact, does not appear as a 'divine man' in any real sense: the emphasis was not on apprehending who he was by virtue of unassailable proofs, but on the understanding which comes only through disclosure arising from faith.   Once the 'penny had dropped', then there could be a wider appreciation of the deeper symbolism associated with his ministry.

Notes and references

[1]   See in particular, Sigerist, H. (1951). *A History of Medicine.* Vol. 1. Oxford University Press, Oxford; Guthrie, D. (1945). *A History of Medicine.* Nelson, London. pp 39-83; Edelstein, L. (1967). *Ancient Medicine: Selected Papers of Ludwig Edelstein.* (edited by Temkin, O. and Temkin, C.L.) Johns Hopkins University Press, Baltimore; Gordon, B.L. (1949). *Medicine throughout Antiquity.* F.A. Davis, Philadelphia; Preuss, J. (1978=1911). *Biblical and Talmudic Medicine.* (edited by Rosner, F.) Sanhedrin Press, New York; Rosner, F. (1977). *Medicine in the Bible and Talmud.* Ktav Publishing House, New York; Scarborough, J. (1969). *Roman Medicine.* Thames and Hudson, London; Grmek, M.D. (1989). *Diseases in the Ancient Greek World.* ET. Johns Hopkins University Press, Baltimore; Jackson, R.P.J. (1988). *Doctors and Disease in the Roman Empire.* British Museum Publications, London; Lloyd, G.E.R. (1973). *Greek Science after Aristotle.* Norton, New York; Longrigg, J. (1993). *Greek Rational Medicine: Philosophy and Medicine from Alcmaeon to the Alexandrians.* Routledge, London; Amundsen, D.W. (1996). *Medicine, Society and Faith in the Ancient and Medieval Worlds.* Johns Hopkins University Press, Baltimore; Faraone, C.A. and Obbink, D. (Eds). (1991). *Magika Hiera: Ancient Greek Magic and Medicine.* Oxford University Press, Oxford.   Note also the relevant articles in Hornblow, S. and Spawforth, A. (eds). (1996). *The Oxford Classical Dictionary.* Oxford University Press,

Oxford (particularly the articles on medicine (pp 945-949) and disease (p 486)).

[2] Hemer, C.J. (1986). Medicine in the New Testament world. In: Palmer B (ed), *Medicine and the Bible*, Paternoster Press, Exeter. p 43.

[3] Grant, R.M. (1952). *Miracle and Natural Law in Graeco-Roman and early Christian Thought.* North Holland, Amsterdam. p 41.

[4] See Parkin, T.G. (1992). *Demography and Roman Society.* Johns Hopkins University Press, Baltimore (especially pp 82-86) and Bagnall, R.S. and Frier, B.W. (1994). *The Demography of Roman Egypt.* Cambridge University Press, Cambridge (note especially the life expectancy tables in chapter 4). The implications of this high general mortality for the Christian mission have been discussed by Keith Hopkins. He has argued that because sickness and death were such an all-prevailing aspect of existence, the healing and miraculous element of Christianity was a major attraction and central to its rapid expansion (Hopkins, K. (1998). Christian number and its implications. *Journal of Early Christian Studies.* 6. 185-226. See also his earlier (1983) study, *Death and Renewal.* Cambridge University Press, Cambridge).

[5] An estimate of 8% infant mortality has been suggested (French, V. (1986). Midwives and maternity care in the Roman world. *Helios.* (New Series). 13. 69-84). Keith Hopkins made an estimate that 28% of Roman babies had died before their first birthday (*Death and Renewal.* p 225). On the other hand Calvin Wells has argued that maternal mortality, at least, has probably been overestimated and that other factors, such as poor diet and infection generally, were responsible for the shorter lives of women in that period (Wells, C. (1975). Ancient obstetric hazards and female mortality. *Bulletin of the New York Academy of Medicine.* 51. 1235-1249).

[6] Lambourne, R.A. (1963). *Community, Church and Healing.* Darton, Longman and Todd, London. p 37

[7] Wright, N.T. (1992). *The New Testament and the People of God.* SPCK, London. p 3.

[8] See for example, Schürer, E., Vermes, G., Miller, F. (1975). *The History of the Jewish People in the Age of Jesus Christ.* T & T Clark, Edinburgh. Vol 2. pp 7-10.

[9] Note the discussion in Freyne, S. (1988). *Galilee, Jesus and the Gospels: Literary Approaches and Historical Investigations.* Fortress Press, Philadelphia. pp 167-171. Note also the evidence of funerary inscriptions in Galilee (Meyer, E.M. and Strange, J.F. (1981). *Archaeology, the Rabbis and Early Christianity.* SCM, London. p 102).

[10] Freyne remarks, 'Diversity has been recognised as one of the hallmarks of pre-70 Jewish religion'. Freyne, S. (1988). *Galilee.* p 176.

[11] Hengel, M. (1974). *Judaism and Hellenism,* SCM, London. Vol 1. pp 1ff and 104. Note however the critiques of his position in Feldman, L.H. (1986). How much Hellenism in Jewish Palestine? *Hebrew Union College Annual.* 57. 83-111 and Millar, F. (1978). The background of the Maccabean revolution: Reflections on Martin Hengel's 'Judaism and Hellenism'. *Journal of Jewish Studies.* 29. 9.

[12] Ferguson, E. (1987). *Backgrounds of Early Christianity*. Eerdmans, Grand Rapids. p 316.

[13] See further, Sigerist, H.E. (1951). *A History of Medicine*, Oxford University Press, New York. See also Kee, H.C. (1986). *Medicine, Miracle and Magic in New Testament Times*. Cambridge University Press, Cambridge. This provides a good overview, but the present writer disagrees with the attempt to distinguish between magic and miracle as completely separate concepts: in the writer's opinion both relate to a magico-religious world view.

[14] Kee, H.C. (1986). *Medicine, Miracle and Magic*. p. 3

[15] Longrigg, J. (1993). *Greek Rational Medicine*. p 14.

[16] Celsus, *De medicina* 1. Proem B.

[17] See Hippocrates. *Concerning Airs*. 1. B.

[18] Hemer, C.J.(1986). *Medicine and the Bible*. p 44.

[19] See further, Longrigg, J (1993). *Greek Rational Medicine*, pp 31-37.

[20] Sherwin-White, S.M. quoted in Kee, H.C. (1986). *Medicine, Mracle and Magic*, p 31. See also Temkin, O. (1991). *Hippocrates in a world of Pagans and Christians*. Johns Hopkins University Press, Baltimore.

[21] Hippocrates, *On the Sacred Disease*, 3-10. Considerable doubt exists about the authenticity of many of the surviving writings of the 'Hippocratic Corpus'. For a fuller discussion of the Hippocratic school and epilepsy see Temkin, O. (1933). Views on epilepsy in the Hippocratic period. *Bulletin of the History of Medicine*. 1. 41-44 and Temkin, O. (1933). The doctrine of epilepsy in the Hippocratic writings. *Bulletin of the History of Medicine*. 1. 277-322.

[22] Guthrie, D. (1945). *A History of Medicine*. p 57.

[23] Details of plant medicaments of the time can be found in volume 1 of Dioscorides *Greek Herbal* (translated by J Goodyer, edited by R. T. Gunther (1959 = 1934), Hafner, New York). See also Scarborough, J. (1991). The pharmacology of sacred plants and roots. In: Faraone, C.A. and Obbink, D (Eds). *Magika Hiera*. pp 139-161. Other histories discuss the available materia medica briefly, such as A. Rendle Short (1953) *The Bible and Modern Medicine*. Paternoster Press, London. pp 70-73.

[24] Kee, H.C. (1986). *Medicine, Miracle and Magic*. p 28.

[25] Pliny. *Historia Naturalis*. particularly 28 and 30.

[26] Soranus. *Medicus* In: Ilberg, J. (1927). *Corpus Medicorum Graecorum*. Vol 4 (Tuebner, Leipzig) the section on obstetric matters has been translated by Temkin, O. (1956). *Soranus' Gynecology*. (Johns Hopkins University Press, Baltimore).

[27] Cartwright, F.F. (1977). *Social History of Medicine*. p 6.

[28] For illustrations of Roman surgical instruments see Milne, J.S. (1907). *Surgical Instruments in Greek and Roman Times*. Oxford University Press, Oxford.

[29] For details see Kudlien, F. and During, R.J. (Eds). (1991). *Galen's Methods of Healing: Proceedings of the 1992 Galen Symposium*. E.J. Brill, Leiden. It is of interest to note that the amount of Galen's surviving text far exceeds that of all other extant Greek authors: more than four times that of Plato, nearly three times that of Aristotle and twice that of Plutarch (see Berkowitz, L. and

Squitier, K.A. (eds) (1990). *Canon of Greek Authors and Works.* Oxford University Press, Oxford).

[30] Galen. *Opera Omnia* XV. 313. As an aside, things did not change for centuries. In Edinburgh, in the seventeenth century, a mixture of senna, prunes, mercury and liquorice (so-called *electuarium lenitivum*) was a favourite with physicians indicating that things had really not changed very much in all those years. Medical students were still examined on the aphorisms of Hippocrates and disease was still considered to be due to an imbalance in one or more of the four humours of blood, black bile, yellow bile and phlegm (for details of this period see Dingwall, H. (1995). *Physicians, Surgeons and Apothecaries: Medical Practice in Seventeenth Century Edinburgh.* Tuckwell Press, Edinburgh).

[31] The practice of Graeco-Roman medicine is discussed in Scarborough, J. (1969). *Roman Medicine.* Thames and Hudson, London and also Jackson, R.P.J. (1993). Roman medicine: the practitioners and their practice. *Aufstieg und Niedergang der Römischen Welt.* 11. 37. 79-101. Note also the references given at p 10, n 1 above.

[32] Stambaugh, J. and Balch, D. (1986). *The Social World of the First Christians.* SPCK, London. p 71

[33] Celsus. *De medicina* 1. 10

[34] See the discussions in Theissen, G. (1982). *The Social Setting of Pauline Christianity.* Fortress Press, Philadelphia (especially pp 69-120) and also Horrell, D.G. (1996). *The Social Ethos of the Corinthian Correspondence: Interests and Ideology from 1 Corinthians to 1 Clement.* T & T Clark, Edinburgh.

[35] Josephus, *Jewish War,* 1.33.5.

[36] See the discussion in Jeremias, J. (1969). *Jerusalem in the Time of Jesus,* SCM. London, pp 17f, 26f. 304-306.

[37] Josephus, *Life.* 72. Earlier he mentions a female physician (*Life.* 37) which must have been quite unusual at this time.

[38] See the Mishnah tractates *Shekalim* 5.2, and *Erubin* 10, 13f.

[39] Hemer, C.J. (1986). *Medicine and the Bible.* p 57.

[40] See Fletcher, R. (1997). *The Conversion of Europe: From Paganism to Christianity 371-1386 AD.* Harper Collins, London. pp 15-16 and 34-38.

[41] Mishnah tractate, *Kiddushin* 4.14

[42] See Babylonian Talmud *Sanhedrin* 17b, p; *Kiddushin* 66d; 82a: *Pesahim* 113a. Note also the praise given to the physician in Ecclesiasticus 38:1-15.

[43] There is a vast literature on the subject. The following are no more than a selection of the secondary sources and the list excludes journal articles and includes only books. Some additional literature will be cited in relation to the specific exorcisms of Jesus as recorded in the Gospels when these are considered in subsequent chapters. Alexander, W.M. (1902). *Demon Possession in the New Testament.* T&T Clark, Edinburgh; Caird, G.B. (1956). *Principalities and Powers,* Clarendon Press, Oxford; Hengel, M. (1974). *Judaism and Hellenism.* SCM, London; Hull, J.M (1974). *Hellenistic Magic and the Synoptic Tradition,* SCM, London; Kee, H C. (1986). *Medicine,*

Miracle and Magic in the New Testament. Cambridge University Press, Cambridge; McCasland, S.V. (1951). *By the Finger of God: Demon Possession and Exorcism in Early Christianity*, Scribner, New York; Smith, M. (1978). *Jesus the Magician*, Gollancz, London; Twelftree, G.H. (1985). *Christ Triumphant: Exorcism Then and Now*, Hodder and Stoughton, London; and Twelftree, G.H. (1993). *Jesus the Exorcist: A Contribution to the Study of the Historical Jesus.* JCB Mohr, Tübingen/Hendrickson, Peabody MA. This last volume contains an up to date extensive bibliography of relevant literature.
[44] Short, A. Rendle. (1953). *The Bible and Modern Medicine.* Paternoster Press, London. p 109.
[45] Stamburgh, J. and Balch, D. (1986). *The Social World of the First Christians.* p 112. The immense difficulties in interpreting the social background of the original Jesus Movement are discussed in Tidball, D. (1983). *An Introduction to the Sociology of the New Testament.* Paternoster Press, Exeter.
[46] This will be discussed in more detail later. See also the writer's study, Howard, J.K. (1985). New Testament exorcism and its significance today. *Expository Times* 96. 105-109.
[47] That Jesus could be referring to poverty as a state of happiness in itself is patently absurd. As Leon Morris (1992) remarks, 'poverty is not a blessing, nor is powerlessness. Whatever Jesus meant, it was surely not that these states are blessed in themselves' (*The Gospel according to Matthew.* Eerdmans, Grand Rapids. p 96).
[48] On the economic situation in first century Palestine see Jeremias, J. (1969). *Jerusalem in the Time of Jesus,* SCM, London and also Goodman, R. (1983). *State and Society in Roman Galilee,* Rowman and Allanheld, Totawa, NJ.
[49] *Shabbath* 6.6, 10; 6. 1; 14.4.
[50] Pliny, *Historia Naturalis* 28.77.250; 30.43.125; 30.44.129 -130.
[51] Pliny, *Historia Naturalis* 26.90.160-161. The use of herbs was not confined to the practitioners of folk medicine, but the more sophisticated physician also recommended them as necessary (see for example, Celsus, *De medicina* 2.8.16; 5.25.14-15 for recommendations of herbs in association with childbirth problems).
[52] Howard, J.Keir. (1987). Occupationally related cancer. In: Howard, J. Keir and Tyrer, F.H. (eds), *A Textbook of Occupational Medicine,* Churchill Livingstone, Edinburgh. p 170.
[53] German, G.A. (1972). Psychiatry. In: Shaper, A.G., Kibukamusoke, J.W., Hutt, M.S.R. (eds). *Medicine in a Tropical Environment.* British Medical Association, London. pp 329-347.
[54] Spurgeon, A., Gompertz, D. and Harrington, J.M. (1996). Modifiers of non-specific symptoms in occupational and environmental syndromes. *Occupational and Environmental Medicine.* 53. 361-366. For a full discussion of the issues see particularly, Pilowsky, I. (1997). *Abnormal Illness Behaviour.* Wiley, Chichester.

[55] See for example the Mishnah tractates, *Horayoth* 10a; *Yoma* 77b, 83b; *Ta'anith* 20b; *Bekhoroth* 44b; *Gittin* 67b. See also Josephus, *Antiquities of the Jews* 6.8.2, 8,25.

[56] See further Cullmann, O. (1951). *Christ and Time.* SCM, London; Barr, J. (1962). *Biblical Words for Time.* SCM, London and Fawcett, T. (1973). *Hebrew Myth and Christian Gospel.* SCM, London.

[57] Russell, D.S. (1964). *The Method and Message of Jewish Apocalyptic*, SCM, London. p 257. These ideas are discussed in detail in pp 235-262. See also Hanson, P.D. (1975). *The Dawn of Apocalyptic: The Historical and Sociological Roots of Jewish Apocalyptic Eschatology*, Fortress Press, Philadelphia. Revised edn.

[58] Walker, A. (1995). The devil you think you know: demonology and the charismatic movement. In: Smail, T., Walker, A. and Wright, N. *Charismatic Renewal.* SPCK, London. p 89.

[59] Josephus, *Jewish War* 2:136. Two important scrolls from Qumran (4QTherapeia and 4QprNab) possibly reflect Essene thinking, on the assumption that the scrolls actually belonged to the Qumran community. This is a point not yet universally agreed and the only real evidence lies in an ostracon recording a transfer of property which is interpreted in totally different ways by different scholars (see Cross, F.M. and Eshel, E. (1997) Ostraca from Khirbet Qumrân. *Israeli Exploration Journal.* 47.17-28 and Yardeni, A. (1997). A draft of a deed of an ostracon from Khirbet Qumrân. *Israeli Exploration Journal.* 47. 233-237).

[60] Josephus, *Antiquities of the Jews*, 8: 40-49.

[61] See Betz, H.D. (ed). (1986). *The Greek Magical Papyri in Translation.* University of Chicago Press, Chicago.

[62] Among the works listed at p 41, n 43 see especially the discussions in Smith, M. (1976) *Jesus the Magician;* Twelftree, G. (1985). *Christ Triumphant* and (1993). *Jesus the Exorcist* and also Kee H. C. (1986) *Medicine, Miracle and Magic in New Testament Times.* The older, but encyclopaedic, work of Alexander, W.M. (1902). *Demonic Possession in the New Testament.* T&T Clark, Edinburgh, should also be consulted. These works provide examples of the various techniques, incantations, etc used by exorcists roughly contemporaneous with Jesus, as well as the later Greek magical papyri.

[63] See for example Meier, J.P. (1994). *A Marginal Jew: Rethinking the Historical Jesus.* Doubleday, New York. Vol 2. p 574. n 72.

[64] The title is taken from Dodds, E.R. (1990 = 1965). *Pagan and Christian in an Age of Uncertainty.* Cambridge University Press, Cambridge.

[65] Kee, H.C. (1983). *Miracle in the Early Christian World: A Study in Sociohistorical Method.* Yale University Press, New Haven, p 52

[66] Kee, H.C. (1977). *Community of the New Age: Studies in Mark's Gospel*, SCM, London. p 2.

[67] Ignatius, *Ephesians* 7:2. The term is used frequently in Clement of Alexandria (eg *Quis Div Salv* 29).

[68] See Kee, H.C. *Medicine, Miracle and Magic.* p 79. A.E. Harvey (1982) has argued similarly when he writes that the healings of Jesus were carried out

'with the absolute minimum of those technical procedures which would most surely have aroused suspicion about his true credentials and motives' (*Jesus and the Constraints of History*. SCM, London. p 109). See also the discussion in Twelftree, G.H. (1993). *Jesus the Exorcist.* pp 157-165. It will be argued later in this study that traces of the methodologies of Jesus remain, although most have been removed for apologetic reasons from the Gospel records.

[69] See the discussion in Twelftree, G.H. (1993). *Jesus the Exorcist.* pp 157-165

[70] For examples see Bonner, C. (1944). The violence of departing demons. *Harvard Theological Review.* 37. 334-336.

[71] See Sargant, W. and Slater, E. (1963). *An Introduction to Physical Means of Treatment in Psychiatry.* Livingstone, Edinburgh. The use of abreaction has fallen into some disrepute in recent years and was mainly used in post-trauma and battle situations where it achieved significant, although largely temporary, results. This method of therapy will be discussed further in respect of the exorcisms of Jesus (see especially p 60). For the use of catharsis in ancient healing rites, see Nichols, M.P. and Dax, M. (1977). *Catharsis in Psychotherapy.* Gardner Press, New York and also Graves, Robert (1959). Brain washing in ancient times. In: Sargant, W. *Battle for the Mind.* Pan Books, London. Revised edn. pp 156-164.

[72] Kee, H.C. (1986). *Medicine, Miracle and Magic*, p 2ff.

[73] This is argued very cogently by N. T. Wright (1996) (*Jesus and the Victory of God*. SPCK, London) who sees the ministry of Jesus as a programmatic presentation of this reality.

[74] See the discussion of some of these issues in Meier, J.P. (1994). *A Marginal Jew.* Vol 2. especially pp 537-545.

[75] See for example, Manson, W. (1943). *Jesus the Messiah*, Hodder and Stoughton, London. p 44.

[76] Fawcett, T. *Hebrew Myth and Christian Gospel.* p 102.

[77] The exact nature of Jewish messianic expectation in the time of Jesus is a matter for ongoing debate. That there was a 'Messianic' expectation, however, in whatever way this was understood, seems incontrovertible. See further Neusner, J., Green, W.S., Fredrichs, E.S. (eds). (1987). *Judaism and their Messiahs at the Turn of the Christian Era.* Cambridge University Press, Cambridge; Zeitlin, I.M. (1988). *Jesus and the Judaism of his Time.* Polity, Cambridge. pp 38-44 and Collins, J.J. (1995). *The Scepter and the Star: The Messiahs of the Dead Sea Scrolls and Other Ancient Literature.* Doubleday, New York.

[78] Lee, B.J. (1988). *The Galilean Jewishness of Jesus. Retrieving the Jewish Origins of Christianity.* Paulist Press, New York. p 56.

[79] Vermes, G. (1983). *Jesus and the World of Judaism*, SCM, London. p 27.

[80] Sanders, E.P. (1993). *The Historical Figure of Jesus.* Penguin Books, Harmondsworth. p 133. Similarly, G.H. Twelftree (1993) remarks that 'it is difficult to see Jesus' observers connecting what was a common occurrence in their day with Jesus being self-evidently the Messiah' (*Jesus the Exorcist.* p 189). Note however, Kee, H.C. (1989). Magic and Messiah. In: Neusner, J.,

Frerichs, E.S. and Flesher, P.V.M. (eds). *Religion, Science and Magic.* Oxford University Press, Oxford. pp 121-141.

[81] These issues are discussed for example in Robinson, J.A.T. (1985). *The Priority of John,* SCM, London. pp 158-189 and note also the essays by Gerhard Schneider (The political charge against Jesus (Luke 23:2)) and E. Bammel (The trial before Pilate), in Bammel, E. and Moule, C.F.D. (1988). *Jesus and the Politics of His Day.* Cambridge University Press, Cambridge. 1984. pp 403-414 and 415-452.

[82] Sanders, E.P. (1985). *Jesus and Judaism.* SCM, London. p. 172.

[83] Note Kee, H.C. *Community of the New Age,* p 27,

[84] See both his *New Testament and the People of God.* (1992) and *Jesus and the Victory of God.* (1996), both published by SPCK, London.

[85] Wright, N.T. (1996). Jesus' symbols of the kingdom: Thomas Burns Lectures, University of Otago, New Zealand 1996 (3). *Stimulus.* 4 (4). 28

[86] The Messianic Rule (1QSa). In: Vermes, G. (1987). *The Dead Sea Scrolls in English.* Penguin Books, Harmondsworth. p 102. The comment about the tottery old man, 'unable to stay still' is most likely a reference to Parkinson's disease, although the details are insufficient for certainty.

[87] For a detailed discussion of the place of healing in Israel's thought and expectation see Brown, M.L. (1995) *Israel's Divine Healer.* Paternoster Press, Carlisle.

[88] It is remarkable that such a careful and balanced study as Beasley-Murray, G.R. (1986). *Jesus and the Kingdom of God,* (Eerdmans, Grand Rapids) can discuss these issues without any reference whatever to the healing work of Jesus and only a passing nod at the exorcisms.

[89] Kee, H.C. *Community of the New Age,* p 28.

[90] Brandon, S.G.F. (1968). *Jesus and the Zealots.* Manchester University Press, Manchester. p 112.

[91] Josephus, *Jewish War.* 2: 264-265; *Antiquities of the Jews.* 20: 160.

[92] Brandon, S G F.(1968). *Jesus and the Zealots.* p 113.

[93] See the discussion later in this study at chapter 7, particularly pp 234-236.

[94] Sanders, E.P. *Jesus and Judaism.* p 172.

[95] See notably Holladay, C.H. (1977). *Theios-Aner in Hellenistic Judaism.* Scholars Press, Missoula, MT and also the summary discussion in Meier, J.P. (1994). *A Marginal Jew.* Vol 2. pp 595-616.

Chapter 3

THE HEALING MINISTRY OF JESUS: THE MARKAN TRADITION

In the healing miracles of Jesus, we see the saving activity of God himself ... the time of salvation has arrived in the person of Jesus, in whom the renewing, creative Spirit of God is at work.

Morna D Hooker

General considerations about the Gospel narratives

The earliest traditions about the words and works of Jesus make it clear that the accounts of his healings formed an essential part of the presentation of the good news of Jesus the Christ. These stories form an integral part of the Gospel narratives and their telling may possibly have been associated with the performance of healings in the apostolic mission such as those recorded in the Acts of the Apostles (eg 3:1-10; 5:12; 6:8; 13:6-12; 14:8-18), although this would be very much a matter of debate [1].

Questions arise, however, concerning the primary interest of the evangelists and the reasons underlying the prominence given to the healings and exorcisms in the Synoptic Gospels in particular. Some have argued that the stories were an essential part of the primary propaganda of the Christian mission in the Hellenistic world and were based on the models already in existence in the various forms of reports of the great deeds of leaders, heroes, and lawgivers that abounded at the time. In consequence, the written accounts are likely to owe more to imagination than fact on such a view. R.W. Funk and his colleagues are representative as they write, 'The gospels are now assumed to be narratives in which the memory of Jesus is embellished by mythic elements that express the church's faith in him, and by plausible fiction that enhance the telling of the gospel story for first-century listeners who knew about divine men and miracle workers firsthand' [2].

There seems to be little evidence that the primitive Church was concerned with recording miracles by themselves, as stories of marvels and wonders that formed part of a life of a peripatetic thaumaturgist, in the manner of Philostratus and his *Life of Apollonius*. The evangelists were concerned with proclamation and the heart of their writing was the same heart as the Church's preaching: it was to bear witness to what Jesus meant for faith and discipleship, not merely in the years of his own ministry, but more importantly for the people of their own day. This is one of the reasons that the Gospels continue to bear witness to what Jesus is to mean for faith and discipleship today. The healing stories (and other 'miracle' stories for that matter) are set out as part of the proclamation of the gospel and as such they require religious categories for their interpretation, an issue that will be discussed in more detail later.

In view of the essentially religious interest of the evangelists, it is not surprising that little attention was paid to the actual nature of the various diseases and conditions that were met during the ministry of Jesus. The writers saw the healing of different forms of sickness as being part of a programme that both showed and proclaimed the nature of the kingdom of God. N.T.Wright makes the important point that the mighty works were signs of the long awaited fulfilment of prophecy. He writes, 'For a first century Jew, most if not all the works of healing, which form the bulk of Jesus' mighty works, could be seen as the restoration to membership in Israel of those who, through sickness or whatever, had been excluded as ritually unclean. The healings thus function in exact parallel with the welcome of sinners, and this, we may be quite sure, was what Jesus himself intended. He never performed mighty works simply to impress. He saw them as part of the inauguration of the sovereign and healing rule of Israel's covenant god (sic)' [3].

There is thus a pattern to the healings that will become apparent as this study progresses. They were not random events, happening simply as circumstances dictated, but they were actions in almost all cases, that were related to those conditions which effectively removed a person from the holy community.   In other words, the healings were not primarily a matter of compassion or concern, but a proclamation that the day of God's visitation had come and the return from Exile was now a genuine possibility. This is not to suggest that Jesus had no compassion for those who were sick or in pain, evidence of his compassion exists throughout all the Gospels.   What it does say, however, is that emotions were not the primary reason for the healings - they were part of a programme.

This dominant religious theme has meant that the specific details of the individual healings are of only peripheral interest in most cases and the information which would add so much to medical analysis is consequently sparse. Not only so, but these accounts were probably dependent upon a largely unstructured oral tradition, although almost certainly one that existed in cycles of material rather than isolated free-floating pericopae, as the Form Critics thought [4]. It is likely, therefore, that the accounts of the ministry of Jesus reached the synoptic writers in largely fragmented form with no chronological framework, other than the events of Holy Week [5]. By the time that the evangelists took pen to papyrus, the stories, more than likely, had already passed through at least one generation of evangelism and teaching which in some instances seems to have reduced details and in others expanded them. In any case, there will have been 'editorial' activity affecting the structure and content of the story as it was handed down. That is to say, the Gospels do not present a woodenly slavish transmission of stories. They represent the end point of a living tradition that, even after the text had been written down, continued to be altered and adjusted with remarkable freedom and, at times, creativity (as for example in the so-called 'Western' text) [6].

This point is worth emphasising. The traditions at all stages, oral and written, were handled creatively: the writers were authors not merely scribes or copyists. Historical data, therefore, should not be simply read off as though what was in front of the reader was a set of case notes set down by a clinical assistant at the bedside. On the other hand, the fact that the tradition has been modified to meet new situations does not affect the underlying reliability of that tradition. It is a massive leap from recognising a creative handling of an actual event (something that happens everyday in the Press) to saying that the Gospels are simply works of fiction [7]. J.D.G. Dunn contends that the synoptic tradition provides direct access to the ministry of Jesus as it was remembered from the beginning and remarks that the early recorders of the traditions were 'preservers more than innovators ... seeking to transmit, retell, explain, interpret, elaborate, but not to create *de novo*' [8].

The development of the 'Jesus tradition' introduces problems in attempting to elucidate the medical details of the stories. These problems are compounded by the fact that the stories were collected and edited at a time when medical language was imprecise and when symptoms were frequently confused with the disease itself. Furthermore, the primary witnesses, first collectors and later editors of the Gospel traditions were not medically trained, unless Church traditions are correct in ascribing the major editor of the Third Gospel and Acts to Luke 'the beloved physician'. Nonetheless, even should this tradition be correct, he would have had to rely on non-medical sources for his material.

It is always difficult to diagnose at a distance and this is made even more difficult through the length of time that has elapsed since these healings took place. It is, nonetheless, possible, on the basis of the various clues and descriptions that are available, to undertake a cautious reconstruction in a number of the healing stories and provide a reasonable guess at diagnosis. In so doing this study adopts the position that there are no *a priori* grounds for not attempting to investigate or provide a scientific explanation of an event which religious faith classifies as a 'miracle'. Indeed, as Barr has shown, there is evidence that even in biblical times a process of critical evaluation of these events was in process, with explanations that were based upon what a post-Enlightenment world would call 'natural causes' rather than 'miracle', although the biblical writers maintained the reality of divine action [9]. A problem remains, however, in determining the extent to which the first century world separated 'natural' from 'divine' causation and whether the concepts of 'natural' or 'supernatural', which have become so much part of modern thinking, were really foreign to its conceptual models [10].

There is no doubt that the post-apostolic Church regularly appealed to miracles as part of its apologetic [11] and it was found to be something of a double edged sword, but this is not generally true of the New Testament writers as this study will attempt to demonstrate. That the philosophical schools of the Graeco-Roman world took what might be termed a more 'rational' view of events need not be doubted, but even their veneer of 'naturalism' was thin and they were much more subjective and fluid in their thinking and less rational than they appeared, as Grant has shown [12]. A natural explanation for an event was often held side by side with a recognition of the activity of God or the gods and the two need not be mutually exclusive.

In the first century Judaeo-Christian context, at the more popular level of everyday people and everyday events, the reality of divine action as the overarching cause of all events is undeniable, even though the Satanic hordes might challenge God with their limited power to act and do harm. In the world of the first century, while things in general may happen by themselves, there is a place for the intervention of God in ordinary human affairs. Moreover, the fact that a person was able to undertake activities that could be classified in varying degrees as 'miraculous' was an indication that God was with that person (note John 3:2) [13]. This is a matter of prime importance when giving any thought to the activity of Jesus and its significance: it is an anachronism to judge it using post-Enlightenment categories.

The healings of Jesus, it has been noted, were recorded against a background of his ministry of proclaiming the kingdom of God. The evangelists have taken the stories from the traditions they had received and used them as vehicles of their own proclamation. In that context they require religious categories to explain and interpret them. The Christian believer sees in the work of Jesus as well as in his words, a special disclosure of God's power and purposes, which reveals something of the character and significance of the Incarnation. 'Miracle', it is suggested at the outset, is a classification accorded by faith to certain events which may, for a variety of reasons, be classified as 'disclosure events' to use Ian Ramsay's terminology [14]. It is a specifically religious classification that introduces the concept of purpose into the equation and says nothing about the intrinsic nature of the event itself. It may or may not prove possible, on the basis of the data available, to provide a scientific explanation or interpretation of the event, but what is important to emphasise is that there can be no valid reason why the attempt should not be made. In this regard it is worth noting the comments of John Barton: 'The religious world today is full of credulity and a seeking of six impossible things to believe before breakfast. For me the problem is not how to defend the supernatural character of the faith I profess, but how to connect it with knowledge in other fields, both scientific and humanistic. For that task an approach which fences off scriptural revelation from the rest of knowledge has its dangers' [15].

Nonetheless, in spite of the avowed theological purpose of the evangelists, the general historicity of the Gospels requires to be taken seriously. Mark's value as an historical source and its likely closeness to eye-witnesses in the apostles themselves (traditionally Peter) has been discussed elsewhere [16] and does not need to be developed in this study. However, it has been all too fashionable to adopt a position of extreme historical pessimism, which ignores the reality of 'those who were there' when the events were happening and who were still alive when the written traditions were being formed. This applies particularly to Mark which, it is almost universally agreed, predates the fall of Jerusalem in AD 70 and was thus written between thirty and forty years after the events described and at a time when first hand memory still existed. It is perhaps for this reason that Mark draws attention to specific named individuals who were possibly still alive and well known in the congregations to which the Gospel was directed (eg Mark 10:46, 15:21).

Vincent Taylor has observed, 'When all the qualifications have been made, the presence of personal testimony is an element in the narrative process which it is folly to ignore' [17]. Memories are not that short and the activity of Jesus would certainly have caught the popular imagination in the small villages and townships of Galilee, just as it gave rise to blatant vilification on the part those who sought to discredit the whole Jesus Movement. As J.D.G. Dunn puts it, 'for the earliest Christians the most probable source for many of the accounts of Jesus' miracles would be the recollection of episodes in Jesus' ministry circulating in Galilee and among his first disciples and admirers' [18]. The Markan tradition developed, therefore, in a situation in which there was what Kelber has called 'an explosion' of differing opinions and remembered stories proliferating in what was still very largely a verbal world [19]. The continuing presence of the original disciples of Jesus in the early Church communities, however, would have represented a significant check on the amount of creativity that was acceptable in modifying the traditions, something to which some critical scholarship has consistently failed to give sufficient weight [20].

It is not denied that the stories about Jesus collected touches of folklore and legend and developed features of exaggeration or other forms of 'embroidery' in the process of transmission: indeed such a process is to be expected. Some aspects of this process may be seen in the way in which Luke, in particular, handles the Markan material and this will be noted specifically when the text is discussed in detail. Furthermore, the theological interests of the evangelists have also to be taken into account. They were making the stories tell a story so that specific details and even chronology became subservient to the central task of proclamation. Nonetheless, to suggest that the picture portrayed was a deliberate falsification of the facts to push forward some imagined social agenda does violence to the facts, violates common sense and is a negation of scientific procedures, as Dahl, among others, has pointed out [21]. The proclamation of the early Christians was centred in an Easter faith, in the words and works of Jesus interpreted in the light of Good Friday and Easter Day, but, equally, it was a proclamation that was completely grounded in the historical moment of a real Jesus.

Judgments about the theological interpretation of events, however, say nothing about the essential historicity of the events themselves and still less do they indicate the existence of an active early Church propaganda machine bent on inventing stories or sayings of Jesus designed to meet the needs of the community and give bite to the evangelistic programme [22]. It may be noted, in passing, that the generally held assumption that the Gospels were written to meet the needs of specific Christian communities is itself an untested hypothesis that has been called into question [23]. A parallel may be useful. Arguments about the motivations of Second World War generals do not change the facts about the success of the D-Day landings or the failure of the Arnhem offensive: these events happened, they were not invented. At the same time, those facts, from the moment that they were recorded, became subject to bias, to various group interests and to differing perspectives. History is always an interpreted reconstruction of what happened. The facts do not exist in a vacuum to be examined as specimens under the microscope, for there can be no such thing as an uninterpreted fact. It should always be remembered, therefore, that historical reconstructions can be very distorted and fragile and the task must be approached with humility, but reconstruction is the necessary task, nonetheless.

From the standpoint of the New Testament, whatever interpretation, embroidery or bias has been added to the mix to make the stories 'relevant' for the people of the first century world, the stories still represent something that happened. It goes without saying that author bias will exist, that redactional approaches will colour the way material is set out and stories will tend to be developed and elaborated with time. None of this, however, means of necessity that the Gospel records are untrustworthy. It is usual for historians to assume that an author is trying to write history if this is what the document appears to demonstrate and the account is, in general terms, trusted unless there are clear reasons not to do so [24]. Thus, the issue of 'whether the task of extracting historical data from the gospels is impossible or not is for the historian to discover, not for the theologian to tell him' [25]. It is also worth observing that, in looking at origins, the value of Ockham's Razor should not be forgotten and causes not be multiplied. The welter of speculative, conflicting and, at times, mutually exclusive theories about the origins of the different Gospels cannot all be right. Irrespective of the extent of the development of the tradition, as it was used for evangelistic and didactic purposes in the early communities and as it was edited to meet the later evangelists' theological points of view, the fact that behind it were the experiences of the people who were there at the time and possibly still alive when the events were set down, is something that cannot be ignored. It is always a good thing for scholars in any discipline to use their common sense as well as their methods [26].

It has to be recognised, nonetheless, that as noted earlier, the evangelists were creative writers, not mere recounters of unadorned facts. It is worth restating that there is no such thing as an uninterpreted fact in any situation and the very way in which a fact is first presented begins the process of interpretation. The evangelists were, by the nature of their enterprise, interpreters: they were concerned to interpret the words and work of Jesus and present their understanding of his meaning for their contemporaries [27].

Mark was without question writing for Christians in a Greek-speaking world, his Gospel was addressed to Christians in an Hellenistic environment. It was the world to which Paul and his associates had gone in the first major attempt to evangelise the non-Jewish world of the Roman Empire. Indeed, it seems very likely that Mark was attacking christologies of power and heretical ideas about the person of Jesus which arose out of distortions of the Pauline gospel, such as had arisen in Corinth as a result of a mixture of Hellenistic ideas and Jewish speculations. The emphasis in Mark is on a theology of the cross, it is not the mighty acts of healing or exorcism that authenticate the ministry of Jesus: only the cross validates and explains his ministry and no one can begin to understand Jesus apart from the cross. Faith is only real faith as it penetrates behind the outward to the inner realities and the saving activity of God in Jesus which culminated in a cross and the demand that the disciple treads the same *via crucis* to ultimate salvation [28].

The problem will often arise, therefore, as to the degree of interpretation that has occurred in the Gospel narratives. It frequently becomes difficult to decide what has been added for effect or for theological purposes, what is merely the conventional framework for the story and so forth. Bultmann drew attention to the problem of idealised settings, which he considered made it impossible to establish the original meaning of a saying with any precision [29]. While considerable care must be exercised with regard to the suppositions and conclusions of Form Critical theory as exemplified by Bultmann and others, there are certainly occasions when it may be difficult to decide on what was the original core of a story and what has been added for effect or to improve the transmission of teaching. This study will proceed to examine the healing stories in the different Gospel traditions, taking the theological interpretations of the different evangelists into account, as well as attempting the task of providing a medical interpretation of the event as far as possible. In this task, the Markan tradition will be given priority in the synoptic accounts. The Johannine tradition will be examined separately. It is emphasised that this study takes the Gospel traditions seriously and accepts the point of view outlined by A. E. Harvey that 'there is a consistency and originality in the broad outlines of the portrait of Jesus as this emerges from the entire gospel tradition' [30].

The Markan Tradition

The evangelists, as writers rather than recorders, were concerned to turn the randomness of the oral tradition into a coherent narrative that began at the beginning, went on to the end and then stopped (something which Mark did with dramatic effect). Mark, as other biblical writers had done before him, used the journey motif as the linking theme of his story, setting the elements of the tradition into this regular framework, although the centre of the story is the unfashionable region of Galilee and not the religious centre of Jerusalem. Kelber has argued that the traditional material used by Mark was already 'fashioned for mnemonic purposes and selected for immediate relevancy, not primarily for historical reasons' [31]. His concern was to weave a story that would create a powerful effect on the reader and both the acts of Jesus as well as his teaching are integral to this 'evangelistic' purpose. As Ellenburg has put it, 'the miracles function in Mark's world of events in the same way that the parables function in word' [32].

On the other hand, the 'miracle' stories show features that suggest that, at the stage of the Markan tradition, they had undergone less theological editing than the 'sayings collections', for example. They contain a wealth of concrete and, at times, theologically irrelevant detail, together with christological and other theological ambiguities that make it virtually impossible to see them as highly fashioned articles designed solely for the purpose of expressing the faith. That they have a theological purpose is undeniable and at times obvious, but, in Trocmé's phrase, they are 'untamed' [33] and the process of 'domestication' has barely begun with Mark's Gospel. This is probably an understatement, since as will be argued in connection with the individual healing narratives, most of them show a clear theological purpose underlying the way the story has been set out. Nonetheless, in most cases, they are sufficiently close to the events themselves to retain the vividness and down-to-earth qualities that are so characteristic of these stories. They are stories that reflect the exciting events which had happened within living memory in Galilee, events seen and remembered by a far wider circle than the immediate followers of Jesus.

Such a background provides for the substantial historicity of the Gospel narratives even though there has been editing and development and the chronological framework may be lacking. Mark appears to have utilised several collections of these stories about the 'mighty works' of Jesus. The clearest examples are the parallel cycles of stories to be found at Mark 4:35-6:44 and Mark 6:45-8:26, the latter being sometimes called the 'Bethsaida section' from the fact that it begins and ends with the only two references to this town in the Gospel [34]. The parallels become clear when the two sections are compared in tabular form (Table 3:1).

Table 3:1   Cycles of Miracle Narratives in Mark

First cycle		*Second cycle*	
4:35-41	Stilling the storm	6:45-52	Walking on the sea
5:1-20	The Gerasene demoniac		
5:22-43	The daughter of Jairus	7:24-30	The Syrophoenician woman's daughter
5:25-34	A woman with a haemorrhage	7:32-37	Healing a deaf-mute
6:30-44	Feeding the 5,000	8:1-10	Feeding the 4,000
		8:22-26	Healing a blind man

It is of particular interest that the stories of the deaf-mute and the blind man belong to an identifiable single source as they are unique in the Synoptic Gospels both as representing Jesus healing with difficulty and also in providing an insight into his healing methods. These aspects suggest an old and relatively unmodified tradition and it may well be that the second cycle of stories represents an independent tradition that came to be added at a later stage to an original Markan document, perhaps something like the *Ur-Markus* of earlier scholarship [35].

Other healings and exorcisms appear to have circulated as independent units of tradition. For example, the story of the healing of the man with the withered hand (Mark 3:1-6) centres on the associated controversy about the Sabbath rather than the healing itself. The healing is merely the starting point for the argument and the unit may be viewed more as a controversy or pronouncement story than a miracle story. Other stories that seem to have had an independent history are the healing of the sufferer from leprosy (Mark 1:40-45), the paralysed man (2:1-12), the boy with epilepsy (9:14-29) and the story of Bartimaeus (10:46-52).

It also seems likely that there are common traditions in both Mark and John as the following table (Table 3:2,) indicates. There is, however, a much greater transformation in John and the theological function is even more apparent. This will be discussed in more detail in relation to the Johannine healing stories to be considered later in chapter 5. There are further parallels to some of the Markan healing stories in the non-canonical gospels and these will also be noted at the appropriate places in the discussion.

Table 3:2   A Comparison of Miracle Narratives in Mark and John

Mark		*John*	
2:1-12	The paralytic man.	5:1-18	The lame man at the pool
6:35-44	Feeding the 5,000.	6:1-15	Feeding the 5,000.
6:45-52	Jesus walks on the sea.	6:16-21	Jesus walks on the sea.
8:22-26	Healing a blind man.	9:1-7	Healing a man born blind.

The Markan healing narratives

The Capernaum Demoniac: Mark 1:21-28 // Luke 4:31-37

Accounts of exorcism are remarkably few in the New Testament:
limited, in fact, to six specific cases in the Synoptic Gospels and two in
Acts [36]. This story is the first account in Mark of this very limited
number of exorcisms undertaken by Jesus. The high profile that seems
to have been given to demons, exorcisms and magic in first century
Judaism, is thus largely absent from the New Testament. There are a
number of passages that mention exorcism and other healings, forming
editorial link statements in the Synoptic Gospels, but these are no more
than vague and generalised editorial comment on the healing ministry of
Jesus. The low total of exorcisms described is suggestive that only
certain categories of disease were characterised as 'demonic' by the
evangelists. As the study progresses, it will be shown that in each case
of 'possession' in Mark there are elements of the bizarre or the unusual
(such as personality changes and convulsions) which set the illness
apart from other diseases, marking it out as something for which the
powers of evil are to be held specifically responsible, quite separately
from their general involvement in the ills of humanity.   The
implications of this will be investigated later [37].

The story of the Capernaum demoniac is found only in Mark and
Luke and it takes the form of a typical exorcism story with the setting
being given, followed by the account of the exorcism itself. This
consists of a description of the confrontation and battle between Jesus
and the demon that is eventually unable to withstand his superior
authority and power. The final convulsion and cry from the affected
man are designed to show the success of the exorcism, although, as will
be discussed later, what may be judged as the actual reasons for what
seems to be a genuine description of an event, are rather different from
those implicit in Mark's story. The account ends with a description of
the amazement of the crowd.

The text of the story as it appears in Mark has several features of the
style noted as peculiar to the evangelist. These include the use of the
characteristic εὐθὺς (immediately) and the frequent use of participles.
The Lukan version contains a number of expansions which seem
designed to raise the reader's awareness of what might be termed the
'miraculous'. Mark's ἐν πνευματι ἀκαθαρτω ('in the grip of an
unclean spirit') becomes much more specifically ἐχων πνευμα
δαιμονιου ἀκαθαρτου ('having a spirit of an unclean demon'). Luke

was undoubtedly smoothing out Mark's somewhat awkward Semitisms, but in doing so he was placing emphasis on the demonic character of the illness which was holding this man in thrall. Again, in Luke's version, the moment the demon sees Jesus it shouts aloud (ἀνεκραξεν φωνη μεγαλη), an expression that Mark reserves for the later shouts of the man as he convulses. Luke also heightens the sense of the dramatic with his statement that the demon threw the sufferer into the middle of the congregation (῾ριψαν ... εἰς το μεσον ἐξηλθεν) and yet he remained unhurt (μηδεν βλαψαν αὐτον). Mark emphasises that the convulsions were violent in the expression, και σπαραξαν αὐτον. The verb is unusual, elsewhere in the New Testament used only in the story of the 'epileptic' boy (Mark 9:14-29). In both contexts, the word expresses the idea of being torn in pieces by the violence of the convulsions [38], but in this case, no details are added. Luke seeks to increase the sense of awe and wonder expressed by the onlookers in their response which not only focuses on the authority (ἐξουσια) of Jesus, already demonstrated in his teaching, but also on his power (δυναμις), a very characteristic Lukan word in relation to the 'miracles'.

The unequivocal details of this story are limited although there is a recoverable core in which a man in the synagogue at Capernaum who was generally known to be ill, with a condition characterised by abnormal behaviour patterns and episodes of violent convulsions, was considered to be affected by malign spiritual influences. Jesus completely reversed these symptoms by a command in a situation of heightened emotion and stress and in the presence of a large number of people. The picture presented in this incident is that of a person suffering from a classical dissociative reaction, what used to be called 'hysterical' neurosis. Such illness is often associated with histrionic behaviour and, in nearly every case, it arises at a definable time, frequently in response to stressful life events. The condition tends to subside when the basic problem and the conflicts it has created are resolved. It is a common condition in warfare when it is seen in soldiers over-exposed to battle conditions - the so-called 'shell shock' or 'battle fatigue'. The patient exhibits what are called 'conversion' symptoms, a pattern of illness reproduced by the patient in order to escape from some unpleasant or demanding situation. The features closely mimic the signs and symptoms of physical illness, very often diseases of the nervous system, but there is no evidence of the corresponding physical or anatomical pathology of the physical disease itself. This essential element is emphasised in the standard definition produced by the American Psychiatric Association: 'The essential feature of Conversion Disorder is the presence of symptoms or deficits affecting voluntary motor or sensory function that suggest a neurological or other general medical condition' [39].

The sensory symptoms of such conditions are very wide ranging and may include blindness, deafness, and severe pain without pathology. There may be, alternatively, loss of sensation or abnormal sensations in various parts of the body. The motor symptoms may also be varied, but often include paralysis of voluntary muscles, shown as an inability to use a single limb, or even hemiplegia. The patient may show loss of balance, bizarre gaits, tremors and tics. Convulsions are also a frequent manifestation, often severe and happening dramatically in public as in this story [40]. So-called 'multiple personality' may occur in which sharply contrasting patterns of behaviour are displayed, often with quite different speech patterns [41].

It has been suggested that while the background to this story is undoubtedly Palestinian and Mark has given the story a specific setting in the synagogue at Capernaum, the account is a generalisation, representing 'the kind of things Jesus did rather than what he actually did on those occasions' [42]. Even should this judgment be true, it is still possible to say that the description is indicative of the kind of people who were helped (and who might have been expected to be helped) by Jesus. There are no grounds for denying the possibility of making a presumptive diagnosis.

Jesus effects the cure in a dramatic setting in the presence of the synagogue congregation. There is a word of command, couched in the standard expressions of contemporary exorcist practice, φιμωθητι και ἐξελθε ἐξ αὐτου ('Be silent and come out of him'). This is probably to be understood as an 'incantational restriction' which bound the demon and put it in a position where it was unable to do further harm [43]. Bultmann correctly recognised that this story contained 'the typical characteristics of a miracle story, and especially of an exorcism', but he saw it merely as a 'cult legend' designed to 'give a paradigmatic illustration of the ministry of Jesus' [44]. This, however, is to confuse the evangelist's theological intention in recording the event with the event itself. If it be accepted that Jesus was a healer and that he carried out 'exorcisms', then this story is exactly the sort of event that one would expect in the context of the time.

Jesus appears to produce the cure by an abreactive method of deconditioning. The method is one used frequently by modern 'faith healers' and 'exorcists'. The method involves emotional stimulation to the point of collapse, in which the patient relives past terrors, often in an explosive manner, and following which there is a sudden mental and physical relief of symptoms. Mark's details are sparse, but they would appear to be consistent with such an explanation. Jesus issues a dramatic word of command in a situation in which, following preparatory excitation, there is highly raised emotion and a release of affect-driven behaviour, seen in the convulsive collapse and loud cry [45]. The man's behaviour, in fact, looks rather like the result of the momentary deregulation of brain stem centres, inducing complete physical collapse, a phenomenon often found in modern charismatic and similar services.

Such techniques are able to terminate the physical expressions of conversion type disorders and re-integrate the mental state. They were particularly valuable in war situations, for example after the Dunkirk evacuation in World War 2, enabling 'shell-shocked' troops to get back to battle [46]. It is worth noting, however, that such techniques, while often immediately helpful, usually fail to produce long term results unless there is associated supportive therapy aimed at changing the patient's attitudes and behaviour patterns and inducing a conscious integration of the 'cure' into the psyche. Thus, they have largely been abandoned in modern psychiatry, although they still have a place in the treatment of some acute neuroses [47]. Without effective reinforcement, improvement is rarely long lasting and there is likely to be recurrence in which the symptoms may even be worse than before. There is possibly an awareness of this lying behind the parable of Luke 11:24-26.

Neither Mark nor Luke suggest that anything else was involved as it would not suit their theological purposes, nor their aim in setting these healings in the context of the outworking of God's power. There is, however, a hint in John, in a record of the healing of what was likely to have been a similar illness, that Jesus recognised the importance of a changed approach to life to ensure the permanence of the immediate 'cure'. The words, 'sin no more that nothing worse befall you' (John 5: 14) would seem to indicate that the man in this story is being pointed to the way in which his freedom from symptoms may be maintained. This approach is also exemplified in the account of the healing of the paralysed man in Mark 2:1-12 (pp 75-81).

The crowd response to what was an unusual event was one of amazement: everyone was 'astounded' (ἐθαμβήθησαν), a word that the evangelist may be using to underline this healing as a disclosure of God's saving activity. On the other hand, there is no consistency about the use of the verb θαμβεομαι (in the passive only here and at Mark

10:32, as used by Mark), and it has been noted that 'Mark does not seem particularly interested in adding this motif to the miracle stories in general nor to the exorcism stories in particular' [48]. These statements, however, serve to move the story into the context of theological interpretation, Mark's primary and all-important interest. The evangelists wish to emphasise that God's power was at work in Jesus and they also wish to emphasise that the people who saw what had happened did not see Jesus as just another wandering wonder worker, but as a genuine prophet of God in the tradition of Elijah. Vermes [49] has argued, in fact, that Jesus has to be considered as a genuine representative of charismatic Judaism. The prophetic element is emphasised in the fact that the amazement expressed by the crowd is centred on the authoritative teaching (διδαχη) of Jesus. The event is thus set in a context of teaching, a teaching undertaken with authority. Mark is concerned to demonstrate that just as the people who listened to Jesus in the synagogue were expected to hear and obey, so also were the evil spirits. Mark thus links the astonishment of the crowd as they hear Jesus teach with its amazement at the exorcism. It is a demonstration of the verbal and didactic quality of the actions of Jesus giving this exorcism the property of an actualised message [50]. However, it is to be emphasised that 'amazement' is not recognised by Mark as an appropriate response to Jesus. It is not genuine faith, but merely a superficial, short-lived and emotional response to a remarkable event that induces no change in life and behaviour [51].

In both Mark and Luke, this story is the first healing that Jesus undertook after his baptism. The baptism had been the moment when the Messianic vocation of Jesus had been confirmed and he had been endowed with God's Spirit in order that he may be able to fulfil his ministry [52]. Luke has reinforced this by inserting an account of Jesus teaching at his home synagogue in Nazareth and picturing Jesus as being 'armed with the power of the Spirit'. Then comes this event in which the one filled with God's Spirit confronts one who is filled with an unclean spirit. Both Mark and Luke are concerned to ensure that the reader understands that, from the outset of the ministry, there was to be conflict between the power of God and the power of darkness, since in the coming of Jesus the rule of God was present. Twelftree comments that 'we can probably say that this narrative, embracing as it does so many of Mark's themes and being placed first in the public ministry of Jesus, is paradigmatic and programmatic for his story of Jesus' [53]. He notes elsewhere that, 'the importance of exorcism in Jesus' ministry, from Mark's perspective, can be gauged by noting that the first public act of Jesus is an exorcism' [54]. The emphasis is thus, not merely on conflict, but on the victory of Jesus over the forces of evil and the freedom that this brings to all in bondage to such powers.

It is important to recognise, however, that Mark was also concerned to ensure from the outset that the reader would not be diverted from the primary role of Jesus as the proclaimer of God's kingdom by an over emphasis on his combat with demons. In spite of the very high profile given to the 'miracles' of Jesus in Mark, his interest in the extraordinary is essentially limited to its value as a vehicle for the transmission of the central message of 'Jesus, the Messiah, the Son of God' (Mark 1:1) and, at the same time, as a constantly recurring illustration of the total lack of discernment of this central truth on the part of the crowds in general and the religious establishment in particular.

The Gospels were written from faith to faith and started from the position that Jesus was the Christ, the Son of God. The reader has been let into the secret from the outset, but the people in the story have to make up their own minds from the clues given in the words and works of Jesus. This healing, therefore, as with the others, has to be fitted into a presentation of Jesus in these terms. He is the one who has been anointed by God's Spirit and this is the key to his status and is an understanding of Messiahship which seems to have been central to much of the thought of the time (note 1Q2:4; Psalms of Solomon 17:37; Enoch 49:3, etc). The problem is that only the inner circle of disciples actually recognises this and even then only partially. The story of the disciples' developing understanding is one of the major themes of Mark and will be illustrated in some of the later occurring stories.

Mark thus makes the point that while the unclean spirits recognise their downfall in the appearance of the Holy One of God, the response of the crowd is no more than amazement - it is the classic picture of the wrong response, for there is no discernment or understanding of the nature of the events unfolding before it. It requires a genuine spiritual disclosure to be able to understand who Jesus is. Mark regularly draws attention to this distinction between the response of amazement and the genuine response of true faith and commitment that leads on to discipleship. In so doing he underlines the essential ambiguity of the ministry of Jesus. The 'secret' of the kingdom of God is something that is 'given', not worked out from first principles (Mark 4:11). This has important implications for any understanding of the place of 'miracle' in the ministry of Jesus, an issue that will be taken up at a later stage of the discussion.

Simon Peter's Mother-in-Law: Mark 1:29-31 // Matt 8:14-15 // Luke 4:38-39.

This short pericope seems to be quite unrelated to the rest of the ministry and is set out without any obvious theological significance. It is, as Hengel observes, 'a report in the gospel which falls outside its framework and seems very personal' [55] and Fuller sees the account as a 'personal reminiscence of Peter himself' [56]. If the traditional view of the Petrine associations of Mark's Gospel are correct, then it may be assumed that it has been included for personal reasons. It is a story which bears all the hallmarks of an eyewitness account and, as Vincent Taylor noted, the detail 'which is not great, is significant, consisting, not so much of matters connected with malady and its cure, as of unimportant features of interest to those concerned in the event' [57]. Luke's version expands on details to provide a more rounded story, but in doing so, becomes contrived and loses all immediacy. Furthermore, in order to emphasise the 'miraculous' element Luke develops the story with his own details, such as the statement that Peter's mother-in-law was suffering from a 'great fever' (πυρετω μεγαλω) which Jesus 'rebuked' (ἐπετιμησεν) and which then 'left her' (ἀθηκεν αὐτην). With the use of these terms, Luke has transformed the straightforward Markan account of a healing into what is essentially a form of exorcism (he has used the verb ἐπιτιμαω, in his earlier account of the Capernaum demoniac). This is in accord with Luke's general tendency to expand the elements of 'wonder' and 'power' in the work of Jesus. Matthew manages to abbreviate even this short pericope and gives only the very barest of details.

The details that Mark provides of this event are meagre. Peter's mother-in-law was suffering from some sort of febrile illness of sufficient severity to keep her in bed. The word used for 'fever' (πυρετος) merely indicates that she was burning hot and the illness, as so often, is simply described in symptomatic terms: the disease was 'a fever', rather than observing that the fever was a symptom of an underlying pathology. The condition may have been due to any one of a large number of acute infections. Luke's expanded terminology, provides little help and is no more than his characteristic emphasis on the power of God's Spirit at work in Jesus, emphasising his healing ability [58], although there was a general recognition that fevers tended to be either 'major' (μεγαλος) and 'minor' (μικρος). Galen considered this an inadequate and oversimplified description, however [59]. Popular thought also viewed fevers as having a demonic origin and this concept appears in the later Rabbinic literature and the writings of Josephus [60].

It is impossible to provide any confident diagnosis in this case, although there is a reasonable possibility that the illness may have been malaria. This disease was common throughout the Middle East and the Mediterranean regions until very recently and still remains in isolated pockets. There is good evidence to suggest that in Roman times malaria was an endemic disease throughout the region of the eastern Mediterranean [61]. The Greek physicians had described the principle forms in relation to the duration and periodicity of the high temperature, distinguishing tertian, quartan as well as the so-called quotidian forms of the illness [62]. In fact, in Greek medicine, 'fever' was essentially coterminous with malaria. The classic study of W.H.S. Jones at the beginning of the twentieth century [63], although now rather dated, nonetheless showed that the works of Hippocrates consistently linked the term πυρετος with marshy localities, although failing to recognise the importance of the mosquito as the vector. In Palestine, the Jordan Valley, and particularly the region around Lake Huleh and the northern shores of Lake Galilee, was generally swampy and an excellent breeding ground for the anopheline mosquito, the carrier of the malarial parasite [64]. Malaria was rife in this region until swamp draining operations were carried out last century allowing agricultural development to proceed [65].

Although the story does not allow more than a highly speculative guess at the nature of the illness, malaria is the most likely possibility, if for no other reason than common things are common. Whatever the condition may have been, however, it was a genuine physical illness in view of the way that Mark has presented the story. The method of 'cure' was apparently by simply grasping the woman's hand and lifting her from her bed. Perhaps she was in the post-febrile stage of her illness with its concomitant depression and lassitude and this was overcome by the charismatic authority of Jesus.

Mark does not develop any overt theological significance out of this healing, but merely records it and does so, indeed 'in the shortest space possible' [66]. This has not stopped commentators from reading theological interpretations into the story, however, as a glance at many of the standard commentaries will show.

The sufferer from 'leprosy': Mark 1:40-45//Matt 8:1-4//Luke 5:12-16

The story of the sufferer from 'leprosy' is the only account of such a 'cleansing' in Mark. Apart from the synoptic parallels, there is a very closely related non-canonical version of the Markan account in the unknown gospel of *Papyrus Egerton 2*, discovered in Egypt and thought to date from the second century. The two versions are set out for comparison in Table 3.3. There are strong arguments for considering that the papyrus is independent of the Synoptic Gospels and represents a witness to the early stages of the development of the tradition [67].

Table 3:3: Parallel versions of the 'sufferer from leprosy'

Papyrus Egerton 2	*Mark 1:40-44*
And behold a leper came to him and beseeching said, 'Master Jesus, wandering with lepers and eating with them in the inn, I myself became a leper, If therefore [you will] I shall be clean',	And a leper came to him him and kneeling said to him, '[Master] if you will you can make me clean'. And he stretched out his hand and touched him and
The Lord said to him, 'I will, be clean!' [And immediately] the leprosy left him,	said to him, 'I will, be clean!' And immediately the leprosy left him, and he sternly charged him and sent him away immediately,
Jesus said to him,	And he said to him, 'See that you say nothing to anyone:
'Go show yourself to the [priests]	but go and show yourself to the priest
and offer the purification as Moses has commanded,	and offer for your purification what Moses commanded for a proof for the people'.
and sin no more!' (Note Jn 5:14).	

The independence of the two versions is indicated particularly by the absence of the Markan redactional elements that enjoin secrecy, which is such a significant element of the Markan theology. In addition, the absence of the statements about the man kneeling before Jesus and being touched, may also point to independence from Mark, although it is clear that the papyrus version has undergone its own redactional changes, some of which seem to be designed solely to colour the story. This is particularly apparent in the reference to eating in the inn, a most unlikely occurrence, suggesting an editorial hand with little knowledge of Palestinian custom. However, if this papyrus is an independent witness to the story of the man with 'leprosy', then it would suggest that the story existed and circulated as a separate unit of the oral tradition which Mark has incorporated into his narrative at this point [68].

Vincent Taylor sees the Markan story as bridging the gap between 1:21-39 and 2:1-3:6, two sections which may have been self-contained units of tradition circulating before Mark was compiled [69]. Further, if the story of the 'ten leprosy sufferers' at Luke 17: 11-19 is considered to be a development of this tradition rather than being an originally independent tradition, then it is of interest that there is, in effect, only one story relating to 'leprosy' in the Gospel narratives. The story itself contains a number of problems that will be discussed later.

Biblical 'leprosy' is the one disease entity that is given greatest prominence in the Bible, although the New Testament references to it are restricted to the Synoptic Gospels and largely to editorial comment. It is one of the more unfortunate aspects of biblical translation that the Hebrew word *sāra'at* in the Old Testament and the Greek word λεπρα in the New have both been consistently translated by the term 'leprosy' in English versions of the Bible, with the exception the 'Good News Bible' (Today's English Version) [70]. The biblical words appear to refer to the same group of conditions, indicated by the references to the Old Testament at Luke 4:27, Matthew 11:5 and parallel passages, as well as by the reference to the levitical purification rites in this particular incident of healing. Similarly, the LXX regularly translates *sāra'at* by λεπρα in such major passages as Leviticus 13 and 14 which speak of 'the law of the leprosy sufferer' (ὁ νομος του λεπρου) (Lev 14:1), a usage which undoubtedly influenced the Synoptic evangelists. It is likely, however, that the choice of λεπρα in the LXX was a somewhat arbitrary decision on the part of the translators, who were looking for a relatively neutral word that suggested a scaly manifestation, but which did not describe a distinct and recognisable entity [71].

Browne has pointed out that 'the original Hebrew and Greek words and their Latin equivalents naturally lack the scientific precision and delimitation of the word "leprosy" (and its cognates) as now used in English. These old words were generic, non-scientific, inclusive, imprecise, "lay" terms' [72]. Indeed, had the translators of the LXX as well as the evangelists, considered that the Old Testament descriptions referred to the specific disease of leprosy, they would almost certainly have used the Greek word ἐλεφαντιασις [73]. This was the term generally current at that period for what may, with reasonable certainty, be identified as true leprosy, a disease that was then becoming known in the Mediterranean world and possibly introduced originally by Alexander's soldiers. The translation of the biblical words by the English 'leprosy' appears to have arisen because, when the Bible was first translated into English, 'leprosy, because of its mysteriousness, its mutilating power and its incurability was symbolic of all that was dreadful in the life of man' [74]. It is a condition which has still power to generate opprobrium as is well known in many Third World countries where leprosy sufferers are still treated as outcasts from society.

There are numerous references in the classical Greek medical authors to the use of λεπρα for scaly and rough skin eruptions [75] and the essential meaning is 'scaly' or 'scabby' (when applied to skin) or 'rough' and 'uneven' (as applied to the ground for example). On the other hand, the meaning of the Hebrew word is uncertain. It has been argued that it conveys the idea of 'smitten', thus suggesting that those with the disease bore the mark of God's anger and must, therefore, be expelled from the community, for their condition was a 'stroke inflicted by God' and they were under a taboo. This view has been disputed, however, and it has been suggested that a more likely derivation is from the word *sir'a*, meaning a wasp or hornet, suggesting that the sufferers looked as though they had been stung by hornets [76].

Etymology is not of great importance: what is important to recognise is that in the Old Testament the term represents not so much a discrete medical condition, but rather what might be called a 'religious syndrome', visited on those who arrogantly broke God's law. Passages such as Exodus 4:6,7 indicate that the condition, or conditions, represented by this term were seen as visible marks of God's power and displeasure. As such 'leprosy' could not only affect people, but also inanimate objects such as clothing or the walls of houses, a reference presumably to fungal growth. The result of such 'infection' was that either the person or the object was rendered ceremonially unclean and was able to pass on this 'uncleanness' to others. In the Mishnah, 'leprosy' was regarded as the first of the 'fathers of uncleanness' and to be a sufferer from 'leprosy' was to be considered essentially as a dead person, totally cut off from the living members of the community and unable to enter into any social or religious relationships [77].

Modern leprosy, on the other hand, is a chronic, communicable disease caused by a bacillus (*Mycobacterium leprae*), very closely related to the organism responsible for tuberculosis. The organism has a predilection for the peripheral nerves and for skin and mucous membranes. The primary and characteristic feature of the disease is loss of sensation due to the damage of sensory nerves that are usually thickened and easily palpable. Unless treated, paralysis and deformity follow the acute primary damage, mainly as the result of secondary infection and the consequences of unrecognised trauma, especially burns, resulting from the loss of feeling. This very specific picture of what is properly leprosy does not occur in any of the descriptions of the conditions that are characterised as 'leprosy' in the Bible, whether in the Old or New Testaments. It is particularly to be noted that the anaesthesia, or lack of sensation, which is the primary characteristic of true leprosy, is not mentioned anywhere in the Bible. It is highly improbable that such a highly specific and easily recognisable symptom as this would have gone unnoticed had the biblical disease been the specific disease of leprosy as known today.

The biblical descriptions indicate conditions with a scaly discolouration of the skin associated with 'raw flesh' and 'scales like snowflakes' (Lev 13 and 14, Exodus 4:6, etc). However, as Hulse noted, these descriptions were 'not meant to be a description of disease, but a list of differential diagnoses and clinical tests to guide priests, when, for ritual purposes, they had to distinguish between *sâra'at* and diseases which resembled it' [78]. These descriptions do not fit any single disorder as it is known today, although taken together, the various descriptions could fit a number of conditions including psoriasis, vitiligo, post-inflammatory leucoderma, seborrheic dermatitis, together with various other infective and fungal skin diseases. There is no final consensus on which, if any, of these conditions represents biblical leprosy, although there is broad agreement that psoriasis has most points of contact with the biblical descriptions. However, it should be emphasised, as Pilch has pointed out [79], that the biblical condition is not genuinely capable of analysis by biomedical taxonomy. Biblical 'leprosy' may be classified as an 'illness reality' rather than a disease in the modern sense and the extension of the term to inanimate objects, such as houses (probably referring to fungal infestations such as dry rot), clearly means that no one pathology can account for the full meaning of the term.

Psoriasis, however, is a condition which seems to meet many of the descriptive features of biblical 'leprosy'. It is a relatively common condition [80] characterised by thickened, reddened and usually well demarcated areas of skin covered by silvery scales which may range from isolated small lesions to the whole of the body surface [81]. All lesions have the cardinal features of redness, scaling and thickening and it has frequently been noted that what has been termed 'the full rich red' colour of psoriasis is much more intense than in other skin conditions. Further, the whole body may be covered by flaking white skin as in the Old Testament texts that refer to the person with 'leprosy' as having skin like 'snow' (Exodus 4:6, Numbers 12:10, 2 Kings 5:27: Heb: *šeleg*; LXX: χιων). In another place, one sufferer was compared to a macerated foetus (Numbers 12: 12), which not only confirmed the peeling and flaking of the skin, but also suggested that the underlying skin surface was a deep red. Such descriptions are highly suggestive that psoriasis was, with almost total certainty, at least one of the forms of *sâra'at*. It is possible that the loose scales of skin, characteristic of the disease, were thought to be like a discharge and in consequence, the sufferer was considered to be ritually unclean. Whatever reason may lie behind the ritual segregation, it would be an anachronism to relate this isolation to modern concepts of infectious disease control. 'Leprosy' was a social disease which, most likely by its disfigurement, resulted in fear and required the ritual removal of the taboo [82].

It has been suggested by E. W. Massey [83] that biblical leprosy may have included syphilis, noting that the 'leprosy' stigma arose in various areas of the world where the Bible had no influence. He considered that 'it is probable that many of the references to leprosy in the Bible and other ancient writings were actually syphilis'. In several cultures true leprosy has been associated with sexual promiscuity and misdemeanours [84] and, in this regard, it is of interest to note that in the seventeenth and eighteenth centuries, leprosy, which was uncommon in most of Europe by this time, was often confused with eruptive skin disorders including syphilis [85]. This is a suggestion, however, which has found little support and has been strongly contested [86]. There is no certain knowledge as to whether syphilis existed in the Middle East in biblical times and, in general, there is little firm evidence for a pre-Columbian origin of syphilis and the biblical references provide no grounds for theorising [87].

The evangelist's interest was not in pathology, however, but in deriving the theological purpose lying behind the cleansing. As has been emphasised previously, the Gospel writers were engaging in theology and not pathology. Both Matthew and Luke remove much of the awkwardness of Mark's language and expand the man's approach to Jesus by introducing an element of recognition. They use the slightly ambiguous κυριος, which may mean little more than 'sir', but, as those original readers would have been well aware, it may also carry the much deeper significance of the Church's recognition of the supreme lordship of Christ. Characteristically, Luke also expands the Markan ending of the story, so that the crowds, who flock to Jesus as they hear more about him, also come for healing. Matthew, in keeping with his general tendency to play down the element of 'wonder' omits all reference to the crowd response. His emphasis in the story follows directly from his placing it immediately following the Sermon on the Mount in which Jesus is pictured as insisting that the law of Moses must be fulfilled. That insistence is reinforced in the Matthean narrative (following Mark) by the command of Jesus to the patient to show himself to the priest and make the necessary offering for his cleansing as required by the law (as in Lev 13-14 and Deut 24:8-9).

Both Matthew and Luke omit Mark's difficult reference to Jesus being 'filled with anger' (ὀργισθεις) a reading which, in the writer's opinion, should be judged more preferable to the easier 'filled with pity' (σπλαγχνισθεις) given in the majority of texts [88]. The idea of anger also seems to link better with the comment that Jesus 'sternly warned' (ἐμβριμησαμενος) the sufferer, a rare word applied to Jesus on only three other occasions in the Gospel tradition (Matthew 9:30; John 11:33, 38) and which suggests extreme agitation in these contexts. The fact also that both Matthew and Luke have no reference to the idea of pity is also surprising if it was original to Mark. Mark, however, seems to say in effect that Jesus 'snorted with anger or indignation' at the man and sent him away. The statement does not seem to fit very well with the previous comment about making the man clean, but it would have been an appropriate response had Jesus been asked to 'declare' the man clean on the basis that he was an 'authorised teacher'. It would appear that the story has undergone some modification, a point discussed later

There is an important consequence deriving from the preferred text. If 'anger' is the correct reading against 'pity' or 'compassion', then nowhere in the Gospel traditions is Jesus credited with performing a healing or exorcism out of his compassion for the sufferer. Arguments in support of the Church's healing ministry make frequent allusion to compassion as the basis for action on the model of Jesus, but Mark, at least, provides no valid grounds for attributing such a motivation to him. As will be discussed later, the primary motivation is 'theological' and relates to the new revelation of the rule and authority of God that he understood to be in process of arrival in his own activity. The healings were part of the programme adopted from the beginning, to demonstrate by action, as well as word, that God was gathering his people together for a new release from exile and bondage. The diseases healed were, by and large, specific to this programme, they were diseases which cut people off from the life of the community and separated them from an active part in its worship.

The word used to mark the restoration to health is significant. In distinction from other illnesses, those suffering from 'leprosy' were 'cleansed', not 'healed'. In this story, the patient entreats Jesus either to make him clean or to pronounce him clean. In the LXX version of Leviticus 13 and 14, the verb καθαρίζω is used to mean 'declare clean' (as it is at Mark 7:19 and Acts 10:15). It has been argued by Cave [89] that this story is an interpretation of an occasion when a leprosy sufferer came to Jesus as though he were an 'authorised teacher' able to provide both a valid legal decision and also a temporary certificate of cleansing. It is suggested that Mark (or the tradition he was following) has turned this into an account of an actual cleansing or healing of the man's disease. He thus brought it into the ambit of the activity of Jesus as the one who has come to establish the rule of God and bring all God's people, even those 'outside the pale', back into the family, thus removing the artificial barriers which destroyed fellowship and caused alienation. It may well be, therefore, that this story was originally a 'conflict' story centred around the role of Jesus in respect to the law and the traditional requirements for establishing ritual purity, rather than an account of an actual healing and its present format, therefore, belongs to an interpretive process [90].

In New Testament times the observance of the laws of uncleanness and purity represented a significant problem in the regions outside the immediate environs of Jerusalem. In order to make life bearable it seems that provision was made for a specially authorised teacher to inspect those leprosy sufferers claiming to be 'cured' and give them a temporary certificate of cleansing [91]. Because of the reputation of Jesus as both prophet and healer, the leprosy sufferer came to Jesus to seek his opinion on whether he was in remission, as it would be put today, and he was thus able to re-enter normal society once again. He responded to this request with anger and indignation because of its total misunderstanding of the nature of his activities and he tells the man to go to the priests in order to fulfil the demands of the Torah, rather than accepting a 'makeshift declaration'. Elsewhere in the tradition, Jesus has refused to accept the position of an authorised teacher in firmly rejecting the role of a lay arbitrator (Luke 12:14) and this story of the leprosy sufferer may well represent a similar situation.

It is interesting to note, however, that in whatever way we may interpret the story, Jesus is clearly presented as acting in accordance with the law [92]. Mark, however, has either received this story as an account of a cleansing, in the traditions he used, or else he has turned it into one to suit his own purposes with regard to the way in which he wishes to present the healing activity of Jesus within the clear framework of his programme to restore the whole people of God to godly wholeness. As a cleansing, it meets his theological purposes, but at the same time, it is not difficult to understand how such a change in the character of the tradition could occur.

In the Markan version, Jesus responds to the man's request with the words, 'I will, be clean' (θελω καθαρισθητι). The emphasis was on the fact that this was not a normal disease for which healing or curing were the appropriate words; this was a defiling condition which required cleansing before the sufferers could escape from the rigorous exclusion imposed upon them and resume their rightful places in society, an exclusion which required banishment from the city to a separate encampment (Num 5:2-3 and confirmed by Josephus as the continuing rule in the first century [93]). Luke develops this theological theme in the familiar story of the 'ten leprosy sufferers' (Luke 17:11-19). All ten λεπροι were cleansed (v 14), but only one was healed (ιασθη, v 15) and the climax comes as Jesus says to him, 'your faith has saved (σεσωκεν) you'. There is a progression of thought from the inadequacies of ritual cleansing to the fullness of healing or salvation that comes from faith in Jesus. There can be little doubt that this would have been early Church sermon material!

From a medical point of view, however, and on the assumption that psoriasis is a reasonable diagnosis for the condition from which the man was suffering, then it needs to be remarked that this condition is not a static disease. Psychological factors, in particular, are important in the maintenance of the condition, and a person's physical and emotional well being have marked effects on the manifestation of the condition as well as seasonal fluctuations. There is no doubt, for example, that 'in patients with the genetic predisposition to psoriasis, stress may precipitate psoriasis and aggravate existing disease' [94]. This probably occurs through hormonal, immune system and autonomic nervous system effects that lead to alterations of the mechanisms that control epidermal proliferation. Spontaneous remissions are very much part of the pattern of the illness, and these may last for considerable lengths of time, although permanent remissions occur in perhaps only some 13 per cent of cases [95]. Such a remission would fit particularly well with the man's request for a declaration from Jesus confirming that he was 'cleansed'.

On the other hand, should it be accepted that Mark provides us with a genuine account of a person 'healed' of a skin disorder, then it is likely that underlying the problem and acting as a trigger mechanism, was some form of psycho-social stress which had caused an unresolved exacerbation of the condition. The authority of Jesus was able to deal with this through the removal of the anxiety, stress or guilt factors that may have both precipitated and aggravated the condition [96]. Against this view, however, should be placed the fact that although guilt and anxiety may be responsible for the onset or maintenance of symptoms, they are not the cause, and an immediate response to changed circumstances would not produce an immediately observable remission, although the time scale may simply be part of Mark's normal compression of events. However, in terms of probability, it seems more likely that the original event was a request for a declaration of cleansing which evoked a response of anger on the part of Jesus.

From the standpoint of the theological 'moral' of the story Lightfoot has suggested that the best commentary on this story is Romans 8:3 [97]. Mark is emphasising the powerlessness of the Law to deliver people from the power of sin and death and to emphasise the victory that God had brought about in Christ. The Torah could only protect society and maintain its ritual purity. It excluded those it considered unclean and readmitted to the community only those who were 'cleansed' and had fulfilled their ceremonial obligations, 'as Moses commanded'. By itself, the Law was unable to restore the outcasts to their rightful place in society: Judaism professed itself powerless in the face of this living death, it could only recognise the cleansing, not effect it. The coming of Christ transformed the situation. The message that Mark was underlining in his treatment of this event was that Jesus both fulfilled and superseded the law and his authority was demonstrated in the cleansing and restoration of those condemned to the living death of 'leprosy' [98]. The rule of God, which Jesus understood as being present in his ministry, was removing the old barriers of ritual uncleanness and was also restoring the outcasts and rejected to the heart of God's people and to a place within his purposes. There is a sense therefore in which Crossan's judgment is correct in seeing that Mark 'sets Jesus' power and authority on a par with or even above that of the Temple itself' [99].

Mark's account ends with a statement about the amazement of the onlookers and the spread of Jesus' fame. These were normal features of 'miracle stories', but Mark uses them to make the point that Jesus wished to keep this response at as low a key as possible. As Hengel has emphasised, Jesus consistently 'wards off the press of the masses, in contrast to the popular miracle workers and magicians' [100]. The command to keep silent emphasised the 'hiddenness' of the ministry. Mark is insistent that Jesus was not looking for personal propaganda or self-aggrandisement. Nor, in Mark's understanding, were the healings open revelations of the divine glory. They were to be understood only by those with eyes to see and ears to hear: as with the parables, true understanding came from disclosure. Whatever Jesus did was met with misunderstanding about the true significance of his person. His mighty acts were in no sense to be understood as proofs of who he was. This element of deliberate ambiguity was an essential part of the work of Jesus as Mark has presented it and the recognition of who Jesus is comes only through disclosure and not because his actions make it obvious.

The paralysed man: Mark 2:1-12// Matt 9:1-8// Luke 5:27-32.

This particular act of healing is recorded by each of the three synoptic evangelists although with a number of marked differences that derive, in part at least, from the differing theological interests and viewpoints of the writers. Luke's characteristic emphasis on the revelation of God's power (δυναμις) is evident at the outset. In his account, Mark's vigorously impressionistic opening, with the bustle and hubbub of a crowd shoving and pushing around the door of the house where Jesus was, gives way to a stereotyped 'conflict' scene in which Jesus is faced by his critics, namely, the scribes and Pharisees. Luke emphasises that God's power is present to heal from the start of the story. His account ends with Christ's triumph over his opponents and the crowds being filled with fear and glorifying God. In place of Mark's vividness (eye witness memory or just good story telling?) there is an expanded (about 10 per cent longer) and rather flat and stylised account in which the element of 'wonder' is deliberately emphasised to suit what might be called Luke's 'charismatic' theology.

Matthew has problems with this story from the start due to the way in which he has rearranged the order of events. He has placed this story immediately after the exorcism of the Gerasene demoniac and consequently he has had to incorporate an additional geographical setting with Jesus being required to sail back across the Lake of Galilee to 'his own city'. Matthew has also considerably abbreviated the story in keeping with his tendency to play down the 'miraculous' element of the Gospel stories. The account, in fact, is almost 40 per cent shorter than Mark's version and with an almost total omission of detail.

A number of other changes have been made to the Markan account by both Luke and Matthew. Mark's authentic picture of the paralysed man's friends breaking up the simple daub and wattle, or possibly turf, roof of a Palestinian peasant home is replaced by Luke with a description that is much more relevant to a sophisticated Graeco-Roman readership. In this version, the man is let down through the roof tiles (διὰ τῶν κεράμων) and not on a simple bed roll or pallet (κραββατον), but on a couch (κλινη)! However, in view of the problems of manoeuvrability for the four friends and the extreme difficulty for the man himself to struggle away with it after his healing, Luke has tempered the situation somewhat by calling it a 'little couch' (κλινιδιον) later in the narrative. Matthew also refers to the man as lying on a 'couch' (κλινη), but he does not suggest that the healed men was expected to carry it home, nor do his friends let it down through the roof. In fact, there is no reference to this episode in Matthew's version, in which Jesus simply responds to the faith displayed by the paralytic's friends in bringing him for healing.

Another point of interest is that Mark refers to the paralysed man as a child (τεκνον), a point that Matthew has copied faithfully. Luke, however, has changed this to 'a man' (ἀνθρωπος). This original characterisation of the patient raises interesting possibilities in respect of diagnosis, although the actual information is so limited that reconstruction will be largely speculative. All that is said is that the person was paralysed to such an extent that he had to be carried around on a pallet, suggesting something in the nature of a paraplegia.

The physical causes of paraplegia are many, the most common in the western world being trauma. There is no evidence of such a background in this story since causative agents, real or imagined, tend to be remembered and recorded when such information is available. A good example of this is the story of Mephibosheth in the Old Testament, whose lameness was blamed on the fact that he was dropped by his nurse as a young child (2 Samuel 4:4). For similar reasons it is unlikely that the condition was due to a birth defect and, in the absence of pain, which one would have expected to be mentioned had it been present, it is unlikely that compression of spinal nerve roots by a tumour, for example, was responsible for the condition. Poliomyelitis has been suggested [101], but as J.R. Paul has argued [102], this is a disease that may not have existed in biblical times and only appears in medical descriptions from about the eighteenth century onwards. Guillaume-Barré Syndrome (a self-limiting, post-viral inflammation of the peripheral nervous system) has also been suggested as meeting the pattern of this man's illness as well as the resolution of the problem at a time when he had probably already recovered local function without realising it, a not uncommon situation [103]. This suggestion seems to be the most likely possibility if a true organic pathology lay behind this man's condition.

However, it seems much more likely that the underlying cause of the illness was functional rather than organic and a number of considerations suggest that this case represents another example of a conversion or somatisation disorder, especially if, as Mark suggests, the patient was a young adolescent, a matter discussed in more detail later. As was discussed in the case of the Capernaum 'demoniac', many of the physical symptoms of these conditions resemble those of diseases of the central nervous system. Either partial or complete paralysis of voluntary muscles is a frequent manifestation and the attention given to the patient from being carried about by four friends would be welcome to a person with what used to be called an 'hysterical' type disorder and would provide reinforcement of his conviction that he was physically ill. The existence of symptoms and signs without any clear pathology is a common phenomenon in medical practice and represents a continuing diagnostic and management challenge to medical practitioners. The use of 'cognitive-behavioural' therapy [104] is often effective where other methods have failed and it is of particular interest that the approach of Jesus to the problem has much in common with this methodology.

The second point to note is the unusual form of address that Jesus used to the patient in the Markan account. This is the only occasion in Mark where Jesus addressed someone as 'child' (τεκνον). On the occasions where the term is used in other places in the Gospel, it carries the normal meaning of child or is used as a familiar term between parent and a grown up member of the family (eg. 7:27; 10:24,29, 13:12 etc.). It is difficult to see why Mark used the expression unless there was a clear memory in the tradition that the person healed was young, probably an adolescent and not a full adult. As noted earlier this may provide some additional weight to a diagnosis of conversion illness, as such conditions tend to be much more common in younger people [105].

Finally, it should be noted that there does appear to be some evidence of the typical 'flight from a conflict' situation in this case. The illness appears to be associated with strong feelings of guilt and was seen as a direct punishment for some sin, real or imagined. Jesus recognised that the patient's primary need was for the assurance that he was forgiven. Once that was accepted then the 'physical' cure could follow, for the root problem would have been resolved. Consequently, by virtue of his delegated authority from God, Jesus began by removing the central cause of the anxiety and the resultant symptoms ('your sins are forgiven') and this opened the way for the word of authority and the subsequent 'cure' ('take up you pallet and go home'). F.F. Bruce commented, 'When the paralytic did just that, Jesus' power as a healer was confirmed - but more than that, it was the assurance that his sins were forgiven that enabled the man to do what a moment previously would have been impossible, so Jesus' authority to forgive sins was confirmed at the same time' [106]. The command was issued in front of a large and enthusiastic crowd and in a situation of high emotion, thus reinforcing the whole process.

Once again, it is suggested, Jesus was making use of abreactive techniques, well known to all engaged in such healing practice as was discussed earlier. It is interesting to note that in this case there is no suggestion that the illness was the result of demon possession, probably because, even though it seems to have been 'hysterical' in nature, it was not associated with bizarre symptoms such as seizures or deranged personality. From Mark's point of view as an evangelist, the inclusion of this story, together with the related discussion about authority and forgiveness, was crucial to his elaboration of the central theme of the good news of Jesus Christ. What was the source of his authority? This question was central to any understanding of his mission and the claim to be able to forgive sins as a divine representative immediately precipitated an argument as to the source and nature of Christ's authority and status.

There are a number of difficulties in this story, particularly in relation to the (admittedly unexpressed) charge of blasphemy. What was the basis of this assessment? It should be noted that Jesus in fact does not claim to forgive sins on his own authority - the statement is in the passive: 'your sins are forgiven' (ἀφιενται σου αἱ ἁμαρτιαι). There is no immediate claim at this stage of the divine authority to forgive. E.P. Sanders has argued that the most likely ground for considering that Jesus was speaking blasphemy would have been arrogant presumption - 'the claim to speak for God and to be supported by him, were it made by a wicked person, might be considered blasphemy: denigrating God by association' [107]. There is certainly evidence that Jesus was considered to be a magician, gaining his powers from Beelzebub, and this would possibly have been enough to earn him the epithet 'wicked' among the members of the religious establishment. Crossan, however, has argued that 'magic' is the 'deviant shadow' of official religion and may be seen, therefore, as the activity of a subversive and unapproved religion [108]. In these terms, Jesus may well have been considered a totally inappropriate person to act as a mediator of God's forgiveness. He was outside the system and had no official sanction for what he was doing and hence the other arguments about authority.

It seems more likely, therefore, that the real offence lay in the fact that Jesus was identifying the rule of God with himself and, furthermore, was doing so outside the properly constituted channels of divine action in Temple and Torah. Not only so, but the blessings of the eschatological kingdom were being offered to all the wrong people. In the previous story, they were offered to someone suffering from a disease that from the beginnings of Israel's history had placed such sufferers outside the community. Now these same blessings were being offered to a paralysed person, someone incomplete and hence not fit to enter the community. Through these actions, however, cure was becoming salvation, it was *shalôm* and restoration to God's people. The problem was, as N.T.Wright points out, that 'he was offering this final eschatological blessing outside the official structures, to all the wrong people, and on his own authority. This was his real offence' [109].

It would also seem, however, that in this context Mark was concerned to demonstrate that God's authority could be delegated, and, furthermore, it had been delegated to the Son of Man. The story of the healing is thus presented in such a way that in order to underline his authority to act in the moral sphere (the forgiveness of sins), Jesus is shown as exerting his authority in the physical sphere (by healing or by assuming the authority to pronounce healing/cleansing). In the culture of the time, it is unlikely that these two ideas would have been quite so compartmentalised as they tend to be in modern western thought, but the two events of the forgiveness of sins and the healing of sickness are sufficiently separated in the story as to make the point valid.

Matthew develops this further. In his account, the crowd glorifies God who had given such authority (ἐξουσια) to mankind (ἀνθρωποις -

literally, 'to men'). The authority that Matthew has in view has to relate
to the argument about the delegation of God's authority to forgive and
the use of the plural (men) in this context suggests the widening scope
of this delegated authority to the infant Church. His Gospel ends with
the authority of the risen Christ being passed to the apostolic nucleus of
the new community (Matt 28:18-20). This included the authority to
forgive, delegated originally to Christ and then by him to Peter, as the
representative of the future Church (Matt 16:19).

There is, however, another issue raised in this story. The emphasis,
as throughout Mark's gospel, is on faith, but here the faith is not that of
the actual recipient of the divine forgiveness and restoration, but rather
the emphasis is on the faith of the paralysed person's friends who
brought him to Jesus and would not be put off by any obstacles in the
way. Mark makes the point that God honours all true faith including
that of those who bring to Christ such persons as could not bring
themselves. It is worth making the point that in first century society (as
in many non-western societal groups today) decisions were taken by
those who were recognised as being able to make decisions. This was
frequently the head of the household. Tidball has noted that a Roman
household 'expressed its solidarity through its adoption of a common
religion. The religion would be that one chosen and practised by the
pater familias. He was the key decision maker regarding any decision,
religion included'[110].

In spite of the normal practice of making corporate multi-personal
decisions, it may be that questions had arisen over the status of children
within the Christian communities. There seems to be an indication that
this issue had arisen as early as the mid-50s (note 1 Cor 7:14). In view
of the use of 'child' as the designation of the paralysed person, it is not
beyond possibility that Mark is using the story to specify the position of
children in a 'post-missionary' church. The faith of their sponsors or
parents is sufficient to bring them to Christ and into the community of
faith and make them 'holy'. Whether this also involved baptism has
been an issue much debated and is outside the subject of this study [111].
Further instances of vicarious faith will be noted in the course of the
study.

The man with the 'withered' hand: Mark 3:1-6 // Matt 12:9-14 //
Luke 6:6-11

This story appears in the Markan context essentially as a conflict
story, centred in the attitude of Jesus to Sabbath observance. R.H.

Fuller has remarked that the 'description of the sickness and cure are reduced to a minimum and all the emphasis is thrown upon Jesus' question, "Is it lawful on the Sabbath to do good or to do harm, to save life or to kill?" ' [112]. Mark uses the verb σωζειν for 'cure', probably because it can carry this double meaning of normal 'cure' and the deeper 'healing' of damaged relationships between God and mankind. The specific activities of 'saving life' and 'doing good' look forward to the Messianic age and the kingdom of God. The Sabbath, the prefigurement of the Future Age (note Heb 4:9-11), was the ideal day for such saving activity to be brought to the people of God. Further, the man who was restored to wholeness was an example of just the sort of person who had been excluded in the past from the covenant community (Lev 21: 16-24), but was now being made welcome through the proclamation of the eschatological kingdom of God, made present in the ministry of Jesus.

Matthew emphasises the conflict situation by turning the opening story round so that it is the opponents of Jesus who ask the question about the Sabbath and not Jesus himself. In addition, he brings in an isolated saying (perhaps from the Q collection) about rescuing sheep on the Sabbath and uses this to underline the reality that every day, and perhaps especially the Sabbath, is a day for doing good.

Mark describes the man at the centre of the dispute as suffering from a 'withered (ἐξηραμμενην) hand'. Luke, as expected, develops the details of the story and adds that it was the man's 'right hand' that was affected. Perhaps he was influenced by another early tradition that made the man a stonemason [113] and thus emphasised the economic importance of the loss of his right (presumed dominant) hand. There is little doubt that these are embellishments designed to increase the human interest value and 'improve' on the starkness Mark's account. Hobart's attempt to describe Luke's statement specifying that it was the man's right hand which was affected, as a 'mark of particularity ... such as a physician would observe' [114], part of his effort to prove that the Third Evangelist was a physician and by implication Luke 'the beloved physician', is unconvincing to say the least.

The verb ξηραινω, that Mark uses to describe the 'withered' state of the hand, commonly means to be dried up or parched and hence, by extension, to waste or wither away. It is used, for example, at Mark 4:6 to describe the desiccated state of the seed that fell on stony soil and at Mark 5:29 to refer to the 'drying up' of the woman's haemorrhage. However, at Mark 9:18 the verb means no more than to be stiff or rigid. The boy at the centre of that story is said to stiffen in his seizures and the verb is used in this way elsewhere [115]. Thus, although the verb may have been used to refer to a state of muscle wasting or paralysis (the term ξηροι is used absolutely to refer to people with paralysis at John 5:3) it is also possible that the meaning is simply a stiff hand, that is, one in which there was no movement.

The difficulty arises when attempting to decide whether the word has a specific reference to wasting, whether it is merely a general reference to some form of paralysis, which could clearly include functional paralysis as a result of a conversion disorder, or whether the root idea is genuinely that of stiffness and immobility. Certainty is impossible on the basis of such flimsy data, but in the light of the other conditions with which Jesus seemed to deal, the probability that this was some form of functional paralysis must be considered strong. Mark infers that the condition was restricted to the hand and such localised forms of paralysis are not uncommon in 'hysterical-type' illnesses, particularly where some form of 'secondary gain' may be involved, such as a soldier being unable to use his right hand for his sword and hence escape the battle or other unpleasant duties.

Such a pathology seems more likely on the basis of general probabilities than a genuine neurological condition such as the so-called *'main en griffe'* or claw hand which can arise from damage to the ulnar nerve or from similar conditions affecting other nerves in the forearm or wrist. Other less likely causes would include conditions such as progressive muscular atrophy in which there is progressive degeneration of motor nerve cells causing wasting of the intrinsic muscles of the hand and associated weakness. Although it is likely that a conversion/somatisation disorder would be the most likely diagnosis, some writers have opted for a physical cause in this condition, suggesting a long standing nerve injury as the most likely cause or alternatively, anterior poliomyelitis or a birth injury [116]. Poliomyelitis, however, seems a very unlikely choice as there is little evidence of the existence of this disease before the eighteenth century as was noted earlier [117]. The possibility of a focal dystonia (a condition in which there is spasm and cramping of muscles so that the hand may be stiff and useless), however, is a distinct possibility and such conditions may occur in various forms of so-called occupational 'cramps' including 'occupational overuse/repetitive trauma syndrome'. These conditions are also generally associated with a high degree of functional overlay and, in fact, commonly present with the features of a conversion disorder representing the expression in physical symptoms of an underlying neurosis [118].

It is also worth giving consideration to the possibility that the man was suffering from 'frozen shoulder' (adhesive capsulitis). This condition often has a spontaneous origin, although it may be associated with shoulder trauma or other lesions, such as tuberculosis. It is characterised by pain and immobility and there is a global restriction of movement at the shoulder. In addition, the condition is often associated with 'shoulder-hand syndrome', a form of regional, rather than generalised, chronic pain syndrome in which there is an 'immobile painful shoulder associated with a swollen, painful, cold and dystrophic looking hand' [119]. The important aspect of this condition is that improvement is generally spontaneous, occurring over a variable period of time (twelve to eighteen months or more), often with complete recovery and quite frequently without the patient realising that recovery has occurred. It is not unusual for the physician to re-examine the arm some time later and find a patient with ongoing restricted mobility, but a normal range of movement on examination. The patient had become so used to the loss of function that there was no awareness that recovery had taken place. The case of the man with the 'withered' hand could certainly fit this clinical picture and in many ways it represents a very plausible explanation for his condition and the apparent cure.

The action of Jesus restores (ἀποκαθιστημι) the hand to its previous condition of soundness or wholeness (ὑγιης). The classical Greek word for health was ὑγεια and the adjective is derived from this root. The emphasis tends to be on the physical aspect of soundness or wellness, but it is worth noting that on a number of occasions words of this group are used to translate the Hebrew *šalôm* in the LXX (for example Gen 29:6 (twice); 37:14; 2 Sam 20:9; Psa 38:3, etc).

It is, however, the theological importance of the incident that is emphasised. The issue at stake is the status of the Sabbath in relation to the new dispensation of the gospel: an issue of some importance in the Church at least until after the fall of Jerusalem and the destruction of the Temple by the Romans in AD 70. The keeping of the Sabbath was an important sign of identity, as with keeping the Torah in general. It was a boundary marker of Israel as the people of God. The Gospels regularly portray Jesus as flouting the strict conventions of Sabbath observance and this story is placed by Mark immediately after the episode of the disciples picking the grains of wheat on a Sabbath. That had culminated in the enunciation of the principle that the Sabbath was made for the benefit of all mankind and not the other way round.

The later Jewish regulations contained in the Mishnah and Tosefta indicate a rigid approach to dealing with sickness and injury on the

Sabbath, forbidding anything that could be designated a 'minor cure'. For example, it was stated that on the Sabbath day, 'they may not use artificial emetics; they may not straighten a child's body or set a broken limb. If a man's hand or foot is dislocated he may not pour cold water over it' [120]. On the other hand, there were ways of avoiding the strict letter of the law: it was not permitted to put water on a sponge and then place the sponge on a wound, but it was allowed to wash one's feet with the sponge under them so that it became wet and then place the sponge on the wound. Similarly, it was not permitted to suck vinegar through one's teeth to alleviate toothache, but one could place vinegar on one's food and hope that it would do as well! [121]

The practice of medicine was construed as work and the only ground for healing activity was when life was in danger - 'whenever there is doubt whether life is in danger this overrides the Sabbath' [122]. Mark depicted Jesus as introducing a much freer attitude, based on an ethic that escaped from the confines of a rigid legalism. However, E. P. Sanders has argued [123] that the problem with this story is that no work, in fact, was performed. The cure was accomplished by a command to the man to stretch out his hand. Talking is not regarded as work in any Jewish tradition and thus the command did not strictly constitute work. Further, even if some work had been involved, the issue would have been a matter of a minor infringement and there is no suggestion that charges were ever laid with the local magistrates against Jesus, which would have been the proper course of action. Wright has countered this argument by focussing attention on the fact that Jesus was a 'prophet of restoration eschatology' something which Sanders himself accepts. The issue is thus 'not the detailed regulations laid down by the (largely Hillelite) Mishnah, two hundred years later, for what might or might not be done on the Sabbath. What matters is the attitude to the Sabbath evinced by someone leading a kingdom-movement' [124].

While it is thus very difficult to conceive of this incident by itself as being the catalyst which brought Pharisees and Herodians (presumably the Galilean supporters of Herod Antipas) together to plot the death of Jesus, such actions clearly show Jesus as challenging prevailing opinion as he sets out his own agenda of redefining the kingdom of God in terms which denied the key symbols of Israel's self-understanding as God's people and God's agents of transformation. It is hardly surprising that the actions of Jesus were seen to be subversive and seriously threatening [125]. The early Church communities probably used such stories in their polemic against what they saw as Jewish legalism, although it is interesting to note that Paul never refers to these traditions nor to the example of Jesus as a basis for his own attacks on Judaistic legalisers. Even when the issue of Sabbath observance was no longer one of concern, this story would have remained of value in underlining the need to guard against legalism in all its forms and preserve the freedom that God intended for his creation.

The Gerasene demoniac: Mark 5:1-20//Matt 8:28-34//Luke 8:26-39

This incident presents more problems for the modern reader than perhaps any of the other accounts of the healing activities of Jesus. Yet the very difficulties, especially the associated stampede of the herd of pigs rushing headlong to destruction, may be considered evidence of the substantial authenticity of Mark's tradition. The various redundancies and apparent inconsistencies in the text are more likely to be due to his own infelicitous handling of his material (perhaps in order to preserve the story in the form in which he had received it), rather than as a result of any lack of skill in story-telling and should not be seen as evidence of secondary accumulation of material around the original story [126]. Bultmann remarks that 'in all probability this story was known to Mark as part of a complex already in the tradition ... Clearly the story is essentially intact in its original form' [127]. The version in Matthew represents a substantial abbreviation of the Markan version (by more than 50 per cent), with most details totally omitted, although he refers to two men being cured. There is also a different identification of the local town by Matthew which, taken together with the variations in the story, may point to the use of an independent parallel tradition of this event, rather than a substantial redaction of the Markan version. Luke follows Mark reasonably closely and there is little of the usual expansion and theological development.

Although not strictly apposite to the main purpose of this study, the textual problems relating to the site of this event should be noted. The variants give some weight to the possibility of alternative traditions being in circulation and used by the evangelists. The text is extremely uncertain: there are five textual variants on the place name in the texts of Mark, five variants for the texts of Matthew and four in the Lukan manuscripts. Some of these are minor variants with little intrinsic worth, but there remain three major choices - the region of the Gerasenes, the Gadarenes or the Gergasenes [128]. The superior external evidence in early representatives of both the Alexandrian and Western types of text suggests that Gerasenes is the correct Markan reading. The textual evidence is suggestive that the Matthean version of the story used a different tradition. The problem with the probable Markan site is that the town of Gerasa lay some 30 miles to the south east of the Sea of Galilee.

The background of the story, with its reference to the keeping of pigs, the stampede over a cliff into the lake as well as the references to Jesus sailing across the Lake of Galilee, suggests a location on the eastern shore of the Lake in the predominantly gentile region of the Decapolis and it is this essential discrepancy which has probably given rise to the textual variants. It also suggests that the evangelist was not very familiar with Galilean geography. Gadara or Gergesa would be much more likely sites for the event. Both were flourishing fishing ports [129], although geographically, Gergesa (modern Kursi) may be judged the more likely site as it is closer to Capernaum and would have been a more natural 'port in a storm' than Gadara, which was situated at the southern end of the Sea of Galilee.

There are clear differences between the account in Mark (followed by Luke) and that in Matthew. The fact that he refers to two demoniacs, rather than one, has already been noted, but he also makes no mention of chaining, simply saying that the demoniacs were so violent that no one passed that way in order to avoid them. Matthew also makes no mention of the demand of Jesus for the man's (demon's) name, nor of the later plea that he might be allowed to stay with Jesus. The latter comment may, in fact, be no more than a Markan expansion of the original tradition designed to place emphasis on the theme of discipleship that is such a dominant feature of Mark's Gospel.

The story is set out as an account of an exorcism in which Jesus once again apparently does nothing other than command and there is an immediate response. There is nothing of the usual paraphernalia of the itinerant exorcist for, as Stevan Davies has noted, 'roots, and rings, invocations, and other Solomonic magical techniques would not have been necessary if it were understood that a "demon" were confronted face to face with "the Holy One of God", for by cultural definition the spirit of God would be more powerful than any demon of Satan' [130]. Jesus has at his disposal a power that no others can match and Mark draws attention to this by his emphasis on the man's strength and his apparent insensitivity to pain as well as the host of demons that have to be overcome.

Jesus has crossed into gentile territory, the region of the 'Ten Towns' and the fact that pigs are being kept nearby emphasises the gentile locale. The heart of the narrative is a dramatic confrontation between Jesus and the possessed man in the very place (among the tombs) where the demons were thought to live [131]. Jesus thus deals with the enemy on his own ground. He commands the demon to 'come out' (ἐξελθε), but it responds by adjuring (ὁρκιζειν) Jesus in the name of God, attempting in this way to bind him by these words and thus prevent him from inflicting further torment. Taking the development of the story in this way is to put v 8 temporally before v 9, which seems to be the implication of the narrative. It would thus appear that Jesus was unsuccessful in obtaining a resolution of the man's symptoms at the first attempt. Jesus, however, overcomes the demon by the technique of asking for its name. The demon is now forced into a corner and has to recognise the superior power of Jesus. It gives its name, 'Legion', and in so doing puts itself in the power and at the mercy of Jesus. The possession of a person's name was understood, in some way, as giving power over that person [132]. The demon seeks for leniency and requests to be allowed to enter a herd of pigs nearby [133]. The account has so many close parallels with contemporary exorcisms, as well as suggesting difficulty on the part of Jesus in effecting the cure, that, as noted earlier, it may be presumed to be an early and authentic part of the original Jesus tradition [134].

From the standpoint of the time, the transference of the demons to the pigs would have been considered an important part of the cure and there was also the ironic twist that (from a Jewish standpoint) the unclean spirits were being transferred to unclean animals. From the standpoint of Mark's theology, however, the real proof of the cure was not in the flight of the pigs, but in the fact that the man was found 'sitting there, clothed and in his right mind (σωφρονουντα)', a term which emphasised a sobriety of demeanour which was in marked contrast to his previous extravagant and irrational behaviour. This was an important word in the Greek and Hellenistic world, although not one that played a major part in New Testament thought, and it emphasised the Greek ideals of a disciplined, measured and orderly life. The word indicated that this man had recovered or come to his senses [135]. The parallels with Christian religious conversion would make this good preaching material!

In spite of such considerations, however, it is of interest that Mark appears simply to record the tradition, rather than attempting to develop a theological understanding. Thus, the details of the way in which Jesus dealt with the situation and the apparent initial difficulty in exorcism, have remained in the account, rather than being smoothed out as they have been in other stories. The picture they give suggests that Jesus acted in ways that would not have appeared markedly different from other exorcists of his time. There would seem to have been few differences in his methods of sufficient magnitude or character to have warranted an automatic response from those who observed his ministry that here was something new and distinctively different at work. There was no reason to connect what was an ordinary occurrence at that time with Jesus being self-evidently the Messiah of God and Deliverer of Israel. It is suggested, in fact, that the recognition of Jesus as someone other than a prophetic healer required a disclosure situation, just as did the understanding of the parables. One of Mark's consistent emphases is on the fact that very few had sufficient insight to recognise the clues and respond in any other way than with 'amazement'. Even the disciples are represented as being blind most of the time to the significance of what was going on around them. This is brought out almost brutally in this story: the evil spirits acknowledge Jesus as the Messianic king, but the people see him only as a nuisance.

This study, however, is primarily concerned with the medical aspects rather than the theological. The story provides the following framework with regard to the man's illness. Firstly, his behaviour was characterised by unpredictable violence to such an extent that the locals left him well alone and had given up their attempts to restrain and tame him in the brutal and inhumane ways of the time. Secondly, the violence was also inwardly directed and he demonstrated grotesque episodes of self-mutilation, using stones to cut himself. Finally, he appears to have suffered from a gross delusional state associated with what may have been a multiple personality syndrome. So convinced was he that he had become one with the demons that he believed tormented him, that he made his home in the tombs where they were believed to live. Even in his more lucid moments, he continued to think of himself in these terms with what appear to be 'third party' hallucinations.

Such a bizarre and violent illness would have led inevitably to the conclusion that the man was possessed by 'an unclean spirit'. In the aetiological categories of the time, only outside and evil forces could explain such an abnormal condition. From the standpoint of modern diagnostic categories, however, there are three likely conditions that would show the symptom complex that the story outlines. These will be considered in turn.

The first and perhaps most obvious choice, is a diagnosis of acute catatonic schizophrenia, a condition characterised by bizarre behaviour patterns and paranoid delusional states which present with both delusions and hallucinations. The generally accepted criteria for a diagnosis of schizophrenia are two or more of the following: delusions, hallucinations, disorganised speech, grossly disorganised behaviour and negative symptoms [136]. In these states the patient's feelings and actions are often experienced as though influenced by outside sources (in this story by demons). These so-called 'first rank' symptoms all appear to have been present in this case. Outbursts of unpredictable violence may also occur, involving murderous attacks on others as well as self-mutilation. The classic description of the violence of these states taken from one of the older textbooks of psychiatry cannot be bettered: 'The patient cries, hits, bites, breaks and destroys everything he can lay hands on, runs up and down, fights everybody and keeps moving day and night. It is impossible to establish any rapport with him and he continues to rage when left alone, independently of any stimulation' [137]. These features certainly characterised the sufferer in the quite detailed Markan description of the illness. In a modern situation 'patients in catatonic excitement urgently require physical and medical control because they are often destructive and violent towards others and their excitement can cause them to injure themselves' [138].

Secondly, it should be noted that a very similar clinical picture may also occur in the manic phase of bi-polar (manic-depressive) disorder. Particularly in the later stages of such illnesses, there may be marked paranoid and grandiose ideas that escalate into delusional convictions and a loss of all insight. Aggressiveness and irritability are frequent manifestations. Patients with acute mania, in fact, may be very difficult to distinguish from the acute schizophrenic, especially on short term observation rather than over a lengthy period. It has been estimated that between ten and twenty per cent of manic patients may display the 'first rank' symptoms of schizophrenia [139]. It is rare, however, for a manic patient to display the severe violence that seems to have been such a marked feature in this story.

The similar features of these illnesses, in fact, may be nothing other than the final common pathway for many different conditions. In spite of the bizarre pattern of this man's disease, therefore, there remains a third possibility of a diagnosis of a psychiatric conversion disorder. These conditions may also manifest themselves as a psychosis with multiple personality syndrome and problems of personal identity as well as paranoia and violence, especially in the so-called histrionic forms of the disorder. Other less likely diagnostic possibilities may include Torvelte's Syndrome in which there is obsessive-compulsive self-mutilation associated with motor tics and various other rare disorders with bizarre manifestations.

It would be rash to be dogmatic about the likely diagnosis. The present writer had suggested elsewhere that schizophrenia best fits the description of the symptoms described [140], but has modified this view as will be apparent from what follows. Some writers have suggested that a manic illness seems more likely. Kaufmann, for example, notes that self-mutilation would possibly be more frequent in manic-depressive illness and the man's apparent coherence and his ability to make contact with Jesus, as well as his recovery, together suggest a possible diagnosis of manic-depressive illness [141]. The recovery, as a result of an authoritative command in an emotionally charged atmosphere, would certainly suggest a condition less severe than schizophrenia and point towards a conversion disorder. Thus, the likelihood that his illness represents another expression of such an illness should be given serious consideration. Even though extreme in its manifestations in this case, the diagnosis is by no means impossible and the essentially behavioural approach to treatment, together with the ongoing supportive environment that Jesus offered, would be major factors in effecting a remission of symptoms in such a condition. It has been observed that the 'common denominator of successful treatment ... is the building of a caring authoritative relationship' [142] and this is exactly what Jesus provided, although, as always, the Markan time-frame is extremely compressed.

The theological function of this story is not as immediately apparent as in some of the other healing narratives. As noted earlier, it provides some insight into the healing methods of Jesus, suggesting that he used techniques that would have stamped him as a charismatic prophet in the minds of his contemporaries. It is also possible that some of the details of this story, which might well have been felt to be mildly embarrassing to the Church in its expanding mission and its developing christology, have been retained because they illustrated the nature of Christian conversion and the transformation of life that results from the presence and power of Christ. It also demonstrated that gentiles as well as Jews were to be touched by his transforming power and were to become his followers, so that the story may have had some bearing on the life of the Church in a missionary situation, illustrating the tensions that exist between different cultures and how these may be resolved in Christ. Meier comments that, 'as the story stands in Mark, it serves the theological purpose of symbolizing the bringing of the healing, liberating message of the Christian gospel to the unclean Gentiles, a mission undertaken proleptically by Jesus himself' [143].

Theissen [144], however, has expressed the opinion that the story was designed as a parable and was originally a 'sign' of a future liberation from oppression and foreign rule. Thus, the story should be seen as having a political motif. In Theissen's view, the allusion to Roman rule, represented by the herd of pigs running over the sacred ground of Israel, is unmistakable. The whole area of Galilee and the Decapolis was under Roman domination and the reference to 'Legion' would have immediately conjured up a picture of Roman soldiers in everyone's mind. The demonic thus becomes a representative of the oppressed and burdened people of the land whose great desire was to be set free. 'The hostility towards the Roman occupiers is made clear when the demons express their wish to be allowed to remain in the country. This is precisely what the Romans also want ... The story symbolically satisfies the desire to drive them into the sea like pigs. It becomes clear why the successful exorcist is sent away: his presence is a real threat to social peace' [145].

This interpretation may be something of an overstatement, but there certainly seems to be a social context behind this story. The whole situation is totally unclean from a Jewish point of view and the driving of the pigs into the sea may well be regarded as symbolic of what the Jewish people desired to do to the unclean Romans. It thus becomes possible to take the interpretation one stage beyond what Theissen, Crossan and others have proposed and see here a wider picture. As N.T. Wright puts it, 'Jesus is fighting a battle against the enemies of the people of YHWH. But Rome is not the enemy; it is the satan and his hordes, who are deceiving Israel into thinking that Rome is the real enemy, so that she (Israel) will not notice the reality. Jesus is going into what was thought of as enemy territory, taking on (from the Jewish point of view) the demon of uncleanness and hostile paganism, and defeating the real enemy instead, demonstrating that victory in the acted symbolism of the death of the pigs' [146]. The triumph is not final, but rather is prophetic. Nonetheless, for Mark's readers, possibly facing potential, if not real, suffering at the hands of Roman power, the story gives a new direction to their situation. It gives what Dormandy has called a 'fresh and greater perspective' [147] and allows a vision of their Lord as the one whose victory at a cross has made all other sovereignty relative. For the contemporaries of Jesus, such actions also pointed to him as fulfilling a prophetic ministry that required to be ranked alongside that of Elijah or Elisha, at the very least, and to those with eyes to see and ears to hear, it pointed on to something very much greater.

The Woman with the Haemorrhage: Mark 5:25-34 // Matthew 9:20-22 // Luke 8:43-48

The Jewish law classified anyone with what could be considered as a discharge as ritually unclean. For this reason a menstruating woman as well as anyone who touched her were 'unclean' (Lev 15:25-27). Both this story and the story of the 'leprosy' sufferer illustrate an important principle about the nature of true 'holiness'. Jesus affirmed in his actions what he emphasised in his teaching that, 'there is nothing that goes into a person from the outside which can make him ritually unclean. Rather it is what comes out of a person that makes him unclean' (Mark 7:15-23). Defilement is not 'caught' like a contagious disease, nor may 'holiness' be lost by contact with something that is considered ritually unclean. Both defilement and holiness derive from a person's 'inner state', from inner motives, attitudes and relationships, and not from the ritual concepts of what is 'tapu' or 'sacred' and on which social and religious sanctions are placed in order to regulate behaviour and the life of the community. Jesus deliberately steps outside the conventions and again presents a message that is subversive to the accepted norms of society.

According to Mark, the woman's condition had lasted for twelve years with no signs of improvement. Indeed, the evangelist seems to indicate that things were possibly getting worse and the attentions of the physicians had merely added to her misery. Such comments, however, may have been no more than a way of heightening the dramatic impact of the story and emphasising the effectiveness of the healing of Jesus in this desperate situation. Mark wished to underline the fact that she was at the end of her tether and all earthly sources of help had failed her totally. Mark's comment on the ministrations of the physicians of the time is studiously avoided by Luke, although the forms of treatment are well attested from contemporary records [148]. The prescriptions included various vile concoctions as well as requirements for strange actions to be performed. That the woman was not helped, but rather grew worse is not surprising. The Lukan version also lacks his characteristic expansion of the story and Matthew manages to reduce the length of even this short pericope by about one third of the Markan length.

It may be debated whether this story should be seen as a genuinely remembered event, thus accounting for its position within the context of the healing of Jairus's daughter. It may be that the positioning is merely skilful story telling and an example of Mark's characteristic intercalation of related incidents designed, in this case, to add a greater level of suspense to the story of the healing of the young girl [149]. Mark was, after all, a skilled story-teller and the introduction of this narrative provides a reason for the apparently fatal delay in the arrival of Jesus at the house of Jairus. Some weight is given to the view that the stories arise from different sources by the fact that Mark has tended to use the historic present in the story of Jairus's daughter, but in this particular narrative he has used past tenses together with long sentences built up with subordinate participial clauses. On the other hand, the account of the indignant and disrespectful protest of the disciples at the question of Jesus about who had touched him, softened considerably by Luke and totally omitted by Matthew, gives credence to the story's likely authenticity, even though Mark may have inserted it at this point in his narrative for his own purposes in story telling. Vincent Taylor has commented that 'the psychological realism of the account of the woman's fears and her courageous action, the rough question of the disciples, and the portrayal of Jesus, leave upon the mind a strong impression of verisimilitude' [150].

The term which Mark uses (and Luke follows) to describe the haemorrhage (ἐν ῥύσις αἵματος) was used in the medical texts to cover any form of severe blood loss, and meant primarily no more than a 'flow of blood' from any source, although it occurs in the Hippocratic texts specifically in relation to gynaecological bleeding [151]. Matthew uses the more normal verb for haemorrhaging (αἱμορροεω) in its only New Testament occurrence. In addition, Mark adds weight to the severity of the condition by referring to the woman's 'fountain of blood' (ἡ πηγη του αἵματος αὐτης) which suggests a constant and significant level of blood loss. It seems clear that the reader is intended to infer that the blood loss was *per vaginum*, although it is not clear whether that loss was from excessive menstrual bleeding (menorrhagia), bleeding between periods (metrorrhagia) or possibly a combination of both. Such distinctions were improperly understood at the time and may be confused even today. The long history of twelve years makes it clear that the problem was not due to a malignant growth, cancer being a specific cause of uterine bleeding. The statement about the number of years that the woman had been suffering, however, may be no more than an assimilation from the story of Jairus's daughter who is recorded as being twelve years old.

Hurtado, among others, sees the number 'twelve' in these stories as a redactional element that Mark has introduced as a symbol of Israel and he comments that 'the sequence of miracles among those identified with Israel, followed by rejection in Jesus' own village, affords the informed reader with a glimpse of the outcome of Jesus' ministry to Israel' [152]. There is an element of Markan irony in this section, in that these two healings, which so effectively dramatise the mission of Jesus to Israel and provide a degree of real insight into who he was, nonetheless result in rejection and consequently prefigure the way that his mission would end.

The normal menstrual cycle is dependent upon a highly complex and sensitive integration between the brain (the hypothalamus), the pituitary gland and the ovaries. Various emotional and psychosocial stressors, such as anxiety, depression, marital problems, grief and so forth, may profoundly influence the brain centres. Such stresses often seriously affect normal menstruation and result either in amenorrhoea (absence of uterine bleeding) on the one hand or in abnormal and excessive bleeding on the other. Although amenorrhoea is the more common response to psychological factors, excessive bleeding may also occur. Further, excessive menstrual bleeding may also be a manifestation of psychological conversion disorders [155]. It has been suggested already that this group of disorders provided the diagnosis in a number of the previous healings discussed. Indeed, the pattern of illness emerging from the Markan narratives is one of disorders having primarily a psychological basis, rather than diseases arising out of specific anatomical pathology, such as cancers or heart disease. They were essentially conditions rooted in people's minds.

It is very possible, therefore, that this woman's illness would also have been influenced by mainly psychosocial factors and it is a reasonable assumption that she was suffering from psychologically generated dysfunctional uterine bleeding. The increasing anxiety induced by her condition was probably also associated with signfiicant depression and the vicious cycle is easy to envisage in a situation in which the woman was effectively cut off from all normal religious and social contacts. Everything she touched would have been 'unclean' and it is not difficult how her condition becamse essentially self-perpetuating. It is hardly surprising that she approached Jesus in such a surreptitious manner [156]. She was convinced, however, that Jesus could help her, even though her approach was coloured by the magical ideas of her time (in this connection note also Mark 3:10; 6:56 and Acts 5:15).

She appeared 'to believe that Jesus possessed a supernatural power of healing, which resided in him almost as a physical fluid, and coould be tapped by touch, even the touching of his clothes, without Jesus himself being aware of what was happening' [157]. Mark seems to share these ideas as he comments that Jesus was aware that 'power had gone out of him' (την ἐξ αὐτου δυναμιν ἐξελθουσ). The intense desire, the inner conviction that help was near, together with the obstacles to be overcome before she could get near enough to Jesus to touch him, all provide the necessary background towards ensuring that the essential psychological release could take place in order to pave the way for the relief of physical symptoms.

Mark's emphasis on the immediacy of the healing is typical of his time compression, but there is no reason to doubt that the woman began to feel that her health was improving 'immediately' after she had touched Jesus: it is what would be expected in such situations of 'faith' cure. Mark's theological interests are underlined in the response of Jesus when he confirmed the healing to the woman (a necessary aspect of such 'faith healing'). It is to be emphasised that the 'power' (δυναμις) of Jesus was within his control: it was not magic. Jesus is God's agent through whom God's power is active to heal and save. It was important to emphasise this aspect, especially to a largely Hellenistic readership, in order to avoid misunderstandings, for 'power' was a common and characteristic term in the language of pagan devotion, understood as an impersonal, divine or semi-divine energy. Jesus, therefore, was concerned to make the woman articulate her faith, which she did with 'fear and trembling' - the correct approach to the one who was the embodiment of God's saving power in the world.

Her response of faith removed the torment (μαστιξ- literally 'whip' or 'lash') of her defilement and she may therefore 'go in peace'. A new and deeper level of meaning is given to the standard formula of leave taking, for, not only is she 'cured' (ὑγιης), but she has been 'saved' (σεσωκεν) and brought to wholeness (peace) through her faith. She is no longer an outcast, she is no longer defiled, but she has entered again into her true status as 'daughter' within the covenant community. Once again, Jesus shows that, if nothing else, he is at least a prophet of Israel's restoration and homecoming to her God.

The daughter of Jairus: Mark 5:21-24, 35-43//Matthew 9:18-19, 23-26//Luke 8:41,42, 49-56.

In contrast to the intercalated story of the healing of the woman with the haemorrhage, a section that is full of participles, the story of Jairus' daughter is written in simpler syntax. The clear differences in style and language between the two narratives are sufficient to suggest that they were possibly not connected in the tradition [158], even though Mark stamps this story with his characteristic 'immediately' (εὐθυς).

Both stories appear to present clear theological messages so that, as acted parables, they could be used to underline essential elements of the Christian gospel and it seems likely that the Church has used these stories in this way from the very beginning. This is not quite the same as saying, however, that this was the way in which Mark intended these stories to function when he wrote them down. Mark's main purpose would appear to be the setting of these actions within the context of his twin themes of faith and unbelief: the central issue of recognising that in and through Jesus, Israel's God is active, which at the same time raises issues of the authority and status of Jesus himself [159].

Nonetheless, it would seem that the story of the daughter of Jairus, the synagogue official, is designed to emphasise two major issues. In the first instance, along with the stories of the paralysed man (or as has been suggested, 'youth'), the Syrophoenician woman's daughter and the epileptic boy, this narrative deals with the importance of vicarious faith. Throughout his Gospel, Mark has been concerned to show the necessity of faith in any dealings with God. Jesus shared the convictions of the Old Testament prophets that what God required from his people was an attitude of humble dependence, summed up in the words of the prophet, 'to do justice, to love mercy and to walk humbly before God' (Micah 6:8). Further, this faith was to be shown by the recognition of the one whom God had sent and the message of deliverance that he brought. The emphasis in this story, however, shifts from the faith exercised by people in respect of their own need (as in the case of the woman with the haemorrhage) to the reward of faith exercised vicariously on behalf of others, more specifically, it would appear in the Markan context, on behalf of those not able to respond for themselves.

In this story and the others noted above, the persons in need are unable to respond to Jesus directly and personally. The implication in three of the stories, and possibly in that of the paralysed 'youth' as well, is that the person in need was below the 'age of discretion'. In each case, they were passive recipients of the healing and wholeness of God that Jesus brought to them. The active faith that released the blessing, was shown by others on their behalf, and there is an emphasis on the response of the parents which had brought them to blessing. It is interesting to speculate that, at the time the Gospel was written, the issue of the baptism of infants and children of believing parents had arisen in the Markan church (perhaps Rome on the basis of tradition) in the immediate 'post-missionary' situation. It may just be that Mark is attempting to provide a theological basis and a justification for the practice, for which the pericope of the blessing of the children provided additional weight. God rewards true faith and the faith of parents on behalf of their children will be honoured.

The second issue that Mark emphasises is the triumph of Jesus over death. Whether the child was truly dead or was comatose is irrelevant from the point of view of the story and its message. Mark's purpose was to reinforce the conviction that, in the words of the Fourth Gospel, Jesus is 'the resurrection and the life' (John 11:25). He is the one who transforms the hopelessness of the living death of the old world of sin and alienation into the boundless and deathless life of the new world in fellowship with God. In addition, as Cranfield has noted, the story serves as 'a reminder to Christians that death is not the last word, but a sleep from which Christ will wake us at the last day, and therefore a rebuke to those who in the presence of death behave as those that have no hope' [160] (note also 1 Thess 4:13,14). It seems likely that Mark has deliberately chosen the rather ambiguous word 'sleep' in order to develop this theological point. It is likely, therefore, that the simple statement by Jesus that 'the child is not dead, but is sleeping' (v 39) should be taken at its face value. It is certain that those in the house are represented as understanding Jesus to have spoken literally, but, thinking they knew better, they laughed him out of court (note the similar confusion also developed for a theological purpose at John 11:11) [161].

The story begins with Jairus coming to Jesus to plead for his 'little daughter' (θυγατριον). He is called 'a ruler of the synagogue' and was presumably from Capernaum, although this is not stated. The ruler of the synagogue (ἀπχισυναγωγος = Heb. *rôš ha-keneset*) was the lay official responsible for the general supervision of the synagogue services, arranging for suitable people to read the prayers and set lections and, as appropriate, to preach. He was also responsible for the maintenance of the building itself. He was appointed by the local elders and was a person of dignity and consequence within the local community. The term may have been derived from the Greek guilds although this is not certain. Normally each synagogue had only one 'ruler' or 'superintendent' who conducted worship and was the probable model for the later Christian 'president', 'overseer' or 'bishop' (ἐπισκοπος) [162]. Mark, however, uses the plural and seems to consider that the congregation had more than one 'ruler' (note also Acts 13:15). This may reflect some confusion with the body of elders or it may be that there were occasions when a synagogue had more than one president, perhaps acting in rotation, particularly if it were large [163].

The age of the little girl was put at 12 years, but, as was discussed earlier, this may be an assimilation from the intercalated story of the woman with the haemorrhage who is stated to have had her problem for 12 years. In both cases there seems to be a deliberate reference to the idea of 'twelve' being representative of Israel and it may be presumed that one story helps to interpret the other. Both the woman and the girl may be seen as representatives of the faithful remnant that saw God's promised redemption being revealed in Jesus and had the faith to receive the fullness of divine healing and reconstitution that he had come to bring.

On the other hand, it is not impossible that when Mark referred to the child as 'little girl' he was using the technical age descriptor which appears to have been the later Rabbinic classification for a girl of this age [164] and was emphasising that she had not reached an age of genuine responsibility. To what extent this classification was in use in the time of Jesus is a matter for debate, but the specific statement of the age suggests it belonged to the early tradition in some form. Luke puts the age into the body of the story and adds that she was an 'only daughter', thus increasing the 'human interest' value of the incident.

In the Markan version, the child is represented as being *in extremis* (ἐσχατον ἐξει), she was apparently at death's door and certainly not expected to recover. The underlying ambiguities of this version are removed quite specifically by Matthew who states unequivocally that the girl was already dead and, indeed, had been dead long enough for the professional mourners with their musical instruments to have been called. There can therefore be no argument about the nature of the intervention: Jesus was restoring life to someone who was already dead. The event may thus be put into the same bracket as the raising of the widow's son (Luke 7:11-17) and a clear evidence of the outworking of divine power. Matthew is sufficiently true to his sources to allow Jesus to speak of the child as being asleep, but in his context, this part of the tradition has to be given a theological meaning. Similarly, Luke also makes the description of the girl's state more specific by saying that she was dying and there is again a more definite emphasis on the restoration to life and the intervention of divine power as he states explicitly that the girl's 'spirit returned' (Luke 8:55). Matthew and Luke, therefore, have developed the 'wonder' aspects of the story for their own theological purposes and any attempt to make a diagnosis of the girl's condition must be on the basis of what is to be judged the more original account in Mark.

Any discussion of the possible nature of the child's illness based on the vague statements in the story is, of necessity, speculative. Many conditions could result in a terminal comatose state. If the urgency of the approach of Jairus was real and not a literary device of Mark to raise the tension of the story, then it may be presumed that the illness was both of recent onset and of very rapid progress. There is, in fact, no suggestion that the girl had been sick for a long time and had gradually sunk into a coma. It might reasonably be supposed, therefore, that the girl was suffering from a severe febrile illness with central nervous system effects, for example, a disease such as bacterial meningitis or cerebral malaria. Both these conditions were likely to have been relatively common in first century Palestine.

Other possibilities exist, however, which are likely to have a greater level of probability, particularly in the light of the apparently rapid cure. For example, the girl may have been suffering from a conversion or somatisation-type illness associated with the menarche, causing a comatose condition through 'hysterical' overbreathing. When carried on for any length of time this may induce loss of consciousness and a genuine comatose state. Overbreathing leads to an acute alkalosis as a result of 'blowing off' carbon dioxide and this excessive loss of carbon dioxide in expired air causes changes in the blood chemistry. This results in a marked constriction of the cerebral blood vessels and a reduction in the brain levels of oxygen which, if allowed to continue, leads to loss of consciousness, as well as tetanic spasms and various changes in sensation, which together present a very frightening picture. It is a well-documented condition seen frequently in developing countries where it is often put down to demon possession [165]. Normally, however, such unconsciousness is relatively shortlived and it is unlikely that it would have lasted long enough for a crowd to have gathered together and certainly not Matthew's professional mourners. It seems certain, however, that these latter were added to the story in order to emphasise that the 'miracle' was one of genuine resuscitation.

A somewhat similar, although not identical, view is that the girl had an unstable vascular system resulting in an episode of unconsciousness through brain oxygen starvation. Lloyd Davies suggests that the child was 'in the prepubescent stage before the start of the adolescent spurt in growth, in which the hormone balance is unstable with possible effect on the vascular circulation. Left alone she would have recovered' [166]. Once again, however, the probability is that the resulting fainting would have been extremely short unless this was a feigned illness. At a time when medical knowledge was very incomplete, someone lying still and with shallow and almost imperceptable breathing might well be considered dead, but this seems unlikely with a fainting fit which would certainly have been recognised.

Nonetheless, on the face of it, the family seemed to have acted with almost precipitate haste in reaching the conclusion that their daughter was dead and bringing in the mourners, unless this is part of the dramatic dressing of the story. It needs to be emphasised that the diagnoses suggested above are no more than speculative. The story as it stands allows no firm conclusions to be drawn, but, in the light of the other healings accomplished by Jesus, a functional ('psychosomatic') condition is the most likely explanation for the situation as Mark presents it. There can be no certainty and it is probably unwise to try to go behind the very limited information that has been provided. For the evangelist and his readers the theological point was all that mattered, although from the standpoint of this study a reasonable diagnosis needs to be made which fits the available data and is not imposed on them for the sake of a preconceived view of the way that Jesus healed.

Finally, it should be noted that the Aramaic words *talitha coum* ('little girl, get up') that Jesus used to address the girl, have been interpreted as a magical formula [167]. Jesus undoubtedly used simple incantational language, familiar to all exorcists, from time to time, but there is no suggestion here (not even in Luke's account) that the healing of this girl was considered to be an exorcism. The words should be taken at face value. They are likely to be remembered words in what seemed to be an impossible situation to the onlooker. Cranfield remarks, the 'suggestion that this use of the Aramaic words has something to do with the fact that the use of foreign words is a feature of miracle-stories is most unlikely - the fact that they are translated tells against it, and also the fact that Mark elsewhere retains original Aramaic words ... but only on one occasion (7:34) in connection with a miracle' [168].

The Syrophoenician woman's daughter: Mark 7:24-30 // Matthew 15:21-28

This story presents a number of problems, not least being the geographical site at which it takes place. Mark states that Jesus went away to the region of Tyre, but then adds that, 'he entered the house'. This is a phrase which, in relation to Jesus, is used generally as equivalent to 'home', either the sense of the home of one or other of the disciples, or more specifically, the place where Jesus lived when not on his journeys. The important point is that this location always appears to be in Capernaum. The problem is compounded by the geographical comments at the end of the story. Mark notes that Jesus left the region of Tyre and came to the Sea of Galilee through the middle of (ἀνὰ μεσον) the district of the Decapolis. The convoluted trail that this would have involved is rather reminiscent of G K Chesterton's famous poem about the 'Rolling English drunkard' and 'the night we went to Birmingham by way of Beachy Head' [169]. It would seem that this story represents an imperfectly remembered part of the tradition. However, as Martin Hengel has noted, 'without a map it would be difficult even for a man of antiquity like Mark to establish his bearings in a strange area a good seventy miles from his home city, which presumably he had left long before he began to write his work, a strange area which he evidently had never visited' [170]. The place name may be considered to be traditional, therefore, rather than redactional and is another example of Jesus moving out to help those beyond the immediate bounds of the 'house of Israel'. It thus provides a dominical basis for the gentile mission of Mark's own time [171].

Matthew has attempted to smooth out some of the geographical problems by omitting all mention of the Decapolis. The other important differences, such as his statement that the woman was a 'Canaanite', his emphasis on petitionary faith, the duplicating of the petition and its being turned into a solemn appeal as well as the insertion of *logia*, all tend to suggest that Matthew may well have been using an independent tradition at this point, rather than relying solely on Mark.

The second problem raised by the story is the uncharacteristically harsh language that Jesus used to the gentile woman who approached him for help. In spite of deliberate oratorical exaggeration, it still strikes the reader as reflecting a substantial degree of Galilean xenophobia. S.G.F. Brandon remarks that, 'Long familiarity with this story, together with the traditional picture of the gentleness of Jesus, tends to obscure the shocking intolerance of the saying' [172]. The Matthean version is even more liable to misunderstandings. Jesus is quoted as affirming the narrowness of his mission: 'I was sent only to the lost sheep of the house of Israel' (Matt 15:24), possibly introduced from a separate segment of tradition (note Matt 10:6). To some extent the words of Jesus would have reflected Jewish attitudes to gentiles, but would have seemed harsh and uncompromising to the reader. It is, indeed, the very inappropriateness of these words, in a document that would inevitably have had a significant gentile readership, that strongly supports their authenticity.

The words of Jesus do not cause offence, as might have been expected. Perhaps there was something in the way that Jesus had responded that indicated that this was not the final word on the matter. The woman was determined to get what she wanted for her daughter and the emphasis of the story is on her remarkable faith and persistence. When she is told, 'first let the children (ie the members of the covenant community) eat all they want', she responds by agreeing, but points out that the house dogs (κυναριον, the diminutive form of κυνων) under the table can still get the scraps without disturbing any priorities. Incidentally, the fact that she appeared to keep dogs in the house would suggest strongly that she was a Greek and certainly not Jewish [173].

This is a story that would have been likely to have had a prominent place in the early debates about the admission of gentiles to the Church community. It is a story that bears witness to the programme of redefining the people of God that was inherent in the work of Jesus. The gentile who responds to Israel's God in faith will receive the same salvation as Jewish people, even though the order is 'first' (a Markan redactional addition to the tradition) to the original members of God's family. It is the same concept to be reflected in Paul's emphasis that the gospel was to be proclaimed to all - to the Jew first, and also to the gentile (Rom 1:16, 2:9-11, etc).

The important element of this pericope is thus the dialogue between Jesus and the gentile woman: the rest of the story is almost incidental, a vehicle to hold the narrative in a context. Bowman, in fact, has called this 'haggadic midrash', material which may or may not be historical in the classical sense, but which was 'told to indicate what was the teaching of Jesus towards Gentiles and church membership' [174]. It would have been an important part of the tradition at a time when the debate on the status of gentile believers had yet to be finally resolved and when the relationship between the new Christian community and the synagogue was also unresolved. In addition to this, both the key elements of faith and persistence are central to the story. Faith is not mentioned specifically, but there is no doubt that the evangelist wishes the reader to see the woman's response as one of faith [175]. Even more prominent is the necessity of persistence in the face of seemingly insuperable difficulties. In spite of an insulting initial refusal, the woman was not prepared to take 'no' for an answer - and she was rewarded. Further, once again this action is vicarious in nature. The woman's daughter was not in a position to make any request or any response: the mother acted for her daughter and her daughter received the promised healing. This also would form early Christian sermon material, underlining the effectiveness of 'fervent prayer' (James 5:15).

The story is presented as an exorcism at a distance, the only example in Mark. The information about the girl is scanty in the extreme, but, in view of the nature of other conditions that have been characterised as 'demon possession' in this Gospel, it may reasonably be assumed that it was some rather bizarre functional illness. The statement that the mother returned to find her daughter 'lying on the bed and the demon gone' suggests that the illness had been of a violent nature and the new restful state was in sharp contrast to the girl's previous behaviour. However, it is impossible to provide any form of diagnosis on the limited information that is available.

One interesting diagnostic suggestion is worth noting. M and T.A. Lloyd Davies have proposed that it was the mother who was ill rather than the daughter and suggest that she was suffering from a form of Munchausen's syndrome (named after the eighteenth century Baron von Munchausen who gained notoriety for his highly exaggerated stories of his exploits and adventures) [176]. This is a well-known condition in which the patient simulates illness, often producing extraordinary symptoms and undergoing repeated surgery or other forms of uncomfortable treatment, in order to gain attention and affection. Interest has focussed recently on women who demonstrate a form of vicarious Munchausen's syndrome (Meadow's syndrome) in which they invent in great detail and over considerable periods of time, symptoms and signs of disease in their children [177]. In this story Jesus gives the mother the attention she needs herself and the assurances she needs in respect of her daughter and she returns home to find her child well. In reality, she had never been genuinely sick other than in her mother's mind. This is an interesting and not impossible suggestion, but as with any reconstruction of the events in this story, it remains in the realm of speculation, as the data are not sufficient to provide definitive conclusions. Nonetheless, the apparent healing of the daughter 'at a distance' may be a good argument for the healing of the mother rather than the daughter.

The story is usually considered to be an example of healing at a distance. However, there is no suggestion that Jesus used any word of command to the demon nor are any of the other usual features of healing or exorcism present. The woman is told simply to go home and her daughter will be found to be well. To explain what may have happened as some form of telepathy is, as John Wilkinson remarks, merely to confound the problem: it is to 'try and explain the unknown by the uncertain and leads nowhere' [178]. Healings at a distance were not unknown in the ancient literature and the power to heal at a distance had been attributed to others, including Jewish rabbis from the same broad period, particularly Hanina ben Dosa [179]. However, there is no clear indication that Jesus actually performed a healing in this story. If it be assumed that it was the mother rather than the daughter who was sick, then what was apparently a healing at a distance becomes a healing very much along the lines of the normal activity of Jesus in dealing with conditions in which the psychological aspects are paramount, what have been generally referred to as 'psychosomatic', 'psychogenic' or 'functional' complaints.

The man with the speech defect: Mark 7:31-37

This story is unique to Mark's Gospel and contains many of the characteristics of the later story of the blind man at Bethsaida (8:22-26), another story that occurs only in Mark and appears to be from the same source. Cranfield [180] considers that these stories were a pair, for both are part of a complex that contains a feeding miracle and are recorded as being difficult to accomplish (see also Table 3:1, p 56). Not only so, but the tradition provides a glimpse of the physical methods of treatment that Jesus used. It is perhaps for this reason that the other synoptic evangelists did not record this event. Matthew, at this point in his narrative (15:29-31), has provided a summary statement of the activity of Jesus in all forms of healings. It is to be presumed that he was aware of the tradition, but because it represents Jesus as having difficulty in accomplishing the healing, it did not suit his christological purposes to include either of these stories. The retention of details that might be embarrassing to the early Christian community would indicate that it derives from an early (and perhaps, eyewitness) tradition which has undergone very little in the way of redaction. The only redactional elements, in fact, seem to be the notes on geographical context (vv 31) and the final comments about the astonishment of the crowd (v 37). The problematic geography has been discussed earlier and it seems to reflect a general vagueness about Palestinian topography on the part of the evangelist, suggesting that this story was without any particular context in the tradition that Mark received. He has accordingly provided one for it, but became rather lost in the process.

The major interest lies in the methods Jesus used in effecting the healing. Mark records that Jesus took the man aside, touched the affected part, sighed and used the Aramaic word, *ephphatha*. Mark records that 'they' (one assumes that this means the man's friends) brought 'a man who was deaf and could hardly speak'. The problem is to decide whether the man was genuinely incapable of speech or whether he had an impediment and was unable to articulate clearly. At a later point in the story (v 37) he is declared to be dumb (ἄλαλος), but this verse is clearly no more than an editorial meditative comment on the healing rather than a genuine record of a spontaneous exclamation of surprise and praise. Mark uses the word μογιλαλος, at v 32. It is an unusual word essentially giving the meaning of speaking with difficulty or having an impediment in one's speech [181]. This is the only New Testament occurrence of the word and it occurs once only in the LXX, at Isa 35:6.

It is very likely that this verse from Isaiah may have been in Mark's mind in view of the 'end time restoration' motif in that section of the book, as well as the likelihood that those reading this story would have their minds directed immediately by this rare word to the prophet's vision of Messianic salvation. It may be, therefore, that the use of the word is no more than Mark's endeavour to aid 'disclosure' and to direct the reader's attention to the real status of Jesus and the nature of his work as an 'eschatological prophet'. Even in this relatively 'primitive' piece of tradition, the interest is essentially theological because the purpose of writing was essentially proclamation [182].

In view of the likely theological aim behind the use of μογιλαλος it would be dangerous to build too much on the use of the word in this particular narrative. Nonetheless, the later statement in the story that, after the healing had taken place, the man was able to 'speak clearly' (ἐλαλει ὀρθως) suggests that the problem may well have been more in the way of a speech defect or impediment rather than total mutism. The minimal amount of information makes it impossible to provide a firm and definitive diagnosis. In cases of deafness from organic causes, there is frequently an associated speech defect of varying degrees and in cases of profound congenital deafness this may amount to genuine mutism. It seems more likely, however, that, as with other examples of healing, this man was suffering from a conversion/somatiform disorder. Deafness and mutism as well as speech defects are well-documented features of these conditions and it seems likely from the method of healing that this man represents a further case of such an illness. Further, in a case of genuine organic deafness/mutism, the use of a command would seem pointless for it would not have been heard, but in a functional illness, hearing remains intact and the command would be heard. The method of healing, clearly very dramatic, suggests the sort of abreactive technique that would produce an effect in such cases, a point that was made by Micklem many years ago [183].

It seems highly probable that the story presents the reader with one of the very few accounts of the actual methods that Jesus used in healing. In most of the stories the methods have been edited out, probably for theological and apologetic reasons, and only the word of Jesus becomes necessary to produce the cure. Here, however, although Jesus uttered a strong word of command, it was in association with the use of saliva, physical manipulation and prayer. These features are suggestive that the healing did not take place as an immediate event.

The use of saliva in healing is well attested in the ancient world and occurs in three of Jesus' healings (the present occasion, Mark 8:23 and John 9:6). Whether this was understood as a magical action is a moot point. Hull remarks that 'with the use of spittle we are in that shadowy world where medicine fades into magic and no sharp distinction can be made' [184]. On the other hand, saliva was believed to have healing properties in its own right, even though many of the uses were mixed with the sort of superstition that frequently is associated with folk medicine and may still be found in western society today. Twelftree remarks that 'in this aspect of his healing technique, the early Church was clearly not endeavouring to remove or isolate Jesus from his milieu' [185].

It has also been argued that the use of the Aramaic word, *ephphatha*, indicates a magical approach in this healing in which foreign (specifically eastern) words could be demonstrated to have greater power than Greek to a gentile audience [186]. Neither example of Aramaic words being used in this Gospel (here and at Mark 5:41) suggest magical formulae, nor are they used in exorcisms in which such formulae might have been expected. It seems more reasonable and much less complicated, therefore, to see in such words the authenticity of genuine memory, a memory, furthermore, which retained all the difficulties associated with this healing.

The blind man of Bethsaida: Mark 8:22-26 [187]

The story of the healing of the blind man at Bethsaida brings the description of Jesus' itinerant preaching ministry to a close. From this point on his 'way is resolutely directed towards Jerusalem and the necessary encounter with the cross' [188]. The story acts as a bridge between the two halves of the Gospel and stands at the centre both of Mark's teaching on the person of Jesus and the realities and cost of discipleship. As was noted in connection with the story of the deaf-mute, that account and the present healing narrative form a pair in which the healings were accomplished only with difficulty and in which Jesus used some form of physical means to bring about the cure.

The story is also unique in its record of the response of the blind man to his returning sight. Apart from the comment, 'now I see' recorded at John 9:25, which is more of a theological point than anything else, this story is the only one in the Gospel records in which a blind person actually describes the experience of recovery of sight.

The words are sufficiently unusual that it is difficult to see them as anything other than a first hand account remembered and later recorded. Further, as will become apparent later, the words are of quite remarkable significance [189]. The major problem of the story is to determine the significance and meaning of this somewhat enigmatic statement, 'I see people, but they look like trees, walking'.

Blindness is a condition that is capable of several definitions. The biblical narratives are seldom sufficiently explicit to allow a distinction to be made between those who would be termed totally blind and those who were in varying degrees partially sighted. It needs to be remembered also that even partial sightedness may equate with severe functional blindness and no useful vision. It is apparent, therefore, that all the cases in the Gospels would be accommodated within modern definitions of blindness such as, 'loss of vision sufficient to prevent an individual from supporting himself in an occupation, making him dependent upon other persons, agencies or devices in order to live' [190]. The dependence of this man on his acquaintances in Mark's story is illustrated by the fact that he had to be brought to Jesus. The implication is that any vision he may have had was very limited.

In order to be able to interpret the nature of the man's response, it is necessary to consider the nature of his blindness and, in particular, whether it was congenital or had been acquired later in life. In only one case in the Gospel narratives is it stated that a person was born blind (John 9:1), an incident that will be considered later. The absence of any specific statement is not conclusive either way, although it is likely that if this information had been available to Mark it would have been recorded, particularly in view of the background details he provides in other healing narratives. There are, however, a number of reasons for reaching the conclusion that this man's blindness was acquired and not from birth.

It has been argued persuasively (for example by Johnson [191]) that the verb ἀναβλεπω (v 25) has the meaning of regaining sight and the use of the aorist tense there possibly indicates the point at which sight was completely restored. Further, in this verse Mark has also used the verb ἀποκαθιστημι (to 'give back' or 'restore') for the restoration of the man's sight. It is a verb that carries the basic meaning of restoration to an original condition and the evangelist has already used the verb in connection with the man with the 'withered hand' at Mark 3:5. There the meaning clearly indicates a restoration of the hand to how had been before the man's illness. The verb is also used in this way by the other evangelists (see Matt 12:13, Luke 6:10). It is most unlikely that such a verb would have been used of someone who was congenitally blind, as nowhere does the verb appear to have the meaning of restoration to how things ought to have been.

The question arises, nonetheless, as to whether Mark was using the verb with theological connotations in mind. The verb had marked overtones in regard to the Messianic restoration of Israel and it is used in this way on several occasions in the New Testament (Mark 9:12, Acts 1:6 and the noun ἀποκαταστασις at Acts 3:21). As will be discussed in more detail later in relation to the healing of blind Bartimaeus, Mark was well aware of the theological implications of the restoration of sight. It is very likely that Mark is here underlining this spiritual component that seems to be part of every healing that Jesus performed and emphasising the universal need for a restoration of relationships with God. Even so, it seems unlikely that he would have used this verb had the man's blindness been congenital.

Acquired blindness has been common in the Middle East throughout recorded history. According to the World Health Organisation the prevalence of blindness in some of the less well developed areas of this region varied between one and three per cent of the population, reaching as high as five per cent in some rural areas [192]. These figures need to be set against the rates for western countries. In the United Kingdom, for example, the prevalence of blindness is approximately 0.2 per cent of the population and in the former West Germany it was even lower at 0.06 per cent. The great majority of cases in the Middle East and Asia are the result of severe eye infections, such as trachoma, together with cataracts. The evidence of this story suggests that the blind man was suffering from severe and over-ripe cataracts, as will be discussed later.

The cure is recorded as taking place in two stages, both associated with the 'laying on of hands' (vv 23, 25), thus making the story unique in the Gospel narratives and indicating that it is almost certainly a genuine reminiscence. The account markedly plays down any sense of wonder or power, which may be why the other synoptic evangelists have ignored it. In common with the parallel story of the healing of the deaf-mute, Jesus applied saliva to the affected organs (see also on John 9:6,7 at pp 183f below). This may have been to awaken expectation in the blind man that something was about to be done for him, especially as he would be aware of the healing properties ascribed to saliva [193]. There may have been an eminently practical reason for the use of saliva, however, simply to remove the dirt and dried secretions from the eyelids preparatory to the healing.

After the 'laying on of hands', Jesus asks the question, 'Do you see (or perhaps better, recognise) anything?' The man's response comes in somewhat enigmatic words, which might be rendered, 'I can make out (βλεπω) people: they are like trees, except that I can see (ορω) them walking'. It has sometimes been argued that this odd expression means no more than that the man's vision was still very blurred and that both men and trees were vague and shadowy objects, except that men moved and trees did not. This fails to provide a satisfactory answer, for there is no reason for comparing men and trees at all, particularly in view of the size differences between them. They are not usually associated as comparable objects.

The British physicist, R E D Clark, suggested an ingenious solution to the problem [194], based partly on his own experiences following eye surgery and on the classic studies of von Senden [195]. The argument is based on the assumption that the man was born blind, an assumption for which the narrative itself provides no real evidence. Clark takes as his starting point the extreme difficulty experienced by a congenitally blind person in discerning shapes after receiving sight later in life. One story is quoted of a blind man who knew his way about perfectly, but who became lost and had to ask his way home after receiving his sight following surgery. Another case, reported extensively in the press at the time, was of a woman who continued to need her guide dog for some time after regaining her sight because she was unable to interpret the visual images that were new to her experience.

These difficulties arise, in part at least, from the different basis on which congenitally blind people group objects together compared with those who are sighted. The criterion for a blind person is touch and feeling, rather than an object's actual appearance. On this basis, both people and trees become members of a class of similar objects - both have a cylindrical trunk and branch-like appendages arising from it. One case, quoted by von Senden, is of particular interest in this respect. A congenitally blind woman who received her sight through surgery, imparted the important discovery to a blind friend that 'people do not look like trees at all'. Had she remained blind there seems little doubt that she would have gone through life with the vague impression that the tallest tree was little bigger than a man.

It has to be remembered that the sense of form entails not only discrimination between a large number of visual stimuli of differing intensity and position, but, equally importantly, it needs a critical ability, based on learning and experience, to interpret the visual stimuli correctly [196]. Blind people lack the visual acuity necessary to discriminate between visual sensory stimuli, but those who lose their sight after learning to interpret such visual stimuli are able to retain the visual images. On the other hand, those born blind have never been able to develop this interpretive function, possess no retained visual images in the brain and, thus, have to learn from the beginning like an infant if sight is gained. The case that Clark makes out assumes that the man in the story confused the visual images of trees and people, considering them both to be of the same size. The problem thus becomes one of recognition: he was unable to interpret what he saw and was unable to discriminate mentally between men and trees until after the second stage of the healing.

While this interpretation is at first sight an attractive one, particularly in its ability to provide a reasonable link between the man's statement in the narrative and the documented perceptual confusion that may exist on the part of those who have recovered their sight after congenital blindness, it does present a number of difficulties. In the first place, it is almost always the case that those who have been blind from birth and later gain their sight, after the removal of congenital cataracts for example, fail to recognise anything in the immediate post-operative period and the names and nature of objects have to be explained to them. Consequently, had the man been blind from birth, it is unlikely that he would have recognised either people or trees, neither would he have understood the movement of walking. The man's words however, indicate that he was fully aware of the difference between people and trees, even though, initially there appeared to have been some confusion between them. Not only so, he also understood the complex movement of walking. Finally, as was discussed earlier, and as will be developed in more detail in the argument that follows, it is most unlikely that the man's blindness was congenital and the evidence points towards an acquired form of blindness.

It is necessary, therefore, to seek a solution to the problem in which, although a conceptual awareness of the difference between people and trees existed, there was an initial visual confusion about size so that people appeared as trees walking about. The only condition that appears to fulfil these criteria is the loss of the crystalline lens of the eye (aphakia). If this were the case, then it would need to be assumed that the cause of the blindness in the first place was severe cataracts. In cases of over-maturity of the cataract, a posterior displacement of the lens into the vitreous chamber of the eye may occur with relative ease. Fraser [197] has drawn attention to the small degree of trauma necessary to effect such a displacement and has pointed out that the pressure of Jesus' fingers on the eye would have been sufficient to cause the lens to fall back into the vitreous chamber had the man been suffering from severe cataracts. This form of therapy, known as manual couching, was a well-established practice, used in Europe until comparatively recent times, and still used extensively in India, Pakistan, Iran and the Near East. It is of interest to note that the great composer, George Frederick Handel, had his cataracts couched, although in his case, a needle was used and the result was less than successful so that he was effectively blind in his last years.

The loss of the lens from the light refracting pathway produces distortion of size perception, resulting in a marked increase in the size of the retinal image compared with the normal eye: up to twice normal size. In addition, there would be considerable blurring of the image consequent upon the loss of focussing power due to the removal of the lens from the optical system (in technical terms, there would be about a 12 dioptre hypermetropia). As Fraser comments, the man would have remembered the appearance of both men and trees, but 'he would be surprised to see that men looked so large and it would be a natural thing for him to compare them with trees walking about'. Thus, in response to the question of Jesus, 'Do you see anything?' the man effectively responds by saying, 'Yes, I can make out people: I know they are people because they are walking about, but they are as big as trees!'

This was not the end of the story, however. Initially, as with all patients with uncorrected vision following cataract removal, and therefore needing further refraction, this man's vision was blurred and vague. Then Jesus touched his eyes again and he regained his sight as it had been before. Mark states that it was fully restored (the doubly augmented ἀποκαθιστημι) and he was able to see clearly. This may be explained if the patient had been a so-called 'high myope' [198]. These people have a number of physical and optical conditions of their eyes which lend them to this kind of "miracle" cure. The eyes are excessive in length and excessively distendable. The vitreous body is extremely fluid and the cataracts are eminently couchable. Further, traditional healers are often able to recognise those sufferers who will benefit most from their ministrations. After the cataract has been removed, such people tend to see much more sharply and clearly than the normal cataract patient. The length of time that it took for the sharp vision to assert itself may have been a function of the time it took for retinal circulation to return to normal following the pressure on the eye.

This story, therefore, has every sign of a clearly remembered and detailed reminiscence of a very real event [199]. It also suggests very strongly that Jesus utilised the established folk healing techniques of the time in his ministry, the details of which have been largely omitted by the evangelists for apologetic reasons. Mark, however, is not so much concerned about the technique used to restore sight, but the actual fact that a blind man can now see and, furthermore, see clearly.

The healing of this man, as with all cases of blindness in the Gospels, was understood not simply in anatomical terms, but more importantly in functional terms. It was not merely the healing of an ocular lesion, but a full restoration to normal function and perception [200]. The point of the story is that the gift of God gives clarity as well as vision, a reality that is at the heart of the good news, for he who opened the eyes of the blind still removes the cataracts from human eyes so that people may recognise the Christ as he truly is.

It is in this evangelistic potential of the story that Mark's true interest lies. The narrative is almost a parable of the experience of the disciples. The physical healing points to the more important reality that the risen Christ will heal the spiritual blindness of those who follow him. As Johnson puts it, 'throughout the gospel the disciples have only imperfect spiritual vision and although they have a measure of understanding they will require contact with Jesus a second time (the resurrection) before they will see clearly' [201]. This theological approach to the restoration of sight is made much more explicit in the story of Bartimaeus which, as a result, is largely emptied of content in terms of the treatment administered (see below on Mark 10:46-53).

The boy with 'epilepsy': Mark9:14-29 // Matthew17:14-20 // Luke9: 37-43

The great majority of writers on this passage have assumed that the boy in the story was suffering from grand mal epilepsy. Epilepsy was well known in the ancient world and was called the 'sacred' or 'divine' disease by the Greek physicians. Hippocrates, as was noted earlier (pp 15f), devoted a complete treatise to the condition and had little time for the introduction of other than natural causes, considering that epilepsy was as much due to natural processes as any other disease. He described the clinical features, noting eight specific signs of an epileptic seizure [202]. Five of these signs are mentioned in the Gospel accounts of this healing, but these accounts also mention other well established clinical signs omitted by Hippocrates. There are, however, only two clear references in the New Testament to epilepsy: this story (and its parallels) and the passing reference to those described as 'moonstruck' at Matthew 4:24 [203]. Matthew's use of the rare verb σεληνιαζομαι (to be moonstruck), at 4:24 and 17:15, would appear to be another example of his desire to play down the 'wonder' element in the healings of Jesus. The word is derived from the belief that epilepsy was due to the influence of the moon (note the English word, lunatic).

The later Jewish Rabbinic writers were well aware of the tendency of the disease to be familial and recommended that 'a man shall not marry a woman from a family of epileptics' [204]. Nonetheless, as is apparent in the Gospel story, the activity of evil spirits was often considered the cause of the illness [205]. The Markan account provides such graphic detail that there can be little doubt that this is a genuine recollection of a specific and factual event [206]. The apparent relationship with the experience on the Mount of Transfiguration [207], together with the initial abject failure of the disciples, would no doubt have helped to establish the event in the minds of those who witnessed it. Further, not only is there the actual account of the boy having convulsions in front of Jesus and the crowd, but there is also the statement of the father describing the boy's previous experiences. This is just the sort of case record which a physician would find of immense value and as Wilkinson remarks, the physician usually 'is given a description of a fit by a relative of the patient, but rarely sees a fit or obtains an eye-witness account of one from an accurate and independent observer. It is this which makes this account of the epileptic boy so valuable and so convincing to a medical reader' [208].

There has been remarkably little disagreement about the diagnosis of the boy's condition and the comment has been made that the combination of the Gospel descriptions form 'so full a summary of events in epilepsy as to forbid any omission in any history of the subject' [209]. The description of the attack notes the immediate tonic phase with collapse and rigidity, the hoarse cry, a common feature as air is driven out of the lungs, the ensuing clonic phase with jerking and convulsions and, finally, the flaccid phase, often of deep coma. The dangers to life and limb from burning in the fire or falling into water, which so concerned the distraught father, are well documented in major epilepsy [210]. As Wilkinson has underlined, life threatening events are very rarely features of 'hysterical-type' illnesses [211], but these would appear to have been a prominent feature of the boy's condition. It is, however, an interesting point to note that, while the boy's convulsions apparently put him into dangerous and potentially life-threatening situations, they do not appear to have actually caused any significant injury. In fact, such events seem to have occurred frequently and they may have been consciously or subconsciously repeated as attention seeking activities to draw attention to himself and his needs. These factors would sound a warning not to assume too readily that epilepsy is the only tenable diagnosis in this case.

In spite of the apparently overwhelming evidence that strongly favours a diagnosis of major epilepsy, the possibility of some form of conversion disorder cannot be discounted out of hand. Admittedly, these are less common in childhood (note the father's comment at 9:21 that the youth had suffered from childhood), but such conditions may occur at relatively early ages [212]. Further, although in many cases it is possible for a modern physician to distinguish conversion seizures from epilepsy, this would not have been the case at a time when the aetiology of such conditions was not understood and all forms of seizure were lumped together (often as demonic possession). Even today, it is not always easy to make the distinction between so-called peudo-seizures and true epilepsy on clinical grounds alone [213].

There is a further issue. Mark notes that the boy is deaf and dumb. This comment has been seen as evidence of a conflation of two different healing stories [214], possibly represented by 9:14-19(20) and 9:20(21)-27. Less complicated explanations are more likely to be nearer the truth, although less academically sophisticated. Cranfield, for example suggests (on the basis of the normally accepted diagnosis of epilepsy) that the dumbness represented the way in which the prodromal stage of the seizure developed [215]. Wilkinson takes very much the same view and considers that these features belong the aura, the warning phase that an attack is coming. It is normally short-lived, but 'the patient is now so taken up with what is happening to him that he becomes unresponsive to his surroundings, and this becomes even more marked when he loses consciousness with the onset of the second stage. Here we have the explanation of the father's description of the spirit which seizes his son as dumb (Mark 9:17) and also why Jesus addresses the same spirit as dumb and deaf (Mark 9:25)' [216]. Such an explanation, however, is too facile by far, attractive though it may be. Assuming that there has been no conflation (and the flow of the story strongly suggests a single event), then the presence of two additional sensory disorders points, even more strongly, to a diagnosis of conversion disorder, rather than true epilepsy, and as such it would have been very amenable to the forms of treatment used by Jesus.

From the point of view of the evangelist, it would seem that the major lesson of the story, as so often in Mark, relates to faith. This was a 'strong' demon: the disciples had failed miserably to expel it and Jesus was to tell them that 'this sort' could be driven out (rather oddly ἐξελθειν rather than ἐκβαλλειν) only by prayer - presumably the prayer of faith in the sense that it is to be the expression of complete dependence on God. The approach of the disciples (and presumably also that of the father) appears to have been akin to that of a magician and they seemed to have assumed that, provided certain actions were performed and certain formulae were used to carry out the exorcism, then the demon would be forced to obey [217]. If this is a correct understanding of the disciple's failure, then it provides a hint to the way in which the Church saw the activity of Jesus as being intrinsically different from magic, although his detractors understood it in this light (Mark 3:22-26). Admittedly, faith may be imbued with semi-magical powers, but Mark makes it clear that true faith is not a means of manipulating God and trying to turn him into a puppet. For Mark, valid faith is modelled on Jesus who lived a life centred in obedience to the will of God.

Blind Bartimaeus: Mark 10:46-53 // Matt 20:29-34 // Luke 18:35-43.

The familiar story of blind Bartimaeus is one which has undergone very considerable redaction, almost certainly in the phase of oral tradition and before Mark added his own editorial amendments. There is a very clear structured form which seems to be designed to illustrate the realities of what it means to follow Jesus. The story is clearly didactic in character and it emphasises the great themes of faith, salvation and discipleship which are central to all Christian preaching. Steinhauser [218] has argued that all the differing elements of the story take on a pronounced symbolism and the whole narrative may be described as a 'call story'. The casting away of the beggar's cloak, for example, was to be understood as a symbolic act pointing to the renunciation of the old life and the relinquishing of all forms of security except that to be found in Christ, an essential part of the Markan theology of commitment and thus a 'narrative device representing the old order that Bartimaeus had left behind' [219]. Perhaps more than any other of the miracle stories, this story is an acted parable, almost an acted allegory. In view of this degree of redactional activity, it is unlikely that a great deal of the original event can be recovered.

The basic construction of the story consists of a cry for help, an initial rejection (by the crowd), a renewed plea to Jesus, an exhortation and an expression of trust detailed as action in following Jesus in the way. This form is common to each of the three versions, although there are several differences in detail between them. Matthew, for example, has two blind men (note his two demoniacs at Matt 8:28-34) and, as usual, he has reduced the length of the narrative by about 30 per cent.

Only Mark provides the familiar name of Bartimaeus for the blind beggar. The form critics, in particular, saw the giving of names as evidence of a secondary account, on the basis that as the tradition develops there is an interest in providing names for the characters in the stories. Such an historically pessimistic viewpoint is not necessary and there is no valid reason why the tradition should not have retained the names of persons who had become well-known in the primitive Church. Nonetheless, the adaptation of this story to the preaching needs of the Church is clear and more than any other healing narrative in Mark, it is to all intents and purposes a sermon, having as its subject 'the faith that confidently persists in seeking and following Jesus, even to the cross' [220]. It thus forms a fitting transition to the passion narrative that follows.

The account is set in the context of the final journey to Jerusalem and the imminent passion. Mark underlines that it is a blind man who recognises Jesus as the promised Messiah (Son of David) when those who can see are blind to his person. There is a similar point made in the Johannine account of the healing of the man born blind (John 9:35-41). As a result of the response of Bartimaeus to the person of Jesus, his eyes are opened and he is able to see: his faith saves (σεσωκεν) him and he follows Jesus in the way (which the reader will be aware, is the way to the cross, note 8:27; 9:33; 10:17, 32, 52). The story is completely theological and is centred in the need for saving faith in the person of Jesus which moves on into a life of discipleship. The emphasis is characteristically Markan. As Best has remarked, 'Mark's gospel is the gospel of the way. It is a way which Jesus the Lord goes and it is a way to which he calls his followers' [221] and he sees in the arrangement of this central section of the Gospel, sandwiched between two healings of blind men, a symbolic reference to the gradual enlightenment of the disciples as they learn the cost of discipleship.

There is no possibility of arriving at any firm diagnosis in a story that has undergone such a high degree of redaction, especially in terms of its interpretative editing. Cataracts or functional blindness remain the most likely causes on the basis that common things are common. The general impression from the healing narratives is that those whose sight was restored were suffering from advanced cataracts. The emphasis of this story, however, is entirely theological: sight being a metaphor for spiritual understanding.

Markan editorial material

The story of Bartimaeus completes the specific stories of healing and exorcism in the Gospel of Mark. There are, however, a number of editorial and other comments in the Gospel that relate to the healing activity of Jesus and also his disciples. Many of these are little more than link statements, maintaining the flow of the narrative and adding further weight to the fact that the predominant activities of Jesus were as a healer and exorcist [222]. The first of these editorial comments is to be found at Mark 1:32-34. It is set out as a story about Jesus, connected to a definite time and place and details the way in which the people of Capernaum brought their sick to Jesus at his home. However, the details are more likely to be due to Markan story telling than derived from a specific memory. The section acts as a transitional summary of Jesus' activities in healing and it leads on to another set of narratives. The importance of the passage is in its outline of Mark's interests as an evangelist, since it forms a direct editorial comment on the tradition with which he was working. Two emphases come through clearly. Firstly, the fact that Jesus undertook 'many' works of healing on the one hand and secondly, the fact that the demonic forces were silenced simply because they knew who he was, a device designed to create tension in the narrative and draw attention to the failure of people to recognise who this itinerant prophet really is.

Other link statements or transitional summaries occur at 1:39; 3:10-12; 6:5,6 and 6:55,56. The last of these examples is of particular interest in that it pictures people being laid on their pallets in the streets in order that they might touch the fringe or tassel of his clothing as Jesus went by [223]. Mark records this essentially superstitious reverence for Jesus as a wonder-worker without comment, although it forms part of his emphasis on the inadequate response of the crowds who witnessed his acts, but failed to see below the surface. They were concerned merely to get what was available for themselves or their families and friends. The general response is one of amazement, rather than the true commitment and faith epitomised in Bartimaeus. Nonetheless, even when deficient or bordering on the superstitious, the evangelist wishes his readers to understand that God honours what faith there is.

In two places, however, Mark states that Jesus also gave to his disciples the same ability to heal and exorcise that he himself possessed (Mark 3:14,15 and 6:7-13). Mark is quite specific and records that Jesus gave his inner group of followers the 'authority' (ἐξουσία) to heal and exorcise. This is an important word in Mark. It is generally used about Jesus as the one who carried out his work because of the divine authority given to him, specifically through his anointing by the Spirit at his baptism (Mark 1:22, 27; 2:10, etc). Now, however, this authority is also committed to those designated 'apostles', that is the small group of followers specifically commissioned and sent by Jesus to expand his mission to areas that he himself was unable to visit.

The key question is whether Mark saw these 'apostles' as representatives of the post-Easter Church which is thus, by extension, being given the authority to heal and exorcise, or whether this was an activity which Mark saw as restricted solely to the Galilean mission. It is important to note, in this regard, that Mark merely records the mission of the disciples as a single event and places very little emphasis on it (unlike Luke for example).   Mark's emphasis is consistently on the uniqueness of Jesus and the nature of his authority as the revealer of the rule of God in word and action.   Further, there is no suggestion in Mark that the post-Easter Church was ever given a special mandate to heal and exorcise.   There seems little doubt that the mission of the apostles and the healing authority associated with it was a unique commissioning for a specific set of circumstances and it should be seen as an extension of the the local and specific ministry of Jesus.   It is inadmissable to read into it a permanent commission given to the Church for all time and consequently it may not be used as biblical support for what is called the Church's 'healing ministry'.

The only passage that suggests a 'healing ministry' for the post-Easter community is at Mark 16:15-18, one of the alternative endings of the Gospel that describes Jesus' post-resurrection appearances. These verses, however, are universally recognised as secondary and they do not form an original part of Mark's Gospel.   They are not earlier than the second century [224], and they represent an attempt to bring Mark into line with the other Gospels by providing it with a conclusion that at least one scribe found satisfactory.   The section cannot be used to support any dominical authority given to the Church and its language clearly reflects Lukan influence (cf Acts 2:4; 28:1-6). It probably also reflects the shifts toward a greater emphasis on the 'miraculous' that was beginning to be seen in the second century, at least among certain groups in the Church.   The work of the disciples, as presented in Mark, seems to be a specific and limited mission associated with the historical prophetic ministry of Jesus and the post-Easter Church is not given any specific mandate to follow this path.

Notes and references

[1] Among others, see Koester, H. (1990). *Ancient Christian Gospels: Their History and Development.* SCM, London. p 201.

[2] Funk, R.W., Hoover, R.W. and the Jesus Seminar (1993). *The Five Gospels: The Search for the Authentic Words of Jesus. New Translation and Commentary.* Macmillan, New York. pp 4,5.   Note also Smith, M. (1971) Prolegomena to a discussion of aretalogies, divine men, the gospels and Jesus. *Journal of Biblical Literature.* 90. 174-199.

[3] Wright, N.T. (1996). *Jesus and the Victory of God.* SPCK, London. p 191.

[4] See for example, Chilton, B. (1995). Traditio-historical criticism and the study of Jesus. In: Green, J.B. (ed). *Hearing the New Testament: Strategies for Interpretation.* Eerdmans, Grand Rapids. pp 37-60.

[5] For a full discussion of the issues, see Kelber, W.H. (1983). *The Oral and the Written Gospel,* Fortress Press, Philadelphia.. See also Sanders, E.P. and Davies, M. (1989). *Studying the Synoptic Gospels.* SCM, London. A strong proponent of independent oral traditions behind all the Gospels, rather than any literary borrowing is Eta Linnemann (1992). *Is There a Synoptic Problem? Rethinking the Literary Dependence of the First Three Gospels.* ET. Baker, Grand Rapids.

[6] Aland K and Aland B. (1987). *The Text of the New Testament,* Eerdmans, Grand Rapids/E J Brill, Leiden, ET. pp 69ff.

[7] This seems to be the approach of at least certain members of the 'Jesus Seminar'. Burton Mack (1988), for example, describes Mark as a 'fantastic fabrication' and little more than a piece of historical and theological fiction (*A Myth of Innocence: Mark and Christian Origins.* Fortress, Philadelphia. p 296). This seems to be a rehashing the ideas of the old radical scholars of the late eighteenth and nineteenth centuries with as little evidence (see Brown, C. (1985). *Jesus in European Protestant Thought: 1778-1860.* Labyrinth, Durham, NC).

[8] Dunn, J.D.G. (1992). Messianic ideas and their influence on the Jesus of history. In: Charlesworth, J.H. (ed). *The Messiah.* Fortress Press, Minneapolis. pp 371f.

[9] Barr, J. (1984). *Escaping from Fundamentalism.* SCM, London, pp 87f.

[10] The relationship between 'natural law' and 'miracle' as causative factors in events has been extensively examined by Grant, R.M. (1952). *Miracle and Natural Law in Graeco-Roman and Early Christian Thought.* North Holland Publishing. Amsterdam.

[11] On this subject, in addition to Grant, R.M. (1952). *op cit.* see also Lampe, G.W.H. (1965). Miracles and early Christian apologetic. In: Moule, C.F.D. (ed). *Miracles: Cambridge Studies in their Philosophy and History.* Mowbrays, London. pp 203-218; Wiles, M.F. (1965). Miracles in the Early Church. *ibid.* pp 219-234 and Meier, J.P. (1994) *A Marginal Jew: Rethinking the Historical Jesus.* Vol 2. *Mentor, Message and Miracles.* Doubleday, New York. pp 535-616.

[12] Grant, R.M. (1952). *Miracles and Natural Law.* p 268.

[13] This is not the equivalent, however, as saying as Origen did, that 'without miracles and wonders (the apostles) would not have persuaded those who heard new doctrines and new teachings to leave their traditional religion and accept the apostles' teaching at the risk of their lives' (*Contra Celsum* 1:46). Mark has remarkable little to say about 'miracles' as proof of who Jesus was although the apologetic importance grew over the next few centuries.

[14] See Ramsay, I.T. (1957). *Religious Language,* SCM, London. Note R.M.Grant (1952) who quotes Richard Kooner approvingly in this respect : 'miracles happen on a level of meaning where laws of nature have no place at all' (*Miracle and Natural Law.* p 268).

[15] Barton, J. (1988). *People of the Book? The Authority of the Bible in Christianity*, SPCK, London, p 38.

[16] See for example Hengel, M. (1985). *Studies in the Gospel of Mark*, SCM, London, ET; Martin, R.P. (1972). *Mark: Evangelist and Theologian*, Paternoster Press, Exeter; Straudinger, H. (1981). *The Trustworthiness of the Gospels*, Handsel Press, Edinburgh.

[17] Taylor, V. (1957). *The Formation of the Gospel Tradition*. Macmillan, London. 6th edn. p 43.

[18] Dunn, J.D.G. (1985). Demythologizing - the problem of myth in the New Testament. In: Marshall I.H. (ed). *New Testament Interpretation*. Paternoster Press, Exeter. 3rd edn. p 291. One wonders why this aspect has been so consistently ignored in virtually all the recent so-called 'historical' approaches to the Gospels.

[19] Kelber, W.H. (1983). *The Oral and the Written Gospel*. p 31.

[20] See the discussion in Manson, T.W. (1962). The foundations of the synoptic tradition: the Gospel of Mark. In: Black, M. (ed). *Studies in the Gospels*. Fortress, Philadelphia. pp 28-45.

[21] Dahl, N. (1991), *Jesus the Christ: The Historical Origins of Christological Doctrine*. Fortress, Minneapolis. pp 94-95. He remarks that 'Whoever thinks that the disciples completely misunderstood their Master or even consciously falsified his picture may give fantasy free rein'.

[22] The extreme of this approach is seen in the work of the 'Jesus Seminar', exemplified by Mack, Funk and Crossan. Typical are Funk's remarks, 'Miracle stories are added to the Christian repertoire to make Jesus comparable to - in fact, competitive with - other charismatic teachers, exorcists and miracle workers.' And again, 'Because the miracle stories were intended as a means of marketing Jesus to a large and often mostly gentile audience, very few of them are based on actual events'. Funk, R.W. (1996). *Honest to Jesus: Jesus for a New Millennium*. Hodder and Stoughton, London. pp 252-253.

[23] See Bauckham, R. (ed) (1998). *The Gospels for All Christians: Rethinking the Gospel Audiences*. T & T Clark, Edinburgh.

[24] See Reiner, G.J. (1950). *History: Its Purpose and Method*. Allen and Unwin, London. pp 90-91 and also Stein, R.H. (1991). *Gospels and Tradition: Studies on Redaction Criticism of the Synoptic Gospels*. Baker, Grand Rapids. p 156.

[25] Bruce, F F. (1964). History and the gospel. *Faith and Thought*; 93, 121-145. He uses the example of the life of St Patrick to emphasise the point that is all too often forgotten that, irrespective of the purpose for which a document was composed, it is nonetheless available to the historian to use, with all proper safeguards, as a basic source for his work. Thus, the scanty material available for a life of St Patrick may still provide a reasonably clear outline of his career and character. The material relating to the life of Jesus is far more abundant. The comments of a less than sympathetic historian are also worth noting. Morton Smith (1978) (*Jesus the Magician*. Gollancz, London, p 95) points out that while details can never be guaranteed, the general characteristics of a tradition that accord with and explain the opinions of both adherents and opponents have a strong claim to authenticity.

[26] The comments of A.H.N. Green-Armytage (1952) and Dorothy Sayers (1946) on the foibles and follies of the academic mind-set are worth noting (quoted at length in Thiede, C.P. and D'Ancona, M. (1996). *The Jesus Papyrus.* (Weidenfeld and Nicolson, London). pp 46-48).

[27] N.T. Wright (1992) has drawn attention to what he calls 'the Myth of Objective Data or of Presuppositionless History' and has emphasised that 'there is no such thing as "mere history" ' (*The New Testament and the People of God.* SPCK. London. p 88)

[28] See further Martin, R P. (1972). *Mark: Evangelist and Theologian.* Paternoster Press, Exeter, and Hooker, M.D. (1983). *The Message of Mark.* Epworth Press, London. As Larry Hurtado (1989) has put it, 'any acclamation uninformed by the crucifixion is misleading and invalid'. (*Mark. The New International Bible Commentary.* Hendrickson, Peabody, MA. p 10).

[29] Bultmann, R. (1968). *The History of the Synoptic Tradition*, Basil Blackwell, Oxford. Revised edn. ET. p 39. Sean Freyne (1988) remarks that 'Bultmann's lack of interest in the historical Jesus and the Jewish roots of early Christianity created a climate of scepticism in New Testament studies' (*Galilee, Jesus and the Gospels.* Fortress Press, Philadelphia. pp 2,3). It is a climate that still colours a great deal of modern New Testament study.

[30] Harvey, A.E. (1982). *Jesus and the Constraints of History.* Duckworth, London.. p 8.

[31] Kelber, W.H. (1983). *The Oral and the Written Gospel.* p 31.

[32] Ellenburg, B.D. (1995). A review of selected narrative-critical conventions in Mark's use of miracle material. *Journal of the Evangelical Theological Society.* 38. 171-180.

[33] Trocmé, E. (1975). *The Formation of the Gospel according to Mark.* Fortress Press, Philadelphia, ET. p 50.

[34] See the discussion by Achtemeier, P.J. (1970). Towards the isolation of pre-Markan miracle catenae. *Journal of Biblical Literature.* 89. 265-291, and (1972).The origin and function of the pre-Markan miracle catenae. *Journal of Biblical Literature.* 91. 196-221.

[35] Note the discussion by Koester H. (1983). *Ancient Christian Gospels.* pp 275-286.

[36] The accounts are at: Mark 1:21-28//Luke 4:31-37; Mark 5: 1-20//Matthew 8:28-34//Luke 8:26-39; Mark 7:24-30//Matthew 15:21-28, Mark 9: 14-29//Matthew 17: 14-21//Luke 9: 37-43; Matthew 9: 32, 33; Matthew 12:22; Acts 16: 16-18; Acts 19: 11-17.

[37] See the writer's discussion of this phenomenon: Howard, J.K. (1985). New Testament exorcism and its significance today. *Expository Times.* 96. 105-109 and (1993). Exorcism. In: Metzger, B.M. and Coogan, M.D.(Eds). *The Oxford Companion to the Bible.* Oxford University Press, New York. pp 216-217.

[38] See examples given in Liddell, H.G.and Scott, R. (1996) *Greek-English Lexicon.* (Revised by Jones, H.S. and McKenzie, R.) Ninth edition with a revised supplement, 1996. Clarendon Press, Oxford. p 1624. (Hereinafter referred to as Liddell and Scott).

[39] American Psychiatric Association (1994). *Diagnostic and Statistical Manual of Mental Disease. (DSM-IV).* 4th edn. American Psychiatric Association. Washington. pp 452-457.

[40] Gelder, H.C. (1996). Neurosis. In: Weatherall DJ, Leadingham JGJ, Warrell DA (eds). *Oxford Textbook of Medicine*, Oxford University Press, Oxford. 3rd edn. p 25.4

[41] A popular account of a modern case of multiple personality is Thigpen, C and Cleckley, H. (1960). *The Three Faces of Eve*, Pan Books, London. For detailed treatments see Putnam, F.W. (1989). *Diagnosis and Treatment of Multiple Personality Disorder*. Guilford Press, New York and Ross, C.A. (1989). *Multiple Personality Disorder: Diagnosis, Clinical Features and Treatment*. Wiley, New York. The abrupt onset of such a bizarre illness would have fitted well with the contemporary belief in a demonic aetiology.

[42] Fuller, R.H. (1963). *Interpreting the Miracles*. SCM, London. p 35.

[43] Twelftree, G H. (1993). *Jesus the Exorcist: A Contribution to the Study of the Historical Jesus*. J.C.B. Mohr, Tübingen/Hendrickson, Peabody, MA. pp 69-70.

[44] Bultmann, R. (1968). *The History of the Synoptic Tradition*. p 209.

[45] The verb ἀνακράζω seems always to be associated with an emotional response; it is not just to 'shout out'. See Bauer, W. (1979). *A Greek-English Lexicon of the New Testament and Othe Early Christian Literature*. (Revised and augmented by Gingrich, F.W. and Danker, F.W.). Second edition. University of Chicago Press, Chicago. p 56. (Hereinafter referred to as Bauer).

[46] Sargant, W. and Slater, E. (1940). Acute war neuroses. *Lancet* ii. 1-2.

[47] For further details see Sargant, W. and Slater, E. (1963). *An Introduction to Physical Methods of Treatment in Psychiatry*. Livingstone, Edinburgh. Note also Sargant's two more popular discussions: Sargant, W. (1957). *Battle for the Mind: A Physiology of Conversion and Brainwashing*. Heinmann, London and Sargant, W. (1973). *The Mind Possessed*. Heinmann, London. Note also the discussion in relation to New Testament healing in Lloyd Davies, M. and Lloyd Davies, T.A. (1993). *The Bible: Medicine and Myth*. Silent Books, Cambridge. 2nd edn. pp 244-248

[48] Twelftree, G.H. (1993). *Jesus the Exorcist*. p 59 and note references cited. Note however, the view of G Bertram (1965), Θαμβος. In. Kittel, G. (ed). *Theological Dictionary of the New Testament*. Eerdmans, Grand Rapids. Vol III. pp 5-7) who sees the use of the verb as a means to describe the coming of Jesus as an epiphany of Israel's God – 'Expressions of fear and astonishment serve to emphasise the revelatory content and christological content of many incidents in the Synoptic Gospels' (p 6). It should be noted, however, that the verb is used of responses in the Magical Papyri (note the references in Liddell and Scott, p 783).

[49] Vermes, G. (1973). *Jesus the Jew: A Historian's Reading of the Gospels*. Collins, London, p 69.

[50] See further Kelber, W.H. (1983). *The Oral and the Written Gospel*. pp 64ff.

[51] This issue is discussed in detail in Marshall, C. (1989). *Faith as a Theme in Mark's Gospel (SNTS Monograph 64)*. CambridgeUniversity Press, Cambridge.

[52] For a discussion see Witherington, B. III. (1990). *The Christology of Jesus.* Fortress Press, Minneapolis. pp 148-155 and also Gundry, R.H. (1993). *Mark: A Commentary on his Apology for the Cross.* Eerdmans, Grand Rapids. pp 46-53.

[53] Tweftree, G.H. (1993). *Jesus the Exorcist.* p 57.

[54] Twelftree, G.H. (1985). *Christ Triumphant: Exorcism Then and Now.* Hodder and Stoughton, London. p 117.

[55] Hengel, M. (1985). *Studies in the Gospel of Mark.* p 50.

[56] Fuller, R.H. (1963) *Interpreting the Miracles,* SCM, London. p34.

[57] Taylor, V. (1955). *The Gospel according to St Mark* (Macmillan, London). p 178.

[58] Twelftree, G.H. (1985). *Christ Triumphant.* p 101.

[59] Galen, *De diferentiis febrium* 1. See also Hippocrates, *Aphorisms* 2.26; Plato, *Timaeus* 86a; etc.

[60] See for example, Philostratus, *Life of Apollonius,* 4:10, 11 and Josephus, *Antiquities of the Jews,* 8:45-49.

[61] Borza E.N.(1979). Some observations on malaria and the ecology of central Macedonia in antiquity. *American Journal of Ancient History* 4. 102-124. It has been commented that malaria in the Mediterranean world produced a vicious cycle of depopulation, poverty and political upheaval (Grmek, M.D. (1989). *Diseases in the Ancient Greek World.* ET. Johns Hopkins University Press, p 283).

[62] Hippocrates, *Epidemics* 1:24.

[63] Jones, W.H.S. (1909). *Malaria and Greek History,* Manchester University Press, Manchester,

[64] See Shepherd, P.M. (1955). The Bible as a source book for physicians. *Glasgow Medical Journal.* 36. 348-375.

[65] Alon, A. (1969). *The Natural History of the Land of the Bible.* Jerusalem Publishing House, Jerusalem. pp 140-143.

[66] Meier, J P. (1994). *A Marginal Jew.* Vol 2. p 707. He goes on to remark that, 'one cannot ignore the striking, almost paradoxical, combination of brevity and detailed concreteness in the story'. He does not consider this adequate, however, to prove historicity. While accepting that 'proof' of historicity is always extremely difficult, if not impossible, to obtain, the present writer considers that the burden of proof lies with those who deny a historical base to such stories.

[67] The papyrus exists in two separate fragments. The English text, published originally by H.I. Bell and T.C. Skeat in 1935 (*Fragments of an Unknown Gospel and other early Christian Papyri.* (Oxford University Press, Oxford), may be found, with the parallel Greek, in Finegan, J. (1969). *Hidden Records of the Life of Jesus.* (Pilgrim Press, Philadelphia). pp 182-183. See also Cameron, R. (1982). *The Other Gospels: Non-canonical Gospel Texts.* (Westminster, Philadelphia). p 72. The originality of this tradition is discussed in Koester, H. (1983). *Ancient Christian Gospels.* pp 205-216 and note also Neirynck, F. (1985). Papyrus Egerton 2 and the healing of the leper. *Ephemerides Theologiae Lovanienses.* 61. 153-160.

[68] Note, however, J.P. Meier's (1991 and 1994) view that the *Egerton Papyrus 2* represents 'an imaginative retelling of Luke 17:11-19, with traits from elsewhere in the Synoptics'. He suggests that the author of the Papyrus may well have been working from the memory of what he had heard read and preached rather than from a text in front of him (*A Marginal Jew: Rethinking the Historical Jesus.* Vol 1. p 119 and Vol 2. p 746. n 96).

[69] Taylor, V. (1955). *The Gospel according to St Mark (Macmillan New Testament Commentary)*, Macmillan, London, 6th edn. p 185.

[70] Even the New Revised Standard Version (1989) and the New English Bible (1990) continue the tradition to the extent of also using the distinctly pejorative expression 'leper'. It is difficult to justify such translations in the light of current knowledge.

[71] Gramberg, K.P. (1959). Leprosy in the Bible. *Tropical and Geographical Medicine.* 11.127-139.

[72] Browne, S.G. (1979). *Leprosy in the Bible*, Christian Medical Fellowship, London, 3rd Edition, p 7.

[73] Celsus, *De medicina.* 3.25. The situation is made even more complicated in terms of modern medical terminology in that *elephantiasis* is a specific condition of tissue swelling due to lymphatic system blockage by filarial worms occurring in tropical Africa and elsewhere and has nothing whatever to do with leprosy - biblical or modern. The Greek physicians were aware of the two forms and referred to the parasitic disease as *elephantiasis Arabum* and the new disease of leprosy as *elephantiasis Graecorum*. Other terms in use by the Greek physicians were *satyriasis* and *leontiasis* (see references in Liddell and Scott, *sv*).

[74] Cochrane, R.G. (1961). *Biblical Leprosy: A Suggested Interpretation.* Tyndale Press, London. p 11.

[75] See Hippocrates, *Aphorisms* 3.20; *Epidemics* 2:43, etc. One reference exists to the word being used of mould (Aristophanes, *Fragment* 723) and Philo groups it with scabs and similar sores (*The Special Laws.* 1.80). See also the references given in Liddell and Scott, p 1039. Leprosy as a specific disease entity is essentially a modern phenomenon, although knowledge of the disease and special arrangements for sufferers were instituted as early as the fourth century in Rome and elsewhere and in England by 625 AD (see Browne, S. G. (1979). *Leprosy in the Bible.* pp 17-20). He notes that the disease was well established in Britain and Europe long before the first Crusaders returned at the end of the eleventh century.

[76] For a discussion, see Browne, S G. (1979). *Leprosy in the Bible.* p 8.

[77] The extravagant view that our Lord himself suffered from 'leprosy' derives from a mistranslation in the Latin Vulgate of Isaiah 53:4. The Hebrew word *naga* (smitten) was translated as 'leprosy' - *et nos putavimus eum quasi leprosum.* Later Wycliffe was to render this into English as, 'and wee heeldun hym has leprous'. See further Browne, S.G. (1979) *Leprosy in the Bible*, p 7.

[78] Hulse, E.V.(1975). The nature of biblical leprosy and the use of alternative medical terms in modern translations of the Bible. *Palestine Exploration Quarterly.* 107. 87-105.

[79] Pilch, J. (1981); Biblical leprosy and body symbolism. *Biblical Theology Bulletin.* 11: 119-133. See also his later (1988) study, Understanding biblical healing, *Biblical Theology Bulletin* 18: 60-66.

[80] The prevalence in the modern world varies from around 2% in Europe to a much lower level among Chinese of around 0.37%. Arabs have been reported to have a similar prevalence rate to that of Northern Europe (Fry, L. (1992). *An Atlas of Psoriasis.* Parthenon, Carnforth. p 13).

[81] A good, well-illustrated account of the details of the condition is given in Fry, L. (1992). *Atlas of Psoriasis.* and also in Menter, A and Barker, J.N.W.N (1991). Psoriasis in practice. *Lancet.* 338: 231-234.

[82] For a full discussion see Browne, S.G. (1979). *Leprosy in the Bible.* See also Goldman, L., Moraites, R. S, Kitzmuller, K. S. (1966). White spots in biblical times. *Archives of Dermatology*; 93: 744-753. There are also references in Indian Vedic medicine to a similar condition. The documents speak of white spots arising from within the body caused by a curse (see Zysk, K.G. (1985). *Religious Healing in the Veda.* American Philosophical Society, Philadelphia, p 81). These references have usually been related to various forms of vitiligo and illustrate the problem of relating modern technical concepts of disease with conditions defined merely on a symptomatic basis. However, recent skeletal studies indicating the presence of psoriatic arthritis in tombs in a Judaean desert monastery dating from the fifth century, a time when the earlier practice of expelling those with disfiguring diseases was giving way to a caring approach which housed and fed the sick in monasteries, is strongly suggestive that psoriasis was one of the conditions included under the umbrella term of 'leprosy' (Zias, J. Mitchell, P. (1996). Psoriatic arthritis in a fifth-century Judean Desert monastery. *American Journal of Physical Anthropology.* 101. 491-502).

[83] Massey, E.W. (1978). Leprosy, biblical opprobrium? *Southern Medical Journal* 71.1294-1295. On the social opprobrium associated with skin disease see Skinsnes, O.K. (1964). Leprosy in society - II The pattern of concept and reaction to leprosy in oriental antiquity. *Leprosy Review* 35: 106-122.

[84] See Skinsnes, O.K. ibid.

[85] Forbes, T.R. (1981). Births and deaths in a London parish, *Bulletin of the History of Medicine* 55. 371-391

[86] See Goldman, L. (1971). Syphilis in the Bible, *Archives of Dermatology.* 103. 535-536.

[87] The current state of knowledge about the origins of syphilis are set out in Porter, R. (ed). (1996). *The Cambridge Illustrated History of Medicine.* Cambridge University Press, Cambridge. p 35.

[88] Although the reading ὀργισθεὶς is restricted to the 'Western' family of texts, it has a strong claim to originality being much more likely to be changed by an over-scrupulous copyist than the alternative. Both UBS and Nestlé committees opted for the easier reading on a majority decision (see Metzger, B.M. (1971). *A Textual Commentary on the Greek New Testament.* London, United Bible Societies. pp 76-77).

[89] Cave, C.H. (1979). The leper: Mark 1:40-45. *New Testament Studies.* 25. 245-250.

[90] However, note the comment of C.E.B. Cranfield (1977), that the 'suggestion that the original story was of a recovered leper who wanted Jesus, instead of a priest, to pronounce him clean is fanciful'. (*The Gospel according to Mark (The Cambridge Greek Testament Commentary).* Cambridge University Press, Cambridge. revised with additional supplementary notes. pp 91,92). Note also J.P. Meier's (1994) arguments against this interpretation (*A Marginal Jew.* Vol 2. pp 747f. n 104). It would be the writer's opinion that this interpretation is not as fanciful as it appears at first sight and it seems more than likely that Jesus did not intervene in a curative sense in this situation, but simply provided a diagnosis and a declaration of 'cleansing'. Note also the comments of Stevan Davies, (1995). *Jesus the Healer: Possession, Trance and the Origins of Christianity.* Continuum, New York. pp 68,69.

[91] See further Daube, D. (1956). *The New Testament and Rabbinic Judaism.* Athlone Press, London, pp 206-223.

[92] Against Crossan, J.D (1993). *The Historical Jesus* p 323. He sees a challenge in the command to the man to show himself to the priests 'as a witness to (against) them' which would demonstrate to them both who Jesus is and what he can do. He notes the 'striking ambiguity' between being declared clean and being made clean, but then develops a complex history to account for his view that Jesus is not being observant of the law.

[93] Josephus. *The Jewish War*, 5:227,

[94] Fry, L. (1992). *Atlas of Psoriasis.* p 19.

[95] Ibid. p 15.

[96] Ibid. p 19.

[97] Lightfoot, R.H. (1950). *The Gospel Message of St Mark.* Oxford University Press, Oxford. p 26.

[98] For a very different view see Kazmerski, C.R. (1992). Evangelist and leper: A socio-cultural study of Mark 1;40-45. *New Testament Studies* 38. 37-50.

[99] Crossan, J.D. (1991). *The Historical Jesus.* p 322. This is essentially where N. T. Wright (1996) arrives, although by a rather different route (*Jesus and the Victory of God.* pp 129-130, etc).

[100] Hengel, M. (1985). *Studies in the Gospel of Mark.* p 43.

[101] Short, A. Rendle, (1953). *The Bible and Modern Medicine*, Paternoster Press, London, p 105 and see also Hemer, C.J. (1986). Medicine in the New Testament world. In: Palmer, B. (Ed). *Medicine and the Bible,* Paternoster Press, Exeter, p 72.

[102] Paul, J.R.(1955). *Poliomyelitis (WHO Monograph No 26)*, World Health Organisation, Geneva.

[103] I owe this suggestion to Dr. S.Mossman, a neurologist.

[104] See Mayou, R. (1991). Medically unexplained physical symptoms. *British Medical Journal.* 303. 534-535.

[105] Gelder, M.G. (1996). Neurosis. In: *Oxford Textbook of Medicine.* p 25.5.

[106] Bruce, F.F. (1983). *The Hard Sayings of Jesus.* Hodder & Stoughton, London. p 26.

[107] Sanders, E.P. (1990). *Jewish Law from Jesus to the Mishnah.* SCM, London. pp 60-63. He has doubts about the historicity of the pericope and considers anyway that the case for blasphemy is extremely weak.

[108] Crossan, J.D. (1991). *The Historical Jesus.* pp 305-309. He argues that the fact that Jesus actually healed people was an indication in the popular mind, which linked sickness with punishment for sin, that the one who healed has forgiven sin and thus manifested divine power. This, however, would have put any of the healers of the day in the same position as Jesus. This seems rather unlikely.

[109] Wright, N.T. (1996b). *Jesus and the Victory of God.* p 272. Crossan, J.D. (1991), remarks that when Jesus 'cured people of their sicknesses (he) implicitly declared their sins forgiven or non-existent. (He) challenged not the medical monopoly of the doctors, but the religious monopoly of the priests' (*The Historical Jesus.* p 324). As noted above, while this judgment contains an element of truth, it would seem to the present writer that it is far too sweeping a generalisation as there would have been other healers who did not in any way suggest that their healing had moral implications.

[110] Tidball, D. (1983). *An Introduction to the Sociology of the New Testament.* Paternoster Press, Exeter. p 84. See also Malina, B.J. (1983). *The New Testament World.* SCM. London. pp 51-70.

[111] The classic arguments concerning infant baptism were set out by Joachim Jeremias (1960. *Infant Baptism in the First Four Centuries.* SCM, London. ET) and from the opposing point of view by Kurt Aland (1963. *Did the Early Church Baptise Infants?* SCM, London. ET).

[112] Fuller, R.H. (1963). *Interpreting the Miracles.* p 52.

[113] This is found in the so-called *Gospel of the Hebrews*, an early apocryphal Gospel, quoted extensively by Jerome (see his *Comm in Mattheum* 2) and known to some of the earlier Church Fathers. See James, M R. (1924) *The Apocryphal New Testament*, Oxford University Press, Oxford, pp 4,5 and Aland K . (ed). (1976). *Synopsis Quattuor Evangeliorum.* 9th edn. Deutsche Bibelsiftung, Stuttgart. p 158 who gives the Latin text. The man is pictured calling to Jesus for help and saying, 'I was a stone mason pursuing a living with my hands. I beg you Jesus, restore to me my health that I may not have to beg dishonourably for my food'.

[114] Hobart, W.K. (1892). *The Medical Language of St Luke*, Dublin University Press, Dublin, p 7. H J Cadbury (1920) was one of the first to criticise Hobart's work and point to the dangers of using uncontrolled lexical parallels (*The Style and Literary Method of Luke*, Harvard Theological Studies No 6, Harvard University Press, Cambridge, Ma.).

[115] See references in Bauer. p 548. This is not mentioned as an interpretation in Liddel and Scott.

[116] See the comments of, Lloyd Davies, M. and Lloyd Davies, T.A. (1993). *The Bible: Medicine and Myth.* p 210. Similar views are expressed by A Rendle Short (1953). *The Bible and Modern Medicine.* p 104 and John Wilkinson (1980). *Health and Healing.* p 66.

[117] See above p. 77.

[118] One of the first descriptions of such a phenomenon is at 2 Sam 23:10. Note the comments of I. Pilowsky (1997). *Abnormal Illness Behaviour.* pp 127-129.

[119] Hazleman, B. (1993). Soft tissue rheumatism. In· Maddison, P.J., Isenberg, D.A., Woo, P., Glass, D.N. (eds). *Oxford Textbook of Rheumatology.* Oxford University Press, Oxford. p 950.

[120] Mishnah, *Shabbath* 14 and 22.

[121] Tosefta, *Shabbat* 12.14 and Mishnah *Shabbath* 14.4

[122] Mishnah, *Yoma* 8.6

[123] Sanders, E P. *Jewish Law from Jesus to the Mishnah.* p 21 and see also his comments elsewhere, (1985). *Jesus and Judaism.* (SCM, London) pp 264-267 and (1993). *The Historical Figure of Jesus.* (Penguin Books, Harmondsworth) pp 212-218. In this latter volume he makes the very categorical statement that 'even if all these (conflict) stories are precise records of events, there is not a single case of obvious or serious transgression' (p 215)

[124] Wright, N T. (1996). *Jesus and the Victory of God.* p 393.

[125] It is to be noted that the Qumran Community observed very rigid sabbatarian rules as both the Community Rule (1QS3) and the Damascus Document (CD 10-11) make clear. 'In sharp contrast to these regulation formulators who see themselves as the guardians of covenantal purity, Jesus describes God ... as the one who seeks out the lost and as the one who sends messengers to urge the outsiders and the rejected to share in the common life of God's people'. (Kee, Howard C. (1992). Membership of the Covenant People at Qumran and in the teaching of Jesus. In: Charlesworth, J H (ed). *Jesus and the Dead Sea Scrolls.* Doubleday, New York. p 113)..

[126] See the discussion of this story in Twelftree, G H. (1993). *Jesus the Exorcist.* pp 72-87.

[127] Bultmann, R. (1963). *The History of the Synoptic Tradition.* Basil Blackwell, Oxford. ET. p 210.

[128] Of the major variants the so-called 'Majority' (Byzantine) text gives Gadarenes in Mark and Luke and Gergasenes in Matthew. The 'better' texts represented, for example, by p75, א and B, give Gerasenes in Mark and Luke and Gadarenes in Matthew. L and *f*1 and later corrections of א give Gergasenes in Mark and Luke. The pattern suggests a common tradition in Mark and Luke and a variant tradition for Matthew.

[129] Most of the ancient fishing ports around the Sea of Galilee have been identified in the past thrity years or so (see Nun, M. (1999). Ports of Galilee. *Biblical Archeology Review.* 25. (4). 18-31, 64.

[130] Davies, S L (1995). *Jesus the Healer.* p 98.

[131] All places of 'uncleanness' were congenial to demons and graveyards were regarded as their favourite site, as was also the desert. Those visiting such places, especially at night, were exposing themselves to enormous risk. See Babylonian Talmud, *Berakoth* 3a, 62b, *Niddah,* 17a, and Jerusalem Talmud, *Shabbat* 67a, *Sanhedrin* 65b, etc.

[132] See the references given by Twelftree, G H. (1993). *Jesus the Exorcist.* p 84. and his earlier (1985) study *Christ Triumphant.* pp 59-67.

[133] It should be noted, however, that there is a strong body of opinion that sees the 'pig incident' as secondary and not part of the original exorcism (see the discussion in Meier, J.P. (1994). *A Marginal Jew.* Vol 2. pp 650-653 and associated notes).

[134] On the various parallels to contemporary exorcist practice see Twelftree, G.H. (1993). *Jesus the Exorcist.* pp 72-87.

[135] See Luck, U. (1971). Σωφρων. In: Friedrich G. (ed), *Theological Dictionary of the New Testament.* Vol VII. pp 1097-1104. Note also the references in Liddell and Scott. p 1751.

[136] American Psychiatric Association. (1994). *Diagnostic and Statistical Manual of Mental Disorders (DSM-IV).* 4th edn. American Psychiatric Association, Washington. p 285.

[137] Mayer Gross, W., Slater, E. and Roth, M. (eds). (1960).*Clinical Psychiatry,* Cassell, London, p 262.

[138] Kaplan, H. I. and Sadock, B. J. (1995). *Comprehensive Textbook of Psychiatry.* 6th edn. Williams and Wilkins, Baltimore. p 981.

[139] Gelder, M.G., Gath, D.H. and Mayou R. (1983). *Oxford Textbook of Psychiatry,* Oxford University Press, Oxford. p 192.

[140] Howard, J. K. (1985). New Testament exorcism and its significance today. *Expository Times.* 95: 105-109. So also Lloyd Davies, M. and Lloyd Davies, T. A. (1993). *The Bible: Medicine and Myth.* p 211.

[141] Kaufmann, J. C. E, (1964). Neuropathology in the Bible - III. *South African Medical Journal.* 38: 805-808. See also Wilkinson J. *Health and Healing*, p 26. and Short, J. Rendle, *The Bible and Modern Medicine,* p 111.

[142] Kaplan, H. I. and Sadock, B. J. (1995). *Comprehensive Textbook of Psychiatry.* p 1258.

[143] Meier, J.P. (1994). *A Marginal Jew.* Vol 2. p 652.

[144] Thiessen, G. (1983). *Miracle Stories of Early Christian Tradition.* T & T Clark, Edinburgh. ET. p 255f. See also Crossan, J.D. (1989). *Jesus: A Revolutionary Biography.* HarperCollins, Los Angeles. pp 89-91.

[145] Thiessen, G. (1983). *Miracle Stories of Early Christian Tradition.* p 255f. See also his later discussion (1991) *The Gospels in Context: Social and Political History in the Synoptic Tradition.* Fortress Press, Minneapolis. pp 109-111. For a contrary view see Twelftree, G. H. (1993). *Jesus the Exorcist.* p 85.

[146] Wright, N T *Jesus and the Victory of God .* pp 195-196. It goes without saying that any interpretation of the event which includes the pigs as integral to the story is in complete contradiction of the view of those who see that part of the narrative as secondary.

[147] Dormandy, R. (2000). The expulsion of Legion: a political reading of Mark 5:1-20. *Expository Times* 111. 335-337.

[148] For examples see Lane, W. L. (1974). *The Gospel of Mark (The New International Commentary on the New Testament).* Eerdmans, Grand Rapids pp 191-192. See also French, V. (1986). Midwives and maternity care in the Roman world. *Helios* (New Series). 13. 69-84.

[149] See the discussion in Theissen, G. *Miracle Stories in the Early Christian Tradition*, pp 183ff and also Kee, Howard C. (1977). *Community of the New Age: Studies in Mark's Gospel.* SCM, London. pp 54 ff and Taylor, V. *St Mark*, pp 19ff. The technique of intercalation has been used in other places (2:1-12, 3: 1-6). On the other hand, both Van der Loos, H. (1965, *Miracles*, p 509) and Cranfield, C. E. B. (1977, *St Mark*,. p 182) take the view that the arrangement reflects genuine memory or at least a fixed tradition which Mark has used. Van der Loos quotes E. R. Micklem as saying, 'there are few narratives in the Gospels which bear such marks of historical accuracy as does this record'. The present writer sees no reason to dissent from this view.

[150] Taylor, V. *St Mark*. p 289.

[151] Hippocrates. *Aphorisms* 2.14; 3.27. See also Hobart, W. K. *The Medical Language of St Luke*. p 15.

[152] Hurtado, L.W. *Mark*. pp 86-88.

[153] See, for example, Short, A.R. *The Bible and Modern Medicine*. p 30 and Wilkinson, J. *Health and Healing*. p 53.

[154] See further Llewellyn-Jones, D. (1986). *Fundamentals of Obstetrics and Gynaecology*. Faber and Faber, London. Vol 2. pp 76-77.

[155] See *DSM-IV*. p 449.

[156] See further, Sanders, E.P. *Jewish Law from Jesus to the Mishnah*. pp. 205-214.

[157] Nineham, D.E. (1963). *St Mark (Pelican Gospel Commentaries)*. Penguin Books, Harmondsworth. p 157.

[158] See further Achtemeier, P. (1970). Toward the isolation of pre-Markan miracle catenae. *Journal of Biblical Literature*. 89. 265-291 and (1972). The origin and function of pre-Markan miracle catenae. *Journal of Biblical Literature*. 91. 198-221.

[159] Note the discussion in Wright, N. T. (1996). *Jesus and the Victory of God.* pp 186-197.

[160] Cranfield, C. E. B. *St Mark*. p 189.

[161] For cogent arguments in favour of the view that the girl was genuinely dead see Taylor, V. *St Mark*. pp 286ff and also Cranfield, C. E. B. *St Mark*. pp 188ff. Van der Loos, H. (*Miracles of Jesus*. p 569) considers that Mark's words should be taken as they stand, 'the obvious explanation is that Jesus aroused the apparently dead girl from a state of deep unconsciousness'.

[162] See Schrage, W. (1971). Αρχισυναγωγος. In: Friedrich, G. (ed). *Theological Dictionary of the New Testament*. Eerdmans, Grand Rapids. Vol VII. ET. pp 844-847.

[163] In this respect C K Barrett (1994) comments in respect of Acts 13:15 that 'if Luke is right in using the plural it may be deduced that the community in Pisidian Antioch was a large one' (*The Acts of the Apostles (International Critical Commentary)*. T & T Clark, Edinburgh. p 629). There is inscriptional evidence that women were appointed to this position, although it is not clear whether they were appointed singly or whether more than one held the title at the same time (see Sawyer, D. (1996). *Women and Religion in the First Christian Centuries*. Routledge & Kegan Paul, London. pp 73-81). F.F. Bruce

(1990), however, notes that 'Sometimes the title was honorary and might be held by women and children' (*Acts of the Apostles, Greek Text with Introduction and Commentar.* Erdmans, Grand Rapids. 3rd edn. p 302).

[164] See further Van der Loos, H. *Miracles of Jesus*, p 571,

[165] The present writer has seen outbreaks of this type of 'hysterical' behaviour in girls of this age group in boarding schools in Central Africa. It is usually, however, a group phenomenon. Note also the comments in Sims, A. C. P. Demon Possession: Medical perspective in a western culture. In: Palmer, B. *Medicine and the Bible.* p 172. Today's treatment would be a small dose of calcium gluconate!

[166] Lloyd Davies, M. and Lloyd Davies, T. A. *The Bible· Medicine and Myth.* p 212.

[167] So Theissen G. *Miracle Stories*, p 254. He sees the use of Aramaic words here and at 7: 34 as 'intended to demonstrate the superior power of eastern words of healing'.

[168] Cranfield, C.E.B. *St Mark.* p 190.

[168] D. E. Nineham, (*St Mark.* p 203) quotes A E J Rawlinson's statement that it is 'as though a man should travel from Cornwall to London via Manchester': not impossible, but very distinctly improbable. For a discussion of the problems of this section, see Taylor; V. *St Mark.* p 633f. It would seem that Mark is trying to picture an extended 'Gentile mission' to provide the right setting for this exorcism, but to do so he has to isolate Jesus from the disciples who do not appear again until 8:1, having disappeared from the story at 7:17.

[170] Hengel, M. (1985). *Studies in the Gospel of Mark.* SCM, London. ET. p 46.

[171] See Theissen, G. *Miracle Stories.* pp 126-127. He suggests that 'Greek' would be a socio-cultural description placing the woman in the Hellenised upper class of the area and 'Syrophoenician' would be an ethnic classification.

[172] Brandon, S.G.F. *Jesus and the Zealots.* p 172. Note also the useful discussion in D.E. Nineham, *St Mark.* pp 198-200 and also E..P.Sanders, (1985), *Jesus and Judaism.* SCM, London. pp 212-221.

[173] See Dufton, F. (1989). The Syrophoenician woman and her dogs. *Expository Times.* 100. 417

[174] Bowman, J. (1965). *The Gospel of Mark· The New Christian-Jewish Passover Haggadah.* E J Brill, Leyden. p 148.

[175] See the discussion in Schweizer, E. (1971). *The Good News according to Mark.* SPCK, London. ET. p 153.

[176] Lloyd Davies, M. and Lloyd Davies, T A *The Bible: Medicine and Myth.* p 213.

[177] Anon. (1983). Meadow and Munchausen. *Lancet.* i. 417

[178] Wilkinson, J. *Health and Healing.* p 58.

[179] See Vermes, G. *Jesus the Jew.* p 75 and also Van der Loos, H. *Miracles of Jesus.* pp 330-331 for examples.

[180] Cranfield, C.E. B. *St Mark* p 253.

[181] See further Bauer, p 525.

[182] See the discussion in Van der Loos, H. *Miracles of Jesus.* pp 524-529.

[183] Micklem, E.R. (1922). *Miracles and the New Psychology.* London. pp 114-120. The criticisms of this explanation by J.M.Hull (1974) completely miss the point (*Hellenistic Magic and the Synoptic Tradition.* SCM, London. pp 74,75). Psychological techniques are well known to 'folk healers' in all societies because they have been found to work, even though the explanations they would give of why they work may be very different from those of modern scientific medicine.

[184] Hull, J. M. (1974). *Hellenistic Magic.* p 76. On the use of saliva in healing in general see his whole discussion on pp 76-78. Also note, Nicholson, F W. (1897). The saliva superstition in classical literature. *Harvard Studies in Classical Philology.* 8. 23-40. and Van der Loos, H. *Miracles of Jesus.* pp 306-313.

[185] Twelftree, G. H. *Jesus the Exorcist.* p 158.

[186] Theissen, G. *Miracle Stories.* p 254

[187] The discussion of this healing is a slightly expanded form of the author's paper (1984), Men as trees walking: Mark 8:22-26. *Scottish Journal of Theology.* 37. 163-170, and with slightly different conclusions.

[188] Johnson, E S. (1979). Mark 8:22-26: The blind man from Bethsaida. *New Testament Studies.* 25. 370-383.

[189] The present writer has found no case among 'theological' writerss on the historical Jesus who has given these words serious consideration other than to put their own interpretation on them. Had any one of them taken the time to discuss the issues with an ophthalmologist they might have come up with very different conclusions!

[190] Vaughan, D. and Astbury, T. (1977). *General Ophthalmology.* Lange, Los Altos, CA. p 304.

[191] Johnson, E S. (1979). *New Testament Studies* 25. 370-383.

[192] Roy, F.H. (1974). World blindness: definition, incidence and major treatable causes. *Annals of Ophthalmology.* 6. 1049. See also *World Health* for February/March 1976 which is devoted entirely to this problem.

[193] Note the Talmudic saying, 'The saliva of an older son has curative powers for the eye' (*Baba Bathra* 126b). Note also the references to the use of saliva in healing referred to in the previous healing narrative.

[194] Clark, R. E. D. (1963). Men as trees walking. *Faith and Thought.* 93. 88-94.

[195] Von Senden, M. (1960). *The Perception of Space and Shape in the Congenitally Blind before and after Operation.* Methuen, London. ET.

[196] Mackay, D. M. (1973). The psychology of seeing. *Transactions of the Society of Ophthalmology.* 93. 391-405.

[197] Fraser, H. (1973). The gospel of St Mark 8:22-26. *Medical Journal of Australia.* 2. 657-658.

[198] I am indebted to Dr. J.D.G. Worst, an ophthalmologist, for this explanation.

[199] Against the historical pessimists, such as Bultmann for example (*History of the Synoptic Tradition.* p 213).

[200] Valvo, A. (1968). Les guerisons des aveugles de l'évangile. *Annales Oculistique (Paris).* 201. 1214-1222.

[201] Johnson, E S. (1979). *New Testament Studies* 25. 370-383. Meier, J. D (1994). (*A Marginal Jew* 2. pp 691-692) takes a similar view of the underlying symbolism of the story, but also makes the important point that 'historicity and symbolism need not be muitually exclusive terms' (p 740. n 63). For a very different view of the theological symbolism behind this story see Surgitharajah, R S. (1992). Men, trees and walking: a conjectural solution to Mark 8:24. *Expository Times*. 103. 172-174. This author attempts to link the statement about trees with the Old Testament prophetic tree parables. Like the great majority of commentators, he fails to see the remarkable appropriateness of the man's statement in context.

[202] Hippocrates, *On the Sacred Disease*. 10.3-10. According to Herodotus (*Histories* 3.33) the Persian king Cambyses suffered from this disease.

[203] See Ross, J M. (1978). Epilepsy in the Bible. *Developmental Medicine and Child Neurology*. 20. 677-678 and the present author's article (1993), Epilepsy. In: Metzger, B M. and Coogan, M D. (eds). *Oxford Companion to the Bible*. Oxford University Press, New York. pp 190-191. It will be argued later that Paul's 'thorn in the flesh' may have been post-traumatic epilepsy. The Hebrew Bible has no clear references to epilepsy, although the mention of 'moonstroke' in Psa 121:6 may refer to epilepsy, particularly in view of the parallel reference to 'sunstroke', another serious condition. Balaam, Saul and Ezekiel may have suffered from epilepsy, but their conditions and abnormal behaviour patterns are best explained in other ways (see further, Rosner, F. (1975). Neurology in the Bible and Talmud. *Israeli Journal of Medical Science*. 11. 385-397).

[204] Mishnah, *Yebamoth* 64.2

[205] Hes, J P. and Wollenstein, S. (1964). The attitudes of the ancient Jewish sources to mental patients. *Israeli Annals of Psychiatry* 2. 103-116. These authors also draw attention to the Midrash Rabbah Lev 21:5 as evidence for the Rabbinic view. Belief in the activity of ancestral or evil spirits in causing epilepsy is still widespread in unsophisticated societies (see Jilek-Aull, L. (1999). Morbus sacer in Africa: some religious aspects of epilepsy in traditional cultures. *Epilepsia* 40. 382-386).

[206] Against such as Achtemeier, P. (1975. Miracles and the historical Jesus: A study of Mark 9:14-29. *Catholic Biblical Quarterly*. 37. 471,479). He argues on the basis of form and redaction criticism, that there are two separate stories which have been combined into a single narrative.

[207] Vincent Taylor notes, 'Whether the connection with the story of the Transfiguration is as close as Mark represents depends in some measure on whether the singular, ἐλθων ... εἰδεν is read in 14' (*St Mark* p 395).

[208] Wilkinson, J. *Health and Healing*. p 62. See also his study (1967), The epileptic boy. *Expository Times*. 79. 39-42. Although the present writer does not accept several of Dr Wilkinson's conclusions, his discussion from the standpoint of a specialist physician and an ordained minister of the Church of Scotland, is one of the most detailed and useful in the literature. However, one must protest at his attempt to maintain the possibility that what he diagnoses as genuine epilepsy may nonetheless be the result of demonic possession. Such

an approach is irresponsible and capable of causing immense suffering to innocent patients.

[209]   Collier, J S. (1934). Epilepsy. In: Bett, W R (ed). *A Short History of Some Common Diseases.* H K Lewis, London. pp 119-136. J C E Kaufmann remarks that the story 'reads in parts like a modern case history' (Neuropathology in the Bible - II. *South African Journal of Medicine.* 38. 788-789).

[210]   It has been noted that in the phase of deep coma, 'even the most painful stimuli produce no response and shockingly severe burns may result' (Matthews, W B. and Miller, H. (1979). *Diseases of the Nervous System.* Blackwell, Oxford, p 280). In many countries, this still presents a problem with a high proportion of burns treated in hospital being the result of epileptic seizures (See for example, Hampton, K K., Peatfield, R C., Pullar, T. (1988). Burns because of epilepsy. *British Medical Journal.* 296. 1659-1660). A study in Malawi found that 36 out of 100 burns admitted to hospital had been the result of epileptic seizures (Buchanan, R C. (1972). The causes and prevention of burns in Malawi. *Central African Journal of Medicine.* 18. 55-56).

[211]   Wilkinson, J. *Health and Healing.* p 66. See also Gelder, M. Gath, D. and Mayou, R. (1983). *Oxford Textbook of Psychiatry.* p 174.

[212]   See Maloney, M.D. (1980). Diagnosing hysterical conversion reactions in children. *Journal of Pediatrics.* 97. 1016-1020 and Grattan-Smith, P., Fairley, M., Procopis, P. (1988). *Archives of Diseases of Childhood.* 63. 404-414.

[213]   Anon. (1991). Neurological conversion disorders in childhood *Lancet.* 337. 889-890.

[214]   So Bultmann, R. *The History of the Synoptic Tradition.* p 211 and Achtemeier, P. (1975) (see above n 206).

[215]   Cranfield, C. E.B. *St Mark.* p 299.

[216]   Wilkinson, J. *Health and Healing.* p 64.

[217]   The centrality of manipulation and coercion to magic is what Howard Kee (1986) sees as the key distinction between it and miracle (*Medicine, Miracle and Magic in New Testament Times.* pp 3-4). There is a useful discussion of the issue in Crossan, J D. (1991). *The Historical Jesus.* pp 303-320. His Jesus, however, becomes little more than his own image of a stereotyped 'peasant' and his reconstruction of his mission is little more than a personal cultural critique.

[218]   Steinhauser, M. G. (1983). Part of a 'call story'. *Expository Times.* 94. 204-206.

[219]   Culpepper, R. A. (1982). Mark 10:50: Why mention the garment? *Journal of Biblical Literature.* 101. 131-132.

[220]   Sinclair, S. G. (1990). The healing of Bartimaeus and the gaps in Mark's messianic secret. *St Luke's Journal of Theology.* 303. 249-257. Note also the similar approach in Robbins, V. K. (1973). The healing of blind Bartimaeus (Mark 10:46-52). *Journal of Biblical Literature.* 92. 225.

[221]   Best, E. (1970). *Scottish Journal of Theology.* 23. 323-337. See also his more detailed study (1981). *Following Jesus.* (JSOT Press, Sheffield) especially pp 134-145.

[222] On the Markan summaries see further, Hedrick, C. W. (1984). The role of 'summary statements' in the composition of the Gospel of Mark: A dialog with Karl Schmidt and Norman Perrin. *Novum Testamentum.* 26. 289-311.

[223] The use of the word κρασπεδον (fringe, border or tassel) suggests that the tradition saw Jesus as a fully observant Jew who essentially followed the Pharisaic tradition (note Num 15:38f, Deut 22:12 as well as the healing of the woman with the haemorrhage at Mark 5:27). In the Matthean tradition, 'Jesus lashes the Pharisees for their purely outward display of piety. Using wool of the prominent hyacinth blue and white, they made their tassels as long as possible in order to gain a reputation for zealous prayer and strict observance of the commandments' (Schneider, J. (1965). Κρασπεδον. In: Kittel, G. (ed). *Theological Dictionary of the New Testament.* Vol III. p 904).

[224] See Metzger, B M. (1992). *The Text of the New Testament: Its Transmission, Corruption and Restoration.* Oxford University Press, Oxford. pp 226-228. and also Aland, K. and Aland, B. (1987) *The Text of the New Testament.* Eerdmans, Grand Rapids. pp 287-288.

Chapter 4

THE HEALING MINISTRY OF JESUS: THE NON-MARKAN SYNOPTIC TRADITIONS

'The Synoptic writers show ... that they are by no means mere collectors and handers-on of the tradition, but are also interpreters of it'

G Bornkamm

General comments

The role of Mark as an interpreter of the traditions about Jesus was demonstrated in his treatment of the stories of healings and exorcisms undertaken by Jesus during his ministry. The process of interpretation, however, is taken further by both Matthew and Luke. This may be seen in their use of the Markan material to which they appeared to have had access, as well as in their handling of the other traditions, both those which were unique to the individual evangelist and those traditions which they shared in common. This latter set of traditions, most of it comprising segments of the teachings of Jesus, has been denoted the 'Q' source which, by definition, is essentially that material which is common to Matthew and Luke, but not found in Mark.

There have been various attempts to analyse and reconstruct Q, based on the assumption that it represents a written source since many of the Matthew-Luke agreements are verbatim or near verbatim [1]. The history of the problem is long and tortuous and has involved the invention of other sources in an attempt to maintain the priority of Mark and the antiquity of Matthew at one and the same time [2]. However, it is equally as probable, if not more so, that this common material was simply part of the wide-spread pre-canonical oral tradition [3]. Similarly, there are cogent arguments that the existence of Q as a documentary source is an unnecessary hypothesis since it is possible to dispense with Q by presuming a direct use of Matthew by Luke [4]. It needs to be stated quite unequivocally that the document Q remains an untested hypothesis, in spite of the remarkable constructions that have been built on this flimsy foundation [5]. In this study, the term Q source or Q tradition is used simply as a convenient term to denote the material common to Matthew and Luke and not appearing in Mark, without any assumptions about its nature as either a written source or part of common oral traditions circulating at the time.

The point to be emphasised, however, is simply that these various traditions about the work and words of Jesus are not simply retold, but are adapted by the writers to meet the specific pastoral and theological needs of their communities. The way in which they handle these traditions is part of the ongoing process of interpreting the word of God revealed in Jesus, a process of interpretation which has continued throughout the life of the Christian community and which will always remain the task of the Church.

This is not the place to embark on a discussion of the various sources used by the synoptic evangelists, nor of the complexities of the synoptic problem. The matter is certainly a great deal more complex than the somewhat simplistic 'two-source' or 'four source' theories espoused by earlier critics [6]. From the standpoint of this study, these are issues which are not of great moment: what is important is the way that the evangelists have handled their traditions and interpreted them within the context of the whole story they were seeking to pass on to their readers.

The Matthean tradition

There is general agreement that the Gospel of Matthew derives from a Hellenistic Jewish background. This is given weight by the writer's confidence that his readers would be familiar with and understand

Jewish customs (Matt 15:5) as well as by the fact that debates about the Law were still a central issue (Matt 5:17-20) and the Sabbath is still being kept (Matt 24:10). Further, the approach to the interpretation of the Law that 'looses' and 'binds' was still central for Matthew and his community [7] (note especially Matt 16:19, 18:18). The background of the Gospel is probably that of Syrian Hellenistic Judaism and it has been observed that 'the community in which Matthew lived exhibits a highly individual nature, found elsewhere only in the Didache' [8], a document for which a Syrian origin is almost universally agreed. The date of the Gospel, however, remains a matter of discussion. Current thinking about the synoptic problem would tend to make Matthew dependent on Mark, but there is a substantial body of opinion that would place Matthew earlier than the fall of Jerusalem (AD 70) and this would make direct utilisation of Mark much more difficult, although allowing for an independent use of the same oral traditions [9]. The matter is not one of great importance for this study which is concerned solely to examine the way in which Matthew has used the traditions of the healing ministry of Jesus to meet the needs of his community and his own theological purposes.

There is little doubt that Matthew has arranged his material in the pattern of Hellenistic biographies, although with a number of important differences [10]. However, the writer does not use the mighty works of Jesus as a demonstration of his divinity in the style of the Greek heroes. Not only do his disciples share in his healing work (10:8), but the disciples of the Pharisees are also involved in exorcisms (12:27) and the origin of their authority is accepted as being from God in the same sense as that of Jesus and his followers. Indeed, the emphasis in Matthew is that these stories are not simply 'miracle stories' in the usually accepted sense of the term, but have something important to say about response and faith.

The previous discussion of the Markan healing stories noted that it was characteristic of Matthew to abbreviate those stories which either originated from a common source with Mark or which he took over from that evangelist. This is often carried to the point of omitting virtually all detail in the narrative and seems to represent a deliberate policy of compression that ignores or removes all material from the story that is ancillary to its main purpose. Matthew, like Mark, was also telling a story to tell a story: the narratives are bearers of a message, of teaching and admonition for the Christian community with which he was associated [11].

There is general agreement that Matthew is primarily concerned with the life and faith of the Christian community in his own time and place. This is also true of the other evangelists, but much more than is apparent in Mark, Matthew tends to depict Jesus, not so much as the man of Nazareth, but as the risen and living Lord to whom all authority and power has been given and who continues to admonish and teach his people in the present. Furthermore, as the one to whom all authority has been given, he now has delegated that authority, firstly to the original circle of the apostles and then to the Church as a whole. He writes clearly and unequivocally from a post-Easter standpoint and he interprets his data in the light of Easter. In consequence, much of Mark's ambiguity has been lost and a double perspective emerges. The stories are presented as incidents in the life of Jesus, but at the same time, they are also living images of the Jesus who continues to live and speak to the disciples and the crowds of Matthew's own time.

The particular characteristic of Matthew is his abbreviation of the Markan stories. H.J. Held has commented on this Matthean process of abbreviating the Markan tradition. He wrote, 'the abbreviating is done in the interest of concentration on what is essential and must consequently be regarded as a means of interpretation' [12]. In so doing, however, Matthew also raised his reader's consciousness of the importance of what may be called, for want of a better term, the 'miraculous' in the ministry of Jesus. Against Mark, Matthew increases both the number of the healing stories and also their magnitude, doubling, for example, the number of those healed in a particular incident as compared with the Markan original (such as the healing of the two blind men at Jericho at 20:29-34). Further he tends to conflate and retell stories as well as extending other elements of the 'miraculous' such as Peter's walking on the water (14:28ff), the resurrection of the dead after the death of Jesus (27:52f), and the earthquake in relation to the resurrection of Jesus (28:2).

A strong christological emphasis is apparent in these healing narratives, but Matthew is as equally insistent as Mark on the themes of faith and discipleship [13]. It should also be noted that the setting of the main block of healing narratives, occupying chapters 8 and 9, may be seen as complementing the major teaching material set out in the Sermon on the Mount. Thus, the two aspects of the ministry of Jesus in word and deed are presented together as a statement of the continuing presence of Jesus with his people, both to teach and to do.

The assumption is made that Matthew has essentially utilised Mark as the groundwork of his Gospel [14]. It is considered that Matthew has extensively reworked this material through modification, major abbreviations, new formulations as well as with the use of extensive additional material, some of it from his own independent sources and some of it from sources used in common with Luke (the so-called 'Q' source, discussed earlier). The way in which Matthew has handled the specifically Markan material has been discussed in the analysis of the healing narratives in Mark (see chapter 3). The emphasis in this section will be on the material that is specific to Matthew, derived from those sources which were distinct from Mark. The special Matthean material contains three distinct healings stories that are not found elsewhere in the canonical Gospel traditions (Matt 9:27-31; 9:32-34; 12:22), together with a number of summary statements about the healing and exorcising ministry of Jesus which will also be considered.

One further healing story needs notice at this point. Matthew records the healing of the centurion's servant, which is not found in Mark and which has often been assumed to be derived from the so-called Q tradition as it is also found in a closely related form in Luke. The fact that a further variant of the story is found also in John seems to be much more indicative of an oral tradition than it does of a written source. It will be discussed in relation to the Johannine 'signs' (in chapter 5), as there are good grounds for considering that John may have preserved a more accurate tradition of the event.

The Matthean healing narratives

The two blind men: Matthew 9:27-31

This short pericope appears to be a variant form of the story at Matthew 20:29-34. This, in itself, is a variant of Mark's story of blind Bartimaeus, although Matthew transforms the single blind beggar of Mark into two people, both here and in the Jericho narrative. It is possible that there has been a conflation of the Bartimaeus narrative with another healing, especially in view of the changed location from the open road to within a house, but the appeal to Jesus as 'Son of David' [15], retained in all three versions, is particularly noteworthy. The other healing story may also have been derived from a Markan-type tradition in view of the warning to keep the healing secret. It is of particular interest to note the association of the warning here with the rare verb ἐμβριμαομαι, used by Mark in relation to the cleansing of the leprosy sufferer. The word suggests anger or some sort of emotional agitation, as was noted in relation to the Markan context, and it conveys the sense of snorting with anger or indignation [16]. The use of this verb seems inappropriate in the context and suggests that Matthew was taking over part of another story without changing its specific vocabulary.

The story is placed within a section (9:18-24) that forms the third and last of Matthew's accounts of Jesus' acts of power. In the light of the consistent emphasis in Matthew on fulfilled prophetic Scripture, it may well be that this story and the healing of the deaf man which follows it, were presented as fulfilments of Isaiah 35:4-6. In this pericope, Jesus opens the eyes of the blind and in the following paragraph, a dumb man has his speech restored. That Matthew saw spiritual symbolism in such actions seems undeniable and it is of interest that the story of the two blind men is the only healing which is made conditional entirely on the faith of the ones being healed. Schweizer makes the important point in this regard that 'what is most striking is that the content of this faith is indicated by means of a "that I can do this" clause. Apart from John we find this idiom only in Mark 11:23-24, Romans 6:8; 10:9; I Thessalonians 4:14 and Hebrews 11:6. Faith is confidence manifested in every action of life, not just a matter of intellectual assent' [17]. This emphasis on a vital faith, drawn out by Jesus into some form of practical expression, is a common thread in all the evangelists.

As is usual with Matthew's terse and compressed accounts, virtually all details have been removed from the story other than the comment that Jesus touched (ἥψατο) the eyes of the blind men. This comment may well represent part of the original memory of the way in which Jesus healed the blind and if this is correct, then it gives support to the view that those whose sight was restored were likely to have been people suffering from cataracts suitable for manual couching. This particular technique has already been discussed in relation to the healing of the blind man at Bethsaida (Mark 8:22-26) (p 110f) and if this Matthean story represents a variant of the healing of Bartimaeus, then it suggests that his blindness was also due to cataracts. There is no doubt that blindness resulting from cataracts would have been the type of blindness most amenable to cure by a traditional type healer. The story provides additional clues indicating that Jesus undertook his healing ministry as a traditional healer/prophet who, on the surface, did not appear to be different from other similar practitioners. While Matthew may attempt to underline the importance of the miraculous in the ministry of Jesus, he is unable to remove entirely the element of ambiguity from the tradition he has received.

The dumb demoniac: Matthew 9:32-33(34)

This very short pericope is so abbreviated and divorced from any genuine context and without any significant detail, that attempts at a medical reconstruction of the underlying condition are impossible. However, in so far as it represents a tradition of healing someone who was dumb and considered demon possessed, it raises again the likelihood of a psychiatric conversion type disorder and tends to confirm the high proportion of these cases represented in the healings of Jesus. The story is paralleled in Luke 11:14,15 and surprisingly, Matthew has made no attempt to abbreviate (in fact his version is slightly longer). There are minor differences, but the words of Matthew's Pharisees are identical to those of Luke's crowds, except that unusually, Luke does not record any expressions of amazement (Luke 11:14). The story may well be a doublet of the similar healing in Matthew 12:22-24. The story is recounted at breathless speed, so that, as Harrington remarks, 'one gets the impression that Matthew's real interest lay in contrasting the reactions of the crowd (9:33b) and the Pharisees (9:34)' [18].

Some commentators consider that v 34 is an intrusion into the text, but although some doubt must surround its integrity, the evidence for the shorter text, omitting the Beelzebub controversy, is relatively late and somewhat meagre [19]. It will be assumed, therefore, that this verse is original to Matthew and the story is thus seen to be centred in the context of the controversy surrounding the origin of the authority of Jesus. The controversy arises at various points in the synoptic narratives (Matt 12:24, Luke 11:15, Mark 3:22-40) and these references point to a very strong memory in the early Church that Jesus had been accused of using what was essentially witchcraft in his healing ministry, using magical powers and being in league with the demonic forces. He was considered to be a person who posed a significant threat to the establishment and the nature of his actions posed a simple alternative: either he was acting as an agent of God and the works he did were undertaken in the power of God, or else he was a deceiver, a false prophet and leading the people astray through the power of Satan.

Whether it is possible to widen one's definition of magic to include any form of 'mighty work' undertaken without official sanction, as Crossan does, is a matter for debate [20]. What is clear, however, is that the early traditions of the works of Jesus underline the inherent ambiguity of his ministry. Indeed, one might say that the mighty works were simply one aspect of a career that was deliberately ambiguous and which forced people to make a decision based on their interpretation of what was going on. There was no 'proof' and there was no short cut to faith. The healings and exorcisms only took on any evidential character once faith already existed (as with John the Baptist, Matt 11:4-5).

The word that Matthew uses for 'dumb' (κωφος) is one which may describe either deafness or a speech impediment. The word originally meant blunt or dull and, by extension, it came to be applied figuratively to dullness of the mind or senses [21]. The context usually clarifies the condition; in this case it is clear that dumbness is meant (v 33). The man is also described as being demonised (δαιμονιζομενος), a term that was frequently used to describe abnormal forms of behaviour as was noted in the Markan narratives. It would be foolish to speculate about a story of this nature, but in general terms it may be said that the traditions that represent Jesus curing such forms of illness are consistent with various manifestations of those psychiatric disorders classified as dissociative illness, such as conversion/somatisation disorders.

The close association of the healing of both the blind and dumb at this point in the narrative seems to reflect such passages as Isaiah 29:18 and 35:5. The evangelist was thus pointing to the end time expectation, underlining that in the ministry of Jesus the age old prophecies were reaching their long awaited fulfilment and the community of Israel was in process of being restored [22]. Matthew places the restoration of sight to the blind man and speech to the dumb in contrast to the spiritual blindness and dulled senses of the religious establishment who neither wished to see nor understand.

The blind and dumb demoniac: Matthew 12:22-23

The function of this incident in Matthew's story seems to be in order to provide the details of the Beelzebub controversy that was introduced briefly earlier. Mark introduces this particular argument between Jesus and the religious establishment without any specific precipitating event, apart from the incident of Mark 3:20f. in which the family of Jesus accuse him of being mad, something which neither Matthew nor Luke were prepared to record. Matthew, nonetheless, feels the need for something to have happened which acted as the trigger to what was apparently a particularly vicious attack on the integrity of Jesus. The evangelist has brought together the brief statements of Mark about the controversy, together with a number of other statements drawn from the so-called Q source (Luke 11:19, 20, 23). To this he has added a series of further sayings in vv 33-36 which originally do not seem to have had anything to do with demon possession at all. To all this, he has added the story of the blind and dumb demoniac by way of introduction.

The key to the section lies in the concluding statement about speaking against the Holy Spirit. Both the activity and the person of Jesus were ambiguous: he was deliberately hidden and unknown. Therefore, to speak against him was forgivable (the words from the cross are particularly apposite: 'Father forgive them for *they do not know* what they are doing'). But, on the other hand, to speak against what was revealed, the manifestation of God's rule and the activity of his Spirit in making people whole and defeating the power of evil in their lives: this was unforgivable. The preconceptions of the religious leaders blinded them to the person of Jesus, so that at best he was little more than a wandering thaumaturgist or at worst, a black magician. This further endangered them by blinding them to the reality of God's presence and power among them. They were thus left open to the sin of speaking against God's Spirit, actively at work in the ministry of Jesus. The crowds, however, are still at the stage of wondering whether or not Jesus is, in fact, the promised 'Son of David', although the οὗτος of v 23 may be an expression of contempt - 'can this fellow really be the Messiah?' [23]. In general, however, Matthew's crowds are usually presented as being friendly, although, as M'Neile notes, the οὗτος ('this fellow') in the retort of the Pharisees (v 24) corresponds exactly to the comments of the crowd [24].

The exorcism itself is narrated with such brevity that it clearly represents no more than a means of introducing the controversy which is the matter of major interest [25]. It seems possible that the story represents a conflation (and a typical Matthean compression) of the two healings at Matt 9:27-34 discussed above. The account reads almost as though the man's blindness was added as an afterthought, with the main issue being his speech defect. Whatever the source of the story, however, the event is set out as a bald and unvarnished statement of fact that allows little in the way of analysis and interpretation. All details which may have been in the tradition originally, have been removed other than the simple statement that the person cured was 'a blind and dumb demoniac' (δαιμονιζομενος τυφλος και κωφος). However, the description seems representative of the sort of people Jesus healed and it would certainly be quite consistent with the conversion/somatisation manifestations of a dissociative disorder. There is no reason why the man should not have exhibited both blindness and dumbness as signs of his condition and so-called 'hysterical blindness' is a well-documented phenomenon [26]. The association in the story of two very distinct conditions is certainly suggestive of the conversion symptoms of a dissociative disorder.

The removal of the symptoms and consequent 'cure' takes place in a confrontational situation, the sort of situation that was met with on previous occasions in the Gospel narratives in which there was heightened emotion and conditions suitable for the use of abreactive techniques (see pp 60f). The story thus provides further suggestive evidence of the major types of illness with which Jesus dealt in his ministry. It also provides support, albeit circumstantial, for the basic historicity of these narratives.

Matthew's summary statements

Matthew includes a number of editorial and summary statements about the healings of Jesus, in much the same way as did Mark. These are placed in a variety of contexts, emphasising that the healings and exorcisms were an essential component of the ministry of Jesus. Indeed, as Fenton has remarked, 'there is no recoverable presentation of Christianity which is wholly without this miraculous element' [27]. Both followers and enemies of Jesus alike regarded him as possessed of quite remarkable powers and, as Wright puts it, 'The church did not invent the charge that Jesus was in league with Beelzebul: but charges like that are not advanced unless they are needed as an explanation for some quite remarkable phenomena' [28]. However embarrassing it may be to some minds today, this is a factor with which both believer and unbeliever alike have to come to terms. Several of these summary statements are no more than editorial links in the narrative with no intrinsic value in respect of interpreting the activity of Jesus. In this respect, they are very similar to the related editorial statements in Mark. However, in some places Matthew goes beyond simple factual statements and introduces an interpretive element.

This interpretive element is particularly noticeable in the statement at Matt 4:23-25 in which the evangelist seems to suggest that those who were healed by Jesus belonged to identifiable groups of people. This particular section seems to be made up of isolated sentences and phrases which derive from the Markan source and which Matthew has simply brought together for his own purposes and arranged them in his own way. In keeping with his source, he initially refers to 'all those in a bad way' (πάντας τοὺς κακῶς ἔχοντας). He then goes on, however, to narrow this down to two main groups: those with 'chronic pain syndromes' (βασάνοις; a word classically construed with 'diseases' (νοσοις) as here) and the 'demonised' (δαιμονιζομενοις). The demon-possessed group are further broken down into the 'moonstruck' (σεληνιαζομενοις) and the 'paralysed' (παραλυτικοις). The reference to what appear to be chronic pain syndromes is particularly interesting in view of the fact that many of these conditions are now recognised as forms of conversion disorders in which pain is unrelated to any underlying pathology [29]. Matthew seems to be saying that the people Jesus healed fell into two broad categories, both of which today would be recognised as psychogenic-type disorders which would have been amenable to the healing activities of a prophetic healer. The evidence from the Synoptic Gospels is thus consistent and strongly supports the view that Jesus dealt with psychosomatic illness in the form of conversion/somatiform disorders and apparently very little else, other than conditions that could be treated by the methods of the folk healer, such as cataracts.

There is further evidence of Matthew's interpretive approach at Matt 8:16-17, a picture derived from Mark 1:32-34. Mark's version emphasises the crowd impact of the story with large numbers coming to Jesus for healing as the evening comes on. Matthew, however, makes a marked shift in the emphasis and he used the statement about the healings to underline his own theological point of view. He argues that it was inevitable that healing would accompany the ministry of Jesus simple because he was the fulfilment of the 'suffering servant' figure, meeting exactly the functional description of Isaiah 53:4.

Whether these words of Deutero-Isaiah can really sustain the interpretation that Matthew puts on them is beside the point. Matthew believed that Jesus fulfilled the prophetic word of promise in the Old Testament and this particular verse became one of his many 'proof texts', designed to show that all that happened in the ministry of Jesus was laid down beforehand and was part of the inevitable and literal fulfilment of God's word through the prophets. This point of view is further emphasised in the account of the response of Jesus to the question of John the Baptist when he was in prison (derived from the non-Markan source Q). Matthew puts forward the healings of Jesus as evidence of his Messiahship (Matt 11:4-5) and thus sets out a very different understanding of the function of this aspect of the ministry than that displayed by Mark, although with respect to John the Baptist, this is done to confirm faith, not to awaken it.

Nonetheless, Matthew seems to be in general agreement with Mark in not making compassion the primary motive for healing. Matthew uses the verb 'to have compassion' (σπλαγχνιζομαι) on four occasions with respect to Jesus. At Matt 9:36, the reference is to the response of Jesus to the 'harassed and helpless' crowds who were without leadership and guidance. In their situation he was genuinely sorry for them. The verb is again used in relation to the needs of large crowds in the story of the feeding of the five thousand (Matt 14:14) and the duplicate story of the feeding of the four thousand (Matt 15:32). Once more, the context refers to a situation where the crowds were in a helpless and seemingly hopeless situation, without leadership, without food and shelter. On only one occasion is the verb used in relation to a healing. It occurs in the Matthean version of the story of blind Bartimaeus (Matt 20:34) in which Jesus responds with compassion to the cry of the two blind men for pity. In this case there are very clear theological overtones in the formation of the story. Neither Mark nor Matthew, therefore, provide any basis for a theology of healing based primarily on the compassion of Jesus for the sick. This is not to suggest that Jesus did not feel compassion for those who were suffering, but it does emphasise that this was not his primary motive for undertaking his healing work. The Church needs to be much more cautious, therefore, in appealing to the example of Jesus' compassion or similar emotion as the foundation for its own concern for the sick. The healings of Jesus were neither random nor comprehensive. They were an element of a deliberate programme, restricted to function as parables of the kingdom of God. No modern 'healing ministry' functions in this way.

One further issue needs to be addressed. Matthew lays great emphasis on the place of healing in the ministry of Jesus. The question arises, therefore, as to whether he understood the Church of his time to be authorised to continue this ministry. The answer appears to be a somewhat qualified affirmative, particularly when this is considered in relation to the very extended account of the commissioning of the Twelve (Matt 10:1-42). Mark treats this episode very briefly and seems to view it as no more than an extension of the ministry of Jesus in Galilee, which, it seems reasonable to assume, it undoubtedly was. Matthew, however, uses this event as the basis of a lengthy passage designed to encourage and prepare the communities, to which his Gospel was likely addressed, for some form of official persecution. The fact that he retains the conferral of authority (ἐξουσια) to heal and exorcise, in spite of his updating of the commissioning of the original Twelve to a commissioning of the Christians of his own time, is strongly suggestive that the Church of the period was continuing some form of 'healing ministry'. At this distance from that community, it is impossible to know what form of ministry this took and there is little to provide evidence elsewhere in the New Testament. Further, the problem of dating Matthew's community remains and there will always be some doubt in respect of the period in the life of the early Church to which his writing applied. However, in the light of the general statements in this Gospel, it seems reasonable to presume that the 'healing ministry' was directed largely if not entirely, to those conditions that today would be classified as psychogenic in origin. This judgment is borne out by the Lukan material (including Acts) that is now to be considered. Such an approach would also seem to have been the pattern of the Church's 'healing' of the sick in this broad period of the mid to late first century in other Jewish-Christian communities, based on the evidence of the letter of James (see chapter 7, pp 258-266).

The Lukan tradition

The Gospel ascribed to Luke in the New Testament has a number of very clear differences from the other accounts of the life and ministry of Jesus. Luke 'wanted to pass on a certain church tradition which he considered authentic' [30]. In this he was no different from the other evangelists, but it is he alone who claims, in the dedication of his Gospel (Luke 1:1-3), to have written a connected narrative (καθεξῆς γραφαι), based on the oral traditions handed down (καθὼς παρεδοσαν), in contrast with those who had merely drawn up an account (διηγησιν). John A.T. Robinson remarked that Luke was 'essentially the gospel for that imperial world evangelised by Paul "from Jerusalem to Rome" ' [31] and this has coloured his approach to his material. He claimed to have checked his sources and he has attempted to set his narrative into a proper historical context and order with people and events in the empire acting as external reference points. He has endeavoured, in fact, to model his work on the methods of the Hellenistic historians of his time as he passed on the traditions that he had received [32]. The Gospel has been described as 'the work of an educated writer whose artistry was that he knew how to draw on tradition to tell a story that is at once aesthetically pleasing and capable of conveying afresh the truth about the salvation that God has accomplished in Jesus of Nazareth' [33].

Luke has utilised large portions of Markan material that he has reworked stylistically, smoothing and improving the syntax. He often replaces a Markan και with δε and improves the transitions between the pericopes by replacing Mark's characteristic εὐθυς or παλιν with a participial construction or a subordinate clause. In addition, he has also incorporated material from the so-called Q source which he shares with Matthew. In both cases, he has largely taken over this material as he found it, but has reworked the way in which it was formulated. There is also a substantial amount of material that is unique to Luke and was probably derived from a variety of oral sources. All these units of tradition have been fitted together and worked into a coherent narrative with a clear and understandable order designed to 'point out the hand of God at work in the one great path of history that leads from the people of Israel through the ministry of Jesus into the church's present' [34]. Luke thus propounds a Christian view of history that not merely sees the activity of Jesus as the fulfilment of the divine promises, but extends this 'salvation history' into the ongoing life of the Church. It is into this wider context of the divine purposes in the world, being worked out in a universal salvation, that Luke places the healings of Jesus.

The emphasis of Luke is that the saving purposes of God embrace all aspects of human existence, including human suffering (note especially Luke 4:18-19; 7:22; 10:23-24). The healing narratives are thus linked specifically to the theological motif of the ongoing purpose of God to bring deliverance to his people. This theme is present in the birth narratives at the beginning of the Gospel and the resurrection appearances of Jesus at the end. The consistent emphasis of Luke is that God has visited his people in order to bring about the long promised deliverance. It is this that underlines the stark tragedy of a Jerusalem that fails to recognise the day of its visitation in grace and salvation, thus leaving it with nothing other than the visitation of wrath and judgment (Luke 19:44). Further, because it is God who is at work, Luke also points consistently to God as the source of the healing and the one to whom all praise and glory is due (Luke 5:25-26; 7:16; 13:13; 17:15-18). The approach is very much in the tradition of the Old Testament prophets and, as with them, the source of the power that accompanies Jesus and is displayed in his mighty works is his endowment by the Spirit of God, not, as then, in eschatological expectation, but now in eschatological fulfilment. Consequently, from a Lukan perspective, the mighty acts of Jesus 'are signs that God is at work to bring about a fulfilment of a comprehensive hope for Israel and the world, long planned and long prophesied in Scripture' [35].

Luke's emphasis on the work of the Holy Spirit (which Luke in Acts seems to equate with the 'Spirit of Jesus' [eg Acts 16:6,7]) is to be noted. It is through the power of the Spirit poured out upon him at his baptism, as it was upon the ancient prophets such as Elijah and Elisha, that Jesus is able to heal and exorcise. Indeed, Luke portrays Jesus very much as 'a prophet mighty in word and deed' (Luke 24:19) and cast in the form of a new Elijah (note Luke 4:25-27; 7:11-17 and the rather instructive parallel at 9:51-55 where his disciples wish him to call down fire as Elijah had done). In the power of the same Spirit that had empowered Elijah, Jesus seems to adopt the same style and consciously imitate his ministry. What Jesus did was done in the power of the Spirit that had come upon him in his baptism and Luke emphasises that it is by the power of that same Spirit that the Church is able to continue and indeed, should be continuing, the same work of Jesus, manifested in 'mighty acts' [36].

The Lukan healing narratives

The healing material that Luke has obtained from Mark and Q has been discussed earlier in this study and it is the specifically Lukan material, not found elsewhere, which will be discussed in this section. The passages that have no parallel in Mark or Matthew comprise nearly half of Luke's gospel. They include the birth and infancy narratives, elements of John the Baptist's preaching, parts of the Passion narrative as well as long sections within the body of the Gospel. This material contains four healing stories that are not found elsewhere - the raising of the widow's son at Nain (Luke 7:11-17), the crippled (bent) woman (Luke 13:10-17), the man with 'dropsy' (Luke 14:1-6) and the ten leprosy sufferers (Luke 17:11-19). Each will be considered in detail. In addition, Luke describes the temporary loss of speech (aphasia) of Zechariah, the father of John the Baptist, following his vision in the temple, which occurs in relation to the birth narratives (Luke 1:18-23, 59-65) and the restoration of the ear of the high priest's servant after it had been cut off in the Garden of Gethsemane (Luke 22:49-51). These two latter stories are not strictly germane to the thrust of this study in terms of the healing/curing of various diseases, but they certainly merit brief mention.

The story of Zechariah's temporary aphasia is of medical interest. Following an intensely emotional experience, in which he learns that, against all the odds, he is soon to become a father, Zechariah becomes dumb. A full differential diagnosis would embrace several possibilities, but the most likely cause of such a self-limiting condition, particularly in view of the fact that it was not associated with agraphia (inability to write) or alexia (inability to read), although apparently with deafness (vv 61-63), would be a psychogenic disorder. Zechariah was almost certainly suffering from a conversion disorder (hysterical aphasia), a point noted by Margaret and T.A. Lloyd Davies [37]. They suggest that, in addition, that there may well have been a flight from reality in that his lack of speech would have avoided a confrontation with his wife Elizabeth. As is not uncommonly the case in such conditions, a new highly charged emotional experience restores function - in this case the birth of his son in his old age, together with the associated excitement of the circumcision/naming ceremony [38]. Gelma has commented that, 'it seems reasonable that this mutism, intervening after emotion, lasting a certain number of months and suddenly cured, may be truthfully called a functional disorder: it is not possible to see in it a case of (motor) aphasia' [39].

Zechariah's case is classic in that once the threatening situation has resolved and there is no longer any need for him to take refuge in his symptoms, his aphasia dramatically terminates and he is able to speak (and presumably hear) once again. It is not impossible, that as an old man, he may have been deaf to start with, although the story does not make these matters clear. From Luke's point of view, the mutism was not only a punishment for Zechariah's unbelief, but, perhaps more importantly, it was also a sign to him as he had requested, a sign furthermore which concealed the content of God's action from everyone else until the appointed time.

Luke also provides an addition to the story of Peter's action in the Garden of Gethsemane when he severs the ear of the high priest's servant. This event is mentioned in all four Gospels, but Luke is alone is asserting that Jesus restored the man's ear and healed him with a touch. Such a happening in the midst of that dreadful night would have been so obvious and so unexpected that, as Achtemeier has remarked, 'one wonders how the other evangelists could have avoided it' [40]. It seems probable that the Lukan version of the story represents his telling of it as he thought it ought to have happened. It is certainly out of keeping with the general pattern of the healing actions of Jesus. No further comment needs to be made on this particular event.

In common with the other evangelists, Luke also includes a number of summary statements both about the healing mission of Jesus and also that of his disciples. Luke, in fact, lays much greater emphasis on the ministry of the disciples and provides for a much more extensive mission, not merely for the Twelve, but also for the larger group of seventy (or seventy two) who were sent out by Jesus to preach and heal. This uniquely Lukan composition is the vehicle of his understanding of the mission of the Church of his own time which he saw as a continuation of the ministry of 'signs and wonders' that Jesus undertook through the power of God. These passages will be given consideration separately later.

The widow's son of Nain: Luke 7:11-17

This story and the raising of Lazarus in John's Gospel are the only two unequivocal accounts of Jesus restoring dead people to life in the Gospels. It may be significant that these two events are recorded in what are generally agreed to be the latest of the Gospels to be written. The common wisdom would suggest that they were separated by some fifty years from the ministry of Jesus and at a time when any of the few remaining eye-witnesses to his work would have been very old indeed. The earliest traditions are very reticent about raising the dead, with the story of Jairus' daughter being the closest to such an occurrence. Here, however, the widow's son is on his way to the tomb and it is clear that the reader is to have no doubts that he was genuinely dead. In the Johannine story, Lazarus had been dead and buried for four days.

The story is told with considerable circumstantial detail of the sort that Luke tended to add to his narratives in order to provide interest (note 6:6; 7:2; 8:42; 9:38). The dead man was his mother's only son and she was a widow. She was thus helpless, with no husband and now no son, on whom it may be certain she had been totally dependent: there would seem to be little doubt that she had now been deprived of any form of economic support. It is this situation of sorrow and sudden helplessness, with all its attendant uncertainty and loss of security, that produces a response of compassion from Jesus. It is again worth noting, as has been emphasised in respect of the use of the verb σπλαγχνίζομαι in Mark and Matthew, that even in Luke it is used of Jesus only in regard to situations of helplessness, in which people, through circumstances beyond their control, are unable to help themselves and are left rudderless in hostile waters. Even Luke does not use the word of Jesus as a response to sickness *per se* and it is difficult to understand how the commonly held view that compassion was the primary motive for the healings of Jesus has arisen from the New Testament data.

The purpose of the story in the Gospel is developed at v 16. The action of Jesus triggered a response of fear among the people. In view of what the people said, it must be assumed that Luke means the reader to understand in this context that it is fear as the proper response to the power and presence of God (note also 1:12; 1:65; 2:9 etc. where fear is the usual reaction in Luke to manifestations of the divine). The action of Jesus in raising the man from the dead led to glory being given to God and a recognition that Jesus was a divinely-sent prophet. Luke thus underlines that God was again visiting his people and the era of fulfilment in which the dead are to be raised has arrived (see 7:22). In other words, Luke understood this action as having the capacity to validate Jesus and show the source of his power, very much as did the similar actions of the prophets Elijah and Elishah (1 Kings 17:17-24; 2 Kings 4:18-37).

There are reasonable grounds for thinking that Luke is accommodating the traditions to a gentile Hellenistic understanding of a divinely empowered wonder-worker (the so-called 'divine man' [41]). Bultmann, in fact considered that the story was a secondary creation of Hellenistic Jewish Christian circles [42] and there are undoubtedly several parallels in Hellenistic stories, perhaps especially in the life of Apollonius [43]. However, one must be careful not to exaggerate this aspect of Luke. The term 'divine man' is not common in Hellenistic writngs and it needs to be said that so-called 'divine man' terminology has been used with considerable imprecision. Luke would have been well aware of the ambiguities of 'charismatic' behaviour in general and 'miracles' in particular. His clear emphasis, therefore, was on God's activity and not on the person of the wonder worker. The people respond to God, for they recognise that it is his power that lies behind all that Jesus is doing: they do not respond to Jesus as a 'divine man'. Luke thus wishes his readers to understand, not only that this action is part of the validation of Jesus and his ministry, but also that such actions may be the basis of belief and lead to faith. Luke's approach is thus very different from that of Mark.

The story is set out as a typical miracle story as far as its form is concerned. There is the record of a serious situation, the word of command, the success of the 'miracle' and the effect on those who witnessed it. The command itself is couched in emphatic terms. Turning away from the mother, Jesus addresses the young man and says, 'to *you* I say (σοι λεγω), Arise!' [44]. The command is given on Jesus' own authority and is immediately obeyed as the dead man sits up (compare Acts 9:40) and begins to speak. The concern that Jesus expresses, however, is not for the son, but for the widow in her helpless and despairing condition and Jesus gives the young man back to his mother to act once again as her stay and support. As noted above, it is the situation of the widow that calls forth the compassion of Jesus.

It seems clear that in the form that Luke has utilised this tradition, it owes much to the Old Testament narratives of the widows of Zarephath and Shunem. Nain was near the ancient city of Shunem where Elijah's miracle was performed, although to claim that the name of the town is occasioned by Elijah's miracle at Shunem is, as John Meier puts it, 'an act of exegetical desperation' [45]. The close geographical relationship of Nain and Shunem in southern Galilee, however, would have been of significance to the Jewish Christians in Palestine among whom the story originated. More importantly, the words of v 15 (και ἐδωκεν αὐτον τῇ μητρι αὐτου) are identical with the Greek of the LXX of 1 Kings 17:23 and serve to emphasise the Elijah typology which lies behind the story. The question thus arises as to whether the event has been retold to fit in with the Elijah/Elisha stories or whether it represents that stage in the tradition in which stories begin to be told to develop the Old Testament parallels and provide greater emphasis on the way in which the early Church saw Jesus as the fulfilment of the ancient prophetic tradition as well as being God's chosen deliverer. The response of the people who witnessed this action in v 16 is indicative of the way in which Luke reinforces the Messianic implications of this event. Such a happening could only mean that the age of eschatological fulfilment, the Messianic age, had arrived: at last, God had visited his people (a constant Lukan theme) and the long-promised great prophet had come among them.

It is to be noted that Luke has already utilised Old Testament patterns as 'types', for example in the birth narratives in which Luke uses the Samuel traditions to formulate his own stories. It has been remarked that these stories are 'permeated by the narrative patterns and language of the narrator's Scripture' [46]. However, the story has all the appearances of a genuine memory of an occasion in which Jesus restored an apparently dead young man to life and to his grieving mother. Of particular importance is the accuracy of Luke's description of Nain as a walled village with a gate, something which has been questioned in the past, but which, in view of the insignificance of the village, suggests that Luke was in close touch with a local tradition [47]. It is not surprising that the developing tradition has moulded this story to meet certain theological presuppositions. What is surprising, however, is that such an event is to be found in only one strand of the tradition, particularly in the light of the affirmations about Jesus raising the dead in all the Gospel traditions.

It should be noted, however, that there has already been a foreshadowing of the Elijah/Elisha parallels in the narrative of Luke 4:16-30. In that section there are implicit connections to their ministry in the reference to Naaman the Syrian being cleansed from his leprosy and, with regard to the present narrative, to the raising of the widow's son by Elijah, a very specific parallel in terms of a new divine visitation. Luke would appear to be basing his understanding of the prophetic role of Jesus as a re-enactment of the Elijah/Elisha epic and just as this ancient mission touched the outsider, so too does the mission of Jesus reach out to the Gentiles - a very different emphasis from Matthew [48]. It would seem inevitable, therefore, that this story has undergone substantial development and represents a major redaction of any original tradition [49]. Nonetheless, the traditions underlying each of the Gospels agree that Jesus raised the dead, irrespective of the manner in which we may decide to interpret that statement today.

From the standpoint of modern medicine, the issue relates to the physical status of the young man, presuming that the narrative reflects an actual happening and is not a late arising 'legend'. Was the man clinically dead or was this some form of comatose condition closely mimicking death? The rapidity with which persons were (and still are) buried in the Middle East would always increase the likelihood of the untoward event of a comatose person being buried as though dead. Conditions mimicking death are not that uncommon and the clinical diagnosis of death may frequently be difficult, even today. Further, cases still arise (and are not that rare) in which a person has been declared dead on the hospital ward only to come round in the mortuary and make the occasional headline in the press.

There is no way, therefore, in which it may be stated unequivocally that the widow's son was 'dead' in the sense that would satisfy all the criteria of the modern clinician or pathologist. The modern concept of 'brain death' was totally unknown in the ancient world, and it has only been made possible in very recent times as a result of the use of complex electronic equipment. At the same time, it has to be said that there is no way that it can be stated unequivocally that the young man was not 'dead' in the accepted sense of the word. The issue here is not one of historical analysis nor medical diagnosis, for the basic reason that there are insufficient data on which a medical judgment can be made. The interpretation of the event thus becomes one of personal viewpoint and belief. The problem of the accurate diagnosis of death did not represent an important issue for the early Church, but it clearly becomes a very important matter when considered in the context of certain modern pentecostal and charismatic claims of being able to raise the dead and in such situations the modern criteria of determining death must be allowed to apply [50].

The deformed woman: Luke 13:10-17

This story has been discussed in considerable detail by Wilkinson, particularly in relation to the nature of the healing and whether it constituted an exorcism [51]. That Luke placed considerable emphasis upon Jesus as an exorcist need not be doubted and there is a tendency, particularly in his retelling of the Markan stories, to turn what Mark recorded as a straightforward healing into an exorcism.   This is particularly noticeable in the story of Peter's mother-in-law, for example.   Here also, in a story which is not at all characteristic of an exorcism, Luke has introduced ideas which at first sight might suggest that he saw this healing as something that, at least, contained elements of exorcist practice and, in more general terms, as illustrating the defeat of Satan.   Luke describes the woman as having a 'spirit of infirmity' (πνευμα ἀσθενιας) and having been 'bound by Satan' for eighteen years.   As a consequence, Twelftree has concluded that by the use of the such terminology 'Luke not only blurs the distinction between healing in general and exorcism in particular, but (and this may explain why he so readily includes "exorcism" in the summaries of Jesus' healing ministry), he in effect gives all sickness a demonic and cosmic dimension; in all healing God's adversary is being subdued' [52].

Such a judgment, however, does not necessarily mean that Luke saw this healing specifically as an exorcism and there are, in fact, linguistic oddities that suggest that Luke was being deliberately ambiguous.   The phrase 'spirit of weakness' has given problems not only to commentators, but also to translators.   A number of English versions have interpreted the phrase to mean demon possession, such as the *Jerusalem Bible* (1966), *The New English Bible* (1970), *The Good News Bible* (1976) and *The Revised English Bible* (1989).   Such a translation is going well beyond the evidence and cannot be sustained. The phrase is not qualified by an adjective such as ἀκαθαρτος (unclean) nor is there any mention of a demon in the passage.   This is in contrast to those stories that are clear cases of exorcism and in contrast also to the normal usage of all the Synoptic Gospels in which the word 'spirit' by itself never implies an evil spirit or the presence of demon possession.   Wilkinson, in fact has argued convincingly that the phrase relates specifically to the general state of mind produced by the condition from which the woman was suffering[53].

Somewhat similar considerations apply to the other phrase about the binding of Satan. This phrase is unique to Luke and found only in this passage in the New Testament. The meaning is made clear from the context in which Jesus argues with the president of the synagogue over the issue of Sabbath observance. Jesus uses an *a fortiori* argument: if on the Sabbath day it is permissible to untie the bonds which have confined the animals in order to allow them to drink, then how much more is it right and proper to untie this poor woman who has been bound by Satan for eighteen years? It is a beautiful example of the *argumentum a minori ad maius* which was so beloved of the Rabbis - 'if the one, then so much more the other'. The phrase has nothing to do with demon possession or exorcism, but is simply a statement of the general view that Satan is primarily responsible for all human sin and sickness. The use of the word 'bound' is explained by the parallel that has been drawn with the animals tied up in their stalls awaiting release to find refreshment.

From Luke's theological perspective, the important aspect of this story is the emphasis on Satan as the originator of human sickness and thus, by simple extension, on God as the source of all healing. The ministry of Jesus thus represents the triumph of God over evil and Satan. The story functions essentially as a pronouncement or conflict story in which the issue is the proper way in which the Sabbath should be kept to bring God glory. Further, it acts also as an additional demonstration of the comprehensiveness of God's saving purposes in Jesus, which embrace every aspect of human life that has been invaded by the powers of sin and death[54]. It is particularly important to recognise that this story is not an example of the way in which Hellenistic magical beliefs have influenced Luke and his presentation of the ministry of Jesus[55]. Nonetheless, it has to be accepted that in this story, Luke has blurred the clear distinction between healing and exorcism that is seen in Mark, no doubt for his own purposes[56].

The limited details provided in the story do not allow of any definitive diagnosis to be made. The text merely states that the woman was unable 'to stand fully (or properly) erect' (construing εἰς τo πανταλες with ἀνακυψαι in v 11). She thus retained some movement of her spine, but this was clearly limited. It is also not entirely clear what is meant by 'bent', although the term suggests either a lateral curvature of the spine (scoliosis) or one that is forward (kyphosis), the 'hunchback' posture. John Wilkinson, in his very full discussion of the diagnosis [57], has argued that the woman was suffering from ankylosing spondylitis, one of the connective tissue ('rheumatoid') conditions in which a chronic and progressive arthritis of the spine develops, leading eventually to complete fusion and loss of spinal movement. In advanced cases, the patient may be 'bent over' as was the woman in the story.

The argument against this diagnosis has always been the clinical preponderance of young males with the condition. However, although the disease is more common in males than females, the previously accepted ratio of 10:1 is no longer reported and the distribution appears similar in both sexes with perhaps a 2:1 ratio and with a clear genetic component [58]. Rendle Short [59] suggested tuberculosis of the spine (Pott's disease) or osteoarthritis as likely causes, but such specific diagnoses are no more than speculation, although tuberculosis was rife throughout the ancient world [60] and could certainly have been a possible cause of spinal deformity. However, such very clear structural deformities caused by anatomical lesions are not the type of disease that Jesus dealt with, certainly in the earlier traditions. A further possibility, therefore, deserves consideration.

Although the available information is very limited, this woman fits the classical picture of adult scoliosis in which the patient is typically a woman between 20 and 40 years of age [61]. Non-structural forms of this condition are well recognised, including those due to psychological causes, such as conversion/somatisation disorders [62]. Chronic back pain itself, with no evidence of pathology, may induce a functional curvature of the spine, adopted by the patient in an attempt to avoid muscle spasm, and this may become a persistent feature of the person's gait, a feature frequently seen in the writer's own specialist medical practice.

Luke told the story to emphasise a point about the Sabbath and it is very likely that the underlying tradition has changed subtly during the lengthy process of transmission. However, in the light of what has already been gleaned about the healings of Jesus, it seems likely that the origin of the woman's problem was functional rather than anatomical and the case represents another example of either a psychological conversion disorder or, very likely, a response to chronic back pain. Certainty is impossible in a story told with so little detail, but there are features of the narrative that would seem to indicate that this healing fits into the general pattern, seen in all the Gospels, of Jesus dealing with what were essentially functional (psychosomatic) disorders.

The man with 'dropsy':   Luke 14:1-6

This story appears to have an artificial setting in the middle of a dinner party and seems to be in its present position to form a narrative setting for what may have been an isolated saying of Jesus about the Sabbath. G.B. Caird pointed out that 'many of the sayings of Jesus came to Luke without any indication of the context in which they were spoken and he has consistently tried to supply such "orphaned" traditions with a narrative setting' [63]. The saying about the son or ox falling into the well and being rescued on the Sabbath is very similar to the one associated with the healing of the 'bent' woman discussed above. The saying is also very closely related to that at Matt 12:11 which occurs in the context of that Gospel's version of the man with the withered hand [64] and, as in the case of the 'bent' woman, the principle that Jesus uses is the *argumentum a minori ad maius* - if this, then so much more the other. The law of mercy may take precedence over the law of the Sabbath in the case of a domestic animal or a child that needs urgent help, how much more then should the same law apply to all in desperate need [65]. The narrative itself is a mixture of miracle story and dispute story, the former being present simply to act as a lead in to the dispute, which is the important part. It is not surprising, therefore, that there is little information given about the man who was healed - he is essentially incidental and promptly disappears home as soon as he is cured.

The word ὑδρωπικος (generally translated as 'dropsy') used to describe the physical state of the man, is found only here and nowhere else in the New Testament, nor in the LXX version of the Old Testament. Hobart quoted extensively from the Hippocratic corpus and Dioscorides to indicate that this word is 'the usual way in medical language of denoting a person suffering from dropsy' [66]. It was his belief that the use of this word formed part of the evidence of the medical background of the writer of the third gospel, who, by extension, is to be identified with Luke 'the beloved physician'. The use of uncontrolled lexical parallels is a dangerous procedure and H.J. Cadbury showed that much of Luke's so-called 'medical language' had wide parallels in contemporary non-medical literature [67].

The word ὑδρωπικος is not by itself a diagnosis and merely describes a symptom rather than any underlying pathology. It is perhaps surprising to find it translated by the archaic term 'dropsy' as late as the *Revised English Bible* (1989) and the *New Revised Standard Version* (1989) although there appears to be a tendency for Bible translators to use long since outmoded 'medical' words. The term describes a condition in which tissue fluids accumulate in different parts of the body, especially those parts that are dependent, such as the legs or lower abdomen. Modern terminology uses the word 'oedema' to describe this fluid accumulation. It would thus refer to peripheral oedema to denote the accumulation of fluid in the ankles and legs, pulmonary oedema to describe the accumulation of fluid in the lungs and ascites to describe the accumulation of fluid in the abdominal cavity. In biblical times, the use of such terminology was imprecise and frequently vague. Furthermore, symptoms were generally confused with the disease and it is impossible to provide any firm diagnosis of this man's condition.

The causes of oedema are many and include conditions that cause failure of the heart, liver or kidneys, but it is not possible to determine whether any of these diseases was responsible for this man's condition and the term may mean little more than the man appeared swollen. There is little value in speculation, particularly as the story appears to be an isolated unit of tradition that seems out of place in its present context in Luke [68]. It is also likely that this unit of tradition had undergone considerable change before it reached Luke. It is probably one of those stories, arising in, or substantially modified in, the later traditions, which portray Jesus curing more 'physical' illnesses than he did in the earliest traditions, in which the consistent picture is of the cure of conditions which had their roots in a person's psyche.

The ten 'leprosy' sufferers: Luke 17:11-19

Other than the story of the healing of the leprosy sufferer at Mark 1:40-45, this is the only account of Jesus dealing with 'leprosy'. The issue of the relationship of modern leprosy to the biblical conditions subsumed under this term was discussed in detail in relation to the Markan story (see above pp 66-75), which Luke also includes in his narrative although with his characteristic expansions in respect of the response of the crowds (Luke 5:12-16). It is possible that this story represents an expansion and theological development of the original Markan tradition that Luke has included for his own purposes in developing the concept of faith as a response of gratitude to the grace of God. As Marshall notes, the story is not simply 'a testimony to the ability of Jesus to cure lepers ... but is also concerned with the attitude of the person cured' [69]. It is also worth noting that the central person in the story is an outsider, not only in respect of his 'leprosy', but also because he was a Samaritan.

The story contains a number of puzzling features, however, which tend to support the view that it represents some sort of composite narrative built on the basis of the Markan story, the core of which still seems to be present. It is possible that this narrative represents part of the 'continuing and still developing free (oral) tradition of sayings of Jesus and stories about him' [70] to which Luke (and his church) bear remarkable witness as something still existing and remaining unfixed at some considerable distance from the Easter event.

The purpose of the story in Luke represents a major shift from the probable Markan original, with its emphasis on the power of Jesus to transcend the Law with something better, to an emphasis on faith in Jesus that brings about a salvation which is more than cleansing from a condition regarded as 'unclean'. H.D Betz [71] has claimed that the story reflects the insistence of the early Church that a healing miracle is not the same thing as salvation itself. The miracle is ambiguous and is not fully experienced until it has brought about a change of inner orientation - in other words it is not complete until 'healing' has become 'salvation'.

Achtemeier [72] has pointed out that the story sits in a context which has to do with the answer to the question, 'what is faith?' - it forgives (vv 1-4), it can do all things (vv 5,6), it is humble (vv 7-10) and in this story it is also at the heart of the response of genuine gratitude to God's grace. Such a response to what Jesus brings as God's agent in salvation is at the core of salvation: the one who returned merely 'cleansed' of the ceremonial defilement of his condition is, as a result of this deeper transformation of attitudes, enabled to enter into a new relationship with God which may be described not as 'healing', but as 'salvation'. It is worth quoting G.B. Caird's comments on this passage: 'Cleansing came to the lepers from God, but through Jesus; and gratitude demanded that the agent, as well as the source, of healing was acknowledged ... Through Jesus, God was acting and through him God must be thanked. What Jesus actually said to the Samaritan was "Your faith has saved you"; and salvation was more than cleansing, a new relationship with God and his kingdom of grace' [73].

The comments relating to possible diagnosis made in considering the Markan narrative, apply also to this story. Further, assuming that this narrative represents a development of a Markan original rather than a specific event in its own right, then the judgments made in respect of

Mark's story and the nature of the healing or declaration of cleansing in that case will also apply to the present story.

Lukan editorial material

The increased emphasis on the mighty works of Jesus in Luke, when compared with Mark and Matthew, is made evident in the various editorial link passages in the Gospel. More than the other evangelists, Luke pictures Jesus healing *all* those who came to him. At times this power seems to come from Jesus in an almost magical manner (note 6:19) and he inserts a comment on healing where other evangelists have not. For example, Luke could not apparently conceive of a crowd coming to Jesus to hear his teaching unless he was also active in healing the sick. Consequently, his introduction to the Lukan equivalent of Matthew's 'Sermon the Mount' (derived from what may be called the Q material) notes that when the crowd came together, Jesus 'healed them all' (Luke 6:19). Further, Luke does not view the healings of Jesus as an essential element of the total proclamation as Mark does, but rather sees the ministry of Jesus as summarised by his acts of power. The response to the Baptist's query (Luke 7:18-23) and the response to Herod (Luke 13:32) both would suggest that for Luke, the career of Jesus could be described in terms of his healing ministry and his acts of power, rather than in the message of the cross and the burden of discipleship. There is thus a strand of triumphalism running through the Lukan treatment of the ministry of Jesus, even though he has to come to terms with the events of Good Friday.

Luke, however, expands this emphasis on healing and power by arguing that such acts should also mark the subsequent ministry of the Church. This seems evident, for example, from the specifically Lukan account of the mission of the Seventy (or Seventy-two) [74]. That Luke sees this group as the precursor of the Church of his own time seems undeniable and he appears to have developed the story by expanding the basic original tradition of a mission of the Twelve. The stories of that mission in Mark (6:7-13), Matthew (10:5-15) and Luke (Luke 9:1-6) are all roughly parallel and it is a reasonable assumption that a single tradition underlies them all [75]. Whether this tradition in its original form actually included healing and exorcism is a moot point, but from Luke's point of view it seems clear that his special tradition of the seventy disciples is intended to point to a universal mission of the Church which included healings and exorcisms as part of the proclamation of the kingdom of God [76]. The number seventy represented the traditional Jewish view of the number of nations in the ancient world [77]. In addition, the concept of the harvest would appear to echo eschatological expectation and the fact that the disciples are instructed both to heal and to announce the arrival of God's kingdom would suggest that Luke sees the healings as being in themselves an essential element of God's reign as it extends beyond the boundaries of Israel to encompass the world.

Luke would seem to be giving to the Church of his time a warrant to continue the ministry of Jesus in healing and exorcism and in his second volume (Acts) he expands on this theme, showing that the apostles and the early missionaries included these elements as necessary parts of their ministry and mission. The very reason for what they were doing was nothing less than the continuation of the ministry of Jesus in the power of the selfsame Spirit that had empowered his work.

Notes and references

[1] See for example, among recent works, Havener, I. (1987). *The Sayings of Jesus: Good News Studies 19* (Glazier, Wilmington) and Kloppenborg, J.S. (1988). *Q Parallels: Synopsis, Critical Notes and Concordance.* (Polebridge Press, Sonoma, CA).

[2] Note particularly Parker, P. (1952). *The Gospel before Mark.* University of Chicago Press, Chicago).

[3] So such writers as Bo Reicke, (1986). *The Roots of the Synoptic Gospels* (Fortress, Philadelphia); Byrskog, S. (1994). *Jesus the Only Teacher, Didactic Authority and Transmission in Ancient Israel, Ancient Judaism and the Matthean Community.* (Almqvist & Wicksell, Stockholm); E. Linnemann (1992). *Is There a Synoptic Problem? Rethinking the Literary Dependence of the First Three Gospels.* (Baker, Grand Rapids) and Wenham, J. (1991). *Redating Matthew, Mark and Luke: A Fresh Assault on the Synoptic Problem.* (Hodder & Stoughton, London).

[4] See for example, Goulder, M.D. (1974). *Midrash and Lection in Matthew.* (SPCK, London) and (1989), *Luke - A New Paradigm. JSNTSS 20.* (JSOT, Sheffield) and also Farrer, A. (1985). On dispensing with Q. In: Bellinzoni, A.J. (ed). *The Two-Source Hypothesis: A Critical Appraisal.* (Mercer University Press, Macon, GA.).

[5] It is remarkable that a document, apparently so highly prized by the canonical evangelists, should have disappeared without trace. In spite of the very tenuous and indeed speculative nature of Q, members of the 'Jesus Seminar' have given it the status of a 'gospel' originating in its own community of Galilean itinerants (see for example, Mack, B. (1993). *The Lost Gospel.* Collins San Francisco, San Francisco) and even a documentary literary history (so

Kloppenborg, J.S.(1987). *The Formation of Q: Trajectories in Ancient Wisdom Collections.* (Fortress, Philadelphia) and (1988). *Q Parallels.* (Polebridge Press, Sonoma, CA). For a penetrating critique of modern biblical scholarship (including the current efforts to define 'Q') from a distinguished historian, see Akenson, D.H. (2000). *Saint Saul: A Skeleton Key to the Historical Jesus.* McGill University Press, Montreal/Oxford University Press, New York.

[6] For a detailed discussion of the general situation and with a fairly standard set of conclusions see Sanders, E.P. and Davies, M. (1989). *Studying the Synoptic Gospels.* SCM, London. Other approaches include Koester, H. (1982). *Introduction to the New Testament. Vol 2: History and Literature of Early Christianity.* Walter de Gruyter, New York & Berlin (especially pp 44-49) and (1990). *Ancient Christian Gospels: Their History and Development.* SCM, London. Note also the radical solutions proposed by Eta Linemann (1992). *Is there a Synoptic Problem?* who argues for an independent use of primary and secondary oral traditions as the sole sources, and also John Wenham (1991). *Redating Matthew, Mark and Luke,* who resurrects the older view that Matthew was the first of the Gospels and (in company with J.A.T. Robinson, (1976). *Redating the New Testament.* SCM, London) argues for an early date. The controversial claims of Carsten Thiede and Matthew D'Ancona (1996) in *The Jesus Papyrus* (Weidenfeld and Nicolson, London), if substantiated, would also make for a much earlier date for Matthew than usually suggested. Such studies simple underline the immense complexity of the problem and the need to avoid simple answers. The fact is that there are no compelling reasons, other than 'received wisdom', for denying an early date (pre-A.D.70) for any of the Synoptic Gospels.

[7] See Schweizer, E. (1976). *The Good News according to Matthew.* SPCK, London. ET. p 16.

[8] Schweizer, E. (1976). *Matthew.* p 17. The origin of this Gospel in Syrian Antioch was argued strongly by B.H. Streeter (1930). *The Four Gospels: A Study of Origins.* Macmillan, London. Revised edn. pp 500-527. Gunther Bornkamm (1982) has remarked that the evangelist 'may be looked upon as a representative of Hellenistic-Jewish Christianity' (The risen Lord and the earthly Jesus. In: Bornkamm, G. Barth, G. and Held, H.J. *Tradition and Interpretation in Matthew.* SCM, London. 2nd edn. p 323).

[9] The issues are complex and outside the scope of this study. See however, Robinson, J.A.T. (1972). *Redating the New Testament,* SCM, London. pp 13-30; Bo Reicke, (1972), Synoptic prophecies on the destruction of Jerusalem. In: Aune, D.E. (ed). *Studies in New Testament and early Christian Literature: Essays in Honour of Allen P. Wikgren.* E J Brill, Leiden. pp 121-134. He comments that the 'situation presupposed by Matthew corresponds to what is known about Christianity in Palestine between AD 50 and ca. 64, but not after the flight of the Christians ca. 64 and the start of the Jewish war in AD 66' and comments that the normal critical dating of the synoptics to later than AD 70 is 'an amazing example of critical dogmatism'.

[10] See the discussion in Sanders, E.P. and Davies, M. (1988). *Studying the Synoptic Gospels.* pp 252-265.

[11] The assumption that the Gospels were written for specific church communities has been strongly criticised by Richard Bauckham as was noted in respect of Mark.   He argues that 'the gospels were written for general circulation around the churches and so envisaged a very general Christian audience' (Bauckham, R. (ed). (1998) *The Gospel for all Christians: Rethinking the Gospel Audience.* Eerdmans, Grand Rapids. p 1).

[12] Held, H.J. (1982).   Matthew as interpreter of the miracle stories.   In: *Tradition and Interpretation in Matthew.* p 168.

[13] See further Held, H.J. (1982). In: *Tradition and Interpretation in Matthew.* pp 168-211.

[14] The commonly accepted view of Markan priority is accepted here without discussion, although the alternatives and the complexities of the problem are recognised.

[15] For a discussion of the relation of this story to the Markan parallel see M'Neile, A.H. (1915). *The Gospel according to Matthew.* Macmillan, London. pp 128-129. The term 'Son of David' is possibly to be seen as a reference to Jesus as a latter day miracle working Solomon, the only Old Testament king to be actually designated 'son of David'. See further J.P. Meier (1994). *A Marginal Jew: Rethinking the Historical Jesus. Vol 2.* Doubleday, New York. pp 689ff .   He makes the important comment that the 'nearly complete restriction of "Son of David" to Solomon in the OT is significant in the light of the subsequent tradition history both of "Son of David" in the Synoptics and of the image of Solomon as an exorcist and magician' (p 737, n 47). See also Duling, D.C. (1978). The therapeutic Son of David: An element in Matthew's christological apologetic. *New Testament Studies.* 24:392-410 and Kingsbury, J.D. (1976). The title 'Son of David' in Matthew's gospel. *Journal of Biblical Literature.* 95. 591-602.

[16] See the comments on Mark 1:43 (p 71). M'Neile, (1915). (*Matthew.* p 127) also gives a number of classical references to the use of this verb.

[17] Schweizer, E. (1976). *Matthew.* p 230.

[18] Harrington, D.J. (1991). *The Gospel of St Matthew (Sacra Pagina Vol 1).* Liturgical Press, Collegeville. p 133.

[19] The evidence is solely the late fifth century Codex Bezae (D) together with some old Latin and Syriac versions. Nonetheless, the *Revised English Bible* consigns this verse to the margin. It is regarded as non-original by Allen, W.C. (1912). *The Gospel according to St Matthew (International Critical Commentary).* T & T Clark, Edinburgh.

[20] See Crossan, J.D. (1991). *The Historical Jesus.* pp 305-309. His approach seems to be getting very close to a Humpty Dumpty view of language in which words can be made to mean whatever the writer determines and it is certainly not the normal way magic is understood. *The Shorter Oxford English Dictionary* (1970, 3rd edn revised. Clarendon Press, Oxford) defines 'magic' as 'the pretended art of influencing the course of events by compelling the agency of spiritual beings or by bringing into operation some occult controlling principle of nature'.

[21] For references see Liddell and Scott, p 1019 and Bauer, p 462.

22 On this matter see further, B.F. Meyer (1979). *The Aims of Jesus*. SCM, London. pp 157-8.

23 Note also that the question is introduced by μητι which normally expects a negative response, although it may be used in questions in which there is doubt about the answer (see Bauer p 520 and also Moule, C.F.D. (1959) *An Idiom Book of New Testament Greek*. Cambridge University Press, Cambridge. second edn. pp 155-156).

24 M'Neile, A.H. (1915). *Matthew*. p 174.

25 Leon Morris (1992) comments that 'few healings are described as briefly as this one' (*The Gospel according to Matthew*. Eerdmans, Grand Rapids. p 313).

26 See, for example, Turner, R.G. (1976). Hysterical blindness. In: Rose, F.C. (ed). *Medical Ophthalmology*. Chapman and Hall. London. pp 224-237.

27 Fenton, J.C. (1963). *Saint Matthew (Pelican Gospel Commentaries)*. Penguin Books, Harmondsworth. p 20.

28 Wright, N.T. (1996). *Jesus and the Victory of God*. SPCK, London. p 187.

29 See for example, Turk, D.C. (1996). *Psychological Aspects of Pain*. Springhouse Press, Spring House, PA. (especially pp 124-179) and Turk, D.C. and Meichenbaum, D. (1994). A cognitive-behavioural approach to pain management. In: Wall, P.D. and Melzack, R. (eds). *A Textbook of Pain*. Churchill Livingstone, Edinburgh. 3rd edn. pp 1337-1348. Note also the discussion in Issy Pilowsky, (1997). *Abnormal Illness Behaviour*. Wiley, Chichester. pp 50-52.

30 Haenchen, E. (1968). The book of Acts as source material for the history of early Christianity. In: Keck, L.E. and Martyn, J.L. (eds). *Studies in Luke-Acts*. SPCK, London. p 258.

31 Robinson, J.A.T. (1976). *Redating the New Testament*. SCM, London. p 101.

32 On Luke as an historian in the Hellenistic pattern see the extensive treatment in Hemer, C.J. (1989). *The Book of Acts in the Setting of Hellenistic History (Wissenschaftliche Untersuchungen zum Neuen Testament: 49)*. J.C.B. Mohr, Tübingen.

33 Kingsbury, J.D. (1991). *Conflict in Luke: Jesus, Authorities, Disciples*. Fortress Press, Minneapolis. p 1.

34 Lohse, E. (1981). *The Formation of the New Testament*. Abingdon, Nashville. ET. p 150.

35 Tannehill, R.C. (1986). *The Narrative Unity of Luke-Acts: A Literary Interpretation. Vol 1. The Gospel according to Luke*. Fortress Press, Philadelphia. p 87.

36 See Marshal, I.H. (1988). *Luke: Historian and Theologian*. Paternoster Press, Exeter. 3rd edn. pp 181-182. The case for a Lukan 'charismatic' theology is argued by R. Stronstad (1984). *The Charismatic Theology of St Luke*. Hendrickson, Peabody. MA. He contends that the anointing of the Spirit for the individual in Luke's theology is always 'experiential' and separate from Christian initiation in 'conversion-baptism'.

37 Lloyd Davies, M. and Lloyd Davies, T.A. (1993). *The Bible: Medicine and Myth*. Silent Books, Cambridge. 3rd edn. p 201.

[38] This association of name giving with circumcision is apparently otherwise unattested in contemporary Judaism (so I.H. Marshall. (1978). *The Gospel of Luke (New International Greek Text Commentary)*. Paternoster Press, Exeter. p 88). Was Luke reading Christian baptismal/naming practice of his own time back into this event?

[39] Gelma, E. (1932). The transitory mutism of Zecharias: the relation of the condition to motor aphasia. *Paris Medicine*. 86. 237-241 (in French).

[40] Achtemeier, P.J. (1978). The Lukan perspective on the miracles of Jesus: a preliminary sketch. In: Talbert, C.H. (ed). *Perspectives on Luke-Acts*. T & T Clark, Edinburgh. pp 153-167.

[41] See particularly Betz, O. (1972). The concept of the so-called 'divine man' in Mark's christology. In: Aune, D.E (ed). *Studies in New Testament and Early Christian Literature. Essays in Honour of A.P. Wikgren*. E.J. Brill, Leiden. pp 229-234 and also Betz, H.D. (1968). Jesus as divine man. In: Trotter, F.T. (ed). *Jesus and the Historian: In Honour of E.C. Colwell*. Westminster, Philadelphia. pp 114-133. For a comprehensive treatment of the subject, see Carrington, G.P. (1986). *The 'Divine Man': His Origin and Function in Hellenistic Popular Religion*. Peter Lang, New York.

[42] Bultmann, R. (1963). *History of the Synoptic Tradition*. Blackwell, Oxford. ET. p 215.

[43] Note the references given in Marshall, I.H. (1978). *Luke*. p 283 and also Bultmann, R. (1963). *History of the Synoptic Tradition*. p 233-234.

[44] See the comments in Plummer, A. (1915). *The Gospel according to St Luke (International Critical Commentary)*. T & T Clark, Edinburgh. 5th edn. p 199.

[45] Meier, J.P. (1994). *A Marginal Jew. Vol 2*. p 794.

[46] Tannehill, R.C. (1986). *The Narrative Unity of Luke-Acts*. p 18.

[47] J.P. Meier commenting on the obscurity of the place, remarks, 'How did Luke, who does not appear as well informed about Palestinian geography as some of the other evangelists, know about the existence of the obscure southern Galilean town of Nain? Further, how did he know that it was a walled town - as recent archaeological excavations have shown - and therefore had a gate? The very specificity of Nain militates against the theory that Luke has created the whole story' (*A Marginal Jew. Vol 2*. p 795 and see also related footnotes)

[48] Note the discussion in Siker, J.S. (1992). 'First to the gentiles': a literary analysis of Luke 4:16-30. *Journal of Biblical Literature*. 111. 73-90.

[49] See the extensive discussion in Meier, J.P. (1994). *A Marginal Jew. Vol 2*. pp 790-797.

[50] Note the claims reported in Harrell, D.E. Jr (1975). *All Things are Possible: The Healing and Charismatic Revivals in Modern America*. Indiana University Press, Bloomington. (Note especially pp 69, 88, and 199). See also Moriarty, M. (1992). *The New Charismatics*. Zondervan, Grand Rapids, especially p 35.

[51] Wilkinson, J. (1977). The case of the bent woman in Luke 13:10-17. *Evangelical Quarterly*. 49. 195-205 = (1980) *Health and Healing: Studies in New Testament Principles and Practice*. Handsel Press, Edinburgh. pp 70-80.

[52] Twelftree, G.H. (1985). *Christ Triumphant: Exorcism Then and Now*. Hodder and Stoughton, London. p 104. See also his later (1993) comments in

Jesus the Exorcist: A Contribution to the Study of the Historical Jesus. J.C.B.Mohr, Tübingen. pp 55-56 and 138. Note the references given.

[53] Wilkinson, J. (1980). *Health and Healing.* pp 77ff.

[54] See further Tannehill, R.C. (1986). *The Narrative Unity of Luke-Acts.* p 89.

[55] This is the rather unconvincing argument of Hull, J.M. (1974). *Hellenistic Magic and the Synoptic Tradition.* SCM, London. See especially pp 87-115 on Luke.

[56] See the discussion in Marshall, I.H. (1978). *Luke.* pp 556-557.

[57] Wilkinson, J. (1980) *Health and Healing.* pp 71-75.

[58] van der Linden, S. (1997). Ankylosing spondylitis. In: Kelley, W.N., Harris, E.D., Ruddy, S., Sledge, C.B. (eds). *Textbook of Rheumatology.* W.B. Saunders, Philadelphia. 5th edn. p 978. See also Kidd, B., Mullee, M., Frank, A. (1988). Disease expression in ankylosing spondylitis in males and females. *Journal of Rheumatology* 15. 1407-1409.

[59] Short, A. Rendle. (1953). *The Bible and Modern Medicine.* Paternoster Press, London. p 104.

[60] There are numerous references to tuberculosis in the medical texts, for example Pliny, *Ep.* 5.19; 7:19.

[61] Borenstein, D.G. Wiesel, S.W. (1989). *Low Back Pain: Medical Diagnosis and Comprehensive Management.* W.B. Saunders, Philadelphia. p 171.

[62] Bradford, D.S., Moe, J.H., Winter, R.B. (1982). Scoliosis and kyphosis. In: Rothman, R.H., Simeone, Fa. (eds). *The Spine.* W.B. Saunders, Philadelphia. pp 316-439.

[63] Caird, G.B. (1963). *Saint Luke (Pelican Gospel Commentaries).* Penguin Books, Harmondsworth. p 175.

[64] Bultmann, R. (1963) sees this story simply as a variant of the episode of the man with the withered hand and the other Sabbath healings (*History of the Synoptic Tradition.* pp 12 and 62).

[65] Note the discussion in Meier, J.P. (1994). *A Marginal Jew. Vol 2.* pp 756-757 (n 146).

[66] Hobart, W.K. (1892). *The Medical Language of St Luke.* Dublin University Press, Dublin. p 24. Hippocrates used the term to denote an oedematous person (*Aphorisms* 6.27 and note also 3.22; 4.11; 6.27 and 7.47), but it is interesting to note that Galen uses the term ὑδρωψ εις ἀμιδαof diabetes (*De medica* 7.81) although this is clearly not the sense in the present context.

[67] Cadbury, H.J. (1920). *The Style and Literary Method of Luke (Harvard Theological Studies No 6).* Harvard University Press, Cambridge, MA. pp 39-72.

[68] Note however, the specific matters which set this story apart from the other Sabbath healings and which raise issues of historicity, noted in Meier, J.P. (1994). *A Marginal Jew.Vol 2.* p 711.

[69] Marshall, I.H. (1978). *Luke.* p 649.

[70] Koester, H. (1990). *Ancient Christian Gospels: their History and development.* SCM, London. p 337. He sees this narrative as a variant of Mark

1:40-45. Bultmann, R. (1963) considers that the story is secondary and Hellenistic in origin (*History of the Synoptic Tradition.* p 33).

[71] Quoted in Marshall, I.H. (1978), *Luke.* p 649.

[72] Achtemeier, P.J. (1978). The Lukan perspective on the miracles. p 160

[73] Caird, G.B. (1963). *Saint Luke.* p 195.

[74] On the problem of the actual number see Metzger, B.M. (1958). Seventy or seventy-two disciples? *New Testament Studies.* 5. 299-306.

[75] See Hahn, F. (1965). *Mission in the New Testament.* SCM, London. pp 43-44.

[76] Note, however, the contrary view expressed by Marshall, I.H. (1978) *Luke.* pp 412-414. He comments that it 'is unlikely that Luke simply invented the second mission in order to deal with the tension between the call of the Twelve by Jesus and the existence of a larger body of evangelists in the church and more probable that he was following his sources. It seems likely the mission sayings in Q were addressed to a wider group than merely the Twelve, and that Mark has narrowed their scope'. Note also the comments of Plummer, A. (1915). *Luke.* pp 270-271.

[77] Marshall, I.H. (1978). *Luke.* p 415. Seventy was also the number of the specially selected elders who were anointed by the Spirit in order to assist Moses in governing the people (Numbers 11:4-32) and this may also have been the model for the number of disciples, especially as it was a frequent number in administrative groupings from the Sanhedrin down (see Rengstorf, K.H. (1964). Επτα κτλ. In: Kittel, G. (ed). *Theological Dictionary of the New Testament.* (Eerdmans, Grand Rapids). ET. p 634).

Chapter 5

THE HEALING MINISTRY OF JESUS:
THE JOHANNINE TRADITION

The work of Jesus as healer, which bulks so large in the Synoptic narrative ... is but feebly represented in the Fourth Gospel'

C.H. Dodd

The most cursory reading of the Gospel of John is sufficient to make the reader aware of the very different approach of the writer of the Fourth Gospel to the life and ministry of Jesus from that of Mark and the other synoptic evangelists. The almost frenetic activity of the Synoptic Gospels is replaced by a much more measured pace and a very marked reduction in the number of healings that appear in the narrative. Before considering this matter in more detail, however, it is necessary to examine briefly the background and purpose of John's Gospel.

The 'New Look' on John

The past forty years or so have seen a major change in the way in which scholars have approached the Johannine literature in general and the Gospel in particular. The assumptions and presumptions of the critical orthodoxy of the first half of the twentieth century have been seriously challenged and, while no universal consensus has been achieved on all matters of debate, there is increasingly general agreement on many broad background issues [1]. This general agreement applies particularly to the background of the thought forms found in both the Gospel and letters and the relationship of John to the Synoptic Gospels. Few would hold today, for example, that purely 'Hellenistic' concepts dominated John or that it was written to accommodate the good news of Christ to a Greek audience, or even that it was written to fill out or correct the picture of Jesus that the synoptic writers had furnished. Rather, John's Gospel is being treated seriously as an independent witness to the life and teaching of Jesus, based on its own distinctive tradition and its own interpretation of it.

There is a high level of probability that the fourth evangelist neither knew nor used the Synoptic Gospels, but derived his tradition independently, in part from the original sources common to all the evangelists, indeed common to the whole primitive Church or, as Robinson believed, entirely from his own first-hand material, the source, rather than the sources [2]. It should be emphasised that, as Dodd observed, the tradition that lies behind the Fourth Gospel is potentially as near the 'source' as that which lies behind any of the other Gospels. It may be said to rest on, and preserve a tradition shaped originally in the cultural context of a Jewish-Christian community in the early decades of the first century [3].

This basic tradition, probably oral in nature, has been edited and developed to meet the requirements of John's 'circle' of followers, traditionally centred in Ephesus [4]. It has been noted earlier in this study that the Gospels, in common with all the New Testament documents, were rooted in real life situations that helped to shape the basic tradition and led ultimately to the publication of the final documents. In many ways, the writings of John reflect a different Christian tradition from that found in the Synoptic Gospels or the Pauline writings and the Gospel itself is to be seen as an independent historical witness. It should be given at least an equal weight as that given to the synoptic evangelists, although reflecting a greater degree of interpretation and theological reflection and development [5]. As C.H. Dodd put it, 'Behind the fourth gospel lies an ancient tradition independent of the other gospels and meriting serious consideration as a contribution to our knowledge of the historical facts concerning Jesus Christ' [6].

The background of John is being increasingly recognised as that of Palestinian Judaism. Not only do the categories of thought belong to that milieu, but also the tradition which underlies the Gospel shows a far greater and more accurate awareness and knowledge of Palestine and its topography than that shown by the synoptic writers who frequently show a lack of genuine first hand knowledge of places and their relationships. The Fourth Gospel contains a wealth of geographical and topographical references, often given with remarkable precision. The specific sites and places named in the Gospel have been analysed and summarised by C.H.H. Scobie [7] and he has demonstrated that, while many have synoptic parallels, a greater number are peculiar to John and indicate a genuine awareness of topographical relationships. As Westcott remarked over a century ago, John 'moves about in a country he knows'. This local knowledge is displayed particularly in the accurate and detailed descriptions of Jerusalem and its environs.

The thought of the Gospel would also indicate a Palestinian background for John, and it appears more closely related to 'sectarian' Judaism than any other part of the New Testament. The relationships seem to be particularly close to that form of Judaism represented in the literature of the Qumran Community (the so-called Dead Sea Scrolls). The links between Qumran and John are numerous and have been discussed at length by several authors [8].

The 'signs' in John's Gospel [9]

Whatever the number of 'signs' that may be identified in this Gospel, and there are divergent opinions about this, one thing stands out: the number is extremely limited when compared with the accounts of the 'miracles' of Jesus in the Synoptic Gospels. This applies quite specifically to the accounts of healing, which in John, account for only about five per cent of the text, whereas in Mark, for example, the records of healing and exorcisms account for something like twenty per cent of the total material. In addition, John's approach tends to be much more matter of fact and there is little of the wonder, awe and amazement in the response of the crowds as they see the activities of Jesus in the synoptic accounts. Indeed, there is little emphasis at all in John on the crowds that followed Jesus and which are such a prominent feature of the synoptic narratives. The commonest word for crowd in John is ὄχλος, used on only 20 occasions (as against 49 times in Matthew for example) and the word λαος occurs on 36 occasions in Luke and 15 in Matthew, but John uses it on only three occasions.

There is also a further major difference between the synoptics and John in that he reports none of the exorcisms that figure so prominently in the first three Gospels, nor indeed, does he display any interest in demons or demon possession. No reader of John would gain the impression that Jesus was an itinerant 'wonder worker' of the type that was common in the Mediterranean world of the first century, nor indeed is he presented even as a charismatic prophetic healer.

The emphasis in John, in fact, is on the words of Jesus to which the 'works' or 'signs' point as symbolic or prophetic actions, designed to convey the reality of the message. The events are never recorded as 'wonders' (τερατα) as they are in the synoptics, but always as 'signs' (σεμεια), events which illuminate faith or are, in Wilkinson's terms, 'revelations to faith' [10], rather than events which have a specific role in stimulating it. The spiritual symbolism of the 'sign', therefore, is of much greater importance than the actual material effect of the action, which seems to be a direct consequence of John's incarnational theology. However, as in the Synoptic Gospels, faith is a necessary accompaniment of the action and both sets of traditions reflect the early understanding of the 'miracles' as an essential part the proclamation of the good news of Jesus the Christ and as part of the work given to Jesus by the Father.

The very definite Old Testament background to the underlying ideas of the terms 'work' and 'sign' that John consistently uses, cannot seriously be doubted. These are words that are frequently related to the creative and saving activity of God for his people and John's use of them points to his understanding of the continuity between the actions of the Father in creation and salvation and those of Jesus, the Son, who comes from the Father and is one with him. They point also to the person of this one who has been sent from the Father, who comes as the bread of life, the light of the world, the resurrection and the life. John has specifically chosen those stories which meet his purpose and he is much more interested in certain particular signs that Jesus did, rather than being concerned with the simple fact that Jesus did signs.

There are four healing stories in the 'signs' collection and they are used as vehicles for John's emphasis on this saving activity of God in new creation which, in the story of the raising of Lazarus (John 11:1-46), culminates in the final prefigurement of the resurrection of Jesus and the resurrection life that he imparts in his Spirit to his followers. Nonetheless, these actions are somewhat ambiguous, very much as were the stories in Mark, and they play no significant part in the legitimation of Jesus and his claims. Indeed, as in Mark, the signs may occasion either belief or unbelief, producing crisis and division (John 2:11, 11:25,29). It may be argued, therefore, that they play a secondary role, evoking a response in those with minds open to see and understand what is going on, reinforcing and deepening faith where this already exists, but not providing the primary foundation out of which faith will grow. Marianne Thompson has expressed this well, noting that faith 'cannot demand authenticating evidence and cannot believe without risk. But if revelation loses that hiddenness so that it can be seen unambiguously in the signs, then the paradox of the incarnation appears threatened as well. Instead of the Word hidden in the flesh, it would be possible to turn away from the incarnate one to the visible glory of the Word; instead of sheer humanity, one would see only divinity' [11].

John's theology, for all its so-called development, is thus, in this area at least, very close to Mark and appears to retain something of the 'primitive' understanding of the work of Jesus as paradoxical and ambiguous. However, there is a twist in this, for John sees the failure of people to believe to be as much deliberate stubbornness and blindness as it is because of the ambiguity of the actions or words of Jesus (John 9:39-41; 12:37-41). Only the eyes of faith grasp the reality of Jesus; the signs, nonetheless, may help in the process, providing that they are seen as revelations of the divine glory and not just 'miracles'. In spite of the very real differences, John and Mark tend to stand together over against the developments that are to be seen in Matthew and Luke, and in the apocryphal Gospels at an even later stage in the developing tradition.

The Johannine healing narratives

The nobleman's son: John 4:46-54//Matthew 8:5-13//Luke 7:1-10

The story of the healing of the nobleman's son is the only account of healing in John that has a synoptic parallel. In the synoptic tradition it belongs to the non-Markan material designated as 'Q' which, in general, contains only the teaching of Jesus. It is the only 'miracle' story in this material that is given an extended treatment (the very limited account of the healing of the mute demoniac in Matt 12:22,23//Luke 11:14 is merely a 'peg' on which to hang the lengthy dispute on whether Jesus is in league with Beelzebul and it serves no other purpose). The synoptic form of this event is not distinguishable from that of John in any important matter, except that there is more conversation in the synoptic accounts and, perhaps surprisingly, they also show more theological development with the emphasis on the symbolic importance of the healing as a picture of the future salvation of the gentiles. What differences exist between the accounts, as R E Brown has pointed out, are 'susceptible of logical explanation, either in terms of the vagaries of independent traditions, or as a reflection of the peculiarities of the individual evangelists' [12]. The similarities are much more apparent than the differences and suggest strongly that the same incident lies behind each of the three accounts, as Lindars remarked, 'the differences are too great to suggest that John is dependent on the Synoptic accounts. It is better to suppose that it comes from a parallel development of the same original tradition [13].

Each account agrees that the 'nobleman' came from Capernaum. The additional information that Jesus was in Cana of Galilee (a correct designation which John regularly used to distinguish it from other places of the same name) suggests that in its original form this story formed a pair with the story of the wedding at Cana (John 2:1-12), particularly as it is referred to as 'the second sign'. The exact status of the man described by John as a 'nobleman' is not entirely easy to ascertain. Both Matthew and Luke refer to him as a centurion and thus, by inference, assume that he was a gentile. This is borne out by the statements about faith outside the people of Israel and Matthew's additional logion concerning those who would come from east and west and enter the kingdom before those of the original chosen nation (Matt 8:11,12), a saying that occurs in a quite different setting in Luke (13:28-30).

John calls the man a king's officer or 'nobleman' (βασιλικος), a term that may mean a person of royal blood or a royal official. It is probably correct to assume that John intended his readers to understand the status of this man in the latter way. Josephus used the term to describe not only the relations and servants of the Herodian royal households, but also of the soldiers [14]. It seems reasonable to infer, therefore, that he was an officer under Herod Antipas, who while strictly not a king, was frequently referred to in this way (note Mark 6:14). The synoptic use of the term 'centurion' is thus likely to refer to an officer in Herod's army, which was modelled on the Roman pattern, but it seems clear that there has been an accommodation to a Graeco-Roman readership. He may have been a Galilean Jew or a gentile mercenary (possibly Syrian), although the synoptic writers have understood him to be a gentile and have based their theological interpretation of the healing on this assumption. It is possible that John may have had a particular reason of his own in using the term 'royal official' [15] and he certainly presents him as a Jew. Meier remarks that 'both Q's presentation of the "centurion" as a Gentile and John's (implicit) presentation of the "royal official" as a Jew serve the theological goals of the respective writers. Neither presentation can claim to be a theologically neutral reporting of the original event' [16]

All the accounts agree, however, that he was a man of substance and status in the community [17].

The sick person is described as the official's son. John used three words to describe him: παις (v 51) [18], the diminutive παιδιον (v 49) and the regular word υιος (vv 46, 47, 50, 53). There is good reason to think that the original tradition probably used the word παις. Matthew has followed this faithfully and Luke less so. The term has an inherent ambiguity and may mean 'boy' or 'servant'. It is, thus, a reasonable presumption that the man was a personal servant along the lines of an officer's batman. Luke seems to have grasped this point and has replaced παις with δουλος in key parts of his narrative, whereas John has interpreted the word to mean the official's son, particularly obvious in his use of παιδιον when the official entreats Jesus to come before his 'little boy' dies.

There are parallels between this story and the healing of the Syro-Phoenician woman's daughter, particularly in its Markan form [19]. What is interesting is that, as Brown remarks, 'these parallels affect particularly the elements in John's account that were not matched in the story of the centurion's son' [20]. These variations suggest that, although there was a single incident recalled in each of the differing accounts, the form of the tradition used by John differed significantly from that used by the synoptic evangelists. It seems very likely, therefore, that there is thus multiple attestation of this story. That stories should develop differently in different branches of the tradition is not surprising and points to the essential historicity of the core that is common to each account [21]. Attention should also be drawn to the parallel in the Rabbinic traditions of Rabbi Hanina ben Dosa who was also credited with healing at a distance [22]. The story relates the healing of the son of the famous Rabbi Gamaliel, who was also suffering from a severe fever, and it has a number of points of contact with the healing of the official's son. Vermes sees these stories as a reflection of a recognised charismatic healing pattern [23].

The medical details are extremely sparse. The record states simply that the man/boy was suffering from a fever (πυρετος) and was close to death (ημελλεν αποθνησκειν). It is of interest to note that the only two stories of curing people with febrile diseases in the course of Jesus' ministry occur in Capernaum, the other person healed being Peter's mother-in-law (Mark 1:29-31). It was observed in the discussion of that story (see pp 63-65) that there was a strong possibility that such fevers were malarial, given the fact that this was a common condition in the low lying and often swampy areas around the Sea of Galilee and the upper Jordan valley. People with severe attacks of malaria might well be close to death. It is certainly the way they would feel!

It is worth reflecting on the fact that the account does not actually describe a cure taking place, but records the fact that the official's son/servant recovered from his illness: in John's words, 'he got better' (κομφοτερον ἐσχεν: an aorist tense to which English versions fail to do justice). Such a statement might well be in accord with a knowledge of the natural history of malaria and an awareness of what is frequently a self-limiting attack. Jesus reassures the father that the crisis has passed, the fever has gone and rather than being at the point of death, his son now lives and has recovered [24]. Lindars makes the point that the way in which John tells the story really amounts to a refusal by Jesus to do anything and the man must believe without seeing any action being taken [25]. Wilkinson's suggestion that the illness was possibly acute meningitis or encephalitis is solely conjectural and not borne out by any clues in the narrative [26]. The suggestion of malaria is admittedly surmise, but it does at least have some element of historical probability.

The Johannine version of the story provides a consistent account that makes good sense. It is remarkably free from any of the embroidery detectable in the versions of Matthew and Luke, both of which tend to emphasise the miraculous. Although Luke provides no details of the illness, Matthew states that the centurion's son was paralysed and in extreme distress, although he does not imply that he was close to death. Assuming that Matthew's account came from a different oral tradition and making the further assumption that the illness was malaria, then it is not outside the bounds of possibility that Matthew's source retains a memory of the frequent rigors that accompany this disease. The synoptic evangelists also place greater emphasis on the 'distance' element in the incident, the healing taking place as a response to the centurion's faith and his recognition of his own unworthiness as a gentile (and, perhaps, a suggestion that Jesus might not be willing to go to a gentile's house). The element of wonder is thus increased and, at the same time, the whole story is turned into 'a charter for the Gentiles' [27]. It would seem reasonable to suggest, therefore, that the Johannine narrative may well provide an account that is close to what actually happened.

The real interest in the story lies in the interpretation, the theological meaning that John derives from the narrative. As in the synoptic accounts, the main emphasis relates to the nature of saving faith. There is a blunt reminder that faith based on 'signs and wonders' (a conventional expression which occurs only here in John and is presumably taken directly from his source without alteration) is a totally inadequate basis for any commitment to Jesus, a point that Mark has already emphasised. The miraculous is not the ground of faith and only Jesus himself and the word he proclaims can provide an adequate basis for a life giving faith. The story seems to be designed to demonstrate the progression from a wrongly based faith, one based on external signs, through an awareness of what those signs reveal about Jesus the giver of life, to a genuine faith, based now on the life giving words of Jesus and which bring the whole household into blessing (v 53). The story may have been included in the Gospel, therefore, as a symbolic reflection of the characteristic progression to faith of the early Christian households. But John is nevertheless sounding a *caveat* - the adherence of a family to the Christian faith on the basis of 'signs and wonders' is not a satisfactory outcome of the Church's mission. Such a level of belief is too shallow and there must be the more profound response to Jesus as the Word, the one who communicates the creative, life-giving word of God. Such a point would have considerable significance in the environment of the gentile mission with the Hellenistic emphasis on the miraculous.

The healing at the Pool of Bethesda: John 5:1-18

This story and the two remaining healings to be considered are unique to John's Gospel. At the same time, however, there are elements in the narrative that suggest that it derives from the same sort of tradition as did the similar synoptic narratives. The form of the story is close to many of the synoptic stories, as Dodd has noted [28], although to suggest that it is a variant of Mark 2:1-12 on the basis of a few verbal parallels, such as the use of κραβαττος (pallet or bed roll) seems to be overstretching coincidences. The form of a story says nothing about its historicity and it needs to be borne in mind that a common form does not necessarily have to be regarded as something artificially imposed on the material, but simply the natural way in which such events would be described, as Wilkinson has observed [29].

There are a number of textual difficulties in the text of this story, particularly in relation to vv 2-4 [30]. From the point of view of this study, the only issue of importance is the omission of vv 3b and 4 from the better manuscripts. This description of the 'moving of the waters' represents scribal additions to explain v 7, when the man tells Jesus that he has no one to help him when the water of the pool 'moves'. It would appear that v 3b was the first addition and then a later scribe felt that further elucidation was necessary and added the comment about the activity of the angel (v 4). It is likely that these glosses represent an accurate reflection of popular traditions about the pool and its healing properties. There is also uncertainty about the name of the pool itself, although the evidence of the Copper Scroll from Qumran (3Q15) would seem to support the traditional name of Bethesda [31]. There is little doubt that the writer of John knew his Jerusalem very well indeed.

The story centres on a man who had apparently been unable to walk for thirty-eight years, although John is silent on the actual nature of the man's disability. The assumption is made that he was paralysed, but this is simply because later in the story Jesus tells him to pick up his bed roll and walk. John merely says that he had some form of 'sickness' (ἀσθένεια, more correctly perhaps, in this context, 'weakness') that prevented him from getting to the front of the crowd when the water was disturbed. Even though he appears to have no friends to help him, he must have been able to get around to some extent, else how did he manage to get to and from the pool? There seems to be little in the narrative that would actually suggest that the man was paralysed in the normally accepted meaning of the word.

The healing immediately gives rise to accusations of breaking the Sabbath and recalls the similar controversies in the Synoptic Gospels. It is worth noting, however, that the ground of the dispute lies, not in the healing itself, which did not result in the breaking of any Sabbath law, but in the fact that the man, following his cure, went off carrying his bed roll, the last of the thirty-nine works forbidden on the Sabbath day by the later rabbis [32]. John, however, unlike the synoptic writers, does not make the Sabbath issue the crucial matter that set the Jerusalem establishment against Jesus, but rather the issue of blasphemy (v.18) [33].

Although this story is distinct from that of the healing of the paralysed man at Capernaum (Mark 2:1-12), there are, nonetheless, a number of important parallels between them that provide insight into the methods that Jesus used. An important point to note is that in both cases, guilt feelings seem to be strongly associated with illnesses that have very similar symptoms. In both cases, also, the heart of the cure is associated with forgiveness and the consequent removal of the central cause of the anxiety state and its related symptoms. It is suggested, therefore, that the man in the story was suffering from some form of functional illness, which, as in the synoptic examples, was most likely a form of conversion disorder that had developed as a means of escape.

The underlying escape from guilt is admittedly implicit in this story, but the interpretation is given weight in view of the words of Jesus to the man after he had been cured; 'sin no more, in case something worse happens to you' (v 14). As in the synoptic stories, the method of treatment appears to have been a form of abreactive technique (see the notes on this treatment at pp 60f) and freedom from a recurrence of symptoms in these circumstances is dependent upon reinforcement. The words of Jesus thus point to the way in which the man's health may be maintained.

There are further clues to the personality of the man in the initial questioning by Jesus, presuming this is based on a genuine memory retained in the tradition [34]. His friends appear to have left him alone to wallow in his misery and he displays a querulous grumbling about those who can race him to the curative waters. Both these factors seem to reflect the sort of inadequate behaviour patterns which fail to be able to meet the problems of life, but take refuge in a flight from reality manifested in this type of conversion (hysterical) disorder. Jesus, as an experienced healer, would recognise among the many sufferers at the pool those who might benefit from his ministry. Thus, it is this man, with his functional illness, who is singled out for help, rather than others who probably had genuine physical pathology, but who would not have responded to the healing/curative methods of Jesus which were primarily directed to dealing with the psychological aspects of illness.

The importance of these healings, for John as much as for the other evangelists, did not lie in the event itself, but in what it signified. The healing is a sign of the life-giving power of Christ, but it also points on as a sign of the End. This healing belongs 'within the horizon of biblical eschatology as it had been formulated by the prophets of Israel, *Then shall the lame man leap as an hart* (Isa 35:6) ... nor does the Fourth Evangelist pass over from eschatology into symbolism ... The lame man healed is a sign to the Jews that in Jesus they are confronted by the final judgement, by life or death, by the Son of man' [35].

The man born blind: John 9:1-41

Each of the Gospels records an example of Jesus bringing sight to a blind person. This story, however, is the only one in which the blind man is stated to have been born blind. There is undoubtedly a theological point being made. The man who has never seen stands as symbolic of all humanity which has never seen the light of God, but exists in spiritual darkness from the moment of birth. The motifs of light and darkness, faith and salvation are evident throughout the controversy that follows the story of the healing. In itself, the healing occupies only three verses (vv 1, 6, and 7) around which John has constructed a complex theological discussion, as he does in the other 'signs'. Meier has called these compositions, 'superb pieces of literary and theological art that clearly reveal the fine hand of the Fourth Evangelist' [36]. The issue of whether verses 2 to 5 belong to the original narrative is a matter of debate. Some scholars have argued that the dialogue of these verses is not typical of a miracle story and is too overtly Johannine to be part of the original tradition [37]. These remarks of Jesus, however, are characteristic of sayings in the Synoptic Gospels (see for example Luke 13:1-5) and may well belong to the nucleus of the original story that John has not changed.

The statement that the man was *born* blind, however, does appear to belong to the original tradition of the story. There is no *prima facie* reason to doubt the basic historicity of a tradition that remembers the provision of sight to a person who had been blind from birth: such events are well documented in medical history and were noted in the discussion of the blind man of Bethsaida at Mark 8:22-26 (see pp 106-112). However, stories that are long in the telling tend to gain additional features in the process and in this respect, John's use of the verb ἀναβλεπω at v 11 to denote the man's reception of sight is important. The use of this verb was noted in relation to the cure of the blind man of Bethsaida and it has been argued convincingly that the verb always conveys the meaning of regaining or recovering sight [38]. If this is correct, then it would be inappropriate to use it of a man who had never seen before.

Some doubt, therefore, will remain whether John's story has taken on certain additional dimensions for theological purposes, although the rest of the account is clearly an accurate reflection of the methods that Jesus used and these have been attested separately by Mark in the story of the blind man of Bethsaida (Mark 8:22-26). If the man was genuinely suffering from congenital blindness, there are a number of widely different possible causes, although the most likely would have been congenital cataracts in view of the apparent method of cure. The commonest cause of congenital lens opacities in the first century is likely to have been one of the major congenital infection syndromes as it is today. Infections transmitted to the infant from the mother at birth (such as gonorrhoea) or maternal infections transmitted to the foetus (the best known example being rubella or german measles) may give rise to lens opacities of varying intensity [39]. John's statement that the blindness had been present from the time of birth (ἐκ γενετης), if an accurate reflection of the real situation and not merely a 'human interest' addition to the story to heighten the remarkable nature of the cure, would seem to indicate that the condition was present and obvious at birth, rather than something that developed in the post-natal period. It seems very possible, therefore, that the man was suffering from congenital cataracts, the most common cause of which in modern times is maternal rubella.

The likelihood of cataracts (congenital or later developing) being the cause of blindness is enhanced by the account of the healing, brief though it is. The similarities between the actions of Jesus in this story and in relation to the Markan story of the blind man at Bethsaida have been noted. In both cases, Jesus uses saliva and places his hands on the blind man's eyes. The additional features in this story are the use of mud on the eye and the washing in the pool of Siloam [40]. It has been noted earlier that details of the methods Jesus used in healing have very largely been omitted by the evangelists, probably for apologetic reasons, to avoid charges of magic being made against him or to heighten the element of the 'miraculous'. The existence of the details in this story is good evidence of the early nature of the tradition that lies behind it.

The importance of saliva in healing rituals was mentioned earlier in regard to the Markan stories and the later rabbis certainly appeared to believe that it had healing properties in certain circumstances, although there is a suggestion of some ambivalence about its use because of the association with magical practices [41]. What seems clear, however, is that neither the evangelist nor the onlookers in the story, saw the use of saliva by Jesus as being any different from the methods of other healers. As Twelftree remarks, 'in this aspect of his healing technique, the earliest Church was clearly not endeavouring to remove or isolate Jesus from his milieu' [42]. The saliva, however, is not applied directly to the man's eyes, but is used to make a mud paste that is then applied. Such an action would appear to have been an illegal action on the Sabbath [43], although some consider the Sabbath motif in this story something that the Evangelist has added later for his own purposes with regard to Jewish-Christian controversies and to give support to Christians facing expulsion from the synagogues [44]. The exact function of the action is not clear from the story, but if the man was suffering from cataracts, then the putting of the paste on the eyes would have afforded Jesus the necessary opportunity for couching them. There seems to be no reason to think that this was some form of symbolic action and it appears to have been an integral part of the method that Jesus used to heal. The time taken to get to the pool and wash the mud away would also have provided an opportunity for the man's eyes to settle down after the pressure placed upon them.

The major problem with the story is the immediate ability of the man to see and to interpret what he saw. Whether sight, with a genuine functional awareness of objects and an interpretive ability to understand what was being seen, could have come about within the time frame of the story is very debatable if this was truly a case of total congenital blindness. The interpretation of what is seen by the eye is an integrative function of the brain which takes time to develop; it is a learned function, as was discussed in relation to the story of Mark 8:22-26. The immediate problem for a person, blind from birth, who gains sight is one of recognition. Objects may now be seen, but they are not recognised for what they are, and a period of explanation and learning has to follow the ability to see. It would certainly be very remarkable for a person to be able to recognise, as opposed to seeing, an object in the immediate period after the gaining of sight. It would seem therefore, that for apologetic reasons, both restoration of vision and the subsequent visual learning process have become a single act of healing, compressed into an immediate time frame which has the purpose of emphasising the completeness of the healing action of Jesus.

It is not unlikely, however, that there was some degree of vision already present and this is normally the case with congenital cataracts that are rarely so profound as to obscure vision totally. In these circumstances, the man would have been aware of the nature and general shape of objects, even though he would have been seeing them through a fog, and he thus would not have been required to learn these details following the couching of the cataracts. It is likely, however, that his vision would have remained blurred to some degree after the couching because of the loss of the lens from the refractive pathway.

This story presents Jesus as a prophetic healer, very much in the tradition of the Synoptic Gospels. His true nature remains veiled and it is only spiritual insight that reveals him for who he really is. John makes this theological point clear as the story unfolds with the gradual and progressive 'opening' of the blind man's spiritual 'eyes' to the one who is the Light of the world. Indeed, the narrative is a skilful literary and theological development of the theme of growing discernment from knowing Jesus simply as a man (v 11), then as a prophet (v 17) and then moving to the final illumination that recognises Jesus as Son of God to whom one's life is to be committed. This progression stands in stark and total contrast to the blindness of the Pharisees, who should have had a greater spiritual insight and been able to recognise in Jesus, the one sent from God. The narrative never loses sight of the reality of the event, however, and there is, as Marianne Thompson has noted, 'a fine touch of Johannine irony: the Jews seem intent on proving to the man that he had never been blind!' [45]. It is not surprising that there is also an important aspect of condemnation in the story, a motif which is important to the overall purpose of John. As Barrett comments, 'The effect of the true light is to blind them (ie. the Pharisees), since they wilfully close their eyes to it. Their sin abides precisely because they are so confident of their righteousness' [46].

It was noted earlier that this story may also have a bearing on the increasing divorce between Jewish and Christian communities in the wake of the Jewish War. Wayne Meeks, among others, saw the language of the Johannine literature, with its tendency towards sectarianism, as a reflection of the 'actual trauma of the Johannine community's separation from the synagogue and its continuing hostile relationship with the synagogue' [47] which resulted in severe social dislocation. Martyn has developed this theme and argued that the story may be understood as a drama being enacted on two levels simultaneously - at the level of the historical Jesus and at the level of the evangelist's contemporary situation with individuals in dire need as a result of this social disruption [48]. It seems a reasonable hypothesis to consider that John's references to exclusion from the synagogue (ἀποσυνάγωγος at v 22 and also 12:42 and 16:2) refer to the experience of Jewish Christians, at the time he was writing, being expelled from their synagogues due to their acknowledgment of Jesus as Messiah.

Once again in the story, as told by John, the healing event is totally subservient to the theological purpose and becomes a peg for a sermon. Far more than in the synoptic tradition, the story is merely a vehicle for the development of teaching designed to meet the specific needs of the Johannine community. Nonetheless, in doing so John also provides the community with a purpose of its own in proclaiming the glory of Jesus as Son of God to those who recognise him.

The raising of Lazarus: John 11:1-44

Barnabas Lindars has remarked that the 'raising of Lazarus is one of the most dramatic and impressive of the compositions of the Fourth Gospel' [49]. Nonetheless, the story is an account of an event which more than any of the other healing stories has become so woven into the fabric of the theological development that it is virtually impossible to separate the underlying tradition from the Johannine theology it is designed to set out. There is no separate and related discourse, but rather a connected narrative throughout, with interspersed segments of conversation, argument or discussion which bring out the theological meaning. To quote Lindars once again, 'the more prominent the theological aim, the more difficult it becomes to view the narrative simply in terms of history [50]. Thus, quite apart from any consideration of the possibility that such an event as the raising of a dead man to life could actually happen, serious objections have been raised about the historicity of the story as set out.

The most important objection relates to the fact that John provides this account as a great sign of unprecedented importance and, perhaps even more importantly, as the direct occasion of the final plotting to kill Jesus. The event is part of the final revelation of the glory of God and, as Fuller has remarked, since 'the cross is the supreme manifestation of the glory or saving action of God in Jesus, the Lazarus miracle serves as a curtain raiser to the passion' [51]. If this is the genuine historical setting, then it is surprising that there is no mention of such an event in the synoptic narratives. Mark records no instance of a dead person being raised, nor, strictly, does Matthew (although note his presentation of the story of Jairus' daughter and Matt 11:5). Luke records the story of the raising of the widow's son of Nain, but there is little doubt that this is a very different narrative from the raising of Lazarus.

Such considerations have led some scholars to the conclusion that the Lazarus story is a purely Johannine construction, possibly based on the Lukan parable of Dives and Lazarus (Luke 16:19-31). The synoptic relationships, tenuous though they may be, are in respect of names and the geographical setting of the event and if there is a connection, then it may be that John (or his source) has turned the parable into an event [52]. On the other hand, Dodd has argued that the name Lazarus entered the story from a confused memory of an actual event of the raising of a man with this name. He remarks that 'there is nothing exceptional in the occurrence of the name in the Lucan parable that calls for an explanation. Such an explanation would be forthcoming, if there existed in the pre-Johannine tradition a story about the resurrection of a man called Lazarus, with a general implication that this did not win men to faith in Christ. From that it would be an easy step to inserting a name in the adapted folk-tale about the rich man and the poor man in Hades' [53]. Robinson has also argued cogently for the correctness of placing this story in relation to the events of the final days of the life of Jesus [54]. This may be trying to push conclusions beyond the evidence, since it would seem that the form of the original tradition is difficult if not impossible to uncover, particularly in the way the details of the burial, for example, seem have been taken over from the Evangelist's own account of the burial and resurrection of Jesus [55].

It is reasonable to assume, however, that the story of Lazarus represents a sound tradition, at least as sound as that of the widow of Nain's son. Indeed, it is worth making the point that, as the other 'signs' in this Gospel may be shown to be derived from traditional backgrounds, there is no reason why this story should not also be traditional, even though there are no synoptic parallels [56]. What is historical in the Gospels is no longer determined by what is synoptic, as Smalley has pointed out [57]. Thus, 'it can be asserted that John had access to synoptic type traditions which were not identical with the forms of the same or similar traditions in the Synoptics' [58].

John has thus developed this traditional story as the ultimate dramatisation of the theme of Jesus as the giver of life and the revelation of God's glory in him. In the Johannine treatment, the story makes the cross something that is inevitable and it is, at the same time, a profound interpretation of the saving action of God in the incarnation, death and resurrection of the Son. The link between the passion and the resurrection is made quite specific in the details of the story: Lazarus was buried in a tomb covered by a stone, he was wrapped in grave clothes similar to those of Jesus and this extended even to the use of a special cloth wrapped around the head and face (v 44).

The issues surrounding the interpretation of the event as a 'healing' relate to what John may have added to the narrative in order to develop the theological themes. The question has to be asked therefore, whether the story represents a combination of several different strands of tradition in order to produce a composite whole which has been worked together with consummate skill and artistry to produce a single coherent narrative. In this regard note should be taken of Lindar's attempt to see in this story traces of an original exorcism narrative, based on the presence of the unusual verb εμβριμαομαι (deeply moved) at vv 34 and 38, which he relates to a vehement rebuke of a spirit by Jesus [59]. In this writer's opinion such an interpretation requires a degree of rewriting of the tradition which seems to be at variance with the general approach of the evangelists who, while expanding and reinterpreting, did not appear to change substantially the underlying nature of the stories. As Beasley-Murray put it, 'We may, accordingly, hold in view the strong probability of the development of the tradition relating to the death and recall to life of Lazarus, but be modest in our claims to delimit the strata in the tradition and to define their precise relations to one another' [60]. It may well be that John built up his story from more than one source, but there seems to be no good reason to doubt that a real event lies behind the narrative in spite of the problems associated with it.

The story as it stands lacks any statements or information on which any diagnosis of the terminal illness of Lazarus may be made and it is totally pointless attempting to speculate. The tradition suggests that there was a fairly rapid progression, but the main interest focuses on the actual restoration of an apparently dead person to life. John states that Lazarus had been dead for four days before Jesus finally arrived on the scene (v 17), a statement that emphasises that this was not to be understood as merely a comatose state, but genuine death. After three days there was no hope of resuscitation, death was definite and irreversible and the three days of strictest mourning had already passed before Jesus arrived [61]. Nonetheless, at the command of Jesus, the dead man comes out of the tomb and is restored to his family.

The way one approaches this event will depend upon individual preconceptions. If it be assumed *a priori*, that such a thing as the restoration to life of a dead person is impossible, then this narrative can be treated as no more than mythical or legendary and can have no genuine historical basis: its only value lies in the spiritual message that the story conveys. At the other end of the spectrum stands the fundamentalist, who, for equally *a priori* reasons, insists that things must have happened exactly as recorded. Neither extreme represents a sound basis for examining this narrative. The possible developments of the story, making it a literary whole, require to be considered, particularly the extensive conversations that form the vehicle of the expounded theology.

The core of the narrative, however, constitutes a simple story of the raising of a dead man. It is reasonable to ask the question whether Lazarus was really dead in the clinical sense, but this is a question to which no definitive answer may be given on the basis of the existing data. That he was considered dead by family and friends is abundantly clear from the story, but as was pointed out in regard to the story of the widow of Nain's son, the diagnosis of death is not always as straightforward as might be expected. If that be true today, how much less straightforward would it have been in the first century. There are numerous records in recent years of people who have been pronounced dead by qualified staff and who have then revived in the mortuary or some other embarrassing spot. It is not beyond the bounds of possibility that such a situation lay behind this story. This, however, is no more than speculation and it would be claimed by many that the adoption of such a viewpoint, merely represented another attempt to avoid the difficult implications of the narrative as it stands.

The fact is that there are simply not enough data to make any reasonable statement or medical judgment about this story. From John's point of view, the story was a vehicle to emphasise that Jesus was the Lord of life. This sign is the decisive revelation of Jesus as the life giver, not simply as a past event, but in the here and now as he gives life to his people so that they should never die (vv 25,26). The tragedy of the story, however, is that this 'greatest act of revelation in a sign leads to ... an extreme hardening of unbelief into hatred and mortal enmity' [62]. This, however, is in the very nature of revelation as John comprehends it, for it compels a response, a decision about the nature of the disclosure has to be made. As Burge puts it, 'According to the Evangelist, only two options are open: offence or belief. After the raising of Lazarus, some Jews believe (11:45) while other conspire to kill Jesus (11:53). No one simply walks away' [63].

Signs and the disciples in John

There is no account in John of any programme of preaching and healing given to the disciples during the ministry of Jesus. Furthermore, the use of the word σεμειον (sign) is reserved exclusively for the actions of Jesus and at no point in the Gospel is it ever suggested that the followers of Jesus would perform 'signs'. There is one place, however, where John suggests that the disciples will perform the same 'works' (ἐργα) as Jesus and even greater ones (John 14:12). The context for this statement is the lengthy 'upper room discourse', a section which, in John, replaces the synoptic account of the Last Supper and the institution of the Eucharist. It thus forms part of a word of encouragement to a group of disciples aware that things were going badly wrong and designed to help them through the period of the Passion and sustain them in the ongoing community life after Jesus has 'gone to his Father'.

It is clear that there is no emphasis here on any marvellous or miraculous character in terms of the nature of what the disciples will do. The emphasis is on the power that they will receive through the coming of the Paraclete. Indeed, as Brown has noted, the reference to 'greater than these' (μειζονα τουτον) as a description of the disciple's activity, is not a measure of its magnitude. This is a concept totally foreign to the New Testament documents and these words form a reference to the eschatological nature of what the disciples of Jesus will do in the future, because the work of Jesus himself is now complete [64]. Throughout John's Gospel, the 'works' are those acts of Jesus in which the power and glory, as well as the character, of God are made known. It is now given to the followers of Jesus to continue his work in revealing the glory of God seen in Jesus, a glory that stems from the cross and is displayed in grace and truth. Further, there appears to be a direct reference here to the words spoken by Jesus at John 5:20 where the 'greater works' in his own ministry underline the eschatological nature of that ministry and relate to the realisation of the life of the future age, not at a final resurrection, but in the present experience of those who believe.

These 'greater works' of bringing the life of God to men and women are now to be performed by the disciples in their onward and outward mission into the world. 'The greater works therefore are the gathering of many converts into the church through the activity of the disciples (cf 17:20; 20:29), which however is effective only through the continuing power of Jesus' word and the work of the Holy Spirit (15:26f)' [65]. It is the fulfilling of salvation-historical realities, the bringing in of the new people of God into the new Messianic community in a way that was never apparent during the earthly ministry of Jesus. Consequently, the predominant significance of the 'works' has nothing to do with 'signs and wonders', but everything to do with the wider apostolic activity in proclaiming the gospel as the source of light and life and the attendant results of this activity as people respond to Jesus who, now 'lifted up', continues to draw everyone to him (John 12:32).

The history of the apostolic mission, exemplified, say, in the work of Paul, forms the commentary on this statement. John, therefore, not only reduces the element of the 'miraculous' in the ministry of Jesus itself, but also provides no basis for any understanding that miraculous powers were to be given to the disciples to allow them to perform 'signs and wonders' in the post-Easter period. Throughout the Gospel, the importance of the signs of Jesus lies in their spiritual and theological significance and it is solely in this sphere that John sees the 'greater works' of the disciples being performed. John certainly provides no foundation for any ongoing practice of 'miraculous' healing in his community.

Notes and references

[1] See for example, Dodd, C.H. (1953). *The Interpretation of the Fourth Gospel*. Cambridge University Press, Cambridge; (1963). *Historical Tradition in the Fourth Gospel*. Cambridge University Press, Cambridge; Smalley, S.S. (1978). *John: Evangelist and Interpreter*. Paternoster Press, Exeter; Brown, R.E. (1979). *The Community of the Beloved Disciple*, Paulist Press, New York; Barrett, C.K. (1982). *Essays on John*. SPCK, London; Robinson, J.A.T. (1985). *The Priority of John*. SCM, London; Cassidy, R.J. (1992). *John's Gospel in New Perspective*. Orbis Books, Maryknoll; Brodie, T.L. (1993). *The Quest for the Origins of John's Gospel*. Oxford University Press, New York.

[2] See the extensive discussion in Robinson, J.A.T. (1985). *The Priority of John*. pp 36-122.

[3] Dodd, C.H. (1963). *Historical Tradition in the Fourth Gospel*. p 426.

[4] There is a useful summary of the early traditions about John in the little volume by F.F. Bruce (1979). *Men and Movements in the Primitive Church*. Paternoster Press, Exeter.

[5] The issue of whether John was dependent on the synoptic accounts or used his own distinctive tradition has been much debated and the debate is outside the limited boundaries of this study. The dependence of John on his own oral tradition and related sources has been stressed by several scholars including C.H. Dodd, (1953). *The Interpretation of the Fourth Gospel*. pp 457-453; (1963). *Historical Tradition in the Fourth Gospel*. pp 5-6; R.E. Brown, (1966). *The Gospel according to John (Anchor Bible)*. Doubleday, New York. pp xxxv, xliv-xlvii; B. Lindars, (1972). *The Gospel of John (New Century Bible Commentary)*. Marshall, Morgan & Scott, London. pp 25-28 and R. Schnackenburg, (1968). *The Gospel according to St John*. Burns and Oates, London. Vol 1. pp 26-43. Contrary views have been expressed, notably by the Louvain school, especially F. Neirynck (1977). John and the Synoptics. In: de Jonge, M. (ed). *L'Evangile de Jean: Sources, Rédaction, Théologie*. Louvain, Leuven University. pp 73-106 and (1984), John 4. 46-54: Signs source and/or synoptic gospels. *Ephemerides Theologicae Lovaniensis*. 60. 367-375. Note also the discussion in Barrett, C.K. (1978). *The Gospel according to St John*. SPCK, London. pp 42-54 and the views of extensive dependence not only on the synoptics, but also other New Testament documents argued by Brodie, T.L. (1993). *The Quest for the Origin of John's Gospel*. Oxford University Press, New York. The last word goes to J.P. Meier (1994) who remarks that to 'explain John's text simply as a creative redaction ... would involve John in a literary process that would be highly erratic, eclectic and eccentric - some might even say unintelligible' (*A Marginal Jew: Rethinking the Historical Jesus*. Doubleday, New York. Vol 1. p 724).

[6] Dodd, C.H. (1963). *The Interpretation of the Fourth Gospel*. p 423.

[7] Scobie, C.H.H. (1982). Johannine geography. *Studies in Religion*. 11. 77-84.

[8] See particularly, Brown, R.E. (1965). The Qumran scrolls and the Johannine gospel and epistles. *New Testament Essays*. Paulist Press, New York. pp 102-

131; Charlesworth, J.H. (ed). (1972). *John and Qumran.* Chapman, London and Morris, L. (1969). The Dead Sea Scrolls and St John's gospel. *Studies in the Fourth Gospel.* Paternoster Press, Exeter. pp 321-358.

[9] A detailed discussion of the theological issues related to the signs in John's gospel is outside the specific scope and purpose of this study. See the full discussion in Schnackenberg, R. (1968) *John.* Vol 1. pp 515-528.

[10] Wilkinson, J. (1966). A study of healing in the gospel according to John. *Scottish Journal of Theology.* 19. 442-461.

[11] Thompson, M.M. (1988). *The Incarnate Word: Perspectives on Jesus in the Fourth Gospel.* Hendricksen, Peabody. MA. p 81.

[12] Brown, R.E. (1966), *The Gospel according to John (Anchor Bible).* Doubleday, New York. Vol 1. p 193. See also the full discussion of the issue in Schnackenburg, R. (1968). *John.* Vol 1. pp 471-475.

[13] Lindars, B. (1972). *John.* p 44f. This healing story is given an extended treatment by J.P. Meier (1994). *A Marginal Jew.* Vol 2. pp 718-726.

[14] Josephus, *Antiquities of the Jews.* 15.289; 20.214; *Jewish War* 1.45; 2.431, 483, 596; 5.474; *Life.* 400.

[15] Note the discussion Barrett, C.K. (1978). *John.* p 247.

[16] Meier, J.P. (1994). *A Marginal Jew.* Vol 2. p 723. He remarks that 'as the tradition developed both orally and in writing, it was interpreted differently by different groups' (p 724). He suggests that an equally ambiguous Aramaic usage may lie behind the narrative

[17] John Robinson (1982) argued that he may have been a Nabatean and perhaps even to be identified with Chuza (Luke 8:3), but this seems close to a flight of fancy (*Priority of John.* p 69).

[18] This is the only occasion on which John uses this word and the Western texts replace it with υἱος which is regarded as a scribal assimilation to the context by the editors of the UBS and Nestlé editions of the Greek New Testament (see Metzger, B.M. (1971). *A Textual Commentary on the New Testament.* United Bible Societies, New York. p 207).

[19] See the discussion in Dodd, C.H. (1963). *Historical Tradition in the Fourth Gospel.* pp 190ff.

[20] Brown, R.E. (1971). *John.* p 194.

[21] Reviewing the evidence, J.P. Meier (1994) remarks, 'these considerations make it seem more probable that behind the primitive tradition lies a historical event from the public ministry of Jesus' (*A Marginal Jew.* Vol 2. p 726).

[22] Babylonian Talmud *Berakoth* 34b. C.K. Barrett (1978) quotes the passage in full (*John* p 249).

[23] See the discussion of Jesus and charismatic Judaism in Vermes, G. (1983). *Jesus the Jew.* SCM, London. 2nd edn. pp 58-82. Note also the discussion in N.T. Wright (1996). *Jesus and the Victory of God.* SPCK, London. pp 147-197.

[24] A similar, although not identical view, was put forward by J.H. Bernard, (1928). *The Gospel according to St John (International Critical Commentary).* T & T Clark, Edinburgh. p clxxx.

[25] Lindars, B. (1972). *John.* p 203.

[26] Wilkinson, J. (1966). Healing in the Fourth Gospel. p 446.

[27] Lindars, B. (1972). *John.* p 202.

[28] Dodd, C.H. (1960). *Historical Tradition in the Fourth Gospel.* pp 174-180.

[29] Wilkinson, J. (1972). Healing in the Fourth Gospel. p 444. He goes on to remark, 'it is a relevant comment to point out that over the years a set form for the description of a medical case has become almost universal and is taught to all medical students trained in the western tradition of medicine. No one has yet drawn any form-critical conclusions from this fact, and certainly no one has ever suggested that we might judge the truth or otherwise of a medical case history from the form in which it is presented!' The same point is made by René Latourelle (1988) who argues that story telling forms would be stereotyped with the same type of sickness being told with the same formula (*The Miracles of Jesus and the Theology of Miracles.* Paulist Press, New York. p 218).

[30] The textual problems are discussed fully in Barrett, C.K. (1978) *John.* pp 251-253. Note also Metzger, B.M.(1971). *Textual Commentary.* pp 208-209.

[31] Discussion of these issues is outside the purpose of this study. See the excellent summary of recent knowledge in Meier, J.P. (1994). *A Marginal Jew.* Vol 2. pp 729-730 (nn 9-11) and also the extensive discussion in Robinson, J.A.T. (1985). *The Priority of John.* pp 54-59.

[32] See Mishnah tractate *Sabbath* 7:2; 10:5.

[33] Barnabas Lindars (1972) argued strongly for a composite origin to this story in which John has incorporated Markan material into his own tradition in order to produce a 'Sabbath incident' (*John.* 209-210). It seems more likely, however, that the story is a unity containing a passing reference to the fact that it took place on the Sabbath and this fact has been used as the basis of the expanded dialogue that occupies vv 9-18 (so G.R. Beasley-Murray (1987). *John.* p 72, among others).

[34] Note the comments of R.E. Brown (1966), 'The story of the healing seems to stem from primitive tradition about Jesus' and 'A character such as this could have been invented, but one would expect to see clearer motivation for such a creation' (*John.* p 209).

[35] Hoskyns, E.C. and Davey, F.N. (1947). *The Fourth Gospel.* Faber and Faber, London. 2nd edn. p 263 (italics original).

[36] Meier, J.P. (1994). *A Marginal Jew.* Vol 2. p 694.

[37] On the structure of this story see, for example, Dodd, C.H. (1963). *Historical Tradition.* pp 181-188; Fortna, R.T. (1988).*The Fourth Gospel and its Predecessor.* T&T Clark, Edinburgh. pp 109-113; Martyn, J.L. (1979). *History and Theology in the Fourth Gospel.* Abingdon, Nashville. Rev. edn. pp 24-36; Bligh, J. (1966). The man born blind. *Heythrop Journal.* 7. 129-144 and also the major commentaries *ad loc.*

[38] See the discussion in Johnson, E.S. (1979). Mark 8:22-26: The blind man from Bethsaida. *New Testament Studies.* 25. 370-383. Note however, the

examples of the use of ἀναβλεπω with complete loss of the force of ἀνα (again), given in Bauer. p 51.

[39] See Martyn, L.J (1992). Pediatric ophthalmology. In: Behrman, R.E., Kliegman, R.M., Nelson, E.W., Vaughan III, V.C. (eds). *Nelson Textbook of Pediatrics*. 14th edn. pp 1578-1579. See also Vaughan, D. Asbury, T. (1983). *General Ophthalmology*. Lange, Los Altos, p 123.

[40] Incidentally, the mention of this pool is another example of the Evangelist's accurate knowledge of pre-AD 70 Jerusalem. The pool of Siloam was situated at the southwest corner of the eastern hill of biblical Jerusalem and the area is mentioned elsewhere in the Bible at Isa 8:6 and Luke 13:4. See further Meier, J.P. (1994). *A Marginal Jew*. Vol 2. pp 696-697.

[41] Note the discussion in Barrett, C.K. (1978). *John*. p 358.

[42] Twelftree, G.H. (1993). *Jesus the Exorcist..* p 158

[43] See further Harvey, A.E. (1982). *Jesus and the Constraints of History*. SCM, London. pp 37-38.

[44] Note the discussion in Martyn, J.L. (1979) *History and Theology in the Fourth Gospel*. pp 30-36 and Horbury, W. (1982). The benediction of the *minim* and early Jewish-Christian controversy. *Journal of Theological Studies*. 33. 19-61 among others.

[45] Thompson, M.M. (1988). *The Incarnate Word.* p 59.

[46] Barrett, C.K. (1978). *John*. p 354.

[47] Meeks, W. (1972). The man from heaven in Johannine sectarianism. *Journal of Biblical Literature*. 91. 44-72.

[48] Martyn, J.L. (1979). *History and Theology in the Fourth Gospel*. pp 30-36. Note also Carroll, K.L. (1957). The Fourth Gospel and the exclusion of Christians from the synagogue. *Bulletin of the John Rylands Library*. 40. 19-32. R.E. Brown (1966) also sees this section of the gospel as having been written (or rewritten) with the post-Jamnia situation in mind (*John*. Vol 1. p380).

[49] Lindars, B. (1992). Rebuking the spirit: A new analysis of the Lazarus story of John 11. *New Testament Studies*. 38. 89-104.

[50] Ibid. See also Richardson, A. (1941). *The Miracle Stories of the Gospels*. SPCK, London. p 120 and the discussion in Barrett, C.K. (1978). *John.* pp 388-389.

[51] Fuller, R.H. (1963). *Interpreting the Miracles*. SCM, London. p 105.

[52] Note the discussion in Lindars, B. (1972). *John*. pp 383-384.

[53] Dodd, C.H. (1963). *Historical Tradition in the Fourth Gospel*. p 229. Dodd has also demonstrated that the form of the Johannine narrative is essentially the same as that of other miracle stories.

[54] Robinson, J.A.T. (1985). *The Priority of John*. pp 217-223.

[55] Note for example, the mourning women, the rock-hewn tomb, closed by a stone, the mention of the grave clothes and specifically the face cloth. These all find their counterparts in the Resurrection narrative in John 20.

[56] Note the comment of Barnabas Lindars (1972), "All the previous healing miracles have had a basis in the tradition, and there is no reason to deny that this one has too, especially as other cases of raising the dead are recorded'

(*John.* p 384). For a detailed examination of the critical problems of this story see the extensive treatment of J.P. Meier, (1994). *A Marginal Jew.* Vol 2. pp 798-832.

[57] Smalley, S.S. (1978). *John: Evangelist and Interpreter.* p 180. See his whole discussion of the raising of Lazarus (pp 178-184).

[58] Lindars, B. (1981). John and the synoptic gospels: a test case. *New Testament Studies.* 27. 287-294.

[59] Lindars, B. (1992). *New Testament Studies.* 38. 89-104.

[60] Beasley-Murray, G.R. (1987). *John.* p 186.

[61] See Stahlin, G. (1965). Κοπετος. In: Kittel, G. (ed). *Theological Dictionary of the New Testament.* Eerdmans, Grand Rapids. Vol 3. pp 842-845.

[62] Schnackenberg, R. (1971). *John.* Vol 2. p 377.

[63] Burge, G.M. (1987). *The Anointed Community: The Holy Spirit in the Johannine Tradition.* Eerdmans, Grand Rapids. p 79.

[64] Brown, R.E. (1971). *John.* p 633.

[65] Barrett, C.K. (1978) *John.* p 460. Note also the comment of G.R. Beasley-Murray (1987), 'The context reveals that the "greater works" that the Father is to "show" the Son, greater than those given him to do thus far, are manifestations of resurrection and judgment ... Thus the "greater works" that the disciples are to do after Easter are the actualization of the realities to which the works of Jesus point, the bestowal of the blessings and powers of the kingdom of God upon men and women which the death and resurrection of Jesus are to let loose in the world'. *John.* p 255.

Chapter 6

HEALING IN THE EARLY CHURCH: THE WITNESS OF THE ACTS OF THE APOSTLES

There is no way to avoid the problem of miracle in Acts
C J Hemer

Introduction

The Acts of the Apostles sets out to continue the story of the origins of Christianity from the first Easter to the arrival of Paul in Rome. It stands as a unique and pioneering work that had no predecessor and no real successors either. The much later apocryphal Acts of Peter, Thomas and similar works are merely examples of legend, straight fiction and Gnostic propaganda which illustrate how very little the early Church knew of the first circle of apostles and disciples and their later activities. C.C. Smith has remarked that 'the early church resumed interest in "the Twelve" too late to recover the originals, even the most important, or their individual fate. Instead there was spawned the legendizing accounts in the "Apocryphal New Testament" ' [1].

It may be accepted without question that the Lukan portrait was idealistic ('idyllic' was Fitzmeyer's word [2]), for Luke had a point to make. He was concerned to develop a picture that emphasised the way in which God's purposes were being fulfilled as the message of salvation in Christ travelled across the Roman world from the obscure capital of a lowly eastern province to the very centre of Roman imperial rule [3]. In doing so he emphasised, at the same time, the centrality of the Gentile mission to the life and very existence of the Church.

There has been a considerable amount of debate about the historical value of the Lukan sources for Acts. There is no doubt that the author intended to write history and F.F. Bruce remarked that 'of all the Evangelists, it is Luke who approaches most nearly the standards of the classical historians. His work, viewed as a historical document, stands in the line of descent from Thucydides' [4]. The problem he faced as an historian, however, was that, although there was a plentiful stream of tradition for the words and works of Jesus, 'for the time between Easter and the death of Paul ... it was just a trickle' [5]. Moreover, there can be little doubt that Luke had a specific purpose in mind in inspiring and strengthening the faith of his readers. In order to build his picture he has used a variety of sources, which, as in the Gospel, he has brought together to form a coherent narrative. Just as the Gospel sources may be shown to be dependent on reliable traditions, so the sources for Acts form an important source of knowledge of early Christianity. As in the Gospels, however, these reliable traditions are subservient to the author's main purpose and there can be little doubt that Luke has taken liberties, in particular with the chronological framework. This is very apparent in those sections that deal with Paul and his mission, in which 'the chronological framework of Pauline data has to be reconstructed from Paul's letters' [6].

The problem of historicity is particularly acute with regard to the healings and other 'miracles' recorded in Acts. To what extent do these events rest on a secure foundation of genuine historical tradition and to what extent have they been embroidered (even invented) to enhance the standing of the apostles in a Hellenistic world that appeared to give great prominence to wonders, prodigies and 'miracles'? There can be no simple answer to this question. It has to be recognised that the world view of the first century was very different from that of the twenty-first and there would have been different criteria of authentication. Further, while there may have been much popular credulity, there was also much scepticism about such events, as was discussed earlier in Chapter 2, although, as also discussed in that chapter, there was a tendency for a greater emphasis on 'miracles' as the Christian mission focused on the gentile world.

Two things need to be borne in mind. In the first place, it is important to distinguish between the genuinely theocentric views of Luke that understood 'miracles' as demonstrations of the loving power of God and that other impression which he allows to emerge from his narrative, an impression that is ultimately the start of a long and suspect Christian tradition of apologetic based on the power of 'miracles' to persuade [7]. Secondly, there is a need for a properly critical approach to the narrative so that, as Hemer has pointed out, when a 'miracle' story is accepted as having an historical basis, the acceptance of the event will be in spite of the 'miracle' and not because of it [8].

It has already been observed in relation to the Gospel that Luke looks to the Old Testament to provide the matrix for comprehending what was happening with regard to the revelation of God's saving purposes in Jesus Christ. In such a context, it was also the Old Testament that provided the determinative concepts for understanding the purpose of the 'miracles'. The irreducible core of this matrix was the activity of God in providence and in judgment throughout the history of Israel and especially at the critical moment of the Exodus, seen by the biblical writers as the paradigm for all God's future redemptive activity. God had been present to work in this way in the person of Jesus through whom a new Exodus had been accomplished.

Luke now takes these ideas further and shows God to be similarly present and active in the apostolic community that was continuing the words and work of Jesus in the world. If Luke's Gospel was the story of 'all that Jesus began to do and teach' (Acts 1:1), then the Acts represents the continuation of the work of the risen Christ through the presence of his Spirit empowering his people. For Luke, therefore, it was imperative that the apostles not only continued to teach the words of Jesus, but also continued his mighty acts. Healings and exorcisms performed by the apostles in the name of Jesus were thus a theological necessity, for they demonstrated that the same Spirit that had empowered Jesus was now at work in the infant 'Jesus community'. The Spirit that was the Spirit of prophecy and gave power to the preaching of the apostles was also the Spirit that gave the necessary 'power' to accomplish miraculous healings and exorcisms [9].

The apologetic value of 'miracle' for Luke was thus highly important and while it has to be recognised that he was writing for an apparently sophisticated audience, at the same time, it was also one that largely accepted the reality of magic and other powers with that strange mixture of scepticism and popular credulity, noted previously. In such a social context, Luke considered that 'it was part of the evidential force of the miracles to demonstrate the loving and authentic power of God as superior to every rival claim' [10]. This was the direction in which the Church's approach to the miraculous was to move in succeeding years, so that the missionary outreach of the early mediaeval Church, for example, used 'miracles' as a necessary part of the proclamation of the good news. Richard Fletcher has commented, 'Demonstrations of the power of the Christian God meant conversion. Miracles, wonders, exorcisms, ... *were in themselves* acts of evangelisation' [11]. It would seem that Luke was seeking to provide an apostolic base for this practice, one that was certainly apparent by the late second and third centuries as the Church's mission was no longer based within Judaism, but had moved thoroughly into the pagan world [12].

Nonetheless, although Luke undoubtedly considered that there was a legitimate argument from 'miracle', he was sufficiently realistic to know that the unbelieving will not be convinced by remarkable happenings and healings by themselves, nor, it should be added, will they be convinced simply by an argument based on propositions. Those who wished to remain unconvinced would remain unconvinced, regardless of what was said or done. This indeed is the whole point of the story of Dives and Lazarus in Luke's Gospel. People may well recognise that they have seen events which are apparently inexplicable, but this does not mean that they will necessarily accept the explanation that is given to them. No one will deny that events occurred which the early Christians interpreted as 'signs and wonders'; the problem is to decide how such events are to be understood today, recognising that even before Luke set down his history, there would have been a process of expansion and development within the tradition [13].

The degree of expansion that may be considered to have occurred will, to some extent, be dependent on the date that is ascribed to the book of Acts. An early date would be against any significant degree of development in the tradition, whereas a later date would give the opportunity for such expansion to have taken place. Further, an early date for the book would mean that eyewitnesses to the ministry of the apostles and the events described would be still alive and they would have acted as a check against excessive development or exaggeration. A discussion of the involved arguments in favour of early or late dates for the composition of Acts is outside the scope of this study. The assumption will be made, therefore, that Luke-Acts is to be dated towards the end of the first century, probably about AD 80 or a little later. The Lukan history would thus have been composed about one or two generations after the events described and thus at a time when many, if not most, of the performers in the drama would have died [14].

The discussion that follows will examine the nine examples of healing or related events in Acts, but will omit detailed consideration of the sudden death of Ananias and Sapphira (Acts 5:1-11). Paul's blindness and its cure at the time of his conversion will be discussed in chapter 7 as part of the general consideration of Paul's health in the section dealing with both Paul and his writings and not in relation to the accounts in Acts. In addition to the nine specific accounts of apostolic healing of sickness, comment will also be made on the two generalised statements about healings attributed to Peter's shadow and Paul's handkerchiefs.

The healing narratives in Acts

The lame man at the gate of the Temple: Acts 3:1-10

This story is a direct sequel to the account of the remarkable events of the Feast of Pentecost and, as Lüdemann has noted, it attests the miracle of the outpouring of the Holy Spirit on the disciples [15]. It is a sample of the many signs and wonders that the apostles in particular were to be able to perform through the power of the Spirit (Acts 2:43). The story is told with a wealth of detail, a characteristic of Luke's story telling as was noted in the consideration of the Gospel material, and he notes both place and time exactly. Peter and John were going up to the Temple for the second of the stated times of prayer: the ninth hour, about 3.00 p.m. in the afternoon and the time of the evening sacrifice. The so-called Western Text (D) adds a clarifying adverbial comment, το δειλιον ('in the afternoon'), to emphasise this point. As they reach the Beautiful Gate, they meet a man who is stated to have been lame from birth.

The identification of the Beautiful Gate remains a matter of ongoing dispute. Josephus does not mention it in his very detailed descriptions of the Temple, although he refers to a gate made from Corinthian bronze [16]. The later description of the Temple in the Mishnah also makes no specific mention of the Beautiful Gate, although referring to the Nicanor Gate [17], usually taken to be the same gate as that to which Josephus refers. There appears to be a general consensus in favour of identifying Luke's Beautiful Gate with the Nicanor Gate of the Mishnah and the gate of Corinthian bronze described by Josephus. It would appear to have been on the eastern side of the Temple, possibly between the court of the gentiles and the court of women and was clearly close to Solomon's Portico (v 11). The latter seems to have been a general gathering place (John 10:23 and Acts 5:12) [18]. Jews may not have considered that they had entered the Temple proper until they had passed beyond the court of gentiles, an implication that seems to be supported by the text (vv 2,3).

Luke describes the man as lame from birth, literally 'from his mother's womb' (χωλὸς ἐκ κοιλίας μητρὸς αὐτοῦ). It is one of the characteristics of Luke's writings that κοιλια always refers to the uterus (womb), whereas it would appear that the word was more normally used of the body cavities in general (thorax and abdomen) or the intestines [19]. It seems possible that Luke was following the usage of LXX (for example Judges 16:17, Psalm 22:10), but the word is also used to mean the uterus at Matt 19:12, John 3:4 and Gal 1:15 (although this latter example undoubtedly echoes Old Testament usage). It is also possible that Luke is reflecting some form of common parlance. As a lame man, the beggar was unable to participate fully in Israel's worship [20]. There would appear to be a deliberate connection here with the programme apparent in the healings of Jesus, discussed in previous chapters. The emphasis is on the restoration of someone who had previously been cut off and unable to play a full part in the community of Israel so that he may now take up his proper place. Luke is emphasising that the time for the restoration of all things has now dawned and is being displayed symbolically in this healing as it had been in the work of Jesus.

The lame man sees Peter (and John, who appears throughout the story as an afterthought) approaching and begins to ask for alms. It has been suggested that the use of the imperfect, ἠρώτα, may indicate the incompleteness of the action (so Haenchen [21]), but it seems more probable that it reflects the typically reiterated appeal of an eastern beggar (so Bruce [22] and Barrett [23]). Peter is described as fixing the beggar with his eye (ἀτενίζειν is a favourite verb of Luke. It is found in Luke-Acts on 12 of the 14 occurrences of the verb in the New Testament). The way is now opened for the healing to take place.

Instead of the expected monetary donation, the beggar receives restoration to normal function and becomes able to walk. The cure is effected 'in the name of (that is, 'on the authority of', or 'by the power of') Jesus of Nazareth'. It has been suggested that the use of the 'name' in this context represents a form of Christian magic being practised, on the basis of the belief in the power of certain divine names [24]. Luke, however, consistently distinguishes the activity of the apostles from magical practices (note Acts 8:9-11; 19:18-19, etc) and there is no suggestion of magical compulsion in any of the Lukan narratives [25]. Rather, it would seem that Peter has learned from his Master the use of abreactive methods and there is thus an operative command, 'walk', followed by the confirmatory action of Peter who pulls the man to his feet (it is difficult to see how πιασας can have the connotation of a healing touch in this context). The result is that the man becomes able to walk: rather, he is able to 'leap like a hart', thus fulfilling the prophecy of Isaiah 35:6.

Hobart [26] argued strongly that Luke used the words στερεοω ('to make strong'), βασις ('foot' and σφυδρον ('ankle') as medical terms, referring to Galen and the Hippocratic corpus for examples of such technical usage. However, βασις would appear to have many more literary than medical associations and its meaning of 'foot' would seem to have a poetic origin [27]. Similarly, σφυδρον (an unusual form, replaced in later MSS by the more normal σφυρον) does not appear to be in any sense a distinctively medical term [28]. Luke's vocabulary would seem, therefore, to be much more literary than medical. Witherington's comment that 'These terms may ... be taken as one small piece of evidence consistent with and supporting the notion that Luke was a doctor, though by no means proving it' [29] should be considered an overstatement.

The story as set out seems to be a Lukan revision of a traditional story told about Peter. The addition of John to the narrative seems to be in order to provide the necessary additional witness who would be able to stand beside Peter to give account before the Jewish Council (Acts 4:20). The story has the typical construction of a miracle story and closely parallels the synoptic forms, ending with the crowd giving glory to God as it responds to the amazing event it has witnessed. The major emphasis of the story, in fact, is on this result and it is important to note the close parallels between this narrative and the story of the healing of the paralysed man at Luke 5:17-26.

The wonder of the crowd and the response of ordinary people to what they have seen stand in stark contrast to the wilful blindness of the Jewish authorities in the face of the revelation of God's salvation in the person of Jesus, working through his anointed apostles. In order to emphasise this point, Luke has set the story in the context of a lengthy speech to the people of Jerusalem and a subsequent defence by the apostles before the Sanhedrin. The whole is a superb literary construction that reaches its climax, not in the response of the crowd, but in the impressive declaration to the rulers of Israel that only in the name of Jesus is salvation to be found. The whole story thus becomes an example of the 'argument from the lesser to the greater' - if, in the name of Jesus, a beggar may be restored to health ('saved', 4:9), how much more, in the name of Jesus, shall full healing ('salvation', 4:12) be given to all who believe? William Kelly once noted, 'if such was the instant virtue of the name of Jesus for the lame man, what would not follow faith in that name if Israel believed?' [30] The whole narrative is a fine example of Luke's rhetoric, drawing attention to the close links between what Jesus did and what his followers are now doing, in his name and through his power.

While Luke's theological purpose is clear, the medical aspects of the story present more difficulties. There is no reason to doubt the basic tradition of a lame person becoming able to walk. The essential problem lies in the statement that the man had been lame from birth, a statement that suggests some form of congenital anomaly or birth injury. The most common of such conditions would be some form of club foot (talipes) [31]. The severity of the man's condition is further emphasised by Luke's suggestion that he could not walk at all, but had to be brought to his begging pitch by his friends (one wonders whether there is an echo here of the story of the paralysed man who was let down through the roof by his friends). The story as recounted presents serious difficulties. It should be borne in mind that the earliest Gospel traditions do not even present Jesus as healing congenital conditions of such magnitude.

It has been observed earlier that there is a tendency in the later traditions to extend the range of conditions that are healed and Luke in particular enumerates a range of chronic diseases of exceptionally long standing in order to emphasise the triumph of God's power in seemingly impossible circumstances. It seems likely that such a factor is in operation in this story so that the basic tradition of a lame man being healed, becomes the healing of man who had been lame from birth. On the other hand, the man himself may have amplified his condition and its effects by claiming that he had been in that condition from birth. Such exaggerations are not uncommon in situations where it is important to gain the sympathy of passers by and exaggeration is also a feature of the psychological conversion type disorders that have been regularly encountered in previous healing stories. It would seem much more probable, therefore, that the original situation was represented by a healing of a man with a conversion disorder ('hysterical paralysis') affecting his lower limbs, thus forming a parallel to the types of condition that the early traditions show Jesus to have been active in healing (Mark 2:1-12; 3:1-6, etc.). From Luke's point of view it emphasises that what the disciples were doing was not different in kind from what Jesus had done. The issue of conversion disorder as a probable basis for many of the recorded healings was discussed in detail in relation to the Markan narratives in chapter 3.

The paralysed man at Lydda: Acts 9:33-35

The story of Aeneas, the paralysed man at Lydda, is closely associated with the account of the raising of Tabitha at Joppa, and they should probably be treated as a pair, in view of the similarities in language between them. They appear to be two traditional stories about Peter that Luke has incorporated into his narrative at this point to give 'the opportunity of bringing Peter down from Jerusalem in the direction of Caesarea, which was no small distance away' [32]. Both these stories thus form part of Luke's chronicle of the movement of the gospel away from Jerusalem to the wider world and the related inclusion of the gentiles. In consequence, they represent a stage in the fulfilment of the command to proclaim the good news, beginning at Jerusalem and extending in ever-widening circles to include the civilised world of the time, which, from Luke's point of view, meant the evangelisation of Rome.

Aeneas (a thoroughly Greek name, possibly foreshadowing the imminent move to the gentile mission [33]) was suffering from some form of weakness or paralysis. Luke has used the more technical term παραλελυμενος (as at Luke 5:18) in preference to the more popular παραλυτικος of the other New Testament writers. Hobart has remarked that this usage 'is in strict agreement with that of the medical writers' [34], but that really gives no ground for drawing conclusions about the writer's background. The condition was clearly chronic and had lasted for some 'eight years' (a more probable meaning of the phrase ἐξ ἐτων ὀκτω than 'from eight years old'). Such circumstantial details are typical of Luke's storytelling and probably represent a Lukan elaboration designed to give greater verisimilitude (note Acts 3:2 and 4:22 for similar time comments).

The actual healing is accomplished with a word of authority closely parallel to the statements of Jesus in the Gospels. Essentially, the statement of healing is simply factual: 'Jesus Christ (a noteworthy comment emphasising that the healing has nothing to do with Peter) is healing you' (ἰαται in this context should be considered an aorist present [35]) and this is followed by the command to 'make your ('bed', understood)', presumably a command to get up [36]. The account bears a pronounced similarity to the Gospel healings and the use of εὐθυς ('immediately') and κραββατον ('bed roll') have an almost Markan ring to them [37]: It seems certain that the language owes much to the Gospel healing traditions, although it may well be representing an accurate tradition of apostolic methods: using the same abreactive techniques for healing this type of condition as did Jesus in the Gospel stories. The resultant response of the local populace is typical of Luke's rhetorical hyperbole. His regular use of πας ('all') in such situations is in order to denote a significant response or impression (note Acts 2:43; 3:11; 5:5,11, etc).

The possibility that this narrative represents a retelling of a story from the Gospel traditions that has now become attached to a 'Life of Peter' cannot be discounted, but equally, there is no reason why Peter should not have been involved in the same methods of healing as Jesus. Indeed, one might be surprised if he was not, for it seems highly probable that Jesus passed on the methods that he used in healing to his immediate circle of followers. There is little doubt that, if one assumes the genuineness of the tradition, the healing of Aeneas follows very much the same pattern as the healing of similar conditions in the Gospels. It is reasonable, therefore, to assume that he was also suffering from a psychological conversion disorder, what might be termed an 'hysterical paralysis' [38]. Some eight years before this meeting with Peter, Aeneas had been confronted by some form of intolerable situation, the only answer to which was a flight from reality expressed as this 'hysterical paralysis'. The discussions of the Gospel healings at an earlier stage in this study suggested that such conditions figured highly in the healings of Jesus and there is no need to repeat the discussion of the characteristics of this type of illness or the methods of dealing with them.

It is a reasonable assumption that the apostles utilised the same techniques as Jesus in dealing with this form of illness, as this story would indicate. On the other hand, the possibility that this story derives originally from a Gospel tradition that has become attached to a 'Life of Peter' cannot be discounted entirely.

The raising of Tabitha: Acts 9:36-43.

The parallels between this narrative and the Gospel story of the healing of the daughter of Jairus, particularly in its Markan form (Mark 5:22-43), are almost too close to be accidental, even to the extent of close verbal parallels. Miracle stories frequently follow the same general form, but here the closeness goes beyond form to what appears to be the same story told in two different contexts. The key elements for comparison are set out in Table 6:1.

Table 6:1 Comparative details of the stories of Tabitha and the daughter of Jairus

Mark 5:21-24, 35-43	Acts 9:36-43
Jairus goes to Jesus and beseeches him (παρακουλενται) to come and make his daughter well.	Two disciples are sent to Peter beseeching him (παρακαλουντες) come without delay.
Jesus went with him (και ἀπηλθεν μετ᾽ αὐτου).	Peter rose and went with them (συνηλθεν αὐτοις).
When they came to the house,	When he had come, they took him to the upper room.
He saw a tumult and people weeping and wailing loudly ...	All the widows stood beside him weeping.
But he put them all outside (αὐτος δε ἐκβαλλων παντος).	Peter put them all outside (ἐκβαλλων δε ἐξω παντας).
Taking her by the hand he said, 'Talitha koum'.	Turning to the body, he said, 'Tabitha arise' (= Tabitha koum).
And immediately the girl got up. (και εὐθυς ἀνεστη)..	She opened her eyes and when she saw Peter she sat up and he gave her his hand and lifted her up (ἀνεστησεναὐτην).

It also seems probable that this story of Tabitha has been influenced, in its form at least, by the Elijah/Elisha cycle of stories from the Old Testament; there is certainly an echo of such passages as 1 Kings 17:17-24 and 2 Kings 4:32-37. It is not clear whether this link had belonged to the original tradition as Luke received it, but there is no doubt that in the Gospel narratives, Luke presents Jesus as a prophet in the Elijah/Elisha tradition [39] and such a view seems central to Luke's understanding of Jesus and his mission. It is suggested that in using these identical themes in the narrative, Luke is underlining the essential continuity between what Jesus did and what his disciples were doing. The prophetic ministry of Jesus, itself understood as the fulfilment of the Old Testament prototypes, is now being continued in the ongoing mission of the Church into all the world.

The nature of an event is always more difficult to determine than its interpretation, in this case its underlying theology. It seems highly likely that the Petrine traditions contained the memory of the apostle actually raising someone from the dead, but the reasonably close parallels between this story and the Markan tradition of the daughter of Jairus suggest that, at the very least, there is some degree of conflation between the two or, perhaps more probably, that a Gospel healing has been attributed to Peter. It would certainly be dangerous to make any attempt to delineate the medical circumstances of this story and the possibility that the accounts of both Tabitha and Aeneas are recensions of Gospel traditions remains a strong probability. The problems of interpreting accounts of resucitations or the restoration to life of dead or apparently dead people has been discussed in relation the widow's son of Nain (Luke 7:11-17) and the story of Lazarus (John 11:1-44).

The blindness of Elymas: Acts 13:6-12.

This brief interlude does not fall properly into the category of a healing (indeed, it is quite the opposite), but it requires inclusion in a study of this nature as an example of the way in which Luke contrasts the workers of magic with the power of God operating through the apostles. The magician Elymas (or Bar-Jesus) appeared to have been attached in some way to the court of the Roman proconsul Sergius Paulus, perhaps as a semi-official soothsayer. The narrative presents him as an opponent of the gospel and he is consequently characterised as a 'false prophet' and a 'son of the devil'. Luke thus makes the point that only those filled with the Holy Spirit, the Spirit of Jesus, can be true prophets able to proclaim the word of God. The magician's persistent efforts to influence the proconsul against Paul and his message eventually earn Paul's stinging rebuke. In a hard-hitting attack, using language borrowed from the Old Testament and thereby emphasising Paul's place in the true prophetic succession, he condemns the magician to temporary blindness.

The purpose of the story is to demonstrate the superiority of Christ to all forms of magic and sorcery. The word of Christ prevails against all who would oppose it and it is now reaching to those in high places in Roman society: an important element of the Lukan apologia. It is made clear that 'the hand of the Lord', here in judgment and not blessing, is upon those who would seek to prevent the spread of the gospel. In this case the judgment is immediate and in the form of blindness, something which clearly carries symbolic meaning in this context. Luke uses an unusual word to describe the effects. The word ἀχλύς is found only here in the New Testament and it carries the meaning of gloom, darkness or mistiness. Hobart [40] drew attention to the use of the word as a technical term for blindness by contemporary medical writers, but the expression is found widely in Greek literature and seems to occur more as a poetic word than a technical term [41]. As a medical term, it was used to describe the mistiness of the cornea following ulceration, but that is very different from the situation in this story. In this context, it simply describes the impact of Paul's pronouncement in terms of experience.

Too many commentators, particularly of the older schools, have failed to recognise the intrinsic probability of this story. There is no need to dismiss it out of hand as mere pious legend. There would seem to be little doubt that Luke has obtained the story from traditional sources (possibly from more than one) [42] suggesting a well-remembered event. Sudden blindness induced by an authoritative command is by no means unknown in cultures where the belief exists that certain persons have 'magical' or similar powers and it has already been observed, in the discussion in chapter 2, that Roman society was a culture which accepted the powers of magic and magicians.

The writer has observed similar events in Central Africa induced by traditional healers and they constitute a type of conversion (hysterical) response. Manifestations of this nature are frequent in such cultural groups and arise as reactions to various forms of 'stress', especially fear. The fear of bewitchment or the belief that a person has been bewitched, are particularly frequent precipitating factors in the development of trance states and various forms of conversion symptoms, including blindness, loss of speech and other forms of physical response, including death [43]. The suggestions or commands of the traditional healer, very much the 'authority person' as Paul was in this story, may either induce or remove such conditions.

Luke has a parallel story relating to Peter in the sudden deaths of Ananias and Sapphira in response to a similar word of command (Acts

5:1-11). Intense emotional stress may induce acute heart failure as a result of stimulation of the sympathetic nervous sytem (cardiogenic shock) which in this case was fatal and, as noted above, such sudden deaths occur in societies that believe in the power of words of authority. In the narrative about Elymas, he responded with fear to Paul's scathing denunciations, promptly developing 'hysterical' blindness in response to Paul's strong suggestion. It is important to recognise, therefore that there is nothing intrinsically impossible or improbable about this story. It has all the features of a well-remembered, real event in which temporary hysterical blindness was induced through Paul's authoritative suggestion in a person susceptible to such suggestion. From Luke's point of view, the important thing is its validation of Paul's credentials as an apostle. What happened to Elymas is a demonstration that the power of God resides in Paul, as it did in the other apostles, not only in word, but also in deed.

The crippled man at Lystra: Acts 14:8-10

There are close similarities between this story and the account of the healing of the lame man at the gate of the Temple by Peter. These similarities, however, are more likely to be due to the standardisation of form in miracle stories than they are to any genuine dependence. The story contains a number of specific Lukan features, such as the use of the word, ἀτενίσας ('fixing the eyes on') which occurs also at Acts 1:10, 3:4 and elsewhere and is almost specifically Lukan. In addition, the statement that the man was lame from birth is identical to the expression used at Acts 3:2. The narrative places a threefold emphasis on the impossible and hopeless state of the man - he was powerless (ἀδύνατος), he had been lame from birth and he had never walked. These statements are all designed to underline the magnitude of the mighty act that Paul was about to perform through the power of God.

Paul looks at the crippled man and sees that he has the 'faith to be healed ('saved') (πιστιν του σωθηναι)'. At this point Luke introduces the characteristic ambiguity in the healing stories that was noted in the Gospel accounts. The language turns attention from beyond the mere physical cure of a condition to the salvation that is brought about through faith in the Christ whom the apostles preach. This is further emphasised by the fact that the faith in this story clearly follows from Paul's preaching - Luke carefully notes that the man had heard Paul speaking (v 9). The emphasis has already shifted from physical healing to the underlying theological message and, as in the Gospels, the story becomes essentially a peg on which to hang an evangelistic sermon. The lame man becomes identifiable with all humanity in its moral and spiritual powerlessness that prevents it from walking in the right way from birth. Only the intervention of the power of God can so change the human situation that people may walk in the Way. Luke, however, does not develop this theme in what follows, but uses the story as the introduction to a further account of the progress of the gospel in the gentile world. The story is little more than the occasion for the more important developments that take place from v 11 onwards and which seem to be based on a separate strand of tradition that Luke has blended with the healing story [44].

There is another important apologetic aspect to these stories of Paul's activities. As Bruce remarked, it is 'plain that Paul is Luke's hero, and the main object of some passages of (Acts) seems to be to show how Paul stands head and shoulders above other men' [45]. In particular Luke wished to underline the fact that Paul did not in any way come behind Peter in the evidence of his apostleship (although Luke never actually ascribes this title to Paul) and demonstrates that he too, as much as the original Eleven, had a ministry that was confirmed by the 'signs of an apostle' (2 Cor 12:2). Did Peter heal a lame man (Acts 3:2ff)? - so too did Paul (as in this story)! Did Peter exorcise (Acts 5:16, a summary statement)? - so did Paul (Acts 16:18ff; 19:12, the latter a generalising statement)! Did Peter raise the dead (Acts 9:36ff)? - so too did Paul (Acts 20:9ff)! The list might be extended - encounters with magicians, escapes from prison and so forth. These parallels, however, do not of necessity imply Lukan invention, although there will certainly have been elaboration and development. The core may be viewed as rooted in history, for Paul himself claimed to have preached the gospel with the accompaniment of 'signs and wonders' (2 Cor 12:12; Rom 15:19), which categories are likely to have included healings, although Paul himself says nothing of exorcisms. That a collection of traditional 'Acts of Paul' should have grown up among the churches that he founded is hardly surprising and that such stories grew in the telling may be considered certain. It is a reasonable hypothesis that Luke obtained much of his basic material from such sources.

There is no intrinsic improbability in the likelihood that Paul undertook the sort of healing of psychosomatic and related disorders that seemed to have made up the great bulk of Gospel healings as well as those recorded in Acts. It is likely that this particular case represented another example of conversion disorder that responded to Paul's authoritative command within the heightened tension of the crowd situation. It thus constitutes yet another example of abreactive treatment that features so prominently in these narratives (note the discussion of these disorders and their treatment in relation to the Capernaum demoniac at Mark 1:21-28 as well as other instances in the Gospel narratives).

The Lukan (or perhaps tradition-based) addition about the lameness having been present from birth probably represents a development designed to raise the level of 'wonder' performed and thus bring greater glory to God. In this regard, it is significant that the Synoptic Gospel traditions do not represent Jesus as healing congenital conditions, a point noted earlier in connection with the healing of the beggar at the Temple gate. The only cure of a condition present from birth in the Gospel narratives is that of the man stated to have been blind from birth at John 9:1-7. In the discussion of that cure it was argued that, on the presumption that the story was based on an accurate tradition, the cure probably represented the couching of over-ripe congenital cataracts - one of the few forms of congenital pathology amenable to the ministrations of a traditional healer.

The accounts in Acts, however, show a clear shift towards activities and actions that would be expected from persons endowed with divine power as were the apostles, although they are not presented as 'divine men' on the Greek model (not even at Acts 28:6!). For apologetic and theological reasons, both Wilkinson and Rendle Short [46] assume that the cure took place exactly as set down and the condition was some form of congenital disorder, but the balance of probabilities must be in favour of a functional illness and some form of conversion/somatiform (hysterical) disorder seems most likely.

The girl medium at Philippi: Acts 16:16-18

This story is the only account of an actual exorcism attributed to the apostles. Luke refers to both Peter and Paul carrying out such activities (Acts 5:16; 19:12), but the only example he can find is this particular incident. It is perhaps significant that the only story in which an exorcism takes place is very different in character from those recorded in the Gospel narratives and attributed to Jesus. It seems possible that Luke's summary statements outlined what the writer thought ought to have happened, given who the apostles were and the divine power which was theirs through the Holy Spirit. However, when it came to providing real examples of such activity, he was able only to provide this one very atypical case that does not correspond in any way to the Gospel accounts of how Jesus undertook his exorcisms.

The story concerns a slave girl (παιδισκη, note Acts 12·13. The word is always used of a slave girl in the New Testament) apparently thought to have been possessed by the Pythian god Apollo. She is described as being possessed by a 'pythonic spirit' or 'a spirit named Python' [47]. The Greek god Apollo was believed to be embodied in a snake (the Python) at the oracle of Delphi and those possessed by him were known as πυθωνες, but the term is used here in apposition to 'spirit' (πνευμα) rather than to the slave girl herself. Nonetheless, it seems reasonable to see her as one thought to be possessed by the 'snake spirit' of Apollo which enabled her to speak in inspired speech (μαντευομαι). This is the only New Testament occurrence of this verb, although it was regularly used of pagan divination and prophesy [48]. The text would indicate that she was a highly successful fortune-teller, possibly using the gift of ventriloquism which had been equated with pythonic possession from antiquity [49]. In doing so, she brought her owners a considerable income. In modern parlance, she would have been termed a 'medium' and consequently her 'possession' was of a very different character from that of those people called 'demon possessed' who were encountered in the Gospel stories. Indeed, it is very probable that she was no more than a trickster, as is frequently the case with such people.

The narrative is very much a Lukan construction and it is full of words and phrases that are either unique to Luke or else predominate in Luke-Acts when compared to other portions of the New Testament [50]. It is not impossible, therefore, that Luke has considerably rewritten the story in order to turn an event of one sort (the unmasking of a fraudulent medium) into something else (an exorcism). The links with Luke 4:33-35 and 8:28-35 should be noted especially. It should also be observed that none of the usual features of an exorcism is present, such as the hostility of the demonic powers. In fact, the girl is essentially friendly and she goes about proclaiming the truth about Paul and his colleagues and their message, although admittedly in a somewhat misleading manner, describing them as 'servants of the Most High God'. Whether this term has a Jewish or pagan background is debatable, although in the context, Luke's understanding is clear [51].

The problem was really rather simple: this poor girl was being a nuisance and Paul shows considerable forbearance before eventually coming to the end of his patience. Even the actual 'exorcism' lacks any of the typical features of the head-on confrontation with evil that mark the narratives of the exorcisms of Jesus. It is possible that the girl may have been mentally handicapped in some way and this would explain the persistent way in which she followed Paul shouting about him. It is not certain how Paul actually dealt with the situation, although the narrative seems to suggest something approaching an abreactive type of technique. However, the details are so sparse that it would be foolish to build anything on such limited data and Paul's intervention may have been nothing more than the unmasking of fraud.

Luke, however, has turned the occasion into an exorcism and this must remain suspicious, particularly in view of the fact that Paul never mentions such activity at any point in his correspondence, just as he never mentions the phenomenon of possession. The Pauline letters are completely free of any suggestion that either the apostle himself or his associates were ever involved in any form of exorcism as will be discussed later in relation to these documents. It would seem, therefore, that Luke is allowing himself a certain amount of licence in his handling of his traditions, although his reasoning seems clear. In some way the girl was 'possessed'; therefore any cure of her condition must represent an exorcism and it needed to be set out in that fashion.

The possessed man and the sons of Sceva: Acts 19:11-19

This particular event is not a healing, but it needs to be mentioned in passing as it does provide an example of 'demon possession', although it is not in any way specifically associated with any of the apostles. It is also a story that underlines Luke's purpose in directing such situations to the glory of God. In this case, the result was that, 'the name of the Lord Jesus was extolled' (v 17) and 'the word of the Lord grew and prevailed mightily' (v 20). The story presents many problems and Haenschen has discussed them in some detail [52], but it seems to be part of a tradition that Luke has received and he attempts to fit it into the narrative. It follows a vague and rather indiscriminate statement about the constant wonder-working of Paul and this is now contrasted with the total failure of the Jewish exorcists, even though they use the name of Jesus. The point that Luke wishes to make is that the name of Jesus cannot be put into a bag of magic tricks for the use of professional exorcists - it may be used only by those who have been filled with his Spirit.

The story is the only genuine mention of demonic possession outside the Gospels and the only occasion on which the word 'exorcist' (ἐξορκιστης) is used in the New Testament. Luke seems to be intent on drawing a marked distinction between the professional exorcists who used magical formulae to drive out demons and the work of the apostles who undertook their exorcisms, not to earn money, but to bring glory to God. The details of the story are scanty in the extreme. The violent incident which Luke records suggests that the man may have been in the manic phase of bipolar disorder or possibly schizophrenic. Patients with acute mania may be difficult to distinguish from paranoid schizophrenia, although it is rare for the manic patient to display the marked violence exhibited in this story [53]. On the other hand, a dissociative state cannot be ruled out entirely, although it seems very much less likely. It would certainly appear, from the recorded events, that he did not have a condition that was amenable to abreative techniques and an organic psychosis seems the most likely reason for his behaviour. If this was so, then it is not surprising that he failed to respond to the methods of the exorcists and turned on his tormentors in a manic or paranoid rage. Psychotherapeutic techniques are of little value in treating psychoses that arise from structural, biochemical and genetic factors, such as schizophrenia.

It is of particular significance from the standpoint of this study that, although Paul and his friends were apparently in the city at the time of the recorded event, Luke does not note any contact between them and this violent man. Further, in spite of Luke's statement about the 'extraordinary miracles' that Paul undertook (v 11), it seems clear that Luke cannot find any real evidence that Paul (or Peter either for that matter) ever engaged in a programme of exorcism and he is too honest an historian to invent such stories. It is also to be noted that the only two cases of what Luke describes in terms of 'demon possession' that actually surface in his narrative, are examples of people who most probably suffered from some form of chronic mental disorder, as appeared to be true of the cases recorded in the Gospels.

The fall of Eutychus at Troas: Acts 20:7-12.

This story has all the feel about it of a genuinely remembered event with the sure ring of authenticity. The Christians in Troas have gathered together to hear Paul preach and celebrate the Eucharist with them (Luke may be reading a little of his own later church practice into the narrative at this point!). A young man (νεανεας) named Eutychus sits in a window and, probably tired after a long day at work as well as, possibly, the tedium of a long sermon, dozes off (καταφερομενος). Once he is sound asleep (κατενεχθεις), he falls out of a third storey window to the ground, where he is picked up apparently dead. Luke's clear statement (v 9) that 'he was picked up dead' (ἤρθη νεκρος) certainly implies that those who picked up the young man at least thought he was dead.

At this point in the narrative Luke cannot resist making an Old Testament allusion and, as with the earlier case of Tabitha, he links Paul's activity with the prophetic work of Elijah and Elisha, using the language of the raising of the widow's son (1 Kings 17:17f) and the Shunamite's son (2 Kings 4:34ff). The crux of the story comes with Paul's statement (v 10), 'Stop making a fuss, his life is in him' (ἡ γαρ ψυχη αὐτου ἐν αὐτω ἐστιν). The plain meaning of these words is simply that the young man was not dead, but merely unconscious, probably quite severely concussed. By the time that the eucharistic meal had finished and Paul had completed his converse with the Christians it was dawn and Eutychus had made a sufficient recovery that he could be taken away, presumably to his home. No more is heard of him and he seems to have been very fortunate. It is to be hoped that he escaped the possible later complications of head injury.

There is nothing in this story as it stands to warrant it being called a 'miracle' or even a 'healing' and all attempts to make it so are quite unconvincing [54]. The story is a straightforward account of just the sort of unfortunate accident that may occur all too often and that, happily for all concerned, had no apparent serious consequences. That Luke would like his readers to consider the actions of Paul as he embraced the man as somehow 'miraculous', particularly by introducing the association with Elijah and Elijah, seems reasonably certain, but he is sufficiently true to his source to make it apparent that the reality of the event was a natural recovery from a bad fall. No further comment on this narrative is necessary.

The father of Publius in Malta: Acts 28:8

The context of this story is the aftermath of Paul's shipwreck on the island of Malta.   The incident occurs immediately after Paul's encounter with the snake that came out of the fire, a story strategically placed in the narrative to raise the status of Paul in the eyes of the local people. The 'barbarians', as Luke rather disparagingly calls these non-Greek speakers (v 6), change their minds about Paul and from thinking that he might be an escaped murderer, they transform him into a god. As Bruce has remarked, 'only βαρβαροι in Luke's judgment, would say anything so foolish' [55].   It is worth making the point that there is

nothing intrinsically improbable about the story of the snake and no
reason to consign it to the realm of legend [56].

This incident paves the way for wider contact with the local people
of Malta and especially with Publius, 'the chief man of the island', an
unofficial title to which the inscriptions bear witness [57]. It is possible
that he had made arrangements to billet the survivors of the shipwreck
and Paul and his friends seem to have been singled out for special
tratment. Luke now records that the father of Publius was sick with
dysentery.   The description is quite graphic: he was gripped
(συνεχομενον) with fever (πυρετος) and severe diarrhoea or dysentery
(δυσεντεριον). The description is suggestive of the response to a food
borne bacterial enterotoxin rather than a food borne infection such as
that caused by the typhoid (*Salmonella* spp) or paratyphoid (*Shigella*
spp) groups of organisms or by *Campylobacter* infections. Malta fever
(caused by the organism *Brucella melitensis* and frequently passed on
through drinking infected goat's milk) is an unlikely cause of the illness
described by Luke. Although characterised by high fevers it is not
characteristically associated with dysenteric symptoms (in only about
seven per cent of cases) [58].

The rapid resolution of symptoms, in this case after Paul had laid his
hands on Publius' father (an act probably associated with prayer for
him) and healed him, would seem to point to a toxic type illness rather
than one due to infection. Fly-borne contamination of food by a variety
of common organisms such as *Staphylococcus aureus* and *Bacillus
cereus* is still very frequent in western countries and would have been
much more common in the less sanitary conditions of first century
Malta. Although the bacteria themselves are destroyed by cooking, the
toxins that they produce are not and the consumption of such
contaminated food may produce a severe febrile illness, characterised
by abdominal cramps, vomiting and nausea as well as by severe and
occasionally, blood-stained diarrhoea, which is usually, and fortunately,
self-limiting within twenty-four to forty-eight hours [59]. It would seem
that some such common condition is the most probable explanation for
this illness and its rapid resolution. Paul's actions in this situation are
comforting and reassuring to the patient, but hardly 'miraculous',
although that is clearly the impression that the author wishes to convey.

What is of particular interest in the account of Paul's stay on Malta
is the fact that he is not portrayed as preaching the gospel at all on the
island. The opportunity seems to have been there, for Luke remarks
that the local population came for treatment (εθεραπευοντο, a different
verb from that used of Paul's actions and one that suggests medical

treatment rather than 'cure' in this context and thus the use of different methods from those used by Paul) [60]. If Luke was with the party (and the account forms part of the famous 'we' passages in Acts), the suggestion seems to be that he was supporting Paul and his friends financially by setting up a medical practice on the island and charging for his clinical services during their short stay [61]. It is perhaps for this reason that, very uncharacteristically indeed, Luke makes no mention of glory being given to God for the treatment and presumed cures. The practical result, however, is that Paul and his friends are heaped with gifts before their departure for Rome.

General statements on healing

Luke's approach to narrative is episodic, which was a common approach in ancient historians who were using a variety of sources. The episodes are joined by summary passages that act as links and as positive statements about the life and progress of the early Church [62]. The statements provide continuity in the narrative, but, as Luke's own composition, they are later than the episodes that form the narrative base. There is a small number of these editorial comments which relate to the healing activities of the apostles, of which the two most interesting are those which credit healings to the passing of Peter's shadow over a sick person (Acts 5:15) and the therapeutic value of Paul's sweat bands (συδαρια) (Acts 19:12). There are, in addition, a number of other references to 'signs and wonders' in connection with all the apostles (Acts 2:43; 5:12), and specifically with Stephen (Acts 6:8) and with Paul and Barnabas (Acts 14:3). There are also specific references to healing in relation to Philip's mission to Samaria (Acts 8:6,7) and Paul's time in Ephesus (Acts 19:10-12).

Nonetheless, it is noteworthy that Luke, in spite of his avowed intention of demonstrating the continuance of the words and works of Jesus in the apostolic mission, has significantly fewer references to healing in the Acts than in the Gospel. It would seem that Luke's sources did not place a very high emphasis on the healing work of the apostles or else there were genuinely few examples of such activity. Further, as has been noted in the preceding discussion, several of the specific accounts of healing in Acts raise questions about both provenance and genuine historicity. It is suggested, therefore, that the vagueness of Luke's generalising statements would indicate a lack of substantial evidence to support his thesis of an extensive apostolic healing ministry: in essence, he cannot find examples to prove his contentions.

The reference to the healing virtue of Peter's shadow has been the occasion of much debate and several attempts have been made to avoid the direct implication of Luke's writing here. Wilkinson, for example has argued that the healings were actually at the hands of the apostle and not by his shadow as such. He argues, therefore, that these were healings occasioned by the touch of the apostles [63]. It is difficult to see how the text could support such an interpretation, although Barrett may be nearer the truth in suggesting that 'we should think here not of the effect of Peter's shadow, but of the presence and power of God which Peter represented' [64]. One has to be careful, however, that, as Haenchen has remarked, one does not 'fall back on apologetic devices which, however, well meant, are useless' [65]. Luke, in fact, has shown no real reticence about adopting the popular conceptions of 'miracles' as will be demonstrated again in relation to Paul's clothing. He was deliberately utilising the ideas of the Hellenistic world to emphasise the hand of God at work in the Christian mission. In doing so, however, he comes perilously close to turning the apostles into something akin to the Greek 'divine men' even though he is at pains, elsewhere, to remove such views (note Acts 14:14ff). There is nonetheless a tendency towards a triumphalist gospel that is in danger of avoiding the scandal of the cross. The people 'cured' by being under Peter's shadow were suffering, almost certainly, from psychosomatic disorders that would be highly amenable to this form of 'faith healing'.

Luke pursues the theme in his mention of the use of Paul's clothing for healing purposes. Just as Peter's shadow seems to hold divine virtue, so also did the work clothes of Paul. Paul's touch could bring about healing and thus, by extension, the clothes that have touched his body must contain the same power. Foakes-Jackson remarked with some acerbity that the 'record of these wonders is of interest to us rather as illustrative of the credulity of the age than as serving the purpose of edification' [66]. It is perhaps more to the point to note that credulity occurs in every age and every society and the beliefs and actions of people in contemporary western society at the beginning of the twenty-first century often match those of earlier ages.

The actions that Luke notes are important, nonetheless, because they demonstrate the concept that the power or grace of God can be treated as though it were an impersonal 'substance'. This is an idea that dominated later thought and was evident as early as the second century when clerical ministrations became the channel through which grace was received [67]. It came to a head in mediaeval miracle mongering and it still lingers today in most forms of sacramental theology and such practices as the sacramental anointing of the sick, as well as in Anglican and Catholic liturgies. It is significant perhaps that, in the New Testament, it is Luke who places most emphasis on this concept. It is one that runs totally counter to his hero Paul's own understanding of the position and characteristics of an apostle and the nature of God's grace which, for him, was centred in a person, Jesus Christ. The Lukan statements seem to describe apostolic power in the way in which it was popularly understood and as set out, for example, by Paul's opponents at Corinth. It certainly does not reflect the *theologia crucis* of Paul and, like other Lukan emphases, tends towards a dangerous triumphalism.

Notes and references

[1] Smith, C.C. (1991). Peter, Saint. In: *St James Guide to Biography*. St James Press, Chicago. pp 620-622. See also Haenchen, E. (1968). The book of Acts as source material for the history of early Christianity. In: Keck, L.E. and Martyn, J.L. (eds). *Studies in Luke-Acts*. SPCK, London. p 258. On apocryphal works see, among others, Hennecke, E. and Schneemelcher, W. (1974). *New Testament Apocrypha*. SCM, London and Robinson, J.M. (1988). (ed). *The Nag Hammadi Library in English*. Harper Collins, San Francisco/E.J. Brill, Leiden. third edn.

[2] Fitzmeyer, J.A. (1968). Jewish Christianity in Acts in the light of the Qumran scrolls. *Studies in Luke-Acts*. p 237.

[3] On the plan and purpose of Acts, see Menoud, P.H. (1954). Le plan des Actes des Apôtres. *New Testament Studies*. 1. 44-51.

[4] Bruce, F.F. (1952). *The Acts of the Apostles: The Greek Text with Introduction and Commentary*. Tyndale Press, London. Second edn. p 15. The third edition of this work (1990) has a more detailed analysis of Luke as historian (pp 27-34) and Bruce notes the judgment of Eduard Meyer, the great classical historian, that Luke was 'the one great historian who joined the last of the genuinely Greek historians, Polybius, to the greatest of Christian historians, Eusebius' (p 27).

[5] Haenchen, E. (1968). *Studies in Luke-Acts*. p 258.

[6] Lüdemann, G. (1989). *Early Christianity according to the Tradition in Acts*. Fortress Press, Minneapolis. p 17. For a much more positive view of Lukan chronology see Witherington, B. (1998). *The Acts of the Apostles: A Socio-Rhetorical Commentary*. Eerdmans, Grand Rapids, especially pp 77-97

[7] See further Lampe, G.W.H. (1965). Miracles in the Acts of the Apostles. In: Moule, C.F.D. (ed). *Miracles: Cambridge Studies in their Philosophy and History*. Mowbray, London. p 168.

[8] Hemer, C.J. (1989). *The Book of Acts in the Setting of Hellenistic History.* J.C.B. Mohr, Tübingen. p 439.
[9] See the discussion of Max Turner (1991). The Spirit and the power of Jesus' miracles in the Lucan conception. *Novum Testamentum.* 33. 124-152. This view is contrary to that of E. Schweizer (1981, *The Holy Spirit.* SCM, London. pp 58-64) as well as of J.M. Hull (1974. *Hellenistic Magic and the Synoptic Tradition.* SCM, London. pp 105-109) who both argue for a quasi-magical view of 'power' as a 'substance' that can be poured out to heal. Passages such as Luke 6:19 and 8:46 as well as 5:15 and 19:12 would certainly seem to suggest an understanding of 'power' as substance in the Lukan writings.
[10] Hemer, C.J. (1989). *The Book of Acts.* p 430.
[11] Fletcher, R. (1997). *The Conversion of Europe from Paganism to Christianity: AD 371-1386* Harper Collins, London. p 45. He gives numerous examples of how the bishops, monks and others used the miraculous to show the superiority of the Christian God and turn people away from paganism. As was noted in the Introduction to this study, such an approach is found in the modern pentecostal/charismatic approach to healing which emphasises the evidential importance of its healing claims. When such claims are shown to be ill-founded, there arises an immense credibility gap which inevitably has an effect on people's attitudes to the core message.
[12] For example, Irenaeus *Against Heresies.* 2.31.2-32.4. He contrasts the healings and miracles of the 'brotherhood' (that is the 'true church') with the claims of various heretical groups. He provides no examples and his comments (including claims of raising the dead) are clearly built on hearsay as are other reports from the same period. On the other hand, not all apologists from this period gave a high place to the persuasive power of 'miracles'. Theophilus of Antioch (*Ad Autolycum* 1.8,13) for example, doubted whether any pagan would be persuaded by even first hand testimony that someone had been raised from the dead. At an earlier stage, Quadratus (ca AD 124-128) placed his emphasis on the permanence of Christ's healings rather than any contemporary activities if Eusebius is to be believed (Eusebius, *Ecclesiastical History.* 4.3.2).
[13] On miracles in Acts see, Adams, M.M. (1993). The role of miracles in the structure of Luke-Acts. In: Stump, E. and Flint, T.P. (eds). *Hermes and Athena: Biblical Exegesis and Philosophical Theology.* University of Notre Dame Press, Notre Dame IN pp 235-272; Ford, J.M. (1988). The social and political implications of the miraculous in Acts. In: Elbert, P. (ed). *Faces of Renewal: Studies in Honor of Stanley M. Horton presented on his Seventieth Birthday.* Hendricksen. Peabody. MA. pp 137-160; Pilch, J.J. (1991). Sickness and healing in Luke-Acts. In: Neyrey, J.H. (ed). *The Social World of Luke-Acts.* Hendricksen, Peabody. MA. pp 181-209 and Turner, M. (1991). The spirit and the power of Jesus' miracles in the Lukan conception. *Novum Testamentum.* 33 124-152.
[14] The conservative scholar Donald Guthrie (1990), gives a judicious summary of the arguments in favour of both early and later dates and comments that a 'date between AD 70 and 85 is … preferred by the majority of scholars' and he

clearly tends to this view himself (*New Testament Introduction.* Inter-Varsity Press, Leicester. Fourth edn. p 362).

[15] Lüdemann, G. (1989). *Early Christianity according to the Traditions in Acts.* p 50.

[16] Josephus, *Jewish War.* 5.201. He stated that this gate far exceeded in value those plated in silver and set in gold.

[17] Mishnah, *Middôt* 2.3. The Nicanor gate is described as being of bronze and leading from the outer court to the 'court of women'.

[18] See further, Jeremias, J. (1969) *Jerusalem in the Time of Jesus.* SCM, London. ET. pp 23-24 and 117 and Hengel, M. (1983). *Between Jesus and Paul.* SCM, London. ET. pp 102-104. Note also the comments in Haenchen, E. (1971). *The Acts of the Apostles.* Blackwell, Oxford. ET. pp 198-199; Bruce, F.F. (1990). *Acts.* pp 136-137 and Barrett, C.K. (1994). *The Acts of the Apostles (International Critical Commentary).* T & T Clark, Edinburgh. pp 179-180.

[19] See for example Galen 15.896; Hippocrates, *Joints* 46, although he does use the word of the uterus (*Diseases of Women* 1.38).

[20] Lev 21:17-20; 2 Sam 5:8 as interpreted in the tractate *Shabbath* 6.8

[21] Haenchen, E. *The Acts of the Apostles.* p 199.

[22] Bruce, F.F. (1990). *The Acts of the Apostles.* p 137.

[23] Barrett, C.K. (1994). *The Acts of the Apostles.* p 181.

[24] See for example van der Horst, P. (1989). Hellenistic parallels to Acts (Chapters 3 and 4). *Journal for the Study of the New Testament.* 35. 37-46.

[25] See Barrett, C.K. (1994). *The Acts of the Apostles.* pp 182-183. On the Lukan use of the name of Jesus see Ziesler, J.A. (1979). The name of Jesus in the Acts of the Apostles. *Journal for the Study of the New Testament.* 4. 28-41.

[26] Hobart, W.K. (1882). *The Medical Language of St Luke.* Dublin University Press, Dublin pp 34-35.

[27] The primary meaning is 'a step' and thus by extension, 'that with which one steps', i.e. a foot. There are frequent references to the use of the word in association with the measured and metrical steps of the dance (see Liddell and Scott, p 310).

[28] See the references in Barrett, C.K. (1994). *The Acts of the Apostles.* pp 183-184.

[29] Witherington, B. (1998). *The Acts of the Apostles.* p 175. n44.

[30] Kelly, W. (1914). *An Exposition of the Acts of the Apostles.* F.E. Race, London. Second edn. p 40.

[31] Both John Wilkinson (1980), (*Health and Healing: Studies in New Testament Principles and Practice.* Handsel Press, Edinburgh. p 88) and J Rendle Short (1953), (*The Bible and Modern Medicine.* Paternoster Press, London. p 107) take the view that the lameness was caused by talipes. The laconic dismissal of the lame man as an imposter without further explanation by Margaret and T.A. Loyd Davies (1993) is a rather inadequate treatment of this story (*The Bible: Medicine & Myth.* Silent Books, Cambridge. Second edn. p 242).

[32] Haenchen, E. (1971). *The Acts of the Apostles.* p 341.

[33] Note however, the comment of C.K. Barrett (1994) (*Acts of the Apostles.* p 480) that while the name does not suggest a Jewish origin, neither does it exclude it. He remarks that in view of Peter's treatment of Cornelius we may conclude that Luke did not think of Aeneas as anything other than a Jew.

[34] Hobart, W.K. *The Medical Language of St Luke.* p 6. One cannot be certain whether Luke intends the idea of paralysis to be dominant or whether the man was simply lame, disabled or weak. The verb may be used in each sense (see Liddell and Scott, p 1317 and Bauer, p 620).

[35] Note, however, the discussion in Barrett, C.K. (1994). *The Acts of the Apostles.* p 481.

[36] The expression στρωσον σεαυτω is not found elsewhere in the New Testament. The phrase is usually understood as a reference to packing up his bed, but it could have the sense of 'set the table' which would make sense if Aeneas was at home (for a discussion see Bruce, F.F. (1990) *Acts of the Apostles* (third edn) p 247 and C.K. Barrett (1994). *Acts of the Apostles.* p 481).

[37] Note the comments of F.J. Foakes-Jackson (1931). *The Acts of the Apostles (Moffatt New Testament Commentaries).* Hodder and Stoughton, London. p 86.

[38] A view shared by Margaret and T.A. Lloyd-Davies (1993). *The Bible: Medicine and Myth.* p 244.

[39] See further, Lindars, B. (1968). Elijah, Elisha and the gospel miracles. In: Moule, C.F.D. (ed). *Miracles.* pp 63-79 and Miller, R.J. (1988). Elijah, John and Jesus in the gospel of Luke.*New Testament Studies.* 34. 611-622.

[40] Hobart, W.K. *The Medical Language of St Luke.* pp 44-45.

[41] See the references given in Barrett, C.K. (1994). *The Acts of the Apostles.* p 618 and also Liddell and Scott, p 297 and Bauer, p 128.

[42] Haenschen (1971) remarks that 'if Luke had invented this story himself, he would never have hit upon *this* name (i.e. Bar-Jesus); we have thus here a proof that Luke is following a tradition' (*Acts of the Apostles.* p 402).

[43] See further German, G.A. (1972). Psychiatry. In: Shaper, A.G., Kibukamasoke, J.W. and Hutt, M.S.R. (eds). *Medicine in a Tropical Environment.* British Medical Association, London. pp 329-347.

[44] For details of the possible blending of traditions see Haenchen, E. (1971). *The Acts of the Apostles.* pp 430-434.

[45] Bruce, F.F. (1952). *The Acts of the Apostles.* Second edn. p 32. He makes a similar point in the third edition (1990) p 52.

[46] Wilkinson, J. (1980). *Health and Healing.* p 88 and Short, J. Rendle. (1953). *Bible and Modern Medicine.* p 107.

[47] See further Foerster, W. (1968). Πυθων. In: Friedrich, G. Kittel, G. (eds). *Theological Dictionary of the New Testament.* Vol VI. Eerdmans, Grand Rapids. pp 917-920.

[48] See the references in Liddell and Scott, p 1079.

[49] Plutarch, *De defectu oraculorum* 9.414E. Considerable scepticism existed about such people and the reality of charlatanism for profit was well known (see Apuleius, *Golden Ass.* 8:26-30).

[50] A list of the specifically Lukan characteristics may be found in Twelftree, G. (1985). *Christ Triumphant: Exorcism Then and Now.* Hodder and Stoughton, London. p 198. n 12.

[51] See further Trebilco, P. (1989). Paul and Silas - 'servants of the most high God'. *Journal for the Study of the New Testament.* 36. 51-73.

[52] Haenchen, E. (1971). *The Acts of the Apostles.* pp 564-566.

[53] For the classic description of schizophrenic violence see Mayer Gross, W., Slater, E. and Roth, M. (1960). *Clinical Psychiatry.* Cassell, London. p 262.

[54] See for example, Witherington, B. (1998). *Acts of the Apostles.* pp 607-608.

[55] Bruce, F.F. (1990) *Acts of the Apostles.* p 532. The term is standard Greek for any non-Greek speaker (see references in Bauer, p 133) and while it may be applied without derogatory connotations, these are often present.

[56] T.E. Lawrence ('Lawrence of Arabia'), (1927). (*Revolt in the Desert.* Jonathan Cape, London) describes a similar experience with a snake coming out of the fire, presumably gathered up with the brushwood for burning. There are no venomous snakes on the island of Malta today, although the common viper may have been present in Roman times (see Hemer, C.J. (1975). Euraquilo and Melita. *Journal of Theological Studies.* 26. 100-111 and also Cansdale, G. (1970). *Animals of Bible Lands.* Paternoster Press, Exeter. p 209).

[57] See Bruce, F.F. (1990). *The Acts of the Apostles.* p 532.

[58] So Madkour, M.M. (1996). Brucellosis. In: Weatherall, D.J., Leadingham, J.G.J., Warrell, D.A. (eds). *Oxford Textbook of Medicine.* Oxford University Press, Oxford. pp 612-623.

[59] See Skirrow, M.D. (1996). Enteropathogenic bacteria. *Oxford Textbook of Medicine.* pp 550-560.

[60] For a contrary view see Haenchen, E. (1971). *The Acts of the Apostles.* p 715. He also dismisses the incident with the snake as improbable without adducing any very satisfactory reason for so doing (p 713).

[61] This suggestion goes back at least to Adolf Harnack. (1907). *Luke the Physician.* London, Williams and Norgate. ET. p 16.

[62] See further Cadbury, H.J. (1933). The summaries in Acts. In: Cadbury, H.J. and Lake, K. (eds). *The Beginnings of Christianity.* Macmillan, London. Vol 5. pp 392-402.

[63] Wilkinson, J. (1980). *Health and Healing.* p 100.

[64] Barrett, C.K. (1994). *Acts of the Apostles.* p 277.

[65] Haenchen, E. (1971). *The Acts of the Apostles.* p 246.

[66] Foakes-Jackson, F.J. (1931). *The Acts of the Apostles (Moffatt New Testament Commentary).* Hodder and Stoughton, London. p 179. See further, Case, S.J. (1946). *Christian Supernaturalism.* University of Chicago Press, Chicago.

[67] For details see Torrance, T.F. (1948). *The Doctrine of Grace in the Apostolic Fathers.* T&T Clark, Edinburgh.

Chapter 7

HEALING IN THE EARLY CHURCH: THE WITNESS OF THE NEW TESTAMENT LETTERS

The New Testament letters 'are not private correspondence, but the instrument of early Christian missionary work'

W.G. Kümmel

The witness of the Pauline correspondence

It is virtually axiomatic to state that the New Testament letters were written to address specific circumstances within specific Christian communities, with perhaps the single exception of Paul's personal letter to Philemon. As Kümmel put it, these letters are 'the instrument of early Christian missionary work' [1]. This is particularly apparent in the writings of Paul, most of which were penned as urgent responses to critical situations arising in the local churches he had been responsible for establishing. Both the letter to the Galatians and the Corinthian correspondence are good examples of what might be termed 'fire fighting exercises'. In the letter to the Galatians, for example, 'Paul was dealing in white-hot urgency with a situation which threatened the very foundation of the Gospel' [2] Because of that particular function and also, because of the very specific circumstances of most of the letters, it has to be considered very unlikely that the Pauline corpus presents anything like a complete picture of early belief and practice in those churches associated with the great apostle. What everyone believed and what everyone did would not normally need to be set out in detail: it was only when things were going wrong that pastoral correspondence was required to restore order. It will be extremely difficult therefore, to recapture with any certainty those elements of early Church life that did not feature in these letters. On the other hand, it is, perhaps, a reasonable assumption that things of major importance to the life of the Church would tend to arise as issues and thus be mentioned in the correspondence. Thus, if healing ranked as high in the list of priorities in the life of those early communities as some have claimed it did and if it was considered to be an essential and integral part of the evangelistic mission and the very nature of the Christian message [3], then it might be expected that some echo of this prominence would appear in the letters.

Examination of the Pauline correspondence, however, reveals that there is virtually no mention of the healing of sickness in these letters and no reference at all to demon possession, exorcism or raising the dead. Admittedly, specific incidents of healing, such as those set out in Acts, would not be expected to feature prominently in correspondence unless there was a direct reason. On the other hand, the only references to sick people in Paul's writings make no mention, or even suggestion, that any cure was other than by normal and natural processes. Paul simply makes no mention of the 'miraculous' in respect of his sick friends and no suggestion that specially gifted people (including himself) were able to deal with these sicknesses. Furthermore, there is no mention in any of the Pauline letters, nor, more importantly, is there apparently any expectation, of the type of healing associated with Jesus in the Gospels or with the apostles in the narratives in Acts. Paul's references to the 'signs of an apostle' will be discussed later, but, in general, as Wilkinson has remarked, 'the paucity of specific references to health and healing in the epistles is of great interest in view of the fact that these writings form over a third of the bulk of the New Testament' [4].

It may be argued that the lack of any mention of 'miraculous' healing does not necessarily reflect whether it was a matter of importance in the local churches. There is, after all, no mention of the Eucharist in the Pauline letters, except in 1 Corinthians, and few would argue that the Eucharist was not a prominent part of the worship of the early Church. Nonetheless, the results of the gracious activity of God through his Spirit in the local church communities are mentioned frequently, yet only in 1 Corinthians is there any clear suggestion of a healing gift.

The Pauline letters represent the earliest New Testament documents, written within a generation of the Easter event, although there is still no universal consensus on either the chronology of Paul's life or the dating of his letters [5]. There is also divergence of opinion on the authenticity of such letters as Ephesians, Colossians and the Pastoral Epistles. Fortunately, from the standpoint of this study, these matters are not of major importance. Paul's views on the issues of disease, suffering and death are set out in the so-called 'capital epistles' which are not in dispute and are accepted universally as genuinely Pauline [6].

Illness and human experience

Paul was under no illusions about the reality of disease and death as an unavoidable part of the normal expectation of human existence. He himself suffered from some form of chronic illness or disability that he described as a 'thorn in the flesh' (2 Cor 12:7), the nature of which will be discussed later. Paul did not see this world as a place in which any form of perfection could be reached and freedom from sickness and death belonged only to the future age of resurrection, the time when 'the redemption of the body' (ἀπολυτρωσις του σωματος), as he put it at Romans 8:23, would come about. In the meantime the body was subject to disease, to degenerative change and, ultimately, to death. Paul's understanding is set out in a number of passages, particularly throughout the arguments of Romans 8, in the course of his extended discussion of the work of Christ's Spirit in the believer as a renewing and transforming activity. This renewal, however, can only be partial in the present time. The present universal experience for all humanity, believer and unbeliever alike, is the 'bondage of corruption', a thraldom in which Paul sees the whole creation sharing (Rom 8:19-23). The one 'in Christ' may enjoy the 'firstfruits (ἡ ἀπαρχη) of the Spirit' (Rom 8:23), but the fullness of redemption remains a future hope and is awaited in expectancy. In Paul's mind, only the arrival of the future glory, the age of resurrection, would bring release from suffering.

A similar argument is found in the Corinthian correspondence. In almost dualistic terms, Paul speaks of the 'outward' person being brought to decay and the 'inward' person being renewed day by day (2 Cor 4:16). In language closely related to that of Romans, he talks about the Christian groaning in the present while awaiting the clothing of immortality that will swallow up and negate the mortality that is the common human lot of this life (1 Cor 15:53,54). The certainty that this hope will be realised resides, once again, in the presence of the Spirit, here not the firstfruits of the future harvest, but the 'down payment' or 'deposit' (ἀρραβον) that secures the final purchase.

The emphasis on the contrast between the present and future states is also emphasised in Paul's lengthy discussion of the resurrection in 1 Corinthians 15. Paul contrasts the present experience of corruption (ἐν φθορα), of dishonour (ἐν ἀτιμια) and weakness (ἐν ἀσθηενεια) with the glory of the future to be revealed at the resurrection (1 Cor 15:42,43). In essence, the contrast is between the natural and the spiritual. Paul conceives of these states as two separate modes of existence, the one under the domination of the 'flesh' and the other as life empowered by the resurrection life of Christ through his Spirit (1 Cor 15:44). It seems from his very detailed argument that Paul does not envisage a state in the present time that is ever free from the inherent weaknesses that are the inevitable accompaniment of the human situation. In the light of the common usage of the term 'weakness' (ἀσθενεια) and in this particular context, it requires to be understood as including sickness. Sickness represents one specific form of human weakness, taking its place among the other aspects of life that define human helplessness. It is the term most frequently used in the New Testament for sickness and disease and this parallels its general Hellenistic usage [7]. It is this meaning of the word that is uppermost in such passages as Gal 4:13 where Paul speaks of his own sickness and at 1 Cor 11:30 where he sees sickness as a judgment on the very unspiritual behaviour of the Corinthian Christians at the Eucharist. Paul sees human sickness, therefore, as part of the normal pattern of life and one of that wide range of vicissitudes that may be summed up in the term 'weakness'. Nowhere does he suggest that the Christian community has some special immunity from sickness or that there is a special Providence that brings universal cures or instant healing.

Healing in the Pauline correspondence

On one occasion and on one occasion only, does Paul make reference to 'gifts of healing' (χαρισματα ἰαματων) in the Church. This is at 1 Cor 12:9, 28 and 30 in the context of his extended discussion of the gifts of the Spirit within the local Christian community, a discussion that occupies 1 Corinthians 12 to 14. The concept of such a gift is found nowhere else in the New Testament and it is especially noteworthy that when Paul discusses the gifts of the Spirit elsewhere in his writings, such as Romans 12:3-8 and Ephesians 4:11-16 [8], he makes no reference to healing (nor incidentally to the more flamboyant gifts which had caused such problems in Corinth). However, Paul does mention his own apostolic activity in terms of divine power and, in addition, on one occasion, he refers to 'works of power' (ἐνεργῶν δυναμεις) within the churches in Galatia (Gal 3:5) and there is a similar expression at 1 Cor 12:10. These phrases would indicate the outworking of divine power within specific and concrete circumstances, but their contexts, however, do not allow any conclusions to be drawn as to the exact nature of these 'works'. The assumption is often made that they included acts of healing, but there is no clear indication that they did. It is likely that the term is simply a generalisation; as Bruce remarks, Paul's terminology 'is used comprehensively of the manifestations of the Spirit's power' [9].

Healings may have been included within this broad terminology, but this is not explicitly stated and in the light of his own physical weakness, very much in evidence at the time of his writing to the Galatians, it may reasonably be questioned whether 'healing' figured very highly in Paul's thoughts or actions. There is no suggestion that healing was the primary purpose of the acts of power themselves, which, in fact, pointed on to the wider purposes of God and his redemptive action. Further, the more general moral emphasis of Paul's use of the word 'power' in other contexts should give rise to caution in assuming that the term automatically requires something 'miraculous'.

It is dangerous to argue from silence, but it would not be impossible for the 'gifts of healing' to have been practices peculiar to Corinth among the Pauline churches and not found elsewhere. The Corinthian Christians may have claimed such gifts as evidence of the arrival of the kingdom of God in the 'now' of their experience, thus forming part of their over-realised eschatology. This led them to believe in the transformation of the human state in the here and now through the presence of the Spirit, giving them the power to speak in 'the tongues of angels' and to live in a world in which the resurrection had already arrived and sickness had been defeated.

Any interpretation of what Paul meant by 'gifts of healing' may only be determined from the context and this is not always particularly helpful as Paul assumes an understanding of his terminology on the part of his readers that is not necessarily present today. Two things are of note. Firstly, Paul does not use a noun derived from the common verb for healing (θεραπευω), but rather the unusual noun ιαμα (derived from ιαομαι) that bears the normal meaning of 'a means of healing, a medicine or remedy' [10]. The word occurs at 1 Cor 12:9, 28 and 30 in the New Testament and nowhere else. The cognate verb has a primary application to physical healing in its New Testament use, particularly in Luke's Gospel, as was noted at an earlier stage of this study, but it may also bear a more symbolic meaning. When used in the latter way the thought is much more akin to 'restore' or 'deliver' someone from ills of any kind, including sin and its consequences. In both Heb 12:13 and 1 Pet 2:24 the thought is clearly that of restoration from the effects of sin, pictured as a wound or disease, and the noun is used in the LXX of Ecclesiastes 10:4 to denote calmness or soothing.

In the light of the total absence of any other references to healing in the Pauline correspondence, it may be wise to exercise care in assuming automatically that Paul is necessarily speaking of physical healing in this context of the operation of the Spirit within the worshipping community, even though this is probably the most obvious sense. The other gifts outlined are reasonably specific and there is not a great deal of uncertainty about their meaning. Further, the unusual word that he has used, with its sense of remedy or a means of restoration, does not fit particularly well as a reference to some form of 'miraculous healing'. Against this, however, needs to be set what seems to have been part of the Corinthian understanding that the future state had already arrived in terms of spiritual experience and the future age could be realised in daily living.

The second point to note is that these particular gifts are mentioned in the setting of Paul's discussion of the *charismata* in relation to the corporate life and worship of the Corinthian church as part of God's provision for all aspects of the community's existence. The particular wording in 1 Cor 12:9 indicates that an individual person (ἀλλος) receives these plural 'gifts' which may indicate that Paul is thinking here of a gift available for a specific occasion rather than one belonging to an individual in the way in which there were prophets and teachers [11]. There appears to be no suggestion, therefore, of a group of full time healers within the community, nor is it entirely clear exactly what Paul meant by his use of ιαμα in this context. Further, if the meaning is 'physical healing', then the specific gift stands out rather paradoxically in a list that is dealing essentially with the spiritual functioning of the community.

It is clearly outside the purpose and function of this study to provide a full discussion of the nature of Paul's understanding of 'spiritual gifts' or 'gifts of grace'. Nonetheless, some discussion is necessary in order to set the question of Paul's understanding of healing into the specific context of the Corinthian church and the obvious misunderstandings of the nature of the activity of the Spirit of God within the Christian community. The literature is immense and frequently partisan in its approach [12]. The word used for these 'spiritual gifts' (χαρισματα) is a distinctively Pauline term in the New Testament and seems to relate to a variety of individual endowments that are to be used for the service of the Christian community and for the common good. They are to be understood as concrete manifestations of the grace of God at work in the community through the activity of the Spirit. There have been various attempts to group these activities and manifestations [13], but none are entirely convincing.

Paul's problem was that the Corinthian Christians appeared to be elitist in their understanding of such endowments. They saw them as the sole possession of the 'spiritual' members (πνευματικοι) of the congregation, that is Christians who were to be distinguished from those who had not reached this level of development. The latter remained as ψυχικοι (on the level of the soul) or even σαρκικοι (on the level of the flesh). Thus, ironically, even sarcastically, he addresses the whole section dealing with the manifestations of the Spirit to those who considered themselves to be 'the spiritual', from the opening words (1 Cor 12:1) to the conclusion (1 Cor 14:37). The Corinthians considered these spectacular and episodic manifestations of the Spirit to be the divine endorsement of the spiritual elite. As Pearson puts it, 'the Corinthians claimed to be πνευματικοι on the basis of their ability to manifest certain πνευματικα chief among which was the ecstatic speech which they deemed to be "prophecy" ... it appears that the Corinthians were bent on emphasising a hyper-individualistic approach to worship, bound up as they were with their own individual experiences of tongue-speaking' [14]. Indeed, it appears to have been just this experience of glossolalia that allowed them to conclude that they were already 'as the angels of heaven': they could speak in their language and the normal restrictions of morality and so forth were no longer applicable to those living on this rarefied spiritual plane.

Paul's emphasis, however, is on the fact that the Spirit of Christ is given to the whole body of the Church and within that body, each member has a contribution to make on the basis of the chrism that he or she has received. Further, that gift has nothing to do with merit, nor with ability, nor again with imagined spiritual status: it has been given solely by the grace of God. There is thus a diversity of operation within

the unity of the body of Christ. The Christian community 'is an organic
unity with a multiplicity of parts ... This organic unity demands a view
of Christian diversity of gifts that fits with the oneness of the body of
Christ rather than detracting from it ... (but) not only are there different
gifts, but also different people are used by the Spirit to deliver the
different gifts for the common good' [15]. Such gifts may thus be seen as
'everything that the Spirit wishes to use and presses into service for the
equipping and upbuilding of the church, what can serve for instruction
and admonishing and for ministering to one another' [16]. It is a range of
activity that comprises normal human endowments, 'sanctified' by the
Spirit so that they may become more effective in the general life of the
Church, as well as those manifestations that belong more specifically to
the community at worship.

The natural talents, abilities and aptitudes of the one baptised into
Christ are themselves baptised, as it were, into the service of God and
by virtue of their immersion in the Spirit (1 Cor 6:11; 12:13) become
gifts of God's grace. Thus, in Bittlinger's phrase, they may be seen as
'going beyond the believer's natural ability for the common good of the
people of God' [17]. The gifts of the Spirit are no more (and no less) than
God's 'kindness in action' [18] and under the lordship of Christ, all human
activity is able to become fruitful, so that human endeavour may be
transformed into God's gracious activity at work within the community.

How then, are the gifts of healing to be understood in such a
context? Wilkinson has argued strongly that the basis for the gifts of
healing lies in the created aptitudes and capabilities of human beings as
created by God [19]. Paul has listed among the charismata, gifts that
include basic abilities and natural endowments, such as the gifts of
leadership, administration, financial ability, teaching and so forth.
Healing thus becomes a sharpened and enhanced natural skill coupled
with intuitive knowledge that is able to deal with the needs of the sick
person within a context of prayer. Whether this explanation will fit
with the context of 1 Corinthians 12 is doubtful. The great majority of
commentators [20] have understood the reference as being to some form
of unusual healing activity such as was evidenced in the ministry of
Jesus or that of the apostles, according to Acts. It should also be noted
that in immediate proximity to healing, Paul lists 'workings of power'
(ἐνεργηματα δυναμεων), an expression that seems to indicate some
unusual form of activity induced by the Spirit, an understanding which
also seems to lie behind Gal 3:5.

It would seem, therefore, that the nature of the 'healings' in the
Corinthian church were in some sense out of the ordinary, as might be

expected in a congregation that placed such emphasis on the more florid expressions of spiritual life. The fact of the matter is that there can be no final certainty about what Paul means in this section, although, as indicated earlier, it seems very likely that the gifts of healing represent some form of activity designed to emphasise the expression of the kingdom of God in present experience as part of living 'as the angels of heaven'. Paul is neutral about its value, as he is about other gifts, except those given specifically to build up the community. He accepted its presence without comment as he did not presume to deny its origin in the activity of the Holy Spirit, but that is about as far as he was prepared to go.

What does seem clear, however, is that in other congregations the care of the sick was handled in quite a different manner. For example, the list of very different 'gifts of grace' in Romans 12 suggests that the care of the sick was based on much more formal caring structures. In place of the flamboyance of Corinth, here are characteristics that emphasise the essential reality of Christianity as a religion of service. The evidence of God's grace in this community was seen not in the hyper-individualism and over-realised eschatology of Corinth, but in 'service' (διακονια), in 'teaching' (διδασκαλια), in 'exhortation' (παρακλησις) and so forth (Rom 12:4-8). In this context of practical Christianity, Paul lists three important types of individual (or perhaps groups of individuals) involved in community service: there is the one who gives a share (ὁ μεταδιδους); there is the one who gives aid (ὁ προισταμενος) and the one who does acts of mercy (ὁ ἐλεων). Here, as Dunn remarks, is 'a sequence of three forms of "welfare service" ' [21]. They are, in fact, at the heart of what was to become the ministry of the diaconal order in the later developing church ministry.

It would seem almost certain that the last example of service is a reference to tending and aiding the sick and abandoned [22]. If this is so, then it would strongly suggest that the church in Rome knew nothing of a 'miraculous healing' ministry and was content to deal with sickness by normal means and by showing care and every assistance to those so afflicted. Certainly with respect to the church in Rome, the approach of Wilkinson to the nature of 'spiritual gifts' would seem to be correct. At Rome the specific charisma for dealing with the sick was a cheerful spirit and Cranfield comments, a 'particularly cheerful and agreeable disposition may well be evidence of the presence of the special gift that marks a person out for this particular service' [23]. The fact that the Corinthians seemed to have evidence of 'gifts of healing' may have been no more than part of their quest for things out of the ordinary.

There is no clear evidence elsewhere that such a gift existed in other church communities, nor indeed, that Paul was particularly favourably inclined to such practices as the Corinthians may have followed. His statements are remarkably neutral.

It is of note that Paul gives no information about how the 'gifts of healing' were to be used in the life of the Corinthian church. It may be remarked that, in general, Paul was not particularly enthusiastic about the way in which gifts were exercised within that particular community. He could not reject the gifts out of hand since that would be to deny the operation of the Holy Spirit. He attempts, therefore, to put them into a framework that would govern their use and serve to regulate the more eccentric aspects of church life in Corinth.

The gift of being able to undertake 'works of power', whatever this may have meant, is stated specifically as something that occurred in Corinth and also in Galatia, yet elsewhere in Paul's writings it seems to be stringently restricted and such activity is considered to be part of the evidence of an apostolic ministry - the 'signs of an apostle' (2 Cor 12:12; Rom 15:19). There is, thus, an element of ambiguity in the use of the term. The exact meaning of the phrase has been debated, but it would seem to imply more than merely the ability to perform 'miraculous' deeds [24]. Paul saw his apostleship very much in terms of service and suffering, following the footsteps of his Master. However, he could not deny that his ministry was accompanied by activities that could be described as 'signs and wonders and works of power', but so also had been the ministry of Jesus and as a result of the activity of the same Spirit of God. It has already been noted in relation to the work of Jesus, however, that the healing of the sick was very much a programmatic activity with only certain groups of sick people being included as a specific pointer to the all inclusive nature of the kingdom of God which he saw as having arrived in his own person. The work of healing was to point to the fact that God had returned to his people.

It is difficult to see the healing of sickness as having this value in a pagan society that knew nothing of the kingdom of God, a term, in fact, rarely used by Paul at all (once each in Romans and Galatians and five times in 1 Corinthians) and which did not think of itself as in exile waiting for the coming of its God to deliver and restore. A pagan audience, however, was more likely to have seen such activities as evidence of the genuineness of Paul's apostolic status and the reality of his calling by God. They would have been interpreted as confirming the presence of divine power, a point made in Luke's treatment of healing in the Acts of the Apostles. The New Testament does not take this further and certainly does not attempt to transform the apostles into 'divine men'. It is reasonable to assume that claims of being able to perform 'signs, wonders, and works of power' were the boast of the 'false apostles', in an attempt to authenticate their ministry. Their argument was simple: only those who were able to perform such 'signs' were by definition 'true apostles'. Paul may well have seen a threat to his own apostolic ministry in the exercise of some of these gifts. It would seem that much of the thrust of the Corinthian correspondence is directed to those elements of the Corinthian church who understood his gospel, with its emphasis on what, in their terms, was judged to be 'weakness' and 'powerlessness', as effectively denying in practice Paul's claims to possess any genuine divine authority.

Paul clearly had difficulty in making counter claims that would stand up and it seems possible that, in his encounters with the false apostles who were legitimising their claims by healings and acts of power, he was learning the hard way that evidential 'signs' were very much a double-edged weapon. His opponents placed their emphasis on the 'powerful' manifestations of the Spirit in the life of those who were designated apostles. From their point of view, the Spirit was the source of their 'powerful' lives and consequently, by definition, Paul failed to meet up to the requirements of an apostle by virtue of his 'powerless' life and his adherence to the *via crucis* with its accompanying hardships and persecutions. Paul's opponents, in fact, seem to have been the original proponents of the 'health and wealth' gospel [25] and he found it difficult to counter their claims other than by rhetorical argument (as in 2 Cor 11 and 12).

Paul well knew that 'miracles' could be performed through trickery and deception like conjuring tricks before a gullible audience [26]. He therefore demands that the Corinthians base their assessment of him on the full picture of his life and ministry. They were fully aware, from their own knowledge, that Paul's life did not consist of boasting in his spiritual prowess, but in humble service on their behalf. His emphasis and the emphasis of all true Christianity is on the fact that as, Bornkamm has put it, 'God's Spirit is not the supernatural power that allows a person to transcend the earthly life and its limitations: instead it is the power of God who shows himself mighty in lowliness and weakness' [27].

The life of service is the mark of a true apostle, but Paul's detractors believed that only the evidences of power was the mark of the one commissioned by God. It is of note that much the same sort of problem was to arise in the second century Church over the claims and counter-claims in respect of Jesus and Asclepius and it seems that the Christians quickly found that they were at a disadvantage in trying to discredit Asclepius whose cures were abundant and whose claims were hard to match. The fact is that the early Church soon became aware that the popular appeal of 'miracles' was much less important in gaining converts from paganism than was the creation of a community founded in the love of God and which expressed that love in the care of its own and of others. That, in fact, was the very point that Paul was emphasising in his letter to the Romans and in his self-defence before the Corinthians. It is remarkable that this is a lesson that still has not been learned by some elements of the Church today [28].

Paul as healer

On two occasions in his letters, Paul speaks of preaching the gospel with accompanying 'signs and wonders' (2 Cor 12:12; Rom 15:19). There is no elucidation of this statement and none was presumably necessary, as the recipients of the letter would presumably have known what was intended. The comment in Romans 15:19 would appear to indicate that such signs and wonders were associated with his entire mission, as he refers to his ministry from Jerusalem to the regions of Illyricum. It seems likely, therefore, that the term would have included such events as those portrayed by Luke in Acts, which were predominantly acts of healing.

On his own admission, therefore, as well as based on the secondary sources in Acts, Paul seems to have had some involvement in healing, but it is a remarkably low key approach. It has been noted already, in respect of the Acts narratives, that the stories outline similar patterns to the removal of what may be termed 'psycho-social' symptoms in the Gospels. More importantly, in relation to the emphasis so often placed by modern charismatics on the role and importance of exorcism, nowhere in any of his letters does Paul indicate any involvement with such activity. Paul, in fact, does not elaborate on this aspect of his ministry.

It is possible, because his readers would have been familiar with the nature of his work in the local missionary situation that had probably brought them into the life of the local Christian community, that there was no need for any further amplification. In other words, Paul had no need to do more than remind them that, as an apostle, he had been involved in a ministry that displayed the 'signs of an apostle' and this included these 'signs and wonders'. Nonetheless, it is of interest to note that even in passages in which Paul is to be found vigorously defending his apostleship against his detractors, he still lays little if any emphasis on this aspect of his ministry.

The available information renders it difficult to be certain about the exact nature of the gifts of healing or apostolic works of power. One thing is clear, however, and that is that the use of such gifts in the Pauline correspondence is remarkably restricted. The gifts of healing as such, in fact, do not appear outside the disordered and eccentric church at Corinth - a poor example for any to follow. There is no suggestion from his own writings that Paul was ever involved in exorcism, nor is it something that even the Corinthians were practising as an evidence of the power of the Spirit of Christ over other spirits. Demons, in fact, are mentioned in the Pauline corpus only as a derogatory term for the pagan gods (1 Cor 10:20-21) and he makes minimal use of the conventional terms for spiritual beings, displaying little interest in them. He nowhere mentions demons in the context of human illness nor does he refer to exorcism. The enemies of humanity, in Paul's thought, are not individual demons and spirits, but the great spiritual forces of Sin and Death, seen as the primary powers of evil that have utilised the Law to accomplish humanity's downfall and spiritual slavery.

Paul, in fact, has hypostatised the abstract concepts of salvation history and essentially personalised them. This trait had become very evident in Hellenistic Judaism (particularly in the writings of Philo of Alexandria) with the hypostatisation of the attributes of deity, making it possible for John, for example, to develop his understanding of the Word of God personalised in Jesus and for Paul to identify him with the hypostatised divine Sophia (Wisdom). Paul has thus moved away from the more conventional understandings of the 'spirit world' and the literal demons which populated the world of popular thought, to a more philosophical standpoint with which, as an Hellenistic Jew, he would be more at home and with which his sophisticated Hellenistic readers would be more able to identify. It may be stated with some degree of certainty that the writings of Paul give no basis for any practice in the modern Church for exorcism or other forms of so-called 'deliverance ministry', whether undertaken in accordance with established rituals (as in the Anglican, Catholic and similar traditions) or with the excesses of modern charismatic excitement. It is surely high time that such practices were given the critical attention they require.

Further, and very importantly, Paul himself did not consider it appropriate, or else was unable, to heal his own colleagues when they were ill (Epaphroditus in Phil 2:25-30 and the probably genuine traditions in the deutero-Pauline literature: Timothy in 1 Tim 5:23 and Trophimus in 2 Tim 4:20). The advice given to Timothy, in fact, is very far removed from any concept of special healing. The prescription quite clearly comes straight out of the Hippocratic tradition of treatment for those whose constitution is not strong, even to the provision of a little wine to drink [29]. It is incontrovertible, therefore, on the basis of the evidence of the Pauline writings taken as a whole, that it was the apostle's understanding that 'Christian faith and experience provide no immunity against disease' [30].

One of the important matters to arise from this discussion is that the evidence of the Pauline writings would militate against the view that an emphasis on the healing of physical disease was a major aspect of early Christianity. This has been a common assertion from the days of Adolf Harnack who argued that, 'Deliberately and consciously (Christianity) assumed the form of "the religion of salvation or healing", or of "the medicine of soul and body", and at the same time it recognised that one of its cardinal duties was to care assiduously for the sick in body' [31]. In a similar vein, Nutton has argued that 'from its inception Christianity offered itself as a direct competitor to secular healing' [32]. However, the writings of Paul, which represent the earliest witness to Christian belief and practice, provide no evidence whatever for such views. Nor does Paul suggest that there was any special 'healing ministry' within the early Church other than a general obligation to care for those in need and distress. There can be no doubt that the care of the sick 'was an important part, but only a part, of the general philanthropic outreach of the church' [33], but we look in vain in Paul for any validation of the modern emphasis on physical healing as being an essential part of the Church's ministry. That the pursuit of the 'miraculous', in healing as in other matters, became a feature of the Christianity of succeeding centuries is not in question, and some of the possible reasons for this are briefly discussed in the concluding chapter of this study. This attitude, however, is not apparent in the first century Church as presented in the Pauline letters. The simple fact of the matter is that the practices of the Pauline churches provide no basis for a healing ministry in the Church as that expression is normally understood.

Some consideration will now be given to Paul's own experience of sickness in order to complete this picture. The following discussion will examine his 'thorn in the flesh' that troubled him constantly, at least in the earlier stages of his apostolic ministry, as well as the possibility that he may have suffered from some form of eye disorder.

Excursus: Paul's personal health

No discussion of Paul's understanding of sickness and healing would be complete without some consideration of the information that may be gleaned about his own health. In general, Paul says very little about himself in this regard other than to refer to his 'thorn in the flesh' (2 Cor 12:7), as well as his numerous physical assaults from his enemies and persecutors. The suggestion that he may have suffered from visual problems is largely dependent on the secondary sources of the Acts of the Apostles and there is little first hand evidence. The discussion that follows will examine the data in relation to both the 'thorn in the flesh' and the possible loss of vision.

Paul's constant physical deprivations and his various beatings and stonings would have had an inevitable effect on his health. According to his own testimony he experienced, 'beatings beyond number, at death's door frequently. Five times, I took thirty-nine lashes from the Jews. Three times, I was beaten with rods. Once I was stoned' (2 Cor 11:23-25). He also speaks of numerous physical deprivations in the course of his ministry - cold, hunger, sleeplessness and a life of toil and hard work (2 Cor 11:27). There is, in this list of sufferings, a strong element of rhetoric and it has been compared frequently to the conventional lists of troubles endured by the moral philosophers of the Graeco-Roman world [34]. It need not be doubted that Paul borrowed from such concepts, but this does not mean that his list of both accomplishments and sufferings is simply exaggerated rhetoric for the sake of effect and with no real basis in fact. It would not have been difficult to disprove Paul's claims if they were false and in the light of his defence of his position as a genuine apostle, a series of palpably false claims would indeed have 'left him naked before his enemies'.

Paul's boasting was, for him, an essentially foolish activity, it was contrary to his normal stand that the only ground of boasting was Christ, but in the specific circumstances of his controversies with the Coritnhians, it was a necessary element in his defence against his detractors. Like Philostratus before Domitian [35], Paul may apologise for sounding like a rhetorician and be very uncomfortable with the method (2 Cor 11:1; 17; 21; 23; 12:1; 11), but he recognised that he had to defend his good name and he did so in a fashion well understood by his Corinthian readers. His opponents made exaggerated claims about themselves: Paul's response was to pour disdain on their pretentiousness and assert that he was able lay claim to equal accomplishments. More importantly, he can lay claim to the life of suffering that is the mark of the true servant of Christ, for it follows the pattern of humility, obedience and suffering which he himself had laid down as a perpetual example (cf Phil 2:1-11). Such a life would have left its scars and it is of particular interest that it is in the context of such experiences that Paul speaks of his 'thorn in the flesh', a physical condition that clearly troubled him for an extensive part of his ministry.

Paul's 'thorn in the flesh'

The nature of Paul's 'thorn in the flesh' (2 Cor 12:7) has been a subject of continuing speculation over the years. Quite apart from those theories that consider Paul's 'thorn' to have been some non-physical problem, such as Jewish persecution, it has been remarked that the list of possible physical causes 'reads like the index of a textbook of medicine' [36]. The discussion that follows does not make any claims to provide a definitive solution, since all attempts to do so are, at best, speculative, but it will be argued that the diagnosis of post-traumatic epilepsy (epilepsy following head injury) is one which fits the available evidence and accounts for the scattered clues that Paul provides in a reasonable manner.

There can be no reasonable doubt that the 'thorn' was a specific physical problem. The various ideas which attempt to identify the 'thorn' with some sort of non-physical situation, such as persecution or opposition from others, especially his fellow Jews, spiritual temptations of various sorts, excessive grief or remorse and similar suggestions, all fail to do justice to the text and context [37]. Paul writes of a condition that began to occur at a specific time: in association with an ecstatic vision. Further, it was recurring, disabling and an individual and personal problem. Situations such as opposition and persecution, being the common lot of all Christians, hardly meet the case. It is assumed, therefore, without further discussion that Paul's 'thorn in the flesh' was some sort of physical condition which was humiliating, perhaps even degrading, and which dated from the time of the specific event of the ecstatic spiritual experience he described, which was itself the immediate precursor of the 'thorn'.

It has already been noted that Paul's reference to his 'thorn in the flesh' occurs within the context of a lengthy autobiographical note in 1 Cor 12 in which he contrasts his experiences of weakness and suffering with those of his opponents who boast in their spiritual strength. He describes a series of dire experiences which he has faced, involving severe personal hardship (none of which, incidentally, is reflected in the compressed account of Acts), and he then recounts one particular episode in which he experienced some form of ecstatic vision (2 Cor 12:1-6).

It was following this particular experience that Paul states that he was given 'a thorn in the flesh, a messenger of Satan, to harass me' (ἐδόθη μοι σκόλοψ τῇ σαρκι, ἀγγελος σατανα, ἱνα με κολαφιζῃ). The context makes it clear that the apostle viewed this affliction as the direct will of God in order to keep him humble, in the light of the revelations he had received through his ecstatic experience. 'Paul did not escape from this experience of his unscathed, but because of the spirit in which he accepted its disagreeable consequences, they became a blessing to him instead of a curse (2 Cor. 12:7-10)' [38]. It is the nature of those 'disagreeable consequences' that will be the primary subject of this section of the study. The discussion will focus on the time of onset and the relationship to the ecstatic vision as well as examining the clues in Paul's writings that provide a basis for a diagnosis.

Chronological problems

There are major difficulties in dating Paul's life, difficulties that are exacerbated by the virtual impossibility of reconciling Paul's autobiographical reminiscences (Gal 1:11-2:11 and 2 Cor 11:16-12:10) with the highly compressed and selective treatment in Acts which has been written with certain specific theological points to make [39]. Paul's ecstatic experience, however, appears to have taken place about seven to ten years after his conversion, at a time when he was in 'the regions of Syria and Cilicia' (Gal 1:12), presumably with his base in his home town of Tarsus (assuming the accuracy of the tradition underlying Acts 11:25,26).

This dating is based on the following considerations. There would be general agreement that the Corinthian correspondence was written in the mid-50s of the first century AD. Writing to the Corinthians, Paul dates his ecstatic experience and the subsequent 'thorn in the flesh' to some fourteen years before the time of writing (2 Cor 12:2), which would thus place the events around AD 40. In his letter to the Galatians, Paul dates his conversion/call to at least seventeen years before writing that letter (Gal 1:18; 2:1). There are substantial differences of opinion on the dating and destination of Galatians.

However, if it be assumed that the letter is early and has a 'south Galatian' destination [40], then this would set Paul's conversion in the early 30s. Such a chronology predates by several years what Luke describes as the first missionary journey. Indeed, Acts passes over these post-conversion years of Paul's life, compressing them virtually out of the narrative, other than brief mention of a few events, such as Paul's escape from Damascus (compare Acts 9:23-25 with 2 Cor 11:32,33).

It seems incontrovertible, however, that, however long it may have been, this period of Paul's life was one which involved him in extensive missionary activity (note Gal 1:23) during which he suffered many of the hardships recounted in 2 Cor 11 and 12. These hardships involved persecution that involved physical violence of an extreme nature, such as beatings and stonings, as well as other severe privations arising out of the nature of his extensive travels. Even allowing for some degree of rhetorical exaggeration in his descriptions, it seems certain that Paul endured significant physical abuse in the course of his work. It will be argued that Paul's 'thorn in the flesh' arose as a direct result of one or more of these episodes of physical violence to which he alludes and which occurred at these early stages in his ministry.

The ecstatic experience: 2 Cor12:1-10

Paul is remarkably reticent about the strange experience which he mentions in 2 Cor 12:2-10. It has been noted earlier that the context is one of self-defence against charges made by his opponents in Corinth and he utilises the standard methods of rhetorical defence, especially irony and sarcasm. The details are not of importance for the purposes of this study other than to note that Paul plays down the value of visions in his scheme of things. Visions and other 'spiritual' experiences are not the criteria by which one may judge the validity of apostolic calling and authority. For Paul it is the humiliation, the suffering and weakness which show clearly that he is following in the footsteps of his Lord and the credentials that he offers are those of sharing in the sufferings of Christ. This stance is in contrast to those false apostles against whom he is arguing, who boast in their superior spiritual experiences. It is suggested that this is important for understanding the nature of his experiences. Paul's apostolic ministry had been almost a progression from one beating or stoning to another and it is not improbable, therefore, that this ecstatic experience was a post-traumatic phenomenon, the direct result of a severe beating or stoning, a result of his following the path of 'weakness' in his own *via dolorosa.*

It is not proposed to discuss the language that Paul used to describe his experience in detail as this has been the subject of numerous other studies and is outside the scope of this discussion. The concern of this study relates solely to the possible nature of his 'thorn' [41]. Paul described his experience in language that would appear to borrow from contemporary ideas as would be expected, as all descriptions of reality are coloured by the broad concepts of the contemporary culture. The 'third heaven', for example, is paralleled in Testament of Levi 2:7 and Ascension of Isaiah 6:13, etc., and the concept of a heavenly ascent is found as a spiritual experience in 1 Enoch. What is important is that Paul felt that he had been transported to a different realm of existence and the language he used to describe his ecstasy reflects the concepts and thought of his time.

From the point of view of this study, it is important to observe that Paul's language strongly suggests some form of 'out of the body' experience. He did not know at the time whether he was alive or dead, as he graphically describes it (vv 2,3) and there appears to have been both depersonalisation and derealisation. He places the whole event in the third person as if it had happened to someone else (note the expressions, 'a man in Christ' (v 2) and even more vaguely, 'so and so' (τοιουτον) (v 3). This shift into the third person may be no more than a rhetorical device. R.P. Martin comments, 'by writing in this manner, he diverts any plaudits from himself, for ... he openly speaks of himself ... only in terms of weakness' [42]. His aim is to direct glory to God, not to himself. On the other hand, experiences of this nature are frequently experienced as though they were occurring to someone else and the use of the third person may reflect experience rather than rhetoric. Sometimes the plain meaning of the text may be correct!

Such conditions of altered consciousness may occur following severe trauma, especially head injuries, and they are referred to as the 'acute organic psychiatric syndrome' [43]. The type of depersonalisation that Paul describes is a frequent manifestation. In this state patients exist in a condition of altered consciousness in which there is a sensation of being detached from the body and being able to look down on it as though it were an entirely separate entity. The experience is usually recalled as having been pleasant and is associated with feelings of great elation. In addition, visual hallucinations and rich thought processes are common features, often with fantastic content. There is also a state of disorientation in time and place. Such situations are generally of very short duration, but there is no indication of the length of time that Paul may have been unconscious or semi-conscious and the experience itself is essentially independent of organised time, as dreams are. It is always dangerous to try to read back into an earlier time modern understandings of pathophysiological change, but Paul's experience has many parallels with modern 'out of the body' experiences. It is proposed, therefore, that Paul's ecstatic experience meets the broad criteria of a post-traumatic state of altered consciousness: an acute organic psychiatric syndrome. This would fit well with the statements he made about his various beatings and stonings with their inevitable concomitant of head injury [44].

Experiences of this type may be associated with other conditions and situations, occurring in so-called 'near death' experiences [45]. Persons resuscitated after cardiac arrest, for example, may be able to describe vivid visual and auditory phenomena that are likely to be due to the effects of cerebral anoxia and may occur in other conditions in which there is disturbance of brain oxygenation. In addition, conditions such as temporal lobe epilepsy may also be associated with this type of experience and Landsborough has argued very cogently that this was the nature of Paul's 'thorn in the flesh' [46]. Similarly, Vercelletto has argued that the Pauline texts suggest the possibility of facial motor and sensory disturbances arising after ecstatic experiences and these may have been the pre-seizure aura in his epileptic condition [47]. He notes that such ecstatic auras are uncommon, but are, nonetheless, well documented and he provides a number of case histories of patients who have experienced ecstatic auras before their seizures. However, people tend to have difficulty in recalling auras, although the post-seizure psychoses may be well remembered and may often have a considerable amount of religious content, such as visions of angels, the Virgin Mary and so forth, depending on the patient's background.

Previous attempts to identify the 'thorn'

The suggestion that temporal lobe epilepsy may have been the specific condition to which Paul referred as his 'thorn in the flesh' is, in one sense, a variant of the suggestion that he suffered from generalised epilepsy, a view which seems to go back to 1804 [48]. Temporal lobe epilepsy is a localised or focal form of epilepsy associated with a specific sensory, motor or psychic aberration that reflects the functioning of that part of the brain from which the seizure originates. Landsborough in particular, has made out a well-argued case for considering Paul's 'thorn in the flesh' to have been this very specific form of epilepsy, on the basis of his visionary and ecstatic experiences. There is no doubt that post-seizure hallucinations are common in temporal lobe epilepsy, together with behaviour patterns that are often out of keeping with the individual's normal character. There is often a display of compulsive and obsessive behaviour that is frequently of a religious nature. Individuals may experience sudden religious conversions and display an excessive 'religiosity' with a tendency to rapid anger [49].

There are certainly aspects of Paul's behaviour that seem to conform to this pattern and a number of visionary experiences are related in Acts, starting with his Damascus Road experience (Acts 9:1-9 and parallels) and going on to those which gave him guidance and encouragement in his later missionary work (Acts 9:12; 16:9-10; 18:9-11; 22:17-21; 23:11; 27:23-24). Paul himself seems to suggest that he had a number of 'visionary' experiences apart from the specific experience under discussion here (2 Cor 12:7). Too much should not be built on this foundation, however. The accounts in Acts represent a secondary source for Paul's life and he says remarkably little about such experiences in his own correspondence. Furthermore, there would appear to be very real differences between the ecstatic and apparently 'out of the body' experience which gave rise to his 'thorn' and the dreams and visions from which he gained guidance and encouragement. There is no compelling evidence in Paul's writings or the Acts that Paul ever experienced another ecstatic-type vision. The clear impression from 2 Cor 12:1-6 is that this was a unique experience which had never recurred [50], although the 'thorn', to which the trauma had given rise, was an ongoing condition that continued to trouble him, at least over a fourteen year period.

The close association between the onset of the trouble caused by the 'thorn' and the experience related in 2 Cor 12:1-9 needs to be emphasised. Paul himself recognised that this relationship was not merely associated in time, but also appeared to be causal. Admittedly, Paul's understanding of the connection was in terms of the will and purposes of God, but he was very well aware that the one followed the other - it was because of his ecstatic vision that he now suffered his 'thorn'. Any attempt to identify the nature of the 'thorn', therefore, requires to take these relationships into account. Landsborough and Vercelletto do not give this sufficient weight in their discussions and they rather put the cart before the horse by inferring that it was Paul's 'thorn', in the form of temporal lobe epilepsy, that gave rise to the vision. It would seem more probable that the reverse is the case: the situation that produced the vision also produced the 'thorn'.

Other suggestions made over the years have also ignored this vital connection between the visionary experience and the subsequent development of the 'thorn', or perhaps, more explicitly, between what specific pathology may have caused both the vision and the 'thorn'. Earlier guesses at diagnosis have included, generalised epilepsy of unknown origin, eye conditions, noting the various allusions to possible difficulties with vision in the Pauline correspondence and Acts (Gal 4:15; 6:11, Acts 23:5), as well as a variety of infections, more especially malaria [51] and brucellosis (Malta fever) [52].

It is interesting that few modern medical writers feel that the data compels them to argue a case in support of malaria, although it remains a popular suggestion among commentators. Malaria would certainly have existed in the low lying regions of Asia Minor and indeed it was endemic throughout the Mediterranean basin as was noted earlier in this study in connection with the illness of Simon Peter's mother-in-law (see the discussion at pp 63-65). It is worth noting that malaria continued to exist in this region until very recently [53]. The forms of malaria in the Mediterranean area have been the so-called benign tertian and quartan forms caused by *Plasmodium vivax* and *Plasmodium ovale*. The illness is certainly debilitating and, on occasions, may also be fatal [54], but it hardly seems to have been the type of disease that would merit Paul's description of his condition. Paul seemed to see this as something very distinct and especially humbling to him. It had come to him because of his vision. Fevers (including malaria) were extremely common and very much part of the general experience of life throughout the areas of his travels. It seems very surprising, therefore, that Paul would have thought of such essentially common conditions as being a special attack on his ministry, which is certainly the way in which Paul views his 'thorn in the flesh'. Indeed, it is unlikely that he and his friends would have escaped from malaria and it is very probable that they would have suffered an attack long before Paul's ecstatic vision.

More recently the interesting suggestion has been put forward by S. Levin that Paul suffered from dystrophia myotonica, a congenital disease of muscles [55]. The condition tends to become manifest in the second and third decades of life and is associated with weakness of the facial muscles and the muscles of the hands and feet. It may be associated with cataracts, sleepiness and intellectual impairment - hardly something that Paul exhibited! Apart from this, however, the problem with this proposal is that to arrive at the diagnosis too much reliance has been placed on the famous, but much later description of Paul's appearance in the second century, charming, but nonetheless, apocryphal, story of *The Acts of Paul and Thecla* [56].

Severe migraine has also been suggested from time to time and the case has been argued recently by Margaret and Trevor Lloyd-Davies [57] although in their view this diagnosis does not account for the Damascus Road experience. A more substantial case for migraine, however, has been made out by Gobel, Isler and Hasenfratz [58]. They argue that the evidence suggests that Paul was suffering from bouts of unilateral headache as well as a chronic eye condition, neither of which appeared to give rise to lasting damage. In their opinion, the various descriptions given of Paul's medical problems meet the criteria of 'migraine without aura' according to the 1988 Classification of Headache. They also argue that this fits in with the Damascus road experience. The flashing light, mentioned in the accounts of the experience and which caused Paul to fall down, may be interpreted as a migraine visual aura with the additional symptoms of photophobia (his 'blindness') and anorexia (he did not eat for three days).   On these assumptions, Paul's whole experience falls into place with his later history. The issue of Paul's Damascus road experience, however, will be discussed in more detail later in relation to his apparent visual problems.

F.F. Bruce has underlined the importance of the chronological issue that is not given full weight in many of these foregoing theories. He makes the point that the 'thorn' 'was probably the "bodily ailment" from which (Paul) suffered when he first visited the Galatians - an ailment which was a "trial" to them as well as to him and which might have been expected to repel them or make them spit in aversion' [59]. Neither malaria nor migraine would fit such categories: indeed the response would have been to help the sufferer rather than being repelled by him in such circumstances.

Internal diagnostic criteria for Paul's 'thorn in the flesh'

It is clearly impossible to provide final certainty about the diagnosis of Paul's 'thorn in the flesh'. However, it may be argued that a condition which meets all or most of the criteria that may be discovered in Paul's own account of his ecstatic experience and its aftermath will provide a credible and reasonable diagnosis. The following are the criteria that need to be met and, it would be argued, many of the suggestions about the nature of Paul's 'thorn' have not taken them into account.

a) The condition was a genuine physical illness. The expression τῇ σαρκι ('in the flesh') is perhaps not as clear as one might have wished, but the implication of the dative here is surely to indicate 'physically' as opposed to 'spiritually' (there is a similar construct in Col 2:5).

b) The onset was sudden, beginning at a specific and specified time in association with his visionary experience. The use of the aorist tense (ἐδόθη) for 'given' at 2 Cor 12:7 would seem to support this interpretation.

c) The condition was chronic in that it appears to have been a problem for fourteen years. It was also recurrent, the implication of the present tenses of ὑπεραιρω ('to be elated') and κολαφιζω ('to harass') at 2 Cor 12:7.

d) It was associated with feelings of depression (2 Cor 12:7).

e) Further, whatever the condition may have been, it was not one that was so debilitating as to impede Paul's work and he was able to continue his ministry without any significant hindrance. This would seem to militate immediately against those views that have postulated conditions such as malaria, which would have been likely to have prostrated the apostle for days at a time.

It is not clear whether pain was associated with this condition. It is likely that that 'thorn' and 'beat' are used metaphorically, laying emphasis on the way in which Paul's body felt racked by the condition, rather than indicating that it was a constant source of pain. There seems to be no doubt that the word for 'buffet', 'harass' or 'box the ears' (κολαφιζω) was often used metaphorically and may mean no more than 'ill treat', or 'roughly treat' (so at 1 Cor 4:11 and 1 Pet 2:20) [60].

Other factors also need to be taken into account. There are clues that Paul's illness was plaguing him during his time in Galatia (which would be expected in view of the time relationships already noted). At Gal 4:13 Paul speaks of his bodily 'weakness' (ἀσθενεια), using a term that was frequently used for sickness in general. The problem at this time appears to have been of sufficient severity to bring about a change in his plans (Gal 4:13). Further, this illness was distressing, not only to the sufferer, but also to those who saw him (Gal 4:14), causing feelings of disgust or perhaps even fear. Responses like this, especially from his friends, effectively take out of contention the usual run of general medical conditions: a fever does not arouse such emotions nor would a severe headache. Finally, Paul's condition was something for which no treatment was available. The Galatians, as Paul remarks, would have torn out their own eyes in order to help him, but they could do nothing (Gal 4:15).

Towards a diagnosis

It is suggested that the condition of post-traumatic epilepsy comes close to fulfilling all the criteria listed above. It was noted earlier that epilepsy has been 'a favourite guess' for many years, but this suggestion has not been related to the specific consequences of head injury as far as the writer is aware. The suggestion made here is that the visionary experience was the direct result of severe head trauma, from one of the many beatings or stonings to which Paul alludes (2 Cor 11:23-25), which then left him with post-traumatic epilepsy.

It has been estimated that something in the order of three per cent of all hospital admissions for head injuries (including minor cases) are associated with the development of epilepsy [61]. The condition is thus by no means uncommon in the modern world and there is no reason to assume that human responses to injury were any different in the ancient world. It is also a condition especially related to parietal or temporal injuries, the type of injury that might be expected from blows to the side of the head. Further, it has been shown that closed head injuries, associated with local brain damage and focal neurological signs, have a very high risk of developing epilepsy and these are the very type of injury which would be likely to result from beatings and stonings [62]. The condition usually develops within six months of the causative injury, and generally sooner, and it is also often associated with some degree of personality change, especially increased nervousness, anxiety and irritability [63].

It is noteworthy that Paul seems to have suffered from exactly these problems and there are suggestions of unusual anxiety and fear for example at 1 Cor 2:3. It is also possible to interpret the comments in both 1 Cor 2:3-4 and 2 Cor 10:10 as indicating some sort of speech defect which, might well have been a result of head trauma. It is accepted that these passages may be no more than references to Paul's lack of rhetorical delivery, although Acts 14:12, assuming it to be based on a reliable tradition, would seem to indicate that Paul was a gifted speaker at the very time when, from his own account, Paul's 'thorn' would appear to have been troubling him. Paul, however, must be allowed to speak for himself and he suggests that he made a very bad first impression on people (for example Gal 4:13), indicating that, although his letters were eloquent and impressive, his actual speech was not. As Barrett remarks, Paul's 'letters are so eloquent that it is hard to believe that Paul was a bad speaker unless he suffered from a speech defect' [64].

One further reference is worth noting. When Paul wrote about his experiences with the Galatians, he praises them for not spitting at him (οὐδὲ ἐξεπτύσατε, Gal 4:14). The verb ἐπτύω, described as, 'a vulgar *koine* word' [65] is found only here in the New Testament. The act of spitting was considered to be a way of warding off the evil eye or demonic powers and the verb is used here 'quite literally in the sense of the ancient gesture of spitting out as a defence against sickness or other demonic threats. The Galatians resist the temptation to see in Paul someone who is demonically possessed because of his sickness, but instead they received him as an angelic manifestation, indeed as Christ Jesus himself' [66]. Epilepsy was the disease, *par excellence,* that was always associated with spitting in the ancient world; it was *morbus qui sputator* [67].

It is impossible to do more than surmise: the evidence is thin to say the least, even in Paul's own letters. On the other hand, it is difficult to imagine that the violence that Paul suffered in the course of those early years of his ministry would not have left its mark on even the fittest person, both physically and mentally. His post-traumatic epilepsy may well account for some of the irritability and abrasiveness, as well as the depressive episodes, occasionally revealed in his letters. It is a reasonable conclusion, therefore, that post-traumatic epilepsy arising from head injury would fit the criteria for Paul's 'thorn in the flesh'.

It is possible that such episodes of epilepsy may have been localised in nature and not associated with the major, whole body seizures of grand mal epilepsy. Conditions such as temporal lobe epilepsy, which produce complex partial seizures, may be associated with trauma and it has been estimated that as much as 19 per cent of the incidence of this condition is traumatic in origin [68]. Such trauma may also have left Paul with some facial or other weakness from nerve damage and this might explain such references as Gal 4:14 and 6:17 in relation to his physical appearance. It is also worth noting that all forms of epilepsy, including post-traumatic types, have a marked tendency to remission as time progresses, and the patient may become symptom free [69]. This may explain the lack of further references in Paul's later correspondence. Certainty is impossible, the evidence for any definitive conclusion does not exist and the best guess is but speculation. However, a diagnosis of post-traumatic and probably focal (or localised) epilepsy fits the criteria for determining the nature of Paul's 'thorn in the flesh' and provides a reasonable solution to the problem.

One further comment is worth making. The book of Acts is remarkably silent about any form of disability from which Paul might have suffered. There is no indication at any point that the author's hero suffered from any form of illness, especially one that was associated with humiliating or even degrading manifestations. Paul strides across the pages of Acts, unaffected, it would seem, by even the severest beatings or other forms of physical abuse. Whether this is simply selective reporting in order to maintain a particular view of Paul, or whether it is a reflection of Luke's 'charismatic' type theology in which sickness may be healed miraculously and immediately, can be debated. The reality, however, seems clear and rather different. Paul suffered from a chronic condition for which there was no 'miracle' cure in spite of his ardent prayers (2 Cor 12:8-9). The answer to Paul's prayer was the grace to be able to live with his affliction and glorify God within it. The great apostle was not immune from the normal ills and sufferings that belong to the human state and his condition, whatever it may have been, had to take its course with no special divine intervention to bring immediate relief. The modern protagonists of triumphalist theologies and miracle cures might do well to give more thought to the experience of Paul and his 'thorn in the flesh'.

Did Paul have a visual problem?

Details of Paul's life rest on two groups of sources, as has already been noted. These are the primary sources of his own correspondence, addressed mainly to the Christian communities that he had been instrumental in establishing, and the secondary sources found in the Acts of the Apostles on the one hand, and in the deutero-Pauline letters on the other. Clues to a possible visual problem may be found in both sets of material, although it has to be admitted that the main evidence derives from the secondary sources. The evidence begins with the accounts of Paul's religious conversion/call on the way to Damascus. According to the Lukan sources, Paul was temporarily blinded as a result of this experience.

Paul's conversion: Acts 9:1-19// 22:3-16// 26:9-19

There are three separate accounts of the conversion/call of Saul of Tarsus. The first (Acts 9:1-19) represents Luke's account of the events that took place on the Damascus road and what happened subsequently, while the other two accounts (Acts 22:3-16 and 26:9-19) are cast as part of speeches by Paul in his own defence. There can be little doubt that Luke saw this event as being of supreme importance for the life of the early Church, which is hardly surprising given the centrality of Paul in Luke's account of the gentile mission and the establishment of Christianity as a genuinely universal religion. From Luke's point of view, this event and its consequences form part of his overall thesis, running through both the Gospel and Acts, that the inclusion of the gentiles and the gentile mission itself are fundamental to any proper understanding of the function of the Church in the world.

The three accounts of Paul's conversion contain minor variations of relatively little importance and they make no difference to the key elements of the story which are the same in each version [70]. The variations, in fact, may be accounted for by Luke's skilful story telling and the different contexts in which the event is recounted. Lüdemann has proposed [71] that the original tradition contained three elements: that Saul, as he was then, was near Damascus; that he saw a brilliant light and fell down, and he heard a voice and was struck blind for a time.

In addition to these elements, there is the tradition of the subsequent visit of Ananias and the consequent restoration of Paul's sight. There is no real reason to doubt this tradition and, as Haenchen has remarked, Paul 'having seen Christ in or near Damascus, was baptised by some member of the congregation there - and why should this Christian not have been called Ananias ?' [72].

There is, however, a significant problem with regard to Luke's version of events. Nowhere in any of his extant writings does Paul himself allude to this traumatic experience. Paul certainly refers to the reality of his Christophany in places such as Gal 1:12-16; 1 Cor 9:1f and 15:8. Luke's tradition agrees with Paul's personal testimony that he had seen Christ Jesus the Lord. Paul himself, however, gives no indication that his experience of the risen Christ was associated with the dramatic events of the Lukan narrative.

Elsewhere, Paul recounts his many experiences of suffering, trauma and persecution and he can speak of a specific post-conversion 'out of the body' experience. There would seem to be no reason, therefore, why he should have been particularly reticent about what happened on the Damascus road. Indeed, at 1 Cor 15:8 he is very emphatic that his meeting with the risen Christ belonged to the same category as the other post-resurrection appearances and was not in any way substantially different from them. The experiences of the other disciples were not associated with the sort of dramatic situation with which Luke surrounds Paul's meeting with the risen Christ and the subsequent dramatic change to his life. Indeed, quite the reverse would appear to have been the case and the Gospels certainly give the impression of a set of experiences that were virtually under cover.

The question arises, therefore, did Luke get it all wrong? Was he simply trying to build up the conversion of the apostle to the gentiles into a dramatic and awe-inspiring event that would add status and credibility to his hero? It has already been noted that the three separate versions of Paul's conversion/call may be accounted for by Luke's skilful story telling. If that is so, then there is, in reality, only one version of this story which Luke has developed and used for his own purposes, and which, more importantly, has no independent verification in Paul's own autobiographical statements.

It would be too sweeping a judgment to relegate the story of the Damascus road experience to no more than legend. There are elements in the story that have an authentic ring and among them is the account of Paul's transitory blindness following the bright light that shone around him. Paul, himself, speaks of his confrontation with the risen Christ as an 'apocalypse' (Gal 1:12-16) - 'a glorious manifestation in which Christ revealed himself to Paul in his state as Son of God' [73]. It is not certain whether he intends this terminology to set his own experience apart from the other post-resurrection appearances, but it could be a reference in particular to the blinding light.

There are three essential features of Paul's blindness according to the Lukan tradition. It followed exposure to some form of bright light (Acts 9:8; 22:11; 26:13), secondly, it was essentially transitory, lasting only for a few (three) days (Acts 9:9), and finally, recovery of sight appeared to have been associated with desquamation of the cornea, assuming that the comment about 'scales falling off' (Acts 9:9) represents a genuine statement about real experience.

The tradition will be examined, assuming its essential historicity, but bearing in mind the *caveats* already expressed. The Lukan story seems to make a clear association between the blindness and the appearance of the bright light and this effectively rules out any suggestion that the light was no more than a subjective sensation or that the blindness was a post-seizure phenomenon resultant upon temporal lobe epilepsy or migraine as has been suggested [74]. Paul probably suffered from epilepsy, but, as argued earlier, this was likely to have been post-traumatic epilepsy and a condition that developed later than his call, being, in fact, the direct result of his experiences as a Christian missionary. Further, the Lukan narratives are strongly suggestive that the light was not the result of a personal subjective experience, but rather was a genuine event [75]. The version of the story at Acts 26, for example, speaks of the light being brighter than the mid-day sun (Acts 26:13) and the use of the verb περιλαμπειν ('to shine') in that context 'suggests physical blinding by a dazzling light' [76]. At Acts 9:3 the light is said to have 'flashed around' (περιηστραψεν), a term used normally for the flash of lightning [77].

It is a reasonable suggestion that Paul's blindness at the time of his conversion, resulted from something akin to lightning stroke injury in which there was a mixture of high intensity light injury, thermal burns to the cornea and possibly retina and a possible long term sequel in the development of cataracts. The visible light spectrum may cause flash blindness with temporary retinal dysfunction or moderate to severe degrees of retinal swelling and atrophy, depending on the light intensity and length of exposure [78]. The effects of heat on the cornea may have been even more important. Corneal burns induced by the heat of the high intensity light would produce death of tissue by heat coagulation of the proteins. The cornea becomes opaque causing transient blindness and there may well be additional localised retinal damage [79].

Three days after the exposure Paul's vision returned following the spontaneous sloughing of the scale-like damaged epithelial tissue. Thus, as Luke puts it, 'something like scales (or flakes) fell off' (απεπασαν ... ώς λεπιδες). Most commentators fail to notice the significance of this throw away remark and even Wilkinson misses the point when he writes that the phrase 'need mean no more than that the return of his sight felt to Paul as if scales had fallen from his eyes' [80]. Although the only examples of the use of αποπιπτω in conjunction with λεπιδες appear to relate to skin diseases [81], the description of epithelial desquamation or sloughing would be difficult to better.

In addition to possible retinal damage, the likelihood of delayed cataract development should also be considered as a potential long term outcome of lightning stroke injury. The association between electric shock and delayed cataracts is well documented [82]. The most likely explanation for Paul's immediate blindness after the Damascus road experience would appear to be something akin to lightning stroke injury with associated thermal burns, possible long term retinal damage and late cataract formation. This view is shared by J.D. Bullock [83], who, after considering a variety of other possibilities, such as vertebro-basilar artery occlusion (most unlikely let it be said in an apparently healthy and relatively young man) and damage to the occipital region following the fall (although the tradition suggests the fall took place after the blinding light), considers that lightning stroke injury and heat induced corneal burns are the most likely causes of Paul's blindness.

This view has been endorsed by other writers [84] and it seems to be the explanation which best fits the available evidence. Whether the laying on of the hands of Ananias had any effect in the healing process is an issue that will depend on one's point of view. It is an action associated with healing in the Gospels, but here it is specifically associated with the giving of the Spirit as well as the recovery of Paul's sight. The possibility that the Damascus road event may have produced some permanent damage to Paul's sight seems to be hinted at in such passages as Acts 23:5 where he fails to recognise the high priest as well as his own comments in Gal 4:15 and 6:11 and these passages will now be considered.

Paul's failure to recognise the high priest: Acts 23:5

The accounts of Paul's missionary activities in the Acts of the Apostles contain only one other episode that may be construed with any plausibility as a reference to visual impairment. Following his arrest in Jerusalem, Paul is brought before the Jewish Sanhedrin for questioning. Following a rather heated altercation, Paul indicates that he had failed to recognise the high priest who had been speaking to him and accepts that it was contrary to the Torah to speak ill of him. As with the story of Paul's conversion, there is no independent substantiation of the event, but it has the ring of authenticity and hardly seems the sort of detail that would have been invented. Various suggestions have been as to why Paul failed to recognise the high priest. It may well be that the words represent an ironic comment on his view of the validity of the claim of Ananias to be high priest or simply sarcasm - 'I did not think that a man who spoke like that could possibly be the high priest' [85]. The suggestion that he failed to recognise the high priest because he had changed since his last visit to Jerusalem has little to recommend it. The high priest would have been in the chair whoever he was and the only two alternatives would seem to be that Paul either could not see that far or he was pursuing his attack on the high priest with sarcasm.

The arrest of Paul in Jerusalem is likely to have taken place about AD 56 or 57 and thus some twenty years or more after his conversion and call. Such a time span would have provided ample opportunity for the development of cataracts as a result of his original lightning stroke injury as well as the exposure to the high levels of ultraviolet light that would have been part of his normal life in the eastern Mediterranean world. In general, the degree of visual impairment is proportional to the density of the cataract, although there may be situations in which loss of visual acuity is out of all proportion to the degree of lens opacity and arises from image distortion. There may also be a paradoxical element so that, although distance vision may be markedly blurred in the early stages of cataract formation, near vision may actually improve slightly so that reading or writing will be unimpaired [86]. Such a situation would certainly fit with the Lukan accounts, allowing Paul to read, but to have problems with his distance vision at the same time. Thus, when facing the high priest, all that he saw was a blurred white figure and he was unable to make out sufficient detail to recognise him.

Nothing can be made of Luke's use of the verb ἀτενίζω at Acts 23:1 where Paul 'looked intently' or 'stared' at the Sanhedrin. The word could indicate an eyesight problem and Luke also used it of Paul at 13:9 when he was dealing with the magician Elymas in Cyprus on his first missionary journey with Barnabus. The verb, however, is almost a favourite with Luke in various settings (twice in the Gospel and ten times in Acts, but only twice elsewhere in the New Testament, in 2 Cor 3:7 and 13). It may perhaps give the sense that Paul was straining his eyes to see his accusers or the magician [87], but it would be dangerous to build too much on such an insecure foundation.

Argument on the basis of the secondary Lukan data is admittedly speculative and no firm conclusions may be drawn. Nonetheless, both the story of the conversion and the later incident before the Sanhedrin are consistent with a single underlying pathology and it remains to examine the evidence from Paul's own correspondence.

Paul's personal comments

There are two somewhat ambiguous statements that may have some bearing on the question of Paul's eyesight, both of which occur in his letter to the Galatians. The first is at Gal 4:15 where Paul speaks of the willingness of the Galatian Christians to have even torn out their own eyes if it had been possible to give Paul some benefit. At an earlier stage in the argument, in the context of the discussion of the 'thorn in the flesh', it was pointed out that this phrase may mean no more than a willingness to give what they prized most to help Paul in his weakness. As F. F. Bruce remarks, 'it is most precarious to take the mention of "eyes" too literally, especially to suppose that the language implies Paul's own eye trouble. The most that can be said is that, if it could be established otherwise that he suffered from some eye-affliction, there would be special force in his choice of words here' [88]. Similarly, Fung argues that it 'is unlikely that the language here implies eye trouble on Paul's part; it may be no more than a graphic description of deep affection' [89]. It would be dangerous therefore, to base too much on this statement.

The second reference concerns the large letters to which Paul refers in the final paragraphs, after his secretary had completed the rest of the letter (Gal 6:11). It seems even more difficult to turn this statement into a reference to visual problems than the previous one. Virtually all commentators see the reference to the 'large letters' as nothing other than a method of emphasis [90]. Over a century ago, Sir William Ramsay drew attention to the use of large letters in public proclamations. He wrote, 'attention was often called to some especially important point, especially at the beginning or end, by the use of larger letters' [91], a practice which in varying ways remains widespread to the present day. This remains the most probable reason for Paul's remarks. As Bruce notes, 'whether the "large letters" were due or not to the condition of his (Paul's) eyesight cannot be said' [92]. It would be dangerous, therefore, to force these words beyond their obvious sense and make them refer to Paul's poor eyesight. They do not provide support for the existence of visual problems any more than do Paul's earlier remarks.

The evidence, therefore, for any problems with Paul's eyesight cannot be adduced with certainty from his own first hand testimony, but only from the secondary sources of Acts and even these references do not provide unequivocal statements. The available evidence allows no conclusions to be drawn and perhaps the speculative theories about Paul's eyesight should now be laid to rest. On the other hand, the possibility that Paul's 'thorn in the flesh' was post-traumatic epilepsy is one that fits the evidence on a reasonable basis.

The real issue, however, from the standpoint of this study, lies in the fact that for Paul there was no immediate 'miracle' cure for his condition in spite of his ardent prayers. In the light of what has been gleaned already concerning the nature of those conditions that are most amenable to healing by prayer and 'faith', it is hardly surprising that a chronic physical illness, such as Paul probably suffered, remained unaffected. As was noted earlier, the answer to Paul's prayer was not a 'miraculous' cure, but the grace to be able to live with his affliction, whatever it may have been. Paul's letters provide no evidence of sudden or special intervention to relieve him or his friends from the ills and sufferings that belong to the human state: genuine physical pathology had to take its course. There is little in the Pauline writings that would suggest that healing (and particularly 'miraculous' healing) figured very highly in his thought and nothing whatever to suggest that it was practiced in any church other than Corinth. Euqally certainly, healing does not feature as an indispensable part of the Christian gospel as Paul understood it.

The witness of the non-Pauline documents

The references to healing in the Pauline literature have been shown to be extremely sparse. It was clearly a subject that did not rank highly in Paul's thought either about the nature or the content of the good news of Jesus and its consequences. When one turns to the other New Testament letters one finds even fewer references to healing and, as in Paul, none whatever to exorcism. In fact there are only three clear references to healing in the remaining New Testament works - one apparently in James 5:14-26 and the others in Revelation 3:18 and 22:2. These will be considered in turn and, in addition, some attention will be given to the reference to Isaiah 53:5,6 at 1 Peter 2:24 and its frequent use as a proof text that physical healing is included in the Atonement.

Healing in the letter of James

There has been considerable debate about the dating of the letter of James. Arguments have been advanced both for a very early date (as early as AD 45-50) on the one hand and for a very much later date on the other, towards the end of the first century or possibly even later [93]. The mediating view, put forward originally by F.C. Burkitt [94], suggests that there was an Aramaic original to be dated early and this was later reworked into very elegant Greek. This option admittedly would seem to seek to have the best of both worlds, but there is much to commend it. James may be seen, perhaps, as the work of 'an enterprising editor. He published his master's work in epistolary form as a plan to gain for it credibility as an apostolic letter. And in doing so, he aimed to address a situation of critical pastoral significance in his region' [95]. This is essentially the view adopted in this study. James may be seen, therefore, as a witness to early concepts and practice in the Christian communities (particularly those that were of Jewish origin) and where the letter appears to have made no modifications to such practices, then the suggestion is strong that the later communities of the editor's time continued to follow the same traditions.

If the letter is as early as some have suggested, then it would predate the majority of Paul's correspondence by some years. The apparent attack on antinomian type misconceptions of the Pauline 'no-law' gospel, however, might suggest that the letter should be dated in relation to the spread of Pauline Christianity and it would thus post-date the Pauline correspondence. In its final form, therefore, this document should be considered as a product of Hellenistic Judaism, a codification of Jerusalem-based Jewish Christian thought in the light of new circumstances and new problems, yet reflecting earlier traditions and practice [96]. If the view be accepted that the underlying ideas and general provenance of the book come from a very early stratum of Jewish-Christian and essentially Palestinian, tradition, then the way in which issues of those described as 'the weak' (ἀσθενει) (usually translated as 'sick') are treated here may give some clues about practice in the early Jewish Christian communities. Further, the fact that the approach is not changed by the editor to meet new and later circumstances, suggests that the practices which are described had remained fairly constant over the intervening years.

James 5:14-16

The discussion of the way in which the 'weak' (ἀσθενει) are to be treated (5:14-16) falls into a section of practical exhortation concerned largely with issues of behaviour and which matches the earlier section 1:19-27 in content. The entire pericope into which this short section falls, is dedicated to the issues of pastoral and community prayer, it is about prayer in all the normal circumstances of life. The subject of verses 14-16 is the effectiveness of prayer for those described as 'weak'. The text of this passage begins with the statement, 'is any among you weak' (ἀσθενει τις ἐν ὑμιν) and this has usually been interpreted as requiring the meaning 'sick' in the light of the frequent use of ἀσθενεια as equivalent to sickness. Indeed, the majority of commentators have assumed with little discussion that ἀσθενει means 'those who are sick'. For example, the older commentator J. B. Mayor simply stated that the word meant 'sick' and drew a comparison with Matt 10:8 and considered that the reference was to a 'special case' of κακοπαθια, the 'suffering' or 'affliction' of vv 10 and 13 [97]. More recently, R.P. Martin also prefers the interpretation of 'sick', but he nonetheless has remarked that it is not entirely clear what kinds of affliction are being referred to in the context of v 14 [98].

There seems to be an element of ambiguity present, however, and it is perhaps surprising that the translation 'ill' or 'sick' has been accepted uncritically in all English translations, particularly as the corollary of this translation would suggest rather strongly that the writer is supporting the ancient view that sickness and sin are directly related in a causal fashion.

There seems little doubt, especially in the light of the references to sin, confession and forgiveness, that the writer is supporting a relationship between being 'weak', whatever that may mean, and sin. This is given weight by the use of the present imperatives of 5:16 that suggest that confession and prayer 'will save' (σωσει), a verb that, as has been noted earlier in reference to the Gospel stories, frequently bears the meaning of 'heal' or 'make whole' in a physical context [99]. In fact, the general impression conveyed to the reader is that 'if all Christian were to be admitting their sins to one another and praying for each other, the ultimate remedy of summoning the elders might be avoided' [100]. Although there would appear to be a conditional element in the statement, 'and if (*or* even if) he is in a state of having committed sins' (κἀν [και εαν] ἀμαρτιας ἡ πεποιηκως [a periphrastic perfect participle]), it has to be stated that the overall impression that is gained from the passage, particularly in view of the calling of the elders as the disciplinary body of the local community, together with the general sense of v 16, is that sin and 'weakness' are being seen as closely related. The issue is to determine what James means by 'weakness' and whether this section has anything to do with healing the sick at all, particularly in view of the earlier citation of the ancient hero Job, who patiently endured his physical affliction and is set out as an example for Christians to emulate (James 5:10,11).

It is proposed that the reference in this section is not to physical sickness, but rather to a mental state. Three types of people in three different situations are brought together by the writer. There are those 'in trouble' (κακωπαθει), those 'in good heart' (εὐθυμει) and those who 'are weak' (ἀσθενει). The context suggests that they should be seen together as three separate mental or emotional states and that behind them there stand, as Wright has suggested, three groups of people who manifest these specific forms of mental state arising from within themselves or as a result of outside circumstances [101].

The first group are 'in trouble', but the idea behind κακωπαθια seems to have shifted by the first century, from suffering, misfortune or misery as such, to a more active sense of the endurance of such suffering, usually arising from external forces and situations. This is borne out by the only other New Testament examples of the term, all in 2 Timothy (2:3, 9; 4:5), where in each case the thought is of 'putting up with', or 'enduring hardship'. The passage suggests, therefore, 'not so much the distressing situation as such, but the spiritual burden which it brings with it and which drives us to prayer. Hence the prayer is more for the giving of strength than the removal of the situation' [102]. Those who are facing or enduring trouble, suffering or misery should thus pray for strength. The second group are those who are cheerful and in good spirits. They should praise God (ψαλλετω: literally, 'play the harp'!). The word used for 'the cheerful' (εὐθυμει) is also rare in the New Testament, occurring only here and in Acts 27:22 and 25 where Paul exhorts his companions to take heart, or cheer up, in the face of the impending shipwreck. It thus suggests a sense of being in good heart in spite of facing trouble and this idea fits well with the context of this section in James.

In contrast with the cheerful are the ἀσθενει, a group that Wright has argued means, in this context, 'depressed'. This interpretation is given support in the light of the very unusual word used at v 15 where these people are referred to as τα καμνοντα, that is, burdened, weary, down-hearted or fatigued, even perhaps weary of life [103]. If we are to translate ἀσθενει as those who are sick, therefore, it has to be a sickness of a very special sort. The context suggests that the writer is thinking, in fact, quite specifically of members of the congregation who are depressed and, in the light of this context, their depression would seem to arise from guilt.

On either side of the person who is cheerful, therefore, stand those who are in very different frames of mind. The contrasts are deliberate. On the one hand, there are those who are putting up with the pressures and stresses of external circumstances ('stressed out' perhaps, in modern parlance). They are told to pray for help and strength in their trials. On the other hand, there are those who are burdened from within, attempting to cope with inner pressures and guilt, and becoming depressed. James suggests that the administrations of the local church leadership will have a supportive and therapeutic value in this situation, helping them to find forgiveness and restoration.

The issue of whether the writer was thinking of physical sickness as a specific result of sin within the Christian community, a discussion that frequently arises in relation to this passage, may be seen therefore to be essentially irrelevant. Certainly, such ideas belonged to the culture of the time. It was noted earlier that the disciples of Jesus in the Johannine tradition certainly saw physical disability, in the form of blindness, as the result of sin (John 9:2). Paul also appears to have associated some of the Corinthian excesses with sickness, although it is not entirely clear whether he saw the sickness and occasional death in the Corinthian community as a punishment or as a logical consequence of their actions (1 Cor 11:30). If the argument that James is not thinking of physical sickness at all in this context is correct, then the question of whether he considered sickness to be a result of sin on the part of the sufferer is no longer of concern. It is proposed, therefore, that James was describing a state of depression, a form of *accidie*, that 'deadly sin' of the mediaeval Church which is so often mistranslated as 'sloth'. Those with this problem are not slothful, however, but feel rather that there is no purpose and meaning left for them and no reason for them to 'press on'. It is a state of mind in which guilt (real or imagined) may figure highly as a cause and for which the assurance of forgiveness will be an important factor in aiding recovery [104].

It is significant, therefore, that it is the 'elders' (πρεσβυτεροι) of the congregation who are called to the 'weak' person. The community to which the letter is addressed is generally agreed to have been Jewish, even to the extent that the word 'synagogue' was still being used of a Christian congregation (2:2). There remains a great deal of uncertainty about the ways in which the early Church developed its leadership patterns and general organisation. There is some evidence that, outside Palestine at least, the tendency was to follow the Jewish Diaspora practice of appointing congregational presidents assisted by 'deacons', but with the whole community of city congregations being overseen by a synodical board of elders, chosen from among the congregational presidents [105]. In this context, however, James writes of a single congregation being governed by a number of elders, a practice which seems to mirror more closely the type of community order to be found in some forms of sectarian Judaism, especially perhaps the Qumran community [106]. The elders are to be called to these down-hearted and depressed members in order to pray and anoint with oil. These administrations, particularly the faithful prayer, are expected to restore the one described as 'weak' and bring forgiveness.

Considerable discussion has always focussed on the exact function of anointing in this passage. James writes, 'if any among you (ἐν ὑμιν, that is, in the congregation) is weak (ἀσθενει) let him summon (προσκαλεσασθω) the elders of the church and let them pray over him (προσευξασθωσαν ἐπ' αὐτον), having anointed him (ἀλειψαντες: aorist participle) with oil (ἐλαιω: specifically olive oil) in the name of the Lord (that is, the Lord Jesus)'. James thus sets out a specific

Christian act of prayer in association with the anointing of oil in order to provide what might be termed the therapeutic context for the restoration of the depressed person and give assurance of forgiveness.

The ancient world generally held a high view of the medicinal properties of olive oil. Oil baths and forms of anointing were commonly practised and it was used ritually in exorcisms and other forms of healing and seen as an important supportive measure in sickness [107]. It is not surprising therefore, to find that a medicinal use for oil has been considered in this context. Wilkinson, for example has argued that an analysis of the use of the verb ἀλειφω in the New Testament 'appears to support the medical view rather than the religious one' [108]. The verb is used on only nine occasions in the New Testament, of which eight are in the Gospels and none relates to religious or ritual anointing. The verb χριω might have been expected as the better choice for a religious or symbolic act of anointing., but it is never used in the New Testament for the act of anointing and is always used in a metaphorical sense. The use of the verb ἀλειφω in the Gospels relates to anointing for toilet purposes, with the single exception of Mark 6:13 which refers to the anointing of the sick by the Twelve as part of their ministry. After their commissioning by Jesus, Mark notes that the disciples 'cast out many demons and anointed many sick with oil and healed them'. What is of interest is that although the disciples were apparently given the commission to heal in this way, there is no record that Jesus did. It should also be noted that there appear to be no other references to unction related to healing in the first two centuries of the Christian Church [109].

The use of olive oil, however, was never considered as a panacea in ancient times. It simply represented one form of therapy among many and it is difficult to see why James should be so specific if he was thinking merely in general terms of therapeutic measures to be used in this situation. When the emphasis is on prayer, why should anointing be a significant part of the 'ritual' when, as Shogren has remarked, 'anointing is not the best medicine and in most cases not even good medicine' [110]. Nonetheless, the use of oil could possibly be seen as a general form of therapy designed to show visible care and attention and thus provide support to the person James describes as 'weak'. Furthermore, the general background would underline an important symbolism related to the outpouring of God's grace and such a visible act of caring support would be of considerable psychological benefit for someone suffering from guilt-related depression. The process of anointing, however, was no more than support and as Hemer has remarked the 'reference is grammatically subordinate, and reads like an incidental mention of a current practice which James does not need to explain' [111]. It is clear, however, that there is no suggestion in this passage that anointing conveyed some sort of semi-magical healing property. Nor does this passage give any basis for the practice of sacramental anointing for the sick. Such practices are based on a concept of grace that understands it as an almost physical substance that is contained in the act of anointing, an understanding derived from mediaeval scholasticism rather than the New Testament. It is regrettable to see a practice abandoned by the churches of the Reformation being reintroduced under the influence of both sacramental and charismatic circles in so-called 'healing' services and authorised 'healing' liturgies.

It needs to be emphasised that the central emphasis of this passage is not on anointing at all, but on the prayer that aided the transformation in the person's state. The effect of guilt-laden remorse and depression, for which there was no help or support, may be seen in the suicide of Judas Iscariot. Paul also draws attention to the difference between that form of depression (λυπη) of which God approves, because it leads to a change of heart and 'salvation' (σωτηρια), which in this context is not to be identified with 'cure' or 'healing' in a physical sense, and the depression which is of 'the world' and leads to death (2 Cor 7:10). Paul was without doubt thinking of 'spiritual death', an existence that is separated from God, but the end result of such unrelieved depression may be physical death as the patient is no longer able to face the realities of life and commits suicide. Altschule sees in this a remarkable understanding, based on empirical observation, of the difference between what would be termed a non-psychotic and a psychotic depression in modern medical terminology [112]. Both Paul and James see the proper outcome in terms of 'salvation', the eschatological wholeness of relationships to be experienced in the present by virtue of the activity of God in Christ. This is not physical healing *per se* and James does not use the normal verb for physical cure (ιαομαι) until v 16 when there appears to be a shift in meaning.

If this interpretation is correct, then once again, as in the Gospels, it is the mental aspects of disease that benefit from prayer. The situation may be extended, for in all illness and all true cure, there are more than merely physical aspects. The 'spiritual' effects of illness are part of normal experience and there would be few who had not suffered the depressing effects of a viral illness such as influenza, for example. Illnesses of all forms result in mental, spiritual and social effects whether in general debility, in reactive depression, in anxiety and so forth. In these situations the therapeutic value of confession and the assurance of forgiveness are well known as they doubtless were to James. These considerations underline the often forgotten point that the function of the Church lies, not in the curative aspects of illness, but in the restoration of the spiritual dynamics of life: in mediating forgiveness and the removal of guilt which may act as catalysts in the overall curative process. As was noted earlier, the emphasis of James is not on the 'faith healing' of disease, but rather the need to accept and bear our misfortunes, including sickness, with the same fortitude as did Job in the ancient story (James 5:10,11). The experience of James, it is suggested, simply emphasises the especial benefit for those suffering from guilt-laden depressions or similar conditions to have reassurance of forgiveness. Further, there is little doubt that such reassurance has an important part to play in the whole general area of functional rehabilitation in times of significant sickness.

There is, however, a final statement in this section. The members of the community are exhorted to confess their sins to one another (ἐξομολογεισθε: present imperative) and pray for one another so that they may be healed (ὁπως ἰαθητε) (v 16). Here the more specific medical word for curative healing is introduced, making an apparent assumption of a causal link between sin and sickness. Such ideas were common at the time (and still are) [113] and represented an effort to find a cause for human illnesses in a concept of punishment by a somewhat vengeful God. However, the use of the present imperative here would suggest that the confession is a repeated action possibly taking place within the setting of normal community worship as a public act [114]. Further, the fact that this is something in which the whole community shares, rather than just the elders, suggests that something other than the specific situation envisaged in the preceding verses is in view.

The verb ἰαομαι is generally used of physical cure in the New Testament, but not absolutely, and the idea that sin may be considered a disease needing radical cure appears for example in Heb 12:13 (note also 1 Pet 2:24) [115]. Indeed, the ideas expressed in Heb 12:12,13 are almost identical in thought to those expressed here and emphasise the ethical responsibility of helping the weak in the faith so that they may be 'healed'. The writer to the Hebrews is giving a word of encouragement to the weaker members of the congregation as they strive for the ultimate goal. If those who are strong will move forward in a straight line, then those who are 'lame' will follow more easily and find 'healing' in the community [116]. It is suggested, therefore, that

James is now moving away from the specific to the general and into the wider realm of pastoral care within the community [117]. The reference would thus seem to be to a figurative healing in the sense of restored relationships, both in a vertical sense with God and in the horizontal sense within the community. Such healing comes about through mutual confession and consequent mutual forgiveness and it closely parallels the saying in Matt 5:23. As Tasker put it, 'Christians should always pray for one another, not only in time of illness but in all the vicissitudes of their lives, so that healing, in the fullest and widest sense of that word, may be bestowed upon them' [118].

It is likely that there will always be some doubt as to the exact meaning of this passage. One thing, however, is clear. Whether James is thinking of depressive type illness or more general sickness, at no time does he envisage some miraculous and immediate effect as a result of prayer and anointing. The elders, representing the church in its pastoral function, were told to seek the aid of God in prayer to bring forgiveness, performing a symbolic act which perhaps demonstrated the pouring out of God's grace, thus assuring the individual that God's grace was present in the situation. Further, there is no suggestion from this passage that the communities to which this letter was addressed knew, understood or used some special 'gift of healing', assuming that more general healing is in view here, rather than the very limited situation that this study has suggested. It may also be argued that James is reflecting the institutionalisation of the *charismata* in the officers of the local church and he provides no place for the type of charismatic ministry that existed, for example, in Paul's Corinth.

More probably, however, James knew nothing of special 'gifts of healing' within the communities with which he was associated. Indeed, there is not even 'a specific reference to a particular elder who is looked upon as the conduit for divine healing. All this is to say that James is not describing for us the practice of "faith healing", a charism claimed by some in the Corinthian church' [119]. As was noted earlier, 'healing gifts' are claimed only in the one disordered church at Corinth and nowhere else in the New Testament letters. It is not unreasonable to infer, therefore, that 'charismatic healing' was neither a regular nor a prominent feature of the life of the early Church as some have often assumed. Equally, these passages give no theological basis for the practices of sacramental healing and the ritual use of specially consecrated oil as though this would impart some unique virtue.

Healing in 1 Peter

It is difficult to locate 1 Peter in terms of its historical setting. The emphasis in recent study has been on the social setting and the way in which the author emphasises the immense differences that separate himself and his readers from the social norms and moral values of the surrounding society [120]. The letter seeks to preserve the social cohesion of the Christian communities to which it was sent by setting and maintaining the boundaries between them and the pagan Roman world, but at the same time, it also seeks to show ways in which Christians could adapt to their social setting. Nonetheless, the emphasis is on the people of God living in exile: the writer sees himself in 'Babylon' (1 Peter 5:13) and his readers are similarly a 'diaspora', scattered as strangers throughout the Roman provinces of Asia Minor. Thus, whatever points of contact they may have with local society, they are essentially outsiders.

One reference in this document has been related to healing. It occurs in a context in which the behavioural differences between the Christians and their pagan neighbours are emphasised. In 1 Peter 2:24,25 suffering as a Christian is marked as the path of honour, for it follows the example of Christ and the slave who accepts what seems to be dishonour for the sake of Christ, wins the approval of God. The passage is of importance as it has often been appealed to as a biblical basis for the inclusion of the healing of disease within the specific terms of the Atonement. It is for this reason, and only for this reason, that the passage merits brief consideration in this study.

1 Peter 2:24,25

These verses include a quotation from Isa 53:5,6 and, as noted above, they have often been appealed to as a proof text by pentecostals, charismatics and others in order to provide a biblical basis for the view that physical healing is part of the Atonement [121]. The statement in question reads, 'He himself took up our sins in his body on the cross, that we might die to sin and live to righteousness. By his wounds you have been healed (τῷ μωλωπι ἰαθητε), for you were wandering like sheep, but have now returned to the Shepherd and Guardian of your souls'. The central portion is essentially a citation from the final Servant Song of Deutero-Isaiah (53:5,6) in which the writer has substituted the original first person 'we' for the second person plural in order to adapt the quotation to the needs of his readers. In view of the later use of this passage in the teaching of the Church, it is, rather surprisingly, the only place in the New Testament where this particular statement is cited [122].

The context in which the quotation is used relates primarily to the suffering of those members of the local church who were slaves. They faced frequent brutality from their owners with beatings and other mistreatment. This was part of the normal lot of slaves, but it would also seem that some of the mistreatment was because of their obedience to Christ. The slaves, therefore, are to recall Christ's example of his own patience under suffering and his own obedience that eventually led to their salvation through the ultimate redemptive suffering of the cross.

The imagery of Deutero-Isaiah, as translated in the Septuagint, was especially suited to this situation with its reference to the bruises or welts (μωλωψ) that come from being beaten with a whip. There is encouragement for these slaves in the fact that Jesus himself accepted such brutal and unfair treatment and his way, as their Leader and Shepherd, is the way they should follow. The writer, however, takes this a stage further and makes the profound claim that 'Christ's passion was vicariously beneficial: as a result of his sufferings sinful men (sic) have been healed, i.e. restored to health from the wounds which their sins had inflicted' [123].

The whole emphasis of these verses is thus on the death of Christ as the source of new life. The cross, for these believers, meant nothing less than the origin of their new life of doing what God required (righteousness) because of their death to sin. The cross was the place where they had been healed, not from natural diseases, not from the burdens and beatings of every day and the effects these had on their tired bodies, but rather through their restoration in Christ and their ability to lead a new life with new ideals, new goals and new hopes and aspirations centred in Christ the Shepherd and Guardian of their souls.

There can be no real doubt that in the context of this letter, the reference to Isaiah 53:5,6 and the idea of healing or as it may reasonably be translated, 'restoration', belongs to the realm of the forgiveness of sins and the related verses make this clear. To interpret Peter's use of Isaiah 53 as the basis for a theology that includes physical healing as an integral and essential part of the Atonement totally ignores the context in which the quotation is used and is a prime example of eisegesis based on theological presuppositions, rather then genuine exegesis of the text. The reference is figurative and relates to the remarkable concept that the one bowed down by his own suffering, becomes himself the bearer of the suffering of others and thus opens the way for forgiveness and peace. Neither text nor context would suggest any relationship to physical healing in this passage.

Healing in the book of Revelation

The book of Revelation is undoubtedly a difficult book, but, as Scobie has noted, the introductory letters to the seven churches of Asia 'cannot simply be labelled as "apocalyptic" with the attendant implication that all their imagery and symbolism is nothing more than part of the stock in trade of apocalyptic writing' [124]. The writer was dealing with specific situations and in doing so used imagery that would have meaning for his readers. While the case for local imagery in the book of Revelation has, at times, been exaggerated, its existence may not be simply discounted and as Scobie concludes, 'there is at least a core of local references in the letters' [125]. The specific historical situation is of less importance as far as this study is concerned. There are two references to healing in the book of Revelation, both of which should be seen as essentially figurative in the light of their specific contexts and, in consequence, having nothing to say in respect of any healing ministry within the Church. They occur at Rev 3:18 and 22:2.

Revelation 3:18 [126]

The reference in this passage is to the use of ointment for those with various eye conditions. The context is the letter to the Church at Laodicea, a community beset by many problems and at a low ebb in its spiritual life. The church is described as being neither cold (that is being able to provide refreshing cold spring water) nor hot (that is being able to provide the healing properties of a hot spring), but simply lukewarm, like the city's water supply that was open to the sun. Tepid water was unpalatable and valueless and simply made the drinker nauseous. The church brought neither spiritual refreshment nor healing to those who needed it. Sadly, the members of the community were blind to their faults and failings and imagined that all was well in a state of vaunted prosperity and complacent self-sufficiency. The writer, however, sees them as 'poor, blind and naked' and counsels them to buy gold (a reference to the wealth of Laodicea as a major banking centre), obtain white clothing (a contrast with the prized black and glossy woollen garments for which the city was famous) and obtain an eye ointment to help them see.

This reference, in common with the other exhortations, is clearly metaphorical: it is spiritual vision that is in view, but the reference would have been well understood by the readers. Sir William Ramsay, in his important studies at the end of the nineteenth century, drew attention to the existence of the medical school in Laodicea, established in the time of the Greek geographer, Strabo, probably around the beginning of the first century, at which a noted ophthalmologist, Demosthenes Philalethes, taught. Ramsay also connected 'Phrygian powder' (an ingredient of eye ointments) with Laodicea [127]. The connection of an eye ointment (κολλυριον) with this school, however, is no more than an inference, as neither of the passages that Ramsay quoted (one from Pseudo-Aristotle and the other from Galen) make a direct reference to Laodicea as the source of the material for producing eye ointment. However, the passage in Galen does immediately go on to speak of an ear ointment which was specifically from Laodicea. On the other hand, although properly cautious about the references to 'Phrygian powder', Hemer [128] has shown that there are a number of circumstantial pointers which favour Ramsay's suggestion, namely, the presence of the most famous medical (and ophthalmic) centre in the region within the city, the fact that Laodicea was in Phrygia and the references in other writers to the sale of *collyria* to people who do not know how to use them. This suggests that there may well have been a major commercial enterprise in the manufacture and sale of patent eye ointments that was no doubt extremely lucrative in a world where eye problems were common.

In terms of the letter to the local church, however, spiritual blindness was the problem, although the underlying irony would surely not have gone unnoticed. The members of this community claim to be able to deal with the problems of physical eyesight, but totally fail to deal with the much more profound problem of spiritual insight in spite of the fact that a genuine remedy lies ready to hand. The diagnosis of their spiritual blindness was clear for all to see: the treatment lay in Christ, the source of true light and spiritual vision.

Revelation 22:2

The final chapters of the vision of John of Patmos focus on a 'Paradise regained' and the imagery is largely derived from the prophetic books of the Old Testament, particularly Trito-Isaiah and Ezekiel, with the pictures of the tree of life and the river of life. The picture of living water as a symbol for the life of God is common throughout the Old Testament and, in the New, it is particularly used in the Johannine literature, especially the Fourth Gospel. Life cannot exist without water and John of Patmos presents a picture of water for all who need it. The picture is identical to that of John 7:38 where the evangelist presents Christ as promising his followers that from their inner being, living waters will flow. Flowing from the heart of the Church in the seer's vision is a life-giving river from which all may drink, it is the very life of God himself given to all through the presence of God's Spirit flowing directly from the throne of God and of the Lamb.

Beside this river, as in the vision of Ezekiel (47:1-12), is the tree of life, a picture that takes the reader back to the story of the first garden in Eden. If that story was the image of Paradise Lost, then here John of Patmos introduces the thought of Paradise Regained, in words that are borrowed directly from Ezekiel. He wrote that along the banks of the Temple river of his vision there would be all kinds of trees, 'their leaves will not wither and their fruit will not fail; each month they will produce new fruit, because the water for them flows from the temple. Their fruit will provide food and their leaves will bring healing (εἰς ὑγιειαν in LXX, translating *litrûpâ*)' (Ezek 47:12). John's picture is the same with its multiplicity of fruit, to be gathered all the year round, reminding one of Paul's imagery of the fruit of the Spirit, but, as in the picture of living water, the benefits are not for the dwellers in the New Jerusalem alone, but are for all people. 'The leaves are for the healing of the nations' (Rev 22:2) said the Seer.

It is interesting that John has changed the LXX's εἰς ὑγιειαν to εἰς θεραπειαν, which tends to provide a clearer and more specific statement of healing in the sense of 'cure' or perhaps 'remedy', whereas the use of ὑγιεια has a wider sense and could be translated to make whole or sound [129]. The community of God's people is given a healing mission to bring the wholeness of God's life to the nations. The essential function of God's electing purpose is that through the few, the many will receive blessing and this is the way John of Patmos sees it here. The picture is figurative, as was probably Ezekiel's also, but while Ezekiel seemed to see the blessings of God as restricted to his people Israel, here the Seer pictures the nations, still bearing the wounds of their battle against God and the Lamb, now coming to receive the cure and the restoration which only Christ's redemptive work can provide.

The healing envisaged by John of Patmos is the healing of the inner rebelliousness of the human heart. It is a restoration of the right relationships between God and his creation that had always been his purpose. This is no second hand usage of old symbols. As Kiddle has put it, he 'sees the river and the trees *afresh*. He sees what they stand for. And when he reports what he has seen in the words already used by Ezekiel, he is actually authenticating the earlier revelation of God's will' [130]. The vision, however, has nothing to do with physical healing, but everything to do with the healing of human sinfulness and the restoration of right relationships.

The non-Pauline letters, thus have little to say about physical healing. The emphasis is always figurative when healing concepts are introduced, relating to the restoration of relationships. The therapeutic metaphors relate not to the physical realm, but to the spiritual health of men and women. The emphasis was not upon curing disease, but upon curing the deeper malady of human sinfulness and even though the concept of 'Christ the Physician' became prominent in the early Church, its primary use was always metaphorical in relation to the 'cure of souls' [131]. There seems to be little, therefore, to suggest from either the Pauline or non-Pauline documents that Christianity saw itself as a religion of healing or that it concerned itself with a healing/curing ministry as distinct from a caring ministry in the first century. Further, there is no suggestion that there was a developed healing ministry with a primary function of attesting the gospel to the pagan world outside the community. As far as the sick were concerned, the emphasis was on their care, rather than their cure. The implications of these conclusions will be the subject of the final chapter.

Notes and references

[1]   Kümmel, W.G. (1975). *Introduction to the New Testament*. ET. SCM, London. p 249.

[2]   Bruce, F.F. (1952). *The Acts of the Apostles*. Tyndale Press, London. second edn. p 35

[3]   See for example the claims in such works as Greig, G.S. and Springer, K.N. (eds). (1993). *The Kingdom and the Power*. Regal Books, Ventura, CA; Harper, M. (1965). *As at the Beginning*. Hodder and Stoughton, London; Foot, D.R.P. (1967). *Divine Healing and the Scriptures*. Henry Walters, Eastbourne, U.K.; Baker, J.P. (1973). *Salvation and Wholeness: Biblical Perspectives of Healing*. Fountain Trust, Eastbourne, U.K. and other charismatic and similar writers.

[4]   Wilkinson, J. (1980). *Health and Healing: Studies in New Testament Principles and Practice*. Handsel Press, Edinburgh. p 103.

⁵ The wide variations in dating between such studies as Bruce, F.F. (1977). *Paul: Apostle of the Free Spirit.* Paternoster Press, Exeter and Jowett, R. (1979). *Dating Paul's Life.* SCM, London are evidence of the immense problems associated with Pauline chronology. See also Lüdemann, G. (1984). *Paul, Apostle to the Gentiles: Studies in Chronology.* SCM. London, whose conclusions on dating are somewhat radical.   Note also the article on 'Chronology' by L.C.A. Alexander (1993), In: Hawthorne, G.F. and Martin, R.P. (eds). *Dictionary of Paul and his Letters.* Inter-Varsity Press, Downers Grove, IL. pp 115-123 and the bibliographic material in C.C. Smith (1991) in his article on 'Paul', In: Schellinger, P.E. (ed). *St James Guide to Biography.* St James, Press, Chicago. pp 613-615.

⁶ The title 'capital epistles' (*Hauptbriefe*) for Galatians, 1 and 2 Corinthians and Romans was first coined by F.C. Baur in the last century.   He wrote that these letters 'bear so incontestably the character of Pauline originality, that there is no conceivable ground for the assertion of critical doubt in their case' (quoted in Bruce, F.F. (1982). *The Epistle to the Galatians (New International Greek Testament Commentary).* Paternoster Press, Exeter. p 1).

⁷ See Stählin, G. (1964). Ασθενης, κτλ. In Kittel, G (ed). *Theological Dictionary of the New Testament.* Vol 1. Eerdmans, Grand Rapids. ET. pp 490-493. The word group occurs on 80 occasions in the New Testament of which half refer to sickness as a specific type of human weakness.

⁸ The view is taken here that Ephesians is probably Pauline in origin, although this is far from universally accepted.   For an extended discussion of the arguments on either side see Guthrie, D. (1990). *New Testament Introduction.* Apollos, Leicester. 4th edn. pp 496-535.

⁹ Bruce, F.F. (1982).*The Epistle of Paul to the Galatians (New International Greek Testament Commentary).* Paternoster Press, Exeter. p 151. He suggests, however, that this may have included healings as 'the introduction of the gospel to new territories was regularly accompanied by miraculous healings and other "signs and wonders" ' (ibid).   On the other hand, R.Y.K. Fung (1988), sees these 'workings' as 'part of God's present supply of his Spirit and his continuing works of power among the Galatians' (*The Epistle to the Galatians (New International Commentary on the New Testament).* Eerdmans, Grand Rapids. p 130).

¹⁰ See Bauer, p 368 and Liddel and Scott p 815.

¹¹ See Fee, G.D. (1987). *The First Epistle to the Corinthians (New International Commentary on the New Testament).* Eerdmans, Grand Rapids. p 594.

¹² Among recent literature may be noted, Schatzmann, S. (1986). *A Pauline Theology of Charismata.* Hendrickson, Peabody, MA; Martin, R.P. (1984). *The Spirit and the Congregation: Studies in 1 Corinthians 12-15.* Eerdmans, Grand Rapids; Dunn, J.D.G. (1974). *Jesus and the Spirit.* SCM, London; Bittlinger, A. (1974). *Gifts and Ministries: A Commentary on 1 Corinthians 12-14.* Hodder & Stoughton, London and Käsemann, E. (1964). Ministry and community in the New Testament. In: *Essays on New Testament Themes.* SCM, London.

[13] See the references in Fee, G.D. (1987). *1 Corinthians.* pp 590-591.

[14] Pearson, B.A. (1973). *The Pneumatikos-Psychikos Terminology in 1 Corinthians.* Scholars Press, Missoula, pp 46-47.

[15] Talbot, C.H. (1987). *Reading Corinthians: A Literary and Theological Commentary on 1 and 2 Corinthians.* Crossroad, New York. pp 84-85.

[16] Ridderbos, H.N. (1975). *Paul: An Outline of his Theology.* Eerdmans, Grand Rapids. p 442.

[17] Bittlinger, A. (1974). *Gifts and Ministries.* p 20.

[18] The expression comes from Flood, E. (1989). *All is Ours: Paul's Message to all Christians.* Fount Paperbacks, London. p 80.

[19] Wilkinson, J. (1980). *Health and Healing.* p 109.

[20] Gordon Fee (1987) can go as far as to remark that 'What this refers to needs little comment. Jesus, Paul and the rest of the early church lived in the regular expectation that God would heal people's physical bodies' (*1 Corinthians.* p 594). This seems something of an overstatement and reflects his essentially Pentecostal theology. The argument of this study is to demonstrate quite the opposite!

[21] Dunn, J.D.G. (1988). *Romans 9-16 (Word Biblical Commentary).* Word Books, Waco, Texas. p 731.

[22] So Käsemann, E. (1980). *Commentary on Romans.* Eerdmans, Grand Rapids. ET. p 342. So also Cranfield, C.E.B. (1979). *Critical and Exegetical Commentary on the Epistle to the Romans (International Critical Commentary).* T&T Clark, Edinburgh. Vol II; Bruce, F.F. (1963). *The Epistle of Paul to the Romans.* Tyndale Press, London and note the comment of John Calvin (1539) on this verse: 'By the words *those who show mercy,* he means widows and other ministers, who were appointed to take care of the sick, according to the custom of the ancient church'. (*Commentary on the Epistle to the Romans.* Translated by F. Sibson, Seeley and Sons, London. 1834. p 500).

[23] Cranfield, C.E.B. (1985). *Romans: A Shorter Commentary.* T&T Clark, Edinburgh. p 307.

[24] See the full discussion in Martin, R.P. (1986). *2 Corinthians (Word Biblical Commentary).* Word Books, Waco, Texas. pp 434-438.

[25] See further, Sumney, J.L. (1990). *Identifying Paul's Opponents: The Question of Method in 2 Corinthians (JSNT Supplement No 40).* JSOT Press, Sheffield.

[26] Note, for example, the way in which the ministry of Jesus in terms of 'signs and wonders' (as in Acts 2:22) and the ministry of the apostles in similar terms which bore witness to their authority, is parodied by the same forms of activity associated with the 'man of lawlessness' who is empowered, not by the Spirit of God, but by Satan (2 Thess 2:9 and note also Mark 13:22 and Rev 13:13 etc).

[27] Bornkamm, G. (1971). *Paul.* Hodder and Stoughton, London. ET. p 181.

[28] Note the emphasis on 'power' in much of the modern charismatic literature which sees Corinth as a community to be emulated, rather than one that stands as a warning.

[29] Rutherford, W.J. (1935). Hippocratic allusion in the New Testament. *Glasgow Medical Journal. 14. 71-74.*

[30] Wilkinson, J. (1980). *Health and Healing.* p 111.

[31] Harnack, A. (1904). *The Expansion of Christianity in the First Three Centuries.* Putnam's, New York. ET. Vol 1. pp 131-132.

[32] Nutton, V. (1985). Murders and miracles: Lay attitudes towards medicine in classical antiquity. In: Porter, R. (ed). *Patients and Practitioners: Lay Perceptions of Medicine in Pre-Industrial Society.* Cambridge University Press, Cambridge. p 48. Other writers have taken a similar stance, one of the most recent being the medical anthropologist, H. Avalos (1999). *Health Care and the Rise of Christinaity.* Hendickson, Peabodt, MA. In what can only be regarded as a gross overstatement, he can write, 'the Christian approach to health care was one of the primary factors in the rise of Christianity' (p 119).

[33] Ferngren, G.B. (1992). Early Christianity as a religion of healing. *Bulletin of the History of Medicine.* 66. 1-15.

[34] See for example Judge, E.A. (1968). Paul's boasting in relation to contemporary professional practice. *Australian Biblical Review.* 16. 37-50. See further Forbes, C. (1986). Comparison, self-praise and irony: Paul's boasting and the conventions of Hellenistic rhetoric. *New Testament Studies.* 32: 1-30.

[35] Philostratus. *Life of Apollonius.* 8.7.

[36] Wilkinson, J. (1980). *Health and Healing: Studies in New Testament Principles and Practice.* Handsel Press, Edinburgh. p 120.

[37] See the discussion of these views in Martin, R.P. (1986). *2 Corinthians.* pp. 412-418.

[38] Bruce, F.F. (1977). *Paul.* p 135.

[39] See for example the discussion in Jewett, R. (1979). *Dating Paul's Life.* SCM Press, London. Others, however, (such as Hemer, C.J. (1980). Observations on Pauline chronology. In: Hager, D.J. and Harris, M.J. (eds). *Pauline Studies.* Paternoster Press, Exeter. pp 3-18) consider that it is possible to reconcile Paul's autobiographical comments with the narrative of Acts. See also Lüdemann, G. (1984). *Paul, Apostle to the Gentiles: Studies in Chronology* (ET. SCM, London) and Ogg, G. (1968). *The Chronology of the Life of Paul.* (Epworth, London).

[40] The issue is too complex for discussion in this context. In the writer's opinion the weight of evidence supports a 'south Galatian' destination for the letter. For a fuller discussion see Bruce, F.F. (1982). *The Epistle to the Galatians.* pp 3-18, Hemer, C.J. (1990). *The Book of Acts in the Setting of Hellenistic History.* Eisenbrauns, Winona Lake. pp 277-307 and Guthrie, D. (1990). *New Testament Introduction.* Apollos, Leicester, UK. 4th Edn. pp 465-481. It is interesting that British scholars are almost unanimous in supporting the 'south Galatian' destination and continental scholars in contrast support the 'north Galatian' destination. This would underline Bruce's *caveat* that the 'question of the North or South Galatian destination of our epistle is not one in which it is proper to take up partisan attitudes or indulge in dogmatic assertions' (idem. p 17.)

[41] See for example, Bowker, J.W. (1971). 'Merkabah' visions and the visions of Paul. *Journal of Semitic Studies*. 16. 157-173 and Schaefer, P. (1984). New Testament and Hekhalot literature: The journey into heaven in Paul and in Merkevah mysticism. *Journal of Jewish Studies*. 35. 19-35. There is also a useful discussion in Segal, A.F. (1990). *Paul the Convert: The Apostolate and Apostasy of Paul the Pharisee.* Yale University Press, New Haven. pp 34-71. Note also the full scale study of Tabor, J.D. (1986). *Things Unutterable: Paul's Ascent to Paradise in its Greco-Roman, Judaic and Early Christian Contexts.* University Press of America, Lanham, MD.

[42] Martin, R.P. (1986). *2 Corinthians.* p 406.

[43] Gelder M, Gath D, Mayou R (eds). (1990). *The Oxford Textbook of Psychiatry.* Oxford University Press, Oxford. p 296.

[44] The Talmudic stories of four rabbis who experienced similar states of altered consciousness are not strictly parallel as their experiences appear to have been engendered by the use of contemplative techniques (TB *Hagigah* 14b-15b). However, the pathophysiology in terms of brain oxygen starvation may well have been the same.

[45] There have been several reviews of 'out of the body' and 'near death' experiences, e.g. Greyson, B. (1993). Varieties of near death experience. *Psychiatry*. 56. 390-399.

[46] Landsborough, D. (1987). St Paul and temporal lobe epilepsy. *Journal of Neurology, Neurosurgery and Psychiatry*. 50. 659-664.

[47] Vercelletto, P. (1994). St Paul's illness: ecstasy and ecstatic seizure (in French). *Revue Neurologique*. 150. 835-839.

[48] See Plummer, A. (1915). *The Second Epistle of St Paul to the Corinthians (International Critical Commentary).* T & T Clarke, Edinburgh. p 351. He refers to K.L Ziegler's (1804) 'conjecture' in *Theologische Abhandlungen*, a reference that it has not been possible to verify. The earliest reference to epilepsy that has been verified is W Wrede (1907). *Paul.* ET. P. Green, London. pp 22f.

[49] For details see Waxman, S. and Geschwind, N. (1975). The inter-ictal behaviour syndrome of temporal lobe epilepsy. *Archives of General Psychiatry*. 32. 1580-1586. See also Bear, D. and Fedio, P. (1977). Quantitative analysis of interictal behaviour in temporal lobe epilepsy. *Archives of Neurology*. 34. 454-467. These authors also draw attention to such behaviour traits as obsessiveness, hypergraphia, excessive religious responses and a tendency to anger.

[50] Post-ictal (seizure) psychotic states may be 'one-off' experiences, although they are often recurrent.

[51] Original references may be found in Bruce, F.F. (1977). *Paul.* p 135 and Wilkinson, J. (1980). *Health and Healing.* pp 112-142. The latter is a very full and detailed discussion of the differing diagnostic suggestions. Wilkinson follows Sir William Ramsay (1893) (*The Church in the Roman Empire*, Hodder & Stoughton, London. pp 59-68) and favours malaria as the most likely diagnosis as also does Hemer, C.J. (1986). Medicine in the New Testament

world. In: Palmer B (ed). *Medicine and the Bible,* Paternoster Press, Exeter. pp 78-80.

[52] Alexander, W.M. (1904). St Paul's infirmity. *Expository Times.* 15. 469-473; 545-548. Brucellosis, often contracted from drinking milk or eating milk products from infected cows or goats, is also known as undulant fever from its variable pattern of remission and recurrence over a period of time. The condition is characterised by fever, sweats, weakness, malaise and weight loss, usually without any localising findings. Although the recurrent pattern would meet the criterion of chronicity in the short term, it would be extremely unusual for even an untreated case to continue with symptoms over many years.

[53] As late as 1960 the standard British text on tropical medicine notes the continuing existence of certain forms of malaria in Italy, Macedonia, Egypt and Palestine (Manson-Bahr, Sir Philip H. (1960) *Manson's Tropical Diseases.* Cassell, London. 15th edn. p 32).

[54] It is of particular interest that the German archaeologist, Karl Buresch, died from malaria in this area in 1896 during one of his expeditions to Lydia. Even as late as the nineteenth century 'Once out of the main towns, the rudiments of civilised life in the form of roads, inns and medical resources hardly existed'. (Frend, W.H.C. (1996). *The Archaeology of Early Christianity: A History.* Geoffrey Chapman, London. p 103). Conditions may well have been better in Paul's time!

[55] Levin, S. (1963). St Paul's sickness. *Medical Proceedings.* 9. 264-265.

[56] This is a section of a larger work called simply *The Acts of Paul,* written by a second century presbyter from the Province of Asia. The section in question relates to Onesiphorus waiting to meet Paul at Iconium and relying on the description of Titus to do so. The passage reads, 'He saw Paul coming, a man of small stature, with a bald head and crooked legs, in a good state of body, with eyebrows meeting and nose somewhat hooked, full of friendliness; for now he appeared like a man and now he had the face of an angel' (contained in: Hennecke, E., Schneemelcher, W., Wilson, R.McL. (eds). (1965). *The New Testament Apocrypha.* Lutterworth, London. ET. Vol 2. p 354). Sir William Ramsay (1895) remarked that 'this plain and unflattering account of the Apostle's appearance seems to embody a very early tradition' (*The Church in the Roman Empire to A.D. 170.* Hodder and Stoughton, London. p 32).

[57] Lloyd-Davies, M. and Lloyd-Davies, T.A. (1991). *The Bible: Medicine and Myth.* Silent Books. Cambridge. second edn. pp 257-258.

[58] Gobel, H. Isler, H. Hasenfrantz, H.P. (1995). Headache classification and the Bible: Was St Paul's thorn in the flesh migraine? *Cephalgia.* 15. 180-181.

[59] Bruce FF. (1977). *Paul.* pp 136-137. Similarly, P. Marshall (1983) has referred to the condition as 'a socially debilitating disease or disfigurement which was made the subject of ridicule and invidious comparison' (A metaphor of social shame: ΘΡΙΑΜΒΕΥΕΙΝ in 2 Cor. 2:14. *Novum Testamentum.* 25. 302-317.

[60] See Schmidt, K.L. (1965). Κολαφιζω. In: Kittel G. (ed). *Theological Dictionary of the New Testament.* Eerdmans, Grand Rapids. Vol 3. ET. pp 818-

821. Bauer (p 441) describes this word as a vernacular term to be found almost exclusively in Christian literature.

[61] Jennett, W.B. (1982). Post-traumatic epilepsy. In: Laidlaw J and Richens A (eds). *A Textbook of Epilepsy.* Churchill Livingstone, Edinburgh. second edn. p 147.

[62] This is discussed in detail in Jennett, W.B. (1970). *Epilepsy after Non-missile Head Injuries.* Heinemann, London.

[63] Pryse-Phillips, W. and Murray, T.J. (1986). *Essential Neurology.* Elsevier, New York. third edn pp 447-448.

[64] Barrett, C.K. (1973). *The Second Epistle to the Corinthians (Black's NT Commentaries).* A & C Black, London. second edition. p 315. See also Clarke, W.K.L. (1929). *New Testament Problems.* SPCK, London. pp 136-140.

[65] Schlier, H. (1964). Εκπτυω. In: Kittel G. *Theological Dictionary of the New Testament.* Eerdmans, Grand Rapids. Vol 2. ET. pp 448-449.

[66] Schlier H. ibid.

[67] Plautus. *Captivi*, 549. Note also Pliny's description of epilepsy as *morbus despui suetus* (*Naturalis Historia.* 10.23,33).

[68] Norman R. (1987). Pathogenesis of temporal lobe epilepsy. In: Ounsted C. Lindsay J. Richards P. (eds). *Temporal Lobe Epilepsy, 1948-1986: A Biographical Study.* Clinics in Developmental Medicine No. 103. Blackwell, Oxford. p 101.

[69] Shorvon, S.D. (1984). The temporal aspects of prognosis in epilepsy. *Journal of Neurology, Neurosurgery and Psychiatry.* 47. 1157-1165.

[70] The old notion that the three versions could be explained on the basis of three separate sources was an example of the habit of multiplying sources at will and has been dealt with by E. Haenchen (1971) among others (*Acts of the Apostles.* Blackwell, Oxford. pp 325-327). As E.V. Rieu (1957) has remarked, 'the discrepancies are what one would expect in an often told tale, especially one told to different audiences' (*The Acts of the Apostles.* Penguin, Harmondsworth. p 138). See also Stanley, D.M. (1953). Paul's conversion in Acts: Why the three accounts? *Catholic Biblical Quarterly.* 315-338.

[71] Lüdemann, G. (1989). *Early Christianity according to the Traditions in Acts.* SCM, London. pp 112-113.

[72] Haenchen, E. (1971). *Acts.* p 328.

[73] Dupont, J. (1970). The conversion of Paul and its influence on his understanding of salvation by faith. In: Gasque, W.W. and Martin, R.P. (eds). *Apostolic History and the Gospel: Biblical and Historical Essays presented to F.F. Bruce.* Paternoster Press, Exeter. p 192.

[74] These issues were discussed earlier in connection with Paul's 'thorn in the flesh' (above pp 244-247).

[75] It may be true that Luke has used the tradition to develop his own symbolism (see Hamm, D. (1990). Paul's blindness and its healing: clues to symbolic intent (Acts 9, 22 and 26). *Biblica* 71. 63-72), but to use an event symbolically does not of necessity undermine its historicity.

[76] Barrett, C.K. (1994). *A Critical and Exegetical Commentary on the Acts of the Apostles.* T&T Clark, Edinburgh. p 449.

[77] Bruce, F.F. (1990). *The Acts of the Apostles: Greek Text with Introduction and Commentary.* Eerdmans, Grand Rapids. third edn. p 234. He also suggests that 'Paul no doubt had this light in mind when referring many years later, to the inward illumination produced by "the light of the gospel of the glory of Christ" (2 Cor 4:4, 6; cf. the surpassing glory of 2 Cor 3:8-11)'.

[78] See for example, Paton, D and Goldberg, M.F. (1976). *Management of Ocular Injuries.* W.B. Saunders, Philadelphia. p 179.

[79] For details see Lydahl, E. and Philipson, B T. (1984). Infrared radiation and cataract. *Acta Ophthalmologica,* 62. 961-975 and 976-992.

[80] Wilkinson, J. (1980). *Health and Healing.* p 87.

[81] See Hippocrates *Aphorisms* 4.81 and note the examples quoted in Hobart, W.K. (1882). *The Medical Language of St Luke.* Dublin University Press, Dublin. pp 39-40. Note also the remarkable parallel in Tobit 11:13.

[82] See Paton, D. and Goldberg, M.F. (1976). *Ocular Injuries.* p 178.

[83] Bullock, J.D. (1978). The blindness of St Paul. *Ophthalmology* 85. 1044-1053. See also his more recent study (1994), Was St Paul struck blind and converted by lightning? *Survey Ophthalmology.* 39. 151-160 in which he again affirms that a lightning strike could account for all the features of the story.

[84] See for example, Manchester, P.T. and Manchester, P.T. Jr. (1972). The blindness of St Paul. *Archives of Ophthalmology.* 88. 316-321; Anon (Annotation). (1978). Paul's blindness re-evaluated. *Journal of the American Medical Association.* 240. 98 and Wilkinson, J. *Health and Healing.* pp 86-87.

[85] Bruce, F.F. (1990). *Acts.* p 464. Note also Haenchen, E. (1971). *Acts.* p 640 who attributes this interpretation to Theodor Zahn.

[86] Vaughan, D., Astbury, T., and Tabbara, K.F. (eds). (1989). *General Ophthalmology.* Appleton and Lange, Norwalk, Connecticut. p 145.

[87] Barrett, C.K. (1994) makes the point that ἀτενιζειν is a stronger verb than βλεπειν and at Acts 1:10 it conveys the idea that the disciples 'were straining their eyes to see their departing Lord' (*Acts.* p 82).

[88] Bruce, F.F. (1982). *The Epistle of Paul to the Galatians (New International Greek New Testament).* Paternoster Press, Exeter. pp 210-211. Note also the close comparison with Lucian's story of the Scythian friends, Dandamis and Amizoces, which H.D. Betz (1979) uses as an illustration of the principle (*Galatians: A Commentary on Paul's Epistle to the Churches in Galatia.* Hermeneia, Philadelphia. p 228.).

[89] Fung, R.Y.K. (1988). *The Epistle to the Galatians (NICNT)* Eerdmans, Grand Rapids. p 199.

[90] See, for example, Bruce, F.F. *Galatians.* p 268, Fung, R.Y.K. *Galatians.* p 301, Betz, H.D. *Galatians.* p 312f. etc.

[91] Ramsay, W.H. (1899). *A Historical Commentary on the Epistle to the Galatians.* Hodder and Stoughton, London. p 466.

[92] Bruce, F.F. *Galatians.* p 268.

[93] There is a good account of the opposing views in Kümmel, W.G. (19). *Introduction to the New Testament.* (ET. SCM, London). pp 411-414 and there is a wide discussion of the issues in Martin, R.P. (1987). *James. (Word Biblical Commentary),* (Word Books, Waco, Texas). pp xxxi-lxxvii.

[94] Burkitt, F.C. (1924), *Christian Beginnings* (University of London Press, London). pp 65-71.

[95] Martin, R.P (1987). *James.* p lxxvii

[96] See Martin, R.P. (1987). *James.* pp lxxviii-lxxix.

[97] Mayor, J.B. (1910). *The Epistle of St James.* Macmillan, London. 3rd edn. p 169. I have not been able to find a commentary that takes an alternative view of the meaning of ἀσθενει.

[98] Martin, R.P. (1987), *James.* p 201.

[99] R.V.G. Tasker (1956) is thoroughly representative in his remark that 'shall save' 'in this context must mean" shall restore to physical health"'. *The General Epistle of James.* Tyndale Press, London. p 132.

[100] Shogren, G.A. (1989). Will God heal us? *Evangelical Quarterly.* 61. 99-108.

[101] Wright, F.J. (1991). Healing: an interpretation of James 5:13-20. *Journal of the Christian Medical Fellowship.* 37 (1). 20-21.

[102] Michaelis, W. (1968). Κακοπαθεω. In: Friedrich, G. (ed). *Theological Dictionary of the New Testament.* Eerdmans, Grand Rapids. ET. Vol 5. p 937. The same translation is favoured by Bauer (p 397).

[103] Note the references in Bauer (p 402), although once again there is an automatic assumption that the use of the word in James means the sick. It is interesting that Wilkinson in his thorough study of this passage simply assumes that ἀσθενει and τα καμνοντα are equivalent and remarks 'we may ignore the rare verb *kamnô* in this case' (Wilkinson, J. (1971). Healing in the epistle of James. *Scottish Journal of Theology.* 24. 326-345 (= *Health and Healing* pp 143-160). Similarly, Martin (1986). *James.* p 209) while mentioning alternative views in passing, does not really do other than assume that the reference is to normal sickness and its cure through the prayer of faith.

[104] This is not the same as arguing that the reference is to 'spiritual weakness' followed by a restoration to 'spiritual wholeness'. See for example, Armerding, C. (1958). Is any among you afflicted? A study of James 5:13-20. *Bibliotheca Sacra.* 95. 195-201 and Hayden, D.R. (1981). Calling the elders to pray. *Bibliotheca Sacra.* 138. 258-266.

[105] Among the many studies in this area, note Brown, R.E. (1980). Episkope and episkopos: the New Testament evidence. *Theological Studies.* 41. 322-339 and Giles, K. (1989). *Patterns of Ministry among the First Christians.* Collins Dove, Melbourne. The latter quotes extensively from Chapple, A. (1984). *Local Leadership in the Pauline Churches.* Unpublished PhD Thesis, University of Durham, England.

[106] See for example, Vermes. G. (1981). *The Dead Sea Scrolls: Qumran in Perspective.* Revised edn. Fortress Press, Philadelphia. pp 87-115 with especial reference to 1QSa 1:23-25; 2:16. The situation seems to be an example of Eduard Schweizer's (1961) comment that 'At first, therefore, the Church has no new order, but goes on living in the established Jewish forms' (*Church Order in the New Testament.* SCM, London. ET. p 47).

[107] For details, see Schleir, H. (1964). Αλειφω. In: Kittel, G. (ed). *Theological Dictionary of the New Testament.* Eerdmans, Grand Rapids. ET. Vol 1. pp 229-

232 and note the references in Mayor, J.B. (1910). *James.* pp 170-173 and Davids, P.H. (1982) *A Commentary on James (New International Greek Testament Commentary).* Eerdmans, Grand Rapids. p 193.   Note also Warrington, K. (1993). Anointing with oil and healing. *European Pentecostal Theological Association Bulletin.* 12. 5-22.

[108] Wilkinson, J. (1980). *Health and Healing.* p 153.

[109]   There does not, in fact, appear to be another mention of anointing for the sick before the third century when a Montanist, named Proculus Torpacion, is said to have healed the emperor Septimus Severus by anointing (Tertullian, *Ad Scapulam* 4).   Both Origen (ca 185-254) (*Homiliae in Leviticum* 2.4) and Chrysostom (ca 347-407) (*De Sacerdote* 3.6) refer to this passage in James, but only Chrysostom connects it with physical healing. It appears that anointing of the sick did not become a common practice until the fourth century (see Gusmer, C.W. (1984). *And you Visted Me: A Sacramental Ministry to the Sick and the Dying.* Pueblo Publishing. New York. pp 5-21).

[110]   Shogren, G.S. (1989). ibid. This paper also deals with the understanding of the act as sacramental and shows conclusively that such an understanding is based both on poor exegesis as well as being anachronistic.

[111]   Hemer, C.J. (1986). Medicine the New Testament world. In: Palmer, B. (ed). *Medicine and the Bible.* Paternoster Press, Exeter. p 82.

[112]   Altschule, M.D. (1967). The two kinds of depression according to St Paul. *British Journal of Psychiatry.* 113. 779-780.

[113]   It is regrettable to see that the association between sin and sickness seems to be maintained in the Report of the Review Group established by the House of Bishops of the Church of England (*A Time to Heal: A Contribution towards the Ministry of Healing.* Church House, London. 2000. See especially pp 224-225 and elsewhere in the Report).

[114]   On the importance of this practice in Judaism and the early Church see Davids, P.H.(1982). *James.* p 195. Confession and absolution, of course, still play an important part in the religious life of many communions of the Christian Church.   The Church of England Report on Healing, mentioned above (*A Time to Heal*) places great stress on the importance of confession, repentance and absolution in 'healing' services. This however, would seem to suggest to sick people that their illness is as a result of their sin.

[115] See Baur, p 368

[116] For detailed comment see Lane, W.L. (1991). *Hebrews 9-13. (Word Biblical Commentary).* Word Books, Waco, Texas. pp 427-428.

[117]   This view is somewhat similar to that of Vouga, F. (1984). (*L'Épitre de s. Jacques (Commentaire du Nouveau Testament).* Labor et Fides. Geneva. p 143) who sees the verb ἰαομαι in this context as referring to the healing of breaches within the community.

[118]   Tasker, R.V.G. (1956). *James.* p 134.

[119] Martin, R.P. (1986). *James.* p 207.

[120] See for example, Elliott, J.H. (1981). *A Home for the Homeless: A Sociological Exegesis of 1Peter, Its Situation and Strategy.* Fortress Press, Philadelphia; Balch, D. (1981). *Let Wives be Submissive: The Domestic Code*

in 1 Peter. Scholars Press, Chico, CA. and Goppelt, L. (1993). *A Commentary on 1 Peter.* Eerdmans, Grand Rapids.

[121] MacArthur has observed that, while paying little or no attention to the context, 'Charismatics often use 1 Peter 2:24 to support their strong emphasis on the gift of healing' (MacArthur Jr, J.F. (1992). *Charismatic Chaos.* Zondervan, Grand Rapids. p 103). Some of the more extreme views may be found in such works as, McCrossan, T. J. (1982). *Bodily Healing and the Atonement.* Faith Library, Tulsa.

[122] On the general use of Isa 53 in the New Testament see Liwak, K.D. (1983). The use of quotations from Isaiah 52:13-53:12 in the New Testament. *Journal of the Evangelical Theological Society.* 26. 385-394.

[123] Kelly, J.N.D. (1969). *A Commentary on the Epistles of Peter and Jude (Black's New Testament Commentaries).* A & C Black, London. p 124.

[124] Scobie, C.H.H. (1993). Local references in the letters to the seven churches. *New Testament Studies.* 39. 606-624. See also Hill, D. (1972). Prophecy and prophets in the Revelation of St John. *New Testament Studies.* 18. 405-406. He emphasises that as a prophet John writes with a 'sensitivity to the actualities of his situation'.

[125] Scobie, C.H.H. (1993). ibid.

[126] The writer is indebted to the detailed treatment of the church of Laodicea in Hemer, C.J. (1986). *The Letters to the Seven Churches of Asia in their Local Setting.* Sheffield Academic Press (JSOT Press), Sheffield. pp 178-209.

[127] Ramsay, Sir W.M. (1895). *The Cities and Bishoprics of Phrygia.* Clarendon Press, Oxford. Vol 1. p 52   and (1904). *The Letters to the Seven Churches of Asia.* Hodder and Stoughton, London. pp 419 and 429.

[128] Hemer, C.J. (1986). *The Letters to the Seven Churches.* pp 196-199. He gives extensive references to the relevant classical authors.

[129] Note the discussion of Brown, M.L. (1995). *Israel's Divine Healer.* (Paternoster Press, Carlisle) pp 398-399. nn 168 and 170.

[130] Kiddle, M. (1940). *The Revelation of St John (Moffat New Testament Commentary).* Hodder and Stoughton, London. p 443.

[131] See Dumeige, G. (1972). Le Christ médicin dans la littérature chrétienne des premiers siècles. *Rivisita di Archeologia Cristiana.* 47. 115-141.

Chapter 8

DRAWING THE ENDS TOGETHER

'There is a need to penetrate the incognito of Jesus ...The miracles, like Jesus himself, demand interpretation'.

Colin Brown

The accounts of the healing activity of Jesus and the apostles, when considered as the record of a series of 'miraculous' events, frequently represents a stumbling block to those who wish to approach Christianity in a thoughtful and reasonable manner. As a result, there have been numerous attempts to 'explain away' the narratives in the Gospels and Acts and see them as no more than pious legends dreamed up by the early Christian community, an approach that goes back at least to Spinoza and Hume [1]. At the other end of the spectrum, however, there are those, particularly in the charismatic and pentecostal wings of the Church, who would take the stories of healing literally as inexplicable demonstrations of God's power in the ministry of Jesus. On this basis they attempt to build a theology of a new activity of the Spirit of God in today's Church which is also to be demonstrated by the appearance of such 'signs and wonders' in daily life and particularly as a 'normal' expression of the ministry of the Church in the world [2].

It has been part of the purpose of this study to demonstrate that the accounts of healing, particularly in the Gospels, are neither to be explained away as inventions on the one hand, nor to be seen as inexplicable deeds on the other. It has been argued that there is no need to doubt the essential historicity of the basic traditions that present Jesus as a healer and exorcist and the descriptions of the variety of healings that he undertook, outline exactly the sort of activity that one would expect from a prophetic healer. It has also been argued that these accounts of healing relate to very specific conditions. Jesus did not heal just any disorder, but specifically those conditions that were amenable to healing on the spot by a charismatic prophet. They were also carefully selected to fit in with his programme of announcing the all-inclusive nature of the kingdom of God. The healings undertaken by Jesus were not just healings, but parables of the kingdom. In short, this study has argued that the accounts of healing, while seen as remarkable events by the onlookers, justifying the use of such categories as 'signs and wonders' in terms of the contemporary outlook, are not descriptions of 'miracle' as inexplicable and singular divine interventions. They represent stories of what may be described as straightforward happenings that fit into the plan of Jesus to announce the all-embracing and all-inclusive nature of the kingdom of God.

One of the problems that faced this study was that many of the descriptions of disease in the Gospels and Acts were inadequate to provide a genuinely substantive diagnosis. Furthermore, the narratives are generally so brief that there is often little more than a hint of the methods that had been used in effecting the healing. In addition, the understanding of disease causation and the underlying pathological processes was lacking even amongst the trained physicians of the time. Diseases tended to be classified simply on the basis of symptoms, as was the case until very recent times. As would be expected, therefore, the descriptions of disease in the New Testament are almost invariably symptomatic.

The people who came to Jesus in the Gospels or to the apostles in Acts, are thus described as being paralysed, blind, swollen and so forth: the symptoms are the disease, rather than the underlying pathology which remained unknown. Similarly, those conditions in which convulsions were the primary feature were simply put together so that no distinction would be made between a disease such as genuine epilepsy on the one hand and 'hysterical' pseudo-convulsions on the other. Further, the primary aims of the evangelists were theological and thus the tradition has undergone progressive editorial adjustment to ensure that the evangelistic and didactic needs of the Church were met as it expanded into the Roman world. In only a relatively small proportion of the New Testament examples of healing, therefore, is it possible to provide anything firmer than a reasonable guess in terms of diagnosis or therapeutic method.

Nonetheless, having sounded this warning, there are sufficient clues in the narratives, both in terms of the symptomatology outlined and the methods which Jesus appears to have used in healing, to provide support for the conclusions of this study, namely, that the majority of the conditions which were treated were largely functional in nature. A high proportion were cases of what are called conversion disorders, those conditions that used to be called 'hysterical neuroses'. This terminology is not used in any pejorative sense, but is simply a description of a psychiatric disorder of the type discussed, for example, in relation to the Capernaum demoniac (Mark 1:21-28) (see the earlier discussion at pp 59-61).

These considerations also seem to be true of the illnesses treated by the apostles, although the Lukan witness of Acts cannot be treated with the same degree of confidence as the Markan tradition of the ministry of Jesus. The majority of conditions treated by Jesus and apparently also by the apostles appear, therefore, to have their origin in those forms of mental disorder which closely mimic conditions having a 'physical' pathology. To the untrained observer it would be impossible to distinguish between the pseudo-convulsions of a psychiatric disorder and the genuine convulsions that were the result of true epilepsy, for example. The examples from both the Gospels and Acts consist largely of conditions such as paralysis, lameness and various sensory defects such as deafness and dumbness which may, with reasonable certainty, be ascribed to conversion or somatisation disorders. It is not impossible that some cases of blindness also fall into this category, although it is judged that severe cataracts would account for most cases, particularly in view of the way in which Jesus is recorded as healing them by the use of touch.

It is apposite to remark that somatiform and related disorders continue to be frequently encountered in modern western medicine with a varying proportion of patients complaining of musculoskeletal and neurological symptoms, often parallel to those noted in the New Testament healing stories, with chronic pain and with vague and non-specific problems. No evident physical pathology is usually found on examination and the illness has to be considered as 'functional' and a form of conversion/somatisation disorder (the old fashioned 'hysteria'). These patients do not respond well to physical treatment, but rather to psychological forms of therapy, especially behavioural therapy [3].

It is argued, therefore, that the evidence of the Gospels in respect of the work of Jesus, as well as that of Acts in respect of the apostles, suggests that the following three groups were the principle conditions to be treated or helped.

a) Conditions which may be subsumed under the broad umbrella of the psychological conversion and somatiform disorders, a term that 'refers to the putative process whereby psychological conflicts are transformed into bodily symptoms and complaints' [4]. It has been argued that this group of illnesses included the various forms of paralysis, lameness, dumbness, convulsions and similar conditions dealt with by the use of essentially psychological means, predominantly the abreactive techniques which were discussed in relation to the work of Jesus. For want of a better term, these will be called psychosomatic disorders.

b) Conditions arising from genuine physical pathology, but which were amenable to what may be called 'folk' medicine. In this group may be included, in particular, the cases of blindness which appear to have been due to over-mature cataracts and which appear to have been treated by pressure couching. It may well be that there were other illnesses in this category, but the details have been lost in transmission or the stories were not recorded as they had no theological application.

c) Conditions that may not have been healed at all, but rather *declared* as cured. The specific example is 'leprosy', which is always described as being 'cleansed' or 'declared cleansed'. The original story of the 'leprosy' sufferer may not have been about a healing intervention, but merely the declaration of whether the person was 'cleansed' or not. Further, even allowing for several such instances to have occurred, it is significant that 'cleansing' was the regular word used, and as Davies has remarked, 'cleansing is not a cure, but a positive diagnosis' [5]. Perhaps the 'jury remains out' on this matter, but there is a strong suggestion that Jesus possibly did no more than to confirm to the sufferer that the skin condition had resolved or was in remission and thus the sufferer was 'clean'. It is of interest to note that the Acts of the Apostles gives no example of such 'cleansing' by the apostles (in spite of the claims of Mark 16:15-18).

The limited evidence from Acts would suggest that what healing was undertaken by the apostles followed very much the same pattern and, once again, the predominance of conversion-type disorders in these narratives was noted in the chapter dealing with Acts (chapter 6).

Some comment will be made on the three groupings of diseases that was outlined above.

The necessary ingredients for dealing successfully with conversion type disorders are essentially psychotherapeutic and they have been outlined by Frank [6]. They are enumerated as follows and comments are made in respect of the way in which these prerequisites appear to have been fulfilled in the ministry of Jesus and the apostles.

a) *An intense, emotionally charged confiding relationship with a helping person.* This criterion is met in all the stories about the relationship of Jesus with the people who came to him for help, although it is not so clear in the stories relating to the work of the apostles.

b) *A rationale, which includes an explanation of the cause of the patient's distress and a method for relieving it.* Within the cultural context of first century Palestine, the causal agents of the more bizarre conditions, ranging from paralysis to convulsions, were invariably demons about which there was no debate and the method of dealing with this problem was by 'exorcism'. Again, this is applicable to the work of Jesus, but not to the apostles as there is a remarkable lack of exorcisms in Acts, as was noted. It is worth observing that the patient's beliefs about causation do not require to be correct for successful therapy to take place. On the other hand, it is essential that the therapist respects these beliefs if there is to be a satisfactory resolution of the problem. The writer has experienced this in Africa with cases of 'bewitchment'. It is of no use to tell the patient or the family that the illness has nothing to do with 'spirits' as this would immediately introduce a barrier to communication and trust and prevent any further progress in treatment. Similar fixations about the cause of conversion disorders occur in more sophisticated societies, although the causative agents are more likely to be 'technological' which merely reflects a cultural preference.

c) *Provision of new information concerning the nature and origins of the patient's problems and possible alternative ways of dealing with them.* This criterion does not seem to have been met in all the stories of healing by Jesus or the apostles. There are cases, however, in which guilt and forgiveness seemed to have played a prominent part in the relief of symptoms (the story of the paralysed man and his friends is possibly the best example and the paralysed man in John's Gospel would appear to have been another). This may well have been much more frequent than the stories suggest.

d) *Strengthening the patient's expectations of help through the personal qualities of the therapist, enhanced by his status in society and the setting in which he works.* This particular prerequisite is met in all the stories. Jesus and the apostles were in fact, sought out by people simply because of the expectations which surrounded their ministries. Jesus was recognised as a healer of great power and authority and similar attributes were accorded to Peter and Paul in particular in the narratives of Acts. People came to them with high expectations that they would be relieved of their sickness simply because of who they were.

e) *Provision of success experiences, which further heightens the patient's hopes and also enhances the sense of mastery, interpersonal competence or capability.* Once again, the stories emphasise the way in which crowds gather simply because of the previous success of Jesus and the apostles as healers. The rumour of success goes before them and thus patients' hopes are raised and everywhere they go there is a sense of expectation.

f) *Facilitation of emotional arousal.* This comes across clearly in several of the stories in which a heightened emotional atmosphere surrounded the healing. The 'epileptic' boy is one example, the Capernaum demoniac another, where there is strong evidence of very markedly raised emotions, providing the appropriate setting for the abreactive type of healing that Jesus seems to have used.

All in all, therefore, in the cases of 'psychosomatic' disorders which seem to have made up the bulk of the work of Jesus, he appears to have followed psychotherapeutic methods and met the criteria for a successful application of these methods in individual cases. This is not surprising as such methods have become known and used by traditional healers in most cultures through years of accumulated experience.

The likelihood of a 'psychosomatic' cause also exists in those cases where the condition seemed more 'physical', as for example in the story of the woman with the haemorrhage (Mark 5:26-34 and parallels). It was argued, in fact, that her condition may well have been the physical manifestation of a conversion disorder. Again, it should be emphasised, that to denote a condition as 'psychosomatic' should not be considered as implying the sufferer was not genuinely ill. Neuroses are genuine illnesses, often causing considerable distress and are frequently resistant to therapy. Indeed, few illnesses do not have a psychological component: even the common cold may induce feelings of marked depression.

It needs to be emphasised, however, that descriptions of conditions which may with confidence be considered as true organic disease and occurring without a dominant functional component, are very limited indeed. There are two cases of febrile illness recorded: the account of the fever of Peter's mother-in-law (Mark 1:29-31) and the dysentery of the father of Publius on the island of Malta (Acts 28:8). Both these illnesses appear to bear all the hallmarks of acute and self-limiting conditions and the ministrations of Jesus on the one hand and Paul on the other, were essentially comforting and encouraging. In addition to these, the only other instance of a specific physical pathology is the story of the blind man of Bethsaida (Mark 8:22-26) in which there seems little doubt that Jesus used the classical method of couching by pressure to deal with his severe cataracts. It seems very likely that other cases of blindness were dealt with in the same way, although the details have largely become lost in transmission. One may note, for example, the accounts at Matt 9:27-31 and John 9:1-40 in which touch seemed to have played an important part in the cure and it is reasonable to assume that couching was being employed. It is also probable that in other cases of healing the normal methods of the folk healer were used, although the details have now become lost, either because they were irrelevant or else embarrassing to the central theological message of the healing story.

The importance of physical contact in relieving symptoms and inducing a feeling of well-being in the patient is illustrated in the stories of Peter's mother-in-law and the father of Publius, something only now being rediscovered in modern medicine. The story of the man with 'dropsy' (Luke 14:1-6) also appears as physical disease although the total lack of detail makes it very difficult to draw any genuine conclusions. Similarly, the story of Paul's blindness in relation to his experience on the road to Damascus (Acts 9:1-19 and parallels) bears all the appearance of a natural event, although for Paul it became the vehicle of a deep and permanent religious experience. Luke has made the ministrations of Ananias essentially 'miraculous', but the return to sight was much more likely to have been the normal progression of a natural process. Among other straightforward accounts of natural recovery is the story of Eutychus (Acts 20:7-12). The story simply describes an unfortunate accident resulting in concussion with a (presumed) natural recovery and it would seem clear that the original tradition contained no element of the 'miraculous', although Luke has attempted to give the impression that Paul was responsible for the young man's return to health. In spite of the interpretations given, there is no reason to see other than natural processes at work in any of these cases.

The final category of conditions 'treated' includes only 'leprosy', and it is possible that the traditions contain only one original account of Jesus and a 'leprosy' sufferer, on which the other stories were based. The cleansing of this 'leprosy' sufferer (Mark 1:40-45) seems to be an account of Jesus being asked to determine whether the man's condition was or was not present any longer. The tendency to transmute a relatively straightforward event into something more, occurs more frequently in the Lukan writings than elsewhere. Such developments in the tradition have been noted, particularly the later tendency for Jesus (as well as the apostles) to be involved in the treatment of various chronic illnesses and also to raise the dead; conditions and situations which are absent from the earliest traditions. That the later developing tradition began to expand the picture of the work of Jesus and the ministry of the earliest Christian community is not in doubt. The longer ending of Mark's Gospel is a clear indication of the way things were beginning to move in some circles at least, by the second century, with a much greater emphasis on the miraculous as the Church came into increasing conflict with paganism. A brief comment will be made on this development later in this discussion.

The marked success of Jesus in dealing with the types of illnesses described, acknowledged, it should be noted, by both followers and detractors, and which appears to have been continued to some extent by the apostles, is indicative of great psychological healing skills at the very least. Faith sees in this something more than this basic estimate, because it sees in Jesus someone more than a mere healer. This, however, is ultimately a matter of conviction and commitment, rather than something derived from the historical data alone. The historical record, however, provides a consistent and entirely reasonable picture of Jesus as a healer of certain forms of illness: essentially psychological conversion disorders or physical illness for which the accepted means of folk medicine were appropriate and effective. The picture of Jesus as 'healer' is medically sound and convincing. Similarly, the accounts of healing in the Acts of the Apostles suggest that the same broad conclusion applies to the work of the apostles.

It is apparent that there is a remarkable lack of any accounts of cures of what may be termed genuinely physical disease with true organic pathology in the New Testament narratives, a fact all the more impressive in view of some of remarkable claims of the modern healing movement. The remarks of J.G.D. Dunn are apposite in this context: it is, he remarked, 'striking that no instances of healing purely physical injuries or mending broken limbs are attributed to Jesus in the earliest stratum of tradition - that is to say, there is no instance of a healing miracle which falls clearly outside the general category of psycho-somatic illnesses' [7]. To say 'no instance' is a slight exaggeration in view of the foregoing discussion, where the evidence suggests that Jesus used the techniques of folk medicine to deal with certain conditions, but the broad truth of Dunn's statement cannot be denied. It is only the later traditions with their tendency to elaborate for apologetic reasons, and more particularly in Luke-Acts, that both Jesus and the apostles are represented as dealing with larger numbers of physical and chronic disorders. The end result of this process is seen in the radical and exaggerated claims made for the followers of Jesus in the apocryphal second century, longer ending of Mark (16:9-20) in which the disciples are purportedly given what are virtually magical powers. The claims of the modern healing movement, it should be noted, are based almost entirely on these late arising verses.

The broad picture of the activity of Jesus presented in each of the Gospels, in spite of the apologetic and theological developments, is essentially what one would expect of a person who was operating in a manner that was in essence indistinguishable from other healers and exorcists. Burkill remarks that 'on general grounds one would expect the basic stratum of any collection of reports of miraculous healing to consist mainly of stories which deal with psychogenic disease ... noteworthy successes in treating psychogenic disease generally constitute the factual basis of a miracle worker's reputation' [8]. Such successful treatments provide the nucleus of a collection that tends to expand in the course of time. Such expansive tendencies have been noted in the way in which both Matthew and Luke treat the Markan tradition as well as in some of the extra stories they include, in which, in Thiessen's words, 'there is a tendency to intensify, to make the miraculous even more striking, which goes well beyond the historical and factual' [9].

By the second century these expansive developments had become much more evident as the Church attempted to demonstrate the truth of the Gospel in terms of the strange, the inexplicable or the wonderful to meet what it saw as apologetic needs in a pagan world. G.W.H. Lampe noted that, 'One of the most tiresome features of a certain kind of Christian apologetic, common in the Church from the second century onwards, is a tendency to assume that the truths of Christian doctrine may be proved by the ability of believers to perform apparently impossible feats ... one might easily gain the impression from Bede that the evangelisation of this country (that is England) was carried out, to no small extent, by a series of conjuring tricks' [10].

It is important that this issue be given brief attention. Although the later developments of the Church's 'healing ministry' do not strictly belong within the limits of this study, the fact that the 'miraculous' came to take on a greater importance in the Church's mission has undoubtedly left a significant legacy in the Church's thinking. This, in turn, has a bearing on the way the ministry to the sick is seen and understood today [11]. The question arises as to whether the Church's ministry is simply one of caring for the sick or some form of 'healing ministry' in which there is a level of intervention beyond simple prayer and care, whether this takes the form of 'sacramental healing' or 'faith healing'. In other words, is Christianity (and more specifically, was early Christianity) a religion of healing?

Adolf Harnack, at the turn of last century, laid considerable emphasis on the place of healing in the early Church and on Christianity as a religion of healing [12]. He saw this as a conscious and deliberate move and his views have been followed by others including Shirley Jackson Case [13], and, more recently, by Vivian Nutton and Hector Avalos. Nutton, in particular, has emphasised the 'miraculous' element of the early Christians' work in caring for the sick, seeing it as being set up in direct competition with pagan healing, especially the cult of Asclepius [14].

However, the New Testament documents, themselves, give no evidence of any major interest in healing of the sick outside the specific ministries of Jesus and the apostles. The type of care that is reflected in the letters would appear to have been solely along conventional lines and as Ferngren has remarked, 'If in its earliest phase Christianity emphasized healing, we should surely expect to find evidence of it in the Epistles' [15]. Similarly, the Apostolic Fathers in the late first and into the second centuries (the epistles of Clement, Polycarp and Ignatius) place the emphasis on care for the sick, including prayer, but do not suggest that miraculous healing was in any sense a normal approach to the cure of diseases [16]. Indeed, in these documents healing imagery is largely metaphorical and is applied to spiritual sickness and alienation. The *Shepherd of Hermas* for example refers to the healing of former sins and uses sickness as a picture of spiritual weakness [17].

It is not, in fact, until the late second century and onwards that there is any evidence of a growth of a 'healing ministry' in the sense of something other than caring for the sick. In part, this is likely to represent a reaction to heretical Christian sects, particularly the Montanists (a second century equivalent to the modern charismatic movement) and the growth of healing activities in respect of the pagan cult of Asclepius [18]. It is also likely to be a reflection of the increasing importance of the 'supernatural' in the life and thought of the world of late antiquity and the growth of the cult of the martyrs and other holy men and women who replaced the hero cults of the pagan world [19].

The important thing to notice, however, is the way in which these later references to healing are all couched in the conventional language of apologetic and lack any real examples [20]. In the light of the apologetic importance of being able to cite specific examples against the pagan claims, it is remarkable that not one Christian writer actually does so, suggesting very strongly that the best evidence that could be cited was no more than hearsay or the turning of the New Testament stories into contemporary legends. The fact is that early Christianity either could not, or for reasons unknown, did not, exploit its healing activities and there seems to be little real evidence for any major interest in either miracle or in religious healing (as opposed to the care of the sick) until a much later stage in the development of Christianity.

It has been argued that the New Testament writers would have seen any major emphasis on religious healing as an apologetic 'proof' of the claims of Christianity, as an attempt to avoid the scandal and the offence of a crucified Messiah. Only at a later stage did such ideas become established and even then it was the normal care of the sick that was the paramount concern of the Church [21]. The modern healing movement, and especially 'faith healing', cannot look to the New Testament as a base for its activities, but only to a later stage of development when the Church was trying to be competitive with paganism and apparently using the same methods. It needs to be stated that the characterisation of modern 'faith healing' in terms of 'wonders', 'signs' or 'miracles' is to invest these events with a level of significance which is not merely unjustified, but is, in fact, plain silly. At best, these claims arise from an uncritical naivete that would stand comparison with second century and later apologetics: at worst, from something a great deal more sinister.

However, it is necessary to return to the main argument. If it be accepted that the methods used by Jesus did not differ significantly from those of other healers and exorcists of the time ('the sons of the Pharisees' for example, mentioned at Mark 3:22-27 in the Beelzebub controversy), then this would explain the deep controversies that arose about his ministry. There was no factual dispute about the healings: the contentious issue related to the power by which his healings and exorcisms were accomplished. This issue arose in other disputes over authority and it is important to recognize that the opponents of Jesus were not forced by any incontrovertible proof to acknowledge any special God-given power. Indeed, as the Beelzebub controversy illustrates, there was more than one way of looking at the ministry of Jesus. The importance of this from the standpoint of this discussion is that it was possible to make a choice about Jesus: his healing ministry was conducted in such a way that it was possible to accept it as derived from God's power or from an alternative source. Those with 'eyes to see or ears to hear' recognized that Jesus had come, not as a physician to whom God had imparted knowledge (Ecclus 38:6,7), but as a prophetic healer to whom God had imparted power and who acted as God's agent in bringing the freedom, deliverance and forgiveness that belonged to the rule of God, now present in him. As N.T. Wright puts it, 'these healings, at the deepest level of understanding on the part of Jesus and his contemporaries, would be seen as part of his total ministry, specifically, part of that open welcome which went with the inauguration of the kingdom' [22].

One other factor lends weight to the judgment that the healings and exorcisms of Jesus did not appear to be any different from those of his contemporaries, namely the apparent difficulties and failures that attended his ministry from time to time. As would be expected, these have to some extent been glossed over in the later developing tradition and examples of apparent difficulty and failure are limited to Mark. The surprising admission of both difficulty and failure would suggest that at the earliest level of the tradition there would have been little in the accounts that would have made the work of Jesus obviously different from that of other healers. These admissions also tend to provide corroboration for the view that the healings themselves were largely of functional or psychogenic illness. Consideration should also be given to the very real possibility that the remissions from the various conditions that were 'healed' may not have been permanent, so that, as in the case of psychogenic illness today, it is likely that relapses occurred from time to time. For apologetic reasons the healings of Jesus are generally presented as instantaneous and complete, but there are hints that relapses occurred (note the parable at Matthew 12:43-45 as well as the comments recorded at John 5:15).

There is nothing that is specifically new in adopting the foregoing approach to an understanding of the healings of Jesus and the apostles and it was pioneered by E.R. Micklem and Leslie Weatherhead [23]. This study, however, has examined each case of healing in detail and has attempted to provide a reasonable suggestion for specific diagnoses in as many cases as possible on the basis of the often meagre information available. In adopting this approach, the aim has been to provide a foundation for the interpretation of the healing methods of Jesus and the apostles that is open to refutation, rather than adopting an approach which is simply an assertion. It is argued that none of the healings for which there is a good historical basis could in any way be described as 'miracle' in the usually accepted ways in which this term is defined. These generally take as their starting point the concept of an event for which no explanation can be found other than divine intervention, often described in terms of 'breaking' natural law [24].

Such definitions, however, are time conditioned and would include a wide variety of happenings which are part of normal life in the modern world, but which, in biblical times (or even a hundred years ago or less), would have been seen as events without any reasonable explanation and beyond the ability of the people of the time to perform or comprehend. Such an approach to unexplained phenomena is simply an evocation of the 'God of the gaps', a God who by definition is a shrinking God as the frontiers of knowledge are pushed back. Eventually, God runs out of things to do and then he becomes no longer necessary - progressively dying the death of a thousand explanations as the gaps are filled.

Similar comments may be made about the picture that emerges from the Acts of the Apostles with regard to the healing activity of the apostles, although the evidence is more scanty. The extent of any healing activity by the apostles is difficult to gauge and Luke's accounts are clearly influenced by his apologetic purposes. Nonetheless, there is remarkably little said about healing and very few examples are given. Perhaps even more important (and indeed, remarkable), given Luke's penchant for expanding the Gospel narratives into exorcisms when the original sources suggested a simple 'healing', is the fact that Acts contains no unequivocal story of exorcism as was noted in chapter 6. There is one case recorded of people possessed (the sons of Sceva) and one of a girl who was apparently exorcised, although this seems very largely to have been an interpretation put on the event by Luke: there is no clearly recorded exorcism after the pattern of the Gospels. One is reliant, therefore, on Luke's summary statements that provide no details and cannot be used as proof of an extensive apostolic healing ministry. As in the Gospel picture, the few examples given fall squarely into the same patterns as the healings in the ministry of Jesus and they are examples of entirely explicable events.

Judgments about the extent of any healing ministry in the first century church may be made only on the information in the New Testament letters. The references in Paul's writings suggest that some healing was carried out in the early community, but he did not appear to give it a high profile in his ministry. The other portions of the New Testament give even less foundation for assuming any extensive healing ministry in the early congregations. The relevant portions of these documents have been examined and analysed in this study and it may be said firmly, that there is no evidence in any of the New Testament letters that physical diseases were ever healed by other than natural processes. Further, the New Testament letters make no reference to the practice of exorcism nor indeed to demon possession. There is nothing in the writings of Paul that would suggest that he was ever involved in such practices, nor do any of the other New Testament documents suggest that such practices were part of the normal activities of the Christian community.

On the other hand, prayer for the sick formed an important ingredient in pastoral care and this is made very clear. However, this is very far from saying that there was an automatic assumption that prayer would result in healing - clearly in some cases it did not, including that of Paul himself. It is important to bear in mind that the letters, in general, are among the earliest documents in the New Testament, predating the Gospels by several years, even on the most conservative estimates. It is therefore significant that so little attention is paid to the issue of healing: there is little, if anything, in the New Testament letters to suggest that 'healing', as opposed to 'caring', was considered an indispensable part of the evangelistic or pastoral activity of the primitive Church.

It is suggested that two considerations in particular arise out of this study. In the first instance, a less mechanical approach to the concept of 'miracle' is needed. It has been argued that the use of the label 'miracle' attached to a biblical event is indicative of a perceived purpose and significance rather than an explanation of mechanism. It is suggested that the same considerations apply to events that may similarly be categorised as 'miracle' today. It is a term that is totally inappropriate as an explanation and should be linked solely to religious interpretation in terms of the significance of the event. Consequently it is possible to sustain the concept of 'miracle' providing that it is properly qualified and used, not in terms of something that is unexplained or apparently inexplicable, but as an interpretative term applied to an event by a person or people, which is seen and experienced as a means of grace.

Such terms as 'miracles', 'signs' or 'wonders' have been used far too lightly and by persistent trivialisation have become largely emptied of content. Nonetheless, these are valid categories to use in terms of individual or community experience when an event becomes the mediator of God's grace and salvation. There is a sense in which, like beauty, 'miracle' lies in the eye of the beholder as a category of spiritual significance when some particular happening, such as restoration to health or deliverance from some peril, perfectly explicable in terms of cause and effect, becomes transmuted and acquires a deeper level of theological interpretation. What is essential is to remove the concept of 'miracle' from the realm of explanation in terms of mechanism [25].

The other matter that arises out of this study is the importance of the care of the sick as opposed to the healing of the sick in terms of the Church's ministry. It was the story of the Good Samaritan that furnished the early Church with its model in dealing with the sick and others in need. As Ferngren puts it, 'It was not curing but caring which constituted the chief ministry of the early Christian community to the sick' [26] and, unlike the pagan world, or even the Jewish community, the Christians extended their concern and care to all [27]. In the modern world, this will mean the development of a proper relationship with the normal health care professions of medical and nursing practice and the other para-medical groups. The ministry of the Church must of necessity lie in close association with the practice of medicine, but at the same time, it pursues its different form of ministry with a recognition of the proper boundaries between the different approaches to meeting the needs of the sick.

The emphasis for the Church remains on caring rather than curing. This is of vital importance, for the majority of ministers of the Church are not competent to assess the nature of a person's sickness. The simple symptomatic approach that marked the biblical understanding in which symptoms were understood to be the disease itself, an approach which marked all earlier, prescientific understandings, is simply not acceptable today. Effective therapy is based on rational and adequate diagnosis and it is this absence of any proper diagnosis which makes nonsense of so much that passes for 'healing' in the practice of healing ministries. As Turner has noted, the 'effective management of illness or disability has to be based on the identification of the underlying cause, ie. accurate diagnosis, and not simply on relief of symptoms which is often regarded, mistakenly, as "healing" ' [28]. When, as in charismatic circles, the underlying cause of a person's sickness is identified as a 'demon', then, the way is open for tragedy and disaster, as many physicians can testify.

The primary emphasis of the New Testament is on the necessity for true 'wholeness' within a restored relationship with God. Such an emphasis remains central to the Church's proclamation and herein lies the abiding importance and relevance of these stories of healing. If the Church cannot say today, like its Lord, to those 'dis-eased' by the very real, although very different set of ills of this modern world, 'Go in peace, your faith has saved you', then it may reasonably be asked whether it has anything worthwhile to proclaim.

What at least is clear from the evidence of the New Testament is that God does not act in an arbitrary manner to rearrange the matter of human bodies directly. What he does is to give meaning to the present reality of existence. False fears and false hopes need to be put aside in the recognition that God acts *through* the human situation, *through* pain and sickness and the other ills of life. He does not act or intervene from the outside to heal the body instantaneously. The theological implications of the New Testament accounts of healing and statements about healing can be reduced ultimately to Paul's experience of God: 'my grace is sufficient for you' (2 Cor 12:9).

On the basis of the foregoing considerations, it is argued that the function of the Christian community in relation to the sick, in addition to general care and help, is to deal with the issues of the mind and spirit, particularly the relief of guilt, alienation and anxiety which may have a potent effect on the speed and effectiveness of a person's recovery. The importance of feelings of guilt in illness was illustrated in a number of the healings of Jesus, as well as at James 5 where the prayer for the 'weak' was a prayer for forgiveness as well as for restoration.

In the context of the individual facing the limitations of disease and its associated uncertainties, the Church has an essential task in strengthening or awakening faith in a loving God. It should be providing the powerful support of prayer to help both the patient and the family to come to terms with the inevitable reality of suffering in the human condition, as well as the equally inevitable and totally unavoidable reality of death. The New Testament letters seem to set out such an approach. They provide no basis for any expectation of the 'miraculous' cure of disease. On the other hand, they emphasise a willingness to accept the common experiences of all humanity. For

Paul, it was a matter for rejoicing at the mercy of God when a colleague recovered from a serious illness, rather than a complacent assumption that such recovery was always to be the properly expected outcome of sickness in faithful people (Phil 2:27). The emphasis was on a God who was himself involved in the human situation, however painful and hopeless it may have appeared, and this is the conviction that lies behind the doctrine of the Incarnation. The Church is required to carry that identification with suffering humanity into its own ministry. The ministry to the sick thus becomes an extension of the ministry of Christ, who 'suffers with us in our weaknesses (ἀσθενείαις)' (Heb 4:15), weaknesses that encompass not only sickness but all forms of human suffering.

A properly focussed person will have a better physiology than one who is riddled with guilt, stress and anxiety. The person who is at peace and who is surrounded by loving support, heals better. It is the Church's function to bring that peace which is a measure of the genuine wholeness that comes from God. This is where its 'healing' ministry, or, both more biblically and more correctly, its care for the sick, must be centred, rather than in trying to recapture an imaginary golden era of 'signs' and 'wonders' or proclaim a false gospel that is centred on the cure of the sick [29]. Those who, like the Corinthian Christians of old, emphasise a triumphalist 'healing gospel' should remember that there can be no Easter without Good Friday and no-one is exempt from the path of suffering.

Notes and references

[1] For a discussion of the contributions of Spinoza and Hume see Brown, C (1984). *Miracles and the Critical Mind.* Grand Rapids, Eerdmans. pp 30-34 and 79-100. This approach has again been resurrected (if it was ever dead) by members of the 'Jesus seminar'. See for example, Funk, R.W. (1996). *Honest to Jesus: Jesus for a New Millennium.* Hodder & Stoughton, London. pp 252-253.

[2] See for example, Wimber, J. (1986). *Power Evangelism.* Hodder & Stoughton, London; Wimber, J. (1987). *Power Healing.* Hodder & Stoughton, London; Wagner, C.P. (1988). *The Third Wave of the Holy Spirit.* Servant, Ann Arbor, MI; and White, J. (1992). *When the Spirit Comes with Power.* InterVarsity Press, Downers Grove, IL. Revised edn. See also Grudem, W. (1993). Should Christians expect miracles today? In: Greig, G.S. and Springer, K.N. (eds). *The Kingdom and the Power.* Regal Books, Ventura, CA.

³ See the discussion in Crimlisk, H, Bhatra, K, Cope, H. et al. (1998). Slater revisited: 6 year follow up of patients with medically unexplained motor symptoms. *British Medical Journal.* 316. 582-586 and the related commentary by O'Brien, M.D. (1998). Medically unexplained neurological symptoms. *British Medical Journal.* 316. 564-565. The problem is discussed in detail by Issy Pilowsky (1997). *Abnormal Illness Behaviour.* Wiley, Colchester.

⁴ Pilowsky, I. (1997). *Abnormal Illness Behaviour.* p 1.

⁵ Davies, S.L. (1995). *Jesus the Healer: Possession, Trance and the Origins of Christianity.* Continuum, New York. p 69.

⁶ Frank, J.D. (1972). Common features of psychotherapy. *Australian and New Zealand Journal of Psychiatry.* 6. 34-40.

⁷ Dunn, J.G.D. (1975). *Jesus and the Spirit.* SCM, London. p 71.

⁸ Burkill, T.A. (1973). Miraculous healing in the gospels. *Central African Journal of Medicine.* 19. 99-100.

⁹ Thiessen, G. (1983). *Miracle Stories in the Early Christian Tradition.* T & T Clark, Edinburgh. p 281.

¹⁰ Lampe, G.W.H. (1965). Miracles in the Acts of the Apostles. In: Moule, C.F.D. (ed). *Miracles: Cambridge Studies in their Philosophy and History.* Mowbray, London. p 165.

¹¹ On the later developments of the Church's work among the sick see for example, Barrett-Lennard, R.J.S. (1994). *Christian Healing after the New Testament: Some Approaches to Illness in the Second, Third and Fourth Centuries.* University Press of America, Washington, DC.; Perkins, J. (1995). *The Suffering Self: Pain and Narrative Representation in the Early Christian Era.* Routledge, London.; Amundsen, D.W. (1996). *Medicine, Society and Faith in the Ancient and Medieval Worlds.* Johns Hopkins University Press, Baltimore.; Numbers, R.L. and Amundsen, D.W. (eds). (1986). *Caring and Curing: Health and Medicine in the Western Religious Tradition.* Johns Hopkins University Press, Baltimore. Note also Amundsen, D.W. (1982). Medicine and faith in early Christianity. *Bulletin of the History of Medicine.* 56. 326-350 and Ferngren, G.B. (1992). Early Christiantiy as a religion of healing. *Bulletin of the History of Medicine.* 66. 1-15.

¹² See Harnack, A. (1904). *The Expansion of Christianity in the First Three Centuries.* (translated and edited by James Moffatt). Putnam, New York. Vol 1. pp 121-151.

¹³ Case, S.J. (1923). The art of healing in early Christian times. *Journal of Religion.* 3. 238-255. See also his major studies (1929) *Experience with the Supernatural in Early Christian Times* (Century, New York). especially pp 221-263 and (1946). *The Origins of Christian Supernaturalism.* (University of Chicago Press, Chicago).

¹⁴ Nutton, V. (1984). From Galen to Alexander: Aspects of medicine and medical practice in late antiquity. In: Scarborough, J. (ed). *Symposium on Byzantine Medicine. Dumbarton Oaks Papers No 38.* Dumbarton Oaks, Washington DC. p 5. Note also Nutton, V. (1985). Murders and Miracles: Lay attitudes to medicine in classical antiquity. In: Porter, R. (ed). *Patients and Practitioners: Lay Perceptions of Medicine in Pre-Industrial Society.*

Cambridge University Press, Cambridge. pp 45-51 and Avalos, H. (1999). *Healthcare and the Rise of Christianity.* Hendricksen, Peabody, MD. Both Ramsay McMullen (1984). *Christianizing the Roman Empire.* Yale University Press, New Haven. p 22, and Keith Hopkins (1998). Christian number and its implications. *Journal of Early Christian Studies.* 6. 161-267, consider miracles as being central to early Christian expansion. On the importance of the cult of Asclepius see Edelstein, E.J. and Edelstein, L (1975=1945). *Asclepius: A Collection and Interpretation of the Testimonies.* (Arno Press, New York). 2 Vols.

[15] Ferngren, G.B. (1992). Early Christianity as a religion of healing. *Bulletin of the History of Medicine.* 66. 1-15.

[16] There was clearly prayer for the sick (*1 Clement* 59:4) and the letter of Ignatius to Polycarp (1:2,3) indicates care for the sick as part of Christian duty, but whether the expression, παντων τας νοσους βασταζε means bearing with the sick or delivering them is a moot point. The remarkable lack of references to healing in the Apostolic Fathers was noted specifically by Warfield, B.B. (1918=1972). *Counterfeit Miracles.* Banner of Truth, London. pp 3-31.

[17] *Shepherd of Hermas; Similitudes* 8.11.1 and *Visions* 3.11.4.

[18] See Edelstein, E.J. and Edelstein, L (1975=1945). *Asclepius.* Vol 2. pp 133-134. They argue that Asclepius of all the ancient Greek gods was the foremost antagonist of Christ.

[19] See for example Brown, P. (1971a). *The World of late Antiquity:AD 150-750.* Harcourt Brace, New York, especially pp 49-57 and Brown, P. (1971b). The rise and function of the holy man in late antiquity. *Journal of Roman Studies.* 61. 80-101. On the rise of the martyr cult see van der Meer, F. (1961). *Augustine the Bishop: The Life and Work of a Father of the Church.* Sheed and Ward, London. ET. pp 471-497.

[20] Even Origen, who claims to have seen miracles, gives no specific example (cf *Contra Celsum.* 1:46 and 2:8) and the same is true of Irenaeus (2.31.2-32.4) who was concerned to show the superiority of the 'brotherhood' (the true church) over against Gnostic heretics. He makes great claims, even of people being raised from the dead, but omits one single example. One wonders whether he (and others) may simply have been using earlier writers such as Quadratus (quoted in Eusebius. *Ecclesiastical History.* IV.3.2) in an out of context fashion.

[21] Note passages such as Hippolytus. *Apostolic Tradition.* Canon 20; Tertullian. *To the wives.* 2.4; *Apostolic Constitutions.* 3.19.

[22] Wright, N.T. (1996). *Jesus and the Victory of God.* SPCK, London. p 192.

[23] See Micklem, E.R. (1922). *Miracles and the New Psychology.* Oxford University Press, Oxford, and Weatherhead, L. (1951). *Psychology, Religion and Healing.* Hodder and Stoughton, London.

[24] For example, John Meier (1994), in an otherwise very careful and balanced review of the subject, can define miracle in the following terms: 'A miracle is (1) an unusual, startling, or extraordinary event that is in principle perceivable by any interested and fair-minded observer, (2) an event that finds no reasonable explanation in human abilities or in other known forces that operate

in our world of time and space, and (3) an event that is the result of a special act of God, doing what no human power can do' (*A Marginal Jew: Rethinking the Historical Jesus. Vol 2 Mentor, Message and Miracles.* Doubleday, New York. p 512).

[25] See further the author's discussion: Howard, J.K. (1996). Is healing ever 'miraculous'? *Stimulus: The New Zealand Journal of Christian Thought and Practice.* 4(2). 7-13.

[26] Ferngren, G.B. (1992). Early Christinaity as a religion of healing. *Bulletin of the History of Medicine.* 66.1-15.

[27] Ferngren, G.B. (1988). The organisation of the care of the sick in early Christianity. In: Schadewaldt, H and Leve, K-H. (eds). *Proceedings of the XXX International Conference of the History of Medicine.* Vicom KG, Dusseldorf. pp 192-198.

[28] Turner, G. (1991). Healing in church services. *Journal of the Christian Medical Fellowship.* 37(2). 7-9.

[29] Note the statement of the Church of England Report, *A Time to Heal: A Contribution towards the Ministry of Healing.* (Church House, London, 2000): 'We hope that this report will encourage all Anglicans to embrace what is sometimes called "the full gospel" – that is, the gospel preached with the hope of healing – so that it may become central to our mission' (p xviii). It has been one aim of this study to demonstrate that physical healing was never the central part of the Church's mission at its inception.

SELECT BIBLIOGRAPHY

The literature on healing in the New Testament and related subjects is immense. What follows, therefore, is no more than a selection of material, mainly in English and including only what may be termed 'modern' writers. Inevitably, any selection of material is bound to be coloured by individual preference, quite apart from the need to keep the bibliography to a reasonable length. Nonetheless, it is hoped that the reader may find the bibliography useful as a base for further study, recognising that many of the works listed also have extensive bibliographies that may be utilised as entries into additional literature. The bibliography includes works cited in the text as well as additional titles relevant to the subject. However, the medical literature dealing with diseases and related subjects in the Bible, and in the New Testament in particular, is relatively complete from 1950 to the present. Sadly, this wealth of material tends to be totally ignored by theologians and biblical scholars, often to the significant detriment of New Testament interpretation. The bibliography is arranged in respect of each chapter. This makes for easier consultation of sources relevant to each part of the study, although it does result in some repetition.

Chapter 1: Setting the Scene

Barrett-Lennard, R.J.S. (1994). *Christian Healing after the New Testament.* University Press of America, Lanham, MD.

Chaniotis, A. (1995). Illness and cures in the Greek propitiatory inscriptions and dedications of Lydia and Phrygia. *Clio Medica.* 28. 323-344.

Church of England Review Group. (2000). *A Time to Heal: A Contribution to the Ministry of Healing.* Church House, London.

Davies, S.L. (1995). *Jesus the Healer: Possession, Trance and the Origins of Christianity.* Continuum, New York/SCM, London.

Eisenburg, D.M., Kessler, R.C., Foster, C. *et al* (1998). Unconventional medicine use in the United States. *Journal of the American Medical Association.* 280. 1569-1575.

Fulder, S.J. and Munro, R.E. (1985). Complementary medicine in the United Kingdom: patients, practitioners and consultations. *Lancet.* ii. 542-545.

Greig, G.S. and Springer, K.N. (eds). (1993). *The Kingdom and the Power.* Regal Books, Ventura, CA.

Harrell, D.E. (1975). *All Things are Possible: The Healing and Charismatic Revival in Modern America.* University of Indiana Press, Bloomington.

Harris, P. and Rees, R. (2000). The prevalence of complementary and alternative medicine use among the general population: a systematic review of the literature. *Complementary Therapy and Medicine.* 8. 88-96.

Howard, J. Keir. (1993). Medicine and the Bible. In: Metzger, B.M. and Coogan, M. (eds). *The Oxford Companion to the Bible.* Oxford University Press, New York. p 509.

Kleinman, A. (1980). *Patients and Healers in the Context of Culture.* University of Califormia Press, Berkeley, CA.

Knipschild, P., Kleijnen, J. and Riet, ter G. (1990). Belief in the efficacy of alternative medicine among general practitioners in the Netherlands. *Social Science and Medicine.* 31. 625-626.

MacLennan, A.H., Wilson, D.H. and Taylor, A.W. (1996). Prevalence and cost of alternative medicine in Australia. *Lancet.* 347. 569-573.

Marshall, R.J., Gee, R., Israel, M., *et al.* (1990). The use of alternative therapies by Auckland general practitioners. *New Zealand Medical Journal.* 103. 213-215.

Maxwell, W.H.A. (1989). *Demons and Deliverance.* Whitaker House, Springdale, PA.

McAll, R.K. (1971). Demonosis or the possession syndrome. *International Journal of Social Psychiatry.* 17. 150-158.

Murray, J. and Shepherd, S. (1988). Alternative or additional medicine: a new dilemma for the doctor. *Journal of the Royal College of General Practitioners.* 38. 511-514.

Peterson, R. and Peterson, M. (1989). *Roaring Lion.* OMF, Singapore.

Pilch, J.J. (2000). *Healing in the New Testament: Insights from Medical and Mediterranean Anthropology.* Fortress Press, Philadelphia.

Prince, D. (no date). *Expelling Demons.* Derek Prince Ministries, Fort Lauderdale.

Richards, J. (1984). The Church's healing ministry and charismatic renewal. In: Martin, D. and Mullen, P. (eds). *Strange Gifts: A Guide to Charismatic Renewal.* Blackwell, Oxford.

Smith, T. (1983). Alternative medicine. *British Medical Journal.* 287.307.

Subritsky, Bill. (1986). *Demons Defeated.* Sovereign World, Chichester.

Thomas, K.J., Carr, J., Westlake, L. and Williams, B.T. (1991). Use of non-orthodox and conventional health care in Great Britain. *British Medical*

Journal. 302. 207-210.

Wilkinson, J. (1986). Healing in semantics, creation and redemption. *Scottish Bulletin of Evangelical Theology.* 4: 17-37.

Williams, J.R. (1990). *Renewal Theology 2: Salvation, The Holy Spirit and Christian Living.* Academie Books, Grand Rapids.

Wimber, J. and Springer, K.N. (1987). *Power Healing.* Hodder & Stoughton, London.

Chapter 2: The Historical and Cultural Context

Alexander, W.M. (1902). *Demon Possession in the New Testament.* T&T Clark, Edinburgh.

Amundsen, D.W. (1996). *Medicine, Society and Faith in the Ancient and Medieval Worlds.* Johns Hopkins University Press, Baltimore.

Avalos, H. (1995). *Illness and Health Care in the Ancient Near East: The Role of the Temple in Greece, Mesopotamia and Israel.* Harvard Semitic Museum Publications, Cambridge, MA.

_____. (1999). *Health Care and the Rise of Christianity.* Hendricksen, Peabody, MA.

Bagnall, R.S. and Frier, B.W. (1994). *The Demography of Roman Egypt.* Cambridge University Press, Cambridge.

Bammel, E. and Moule, C.F.D. (eds). (1988). *Jesus and the Politics of His Day.* Cambridge University Press, Cambridge. 1984.

Barr, J. (1962). *Biblical Words for Time.* SCM, London.

Berkowitz, L. and Squitier, K.A. (eds). (1990). *Canon of Greek Authors and Works.* Oxford University Press, Oxford.

Betz, H.D. (ed). (1986). *The Greek Magical Papyri in Translation.* University of Chicago Press, Chicago.

Bonner, C. (1944). The violence of departing demons. *Harvard Theological Review.* 37. 334-336.

Brandon, S.G.F. (1968). *Jesus and the Zealots.* Manchester University Press, Manchester.

Brown, M.L. (1995) *Israel's Divine Healer.* Paternoster Press, Carlisle.

Borza, E.N. (1979). Some observations on malaria and the ecology of central Macedonia in antiquity. *American Journal of Ancient History.* 4. 102-124.

Caird, G.B. (1956). *Principalities and Powers,* Clarendon Press, Oxford.

Cartwright, F.F. (1977). *Social History of Medicine.* Longman, London.

Collins, J.J. (1995). *The Scepter and the Star: The Messiahs of the Dead Sea Scrolls and Other Ancient Literature.* Doubleday, New York.

Conrad, L.I., Neve, M., Nutton, V., Porter, R., Wear, A. (1995). *The Western Medical Tradition, 800BC to AD1800.* Cambridge University Press, Cambridge.

Cullmann, O. (1951). *Christ and Time.* SCM, London.

Dingwall, H. (1995). *Physicians, Surgeons and Apothecaries: Medical Practice in Seventeenth Century Edinburgh.* Tuckwell Press, Edinburgh.

Dioscorides *Greek Herbal.* (translated by J Goodyer, edited by R. T. Gunther). (1959 = 1934), Hafner, New York.

Dodds, E.R. (1990 = 1965). *Pagan and Christian in an Age of Uncertainty.* Cambridge University Press, Cambridge.

Edelstein, L. (1967). *Ancient Medicine: Selected Papers of Ludwig Edelstein.* (edited by Temkin, O. and Temkin, C.L.) Johns Hopkins University Press, Baltimore.

Faraone, C.A. and Obbink, D. (eds). (1991). *Magika Hiera: Ancient Greek Magic and Medicine.* Oxford University Press, Oxford.

Fawcett, T. (1973). *Hebrew Myth and Christian Gospel.* SCM, London.

Feldman, L.H. (1986). How much Hellenism in Jewish Palestine? *Hebrew Union College Annual.* 57. 83-111

Ferguson, E. (1987). *Backgrounds of Early Christianity.* Eerdmans, Grand Rapids.

Fletcher, R. (1997). *The Conversion of Europe: From Paganism to Christianity 371-1386 AD.* Harper Collins, London.

French, V. (1986). Midwives and maternity care in the Roman world. *Helios.* (New Series). 13. 69-84.

Freyne, S. (1988). *Galilee, Jesus and the Gospels: Literary Approaches and Historical Investigations.* Fortress Press, Philadelphia.

Friedenwald, H. (1944). *The Jews and Medicine.* Johns Hokins University Press, Baltimore, 2 vols.

German, G.A. (1972). Psychiatry. In: Shaper, A.G., Kibukamusoke, J.W., Hutt, M.S.R. (eds). *Medicine in a Tropical Environment.* British Medical Association, London. pp 329-347.

Goodman, R. (1983). *State and Society in Roman Galilee*, Rowman and Allanheld, Totawa, NJ.

Gordon, B.L. (1949). *Medicine throughout Antiquity.* F.A. Davis, Philadelphia.

Grant, R.M. (1952). *Miracle and Natural Law in Graeco-Roman and early Christian Thought.* North Holland, Amsterdam.

Graves, Robert (1959). Brain washing in ancient times. In: Sargant, W. *Battle for the Mind.* Pan Books, London. Revised edn. pp 156-164.

Grmek, M.D. (1989). *Diseases in the Ancient Greek World.* ET. Johns Hopkins University Press, Baltimore.

Guthrie, D. (1945). *A History of Medicine.* Nelson, London.

Gwilt, J.R. (1986). Biblical ills and remedies. *Journal of the Royal Society of Medicine.* 79. 738-741.

Hanson, P.D. (1975). *The Dawn of Apocalyptic: The Historical and Sociological Roots of Jewish Apocalyptic Eschatology*, Fortress Press, Philadelphia. Revised edn.

Hardie, J.B. (1966). Medicine and the biblical world. *Canadian Medical Association Journal.* 94. 32-36.

Harvey, A.E. (1982). *Jesus and the Constraints of History.* SCM, London.

Hengel, M. (1974). *Judaism and Hellenism*, SCM, London. 2 Vols.

Holladay, C.H. (1977). *Theios-Aner in Hellenistic Judaism.* Scholars Press, Missoula, MT

Hopkins, K. (1983). *Death and Renewal.* Cambridge University Press, Cambridge.

_____. (1998). Christian number and its implications. *Journal of Early Christian Studies.* 6. 185-226.

Hornblow, S. and Spawforth, A. (eds). (1996). *The Oxford Classical Dictionary.* Oxford University Press, Oxford (particularly the articles on medicine (pp 945-949) and disease (p 486)).

Horrell, D.G. (1996). *The Social Ethos of the Corinthian Correspondence: Interests and Ideology from 1 Corinthians to 1 Clement.* T & T Clark, Edinburgh.

Howard, J.Keir. (1985). New Testament exorcism and its significance today. *Expository Times* 96. 105-109.

Hull, J.M. (1974). *Hellenistic Magic and the Synoptic Tradition,* SCM, London.

Ilberg, J. (1927). *Corpus Medicorum Graecorum.* 4 Vols. Tuebner, Leipzig.

Temkin, O. (1956). *Soranus' Gynecology.* Johns Hopkins University Press, Baltimore.

Jackson, R.P.J. (1988). *Doctors and Disease in the Roman Empire.* British Museum Publications, London.

_____. (1993). Roman medicine: the practitioners and their practice. *Aufstieg und Niedergang der Römischen Welt.* 11. 37. 79-101.

Jeremias, J. (1969). *Jerusalem in the Time of Jesus,* SCM, London.

Kee, H.C. (1977). *Community of the New Age: Studies in Mark's Gospel,* SCM, London.

_____. (1983). *Miracle in the Early Christian World: A Study in Sociohistorical Method.* Yale University Press, New Haven.

_____. (1986). *Medicine, Miracle and Magic in New Testament Times.* Cambridge University Press, Cambridge.

_____. (1989). Magic and Messiah. In: Neusner, J., Frerichs, E.S. and Flesher, P.V.M. (eds). *Religion, Science and Magic.* Oxford University Press, Oxford. pp 121-141.

Kleinman, A (1980). *Patients and Healers in the Context of Culture.* University of California Press, Berkeley, CA.

Kudlien, F. and During, R.J. (Eds). (1991). *Galen's Methods of Healing: Proceedings of the 1992 Galen Symposium.* E.J. Brill, Leiden.

Lambourne, R.A. (1963). *Community, Church and Healing.* Darton, Longman and Todd, London.

Lee, B.J. (1988). *The Galilean Jewishness of Jesus: Retrieving the Jewish Origins of Christianity.* Paulist Press, New York.

Lloyd, G.E.R. (1973). *Greek Science after Aristotle.* Norton, New York.

Longrigg, J. (1993). *Greek Rational Medicine: Philosophy and Medicine from Alcmaeon to the Alexandrians.* Routledge, London.

Majno, G. (1976). *The Healing Hand.* Harvard University Press, Cambridge, MA.

Manson, W. (1943). *Jesus the Messiah,* Hodder and Stoughton, London.

McCasland, S.V. (1951). *By the Finger of God: Demon Possession and*

Exorcism in Early Christianity, Scribner, New York.

Meier, J.P. (1994). *A Marginal Jew: Rethinking the Historical Jesus.* Doubleday, New York. 3 Vols.

Meyer, E.M. and Strange, J.F. (1981). *Archaeology, the Rabbis and Early Christianity.* SCM, London.

Millar, F. (1978). The background of the Maccabean revolution: Reflections on Martin Hengel's 'Judaism and Hellenism'. *Journal of Jewish Studies.* 29. 9.

Milne, J.S. (1907). *Surgical Instruments in Greek and Roman Times.* Oxford University Press, Oxford.

Neusner, J., Green, W.S., Fredrichs, E.S. (eds). (1987). *Judaism and their Messiahs at the Turn of the Christian Era.* Cambridge University Press, Cambridge.

Nichols, M.P. and Dax, M. (1977). *Catharsis in Psychotherapy.* Gardner Press, New York.

Palmer, B. (ed). (1986). *Medicine and the Bible.* Paternoster Press, Exeter.

Parkin, T.G. (1992). *Demography and Roman Society.* Johns Hopkins University Press, Baltimore.

Pilch, J.J. (1988). Understanding biblical healing. *Biblical Theology Bulletin.* 18. 60-66.

_____. (2000). *Healing in the New Testament Insights from Medical and Mediterranean Anthropology.* Fortress Press, Philadelphia.

Pilowsky, I. (1997). *Abnormal Illness Behaviour.* Wiley, Chichester.

Porter, R. (ed). (1996). *The Cambridge Illustrated History of Medicine.* Cambridge University Press, Cambridge.

Preuss, J. (1978=1911). *Biblical and Talmudic Medicine.* (edited by Rosner, F.) Sanhedrin Press, New York.

Riddle, J.M. (1985). *Dioscorides on Pharmacy and Medicine.* University of Texas Press, Austin.

Rihll, T.E. (1999). *Greek Science (New Surveys in the Classics No 29).* Oxford University Press, Oxford.

Robinson, J.A.T. (1985). *The Priority of John,* SCM, London.

Rosner, F. (1977). *Medicine in the Bible and Talmud.* Ktav Publishing House, New York.

_____. (2000). *Encyclopedia of Medicine in the Bible and Talmud.* Aronson, New York.

Russell, D.S. (1964). *The Method and Message of Jewish Apocalyptic,* SCM, London.

Sanders, E.P. (1985). *Jesus and Judaism.* SCM, London.

_____. (1993). *The Historical Figure of Jesus.* Penguin Books, Harmondsworth.

Sargant, W. and Slater, E. (1963). *An Introduction to Physical Means of Treatment in Psychiatry.* Livingstone, Edinburgh.

Scarborough, J. (1969). *Roman Medicine.* Thames and Hudson, London.

_____. (1991). The pharmacology of sacred plants and roots. In: Faraone, C.A. and Obbink, D (Eds). *Magika Hiera.* pp 139-161.

Schürer, E., Vermes, G., Miller, F. (1975). *The History of the Jewish People in the Age of Jesus Christ*. T & T Clark, Edinburgh. 2 Vols.

Short, A. Rendle. (1953) *The Bible and Modern Medicine*. Paternoster Press, London.

Sigerist, H. (1951). *A History of Medicine*. 2 Vols. Oxford University Press, Oxford.

Smith, M. (1978). *Jesus the Magician*, Gollancz, London.

Smith, W.D. (1979). *The Hippocratic Tradition*. Cornell University Press, Ithaca.

Spurgeon, A., Gompertz, D. and Harrington, J.M. (1996). Modifiers of non-specific symptoms in occupational and environmental syndromes. *Occupational and Environmental Medicine.* 53. 361-366.

Stambaugh, J. and Balch, D. (1986). *The Social World of the First Christians*. SPCK, London.

Temkin, O. (1933). The doctrine of epilepsy in the Hippocratic writings. *Bulletin of the History of Medicine.* 1. 277-322.

_____. (1933). Views on epilepsy in the Hippocratic period. *Bulletin of the History of Medicine.* 1. 41-44.

_____. (1971). *The Falling Sickness*. Johns Hopkins University Press, Baltimore.

_____. (1973). *Galenism: Rise and Decline of a Medical Philosophy*. Cornell University Press, Ithaca.

_____. (1991). *Hippocrates in a world of Pagans and Christians.* Johns Hopkins University Press, Baltimore.

Theissen, G. (1982). *The Social Setting of Pauline Christianity*. Fortress Press, Philadelphia

Tidball, D. (1983). *An Introduction to the Sociology of the New Testament*. Paternoster Press, Exeter.

Twelftree, G.H. (1985). *Christ Triumphant: Exorcism Then and Now*, Hodder and Stoughton, London.

_____. (1993). *Jesus the Exorcist: A Contribution to the Study of the Historical Jesus*. JCB Mohr, Tübingen/Hendrickson, Peabody MA.

_____. (1999). *Jesus the Miracle Worker: A Historical and Theological Study.* Inter Varsity Press, Downers Grove, IL.

Vermes, G. (1983). *Jesus and the World of Judaism*, SCM, London.

_____. (1987). *The Dead Sea Scrolls in English*. Penguin Books, Harmondsworth.

Walker, A. (1995). The devil you think you know: demonology and the charismatic movement. In: Smail, T., Walker, A. and Wright, N. *Charismatic Renewal.* SPCK, London. p 89.

Wells, C. (1975). Ancient obstetric hazards and female mortality. *Bulletin of the New York Academy of Medicine.* 51. 1235-1249.

Wright, N.T. (1992). *New Testament and the People of God*. SPCK, London.

_____. (1996a). *Jesus and the Victory of God*. SPCK, London

_____. (1996b). Jesus' symbols of the kingdom: Thomas Burns Lectures, University of Otago, New Zealand 1996 (3). *Stimulus.* 4 (4). 28

Zeitlin, I.M. (1988). *Jesus and the Judaism of his Time*. Polity, Cambridge.

There are no complete English translations of either the Hippocratic or Galenic collections. Partial translations will be found in Lloyd, G.E.R. (ed). (1978). *The Hippocratic Writings.* Penguin Books, Harmondsworth and in Brock, A.J. (1929). *Greek Medicine.* Dent, London. The only English translation of the Mishnah continues to be, Danby, H. (1933). *The Mishnah.* Oxford University Press, Oxford. The Talmud is available as *Talmud of the Land of Israel* (Chicago University Press, Chicago) in 18 volumes, edited by J. Neusner and with various translators, the latest volume published in 2000. The works of Josephus are available in the Loeb Classical Library.

Chapter 3: The Healing Ministry of Jesus: The Markan Tradition

Achtemeier, P. (1970). Toward the isolation of pre-Markan miracle catenae. *Journal of Biblical Literature.* 89. 265-291
_____. (1972). The origin and function of pre-Markan miracle catenae. *Journal of Biblical Literature.* 91. 198-221.
_____. (1975. Miracles and the historical Jesus: A study of Mark 9:14-29. *Catholic Biblical Quarterly.* 37. 471-479).
Aland, K. (1963. *Did the Early Church Baptise Infants?* SCM, London. ET.
_____. (ed). (1976). *Synopsis Quattuor Evangeliorum.* 9th edn. Deutsche Bibelsiftung, Stuttgart.
Aland, K. and Aland, B. (1987) *The Text of the New Testament.* Eerdmans, Grand Rapids/E J Brill, Leiden, ET.
Alon, A. (1969). *The Natural History of the Land of the Bible.* Jerusalem Publishing House, Jerusalem..
American Psychiatric Association (1994). *Diagnostic and Statistical Manual of Mental Disease.* (*DSM-IV*). 4th edn. American Psychiatric Association. Washington.
Anon. (1983). Meadow and Munchausen. *Lancet.* i. 417
Anon. (1991). Neurological conversion disorders in childhood. *Lancet.* 337. 889-890.
Barr, J. (1984). *Escaping from Fundamentalism.* SCM, London.
Barrett, C.K. (1994). *The Acts of the Apostles (International Critical Commentary).* T & T Clark, Edinburgh.
Barton, J. (1988). *People of the Book? The Authority of the Bible in Christianity*, SPCK, London.
Bauckham, R. (ed) (1998). *The Gospels for All Christians. Rethinking the Gospel Audiences.* T & T Clark, Edinburgh.
Bell, H.I. and Skeat, T.C. (1935). *Fragments of an Unknown Gospel and other early Christian Papyri.* Oxford University Press, Oxford.
Best, E. (1970). *Scottish Journal of Theology.* 23. 323-337.
_____. (1981). *Following Jesus.* (JSOT Press, Sheffield).
Bowman, J. (1965). *The Gospel of Mark: The New Christian-Jewish Passover Haggadah.* E J Brill, Leyden.
Borza E.N.(1979). Some observations on malaria and the ecology of central

Macedonia in antiquity. *American Journal of Ancient History* 4. 102-124.

Brown, C. (1985). *Jesus in European Protestant Thought: 1778-1860.* Labyrinth, Durham, NC.

Browne, S.G. (1979). *Leprosy in the Bible*, Christian Medical Fellowship, London, 3rd Edition.

Bruce, F F. (1964). History and the gospel. *Faith and Thought*; 93, 121-145.

_____. (1983). *The Hard Sayings of Jesus.* Hodder & Stoughton, London.

_____. (1990). *Acts of the Apostles, Greek Text with Introduction and Commentary.* Erdmans, Grand Rapids. 3rd edn.

Buchanan, R C. (1972). The causes and prevention of burns in Malawi. *Central African Journal of Medicine.* 18. 55-56.

Bultmann, R. (1968). *The History of the Synoptic Tradition*, Basil Blackwell, Oxford. Revised edn. ET.

Cadbury, H.J. (1920) *The Style and Literary Method of Luke*, Harvard Theological Studies No 6, Harvard University Press, Cambridge, MA.

Cameron, R. (1982). *The Other Gospels: Non-canonical Gospel Texts.* Westminster, Philadelphia.

Cave, C.H. (1979). The leper: Mark 1:40-45. *New Testament Studies.* 25. 245-250.

Charlesworth, J H (ed). (1992). *Jesus and the Dead Sea Scrolls.* Doubleday, New York.

Charlesworth, J.H. (ed). (1992). *The Messiah.* Fortress Press, Minneapolis.

Clark, R. E. D. (1963). Men as trees walking. *Faith and Thought.* 93. 88-94.

Cochrane, R.G. (1961). *Biblical Leprosy: A Suggested Interpretation.* Tyndale Press, London.

Collier, J S. (1934). Epilepsy. In: Bett, W R (ed). *A Short History of Some Common Diseases.* H K Lewis, London. pp 119-136

Cranfield, C.E.B. (1977), *The Gospel according to Mark (The Cambridge Greek Testament Commentary).* Cambridge University Press, Cambridge.

Crossan, J.D. (1989). *Jesus: A Revolutionary Biography.* HarperCollins, Los Angeles.

Culpepper, R. A. (1982). Mark 10:50: Why mention the garment? *Journal of Biblical Literature.* 101. 131-132.

Dahl, N. (1991), *Jesus the Christ: The Historical Origins of Christological Doctrine.* Fortress, Minneapolis.

Daube, D. (1956). *The New Testament and Rabbinic Judaism.* Athlone Press, London.

Davies, S. (1995). *Jesus the Healer: Possession, Trance and the Origins of Christianity.* Continuum, New York.

Dormandy, R. (2000). The expulsion of Legion: a political reading of Mark 5:1-20. *Expository Times* 111. 335-337.

Dufton, F. (1989). The Syrophoenician woman and her dogs. *Expository Times.* 100. 417

Ellenburg, B.D. (1995). A review of selected narrative-critical conventions in Mark's use of miracle material. *Journal of the Evangelical Theological Society.* 38. 171-180.

Elliott, J.K. (1978). The healing of the leper in the synoptic parallels. *Theologische Zeitschrift.*. 34. 175-176.

Finegan, J. (1969). *Hidden Records of the Life of Jesus*. Pilgrim Press, Philadelphia.

Forbes, T.R. (1981). Births and deaths in a London parish, *Bulletin of the History of Medicine* 55. 371-391

Fraser, H. (1973). The gospel of St Mark 8:22-26. *Medical Journal of Australia*. 2. 657-658.

French, V. (1986). Midwives and maternity care in the Roman world. *Helios* (New Series). 13. 69-84.

Freyne, S. (1988). *Galilee, Jesus and the Gospels*. Fortress Press, Philadelphia.

Fry, L. (1992). *An Atlas of Psoriasis*. Parthenon, Carnforth.

Fuller, R.H. (1963) *Interpreting the Miracles*, SCM, London.

Funk, R.W. (1996). *Honest to Jesus: Jesus for a New Millennium*. Hodder and Stoughton, London.

Funk, R.W., Hoover, R.W. and the Jesus Seminar (1993). *The Five Gospels: The Search for the Authentic Words of Jesus. New Translation and Commentary.* Macmillan, New York.

Gelder, M.G. (1996). Neurosis. In: Weatherall DJ, Leadingham JGJ, Warrell DA (eds). *Oxford Textbook of Medicine*, Oxford University Press, Oxford. 3rd edn. p 25.4,5

Gelder, M.G., Gath, D.H. and Mayou R. (1983). *Oxford Textbook of Psychiatry*, Oxford University Press, Oxford.

Goldman, L. (1971). Syphilis in the Bible, *Archives of Dermatology*. 103. 535-536.

Goldman, L., Moraites, R. S, Kitzmuller, K. S. (1966). White spots in biblical times. *Archives of Dermatology*; 93: 744-753.

Gramberg, K.P. (1959). Leprosy in the Bible. *Tropical and Geographical Medicine.* 11.127-139.

Grant, R.M. (1952). *Miracle and Natural Law in Graeco-Roman and Early Christian Thought.* North Holland Publishing. Amsterdam.

Grattan-Smith, P., Fairley, M., Procopis, P. (1988). Clinical features of conversion disorders. *Archives of Diseases of Childhood*. 63. 404-414.

Green, J.B. (ed). *Hearing the New Testament: Strategies for Interpretation.* Eerdmans, Grand Rapids.

Grmek, M.D. (1989). *Diseases in the Ancient Greek World*. ET. Johns Hopkins University Press.

Gundry, R.H. (1993). *Mark: A Commentary on his Apology for the Cross.* Eerdmans, Grand Rapids.

Hampton, K K., Peatfield, R C., Pullar, T. (1988). Burns because of epilepsy. *British Medical Journal.* 296. 1659-1660).

Harvey, A.E. (1982). *Jesus and the Constraints of History*. Duckworth, London.

Hazleman, B. (1993). Soft tissue rheumatism. In: Maddison, P.J., Isenberg, D.A., Woo, P., Glass, D.N. (eds). *Oxford Textbook of Rheumatology*. Oxford University Press, Oxford. p 950.

Hedrick, C. W. (1984). The role of 'summary statements' in the composition of the Gospel of Mark: A dialog with Karl Schmidt and Norman Perrin. *Novum Testamentum.* 26. 289-311.

Hengel, M. (1985). *Studies in the Gospel of Mark*, SCM, London, ET.

Hes, J P. and Wollenstein, S. (1964). The attitudes of the ancient Jewish sources to mental patients. *Israeli Annals of Psychiatry* 2. 103-116.

Hiers, R.H. (1974). Satan, demons and the kingdom of God. *Scottish Journal of Theology.* 27. 35-47.

Hobart, W.K. (1892). *The Medical Language of St Luke*, Dublin University Press, Dublin.

Hollenbach, P.W. (1981). Jesus, demoniacs and public authorities: a socio-historical study. *Journal of the American Academy of Religion.* 49. 567-588.

Hooker, M.D. (1983). *The Message of Mark*. Epworth Press, London.

_____. (1997). *The Signs of a Prophet: The Prophetic Actions of Jesus.* SCM, London.

Howard, J.Keir. (1984), Men as trees walking: Mark 8:22-26. *Scottish Journal of Theology.* 37. 163-170,

_____. (1985). New Testament exorcism and its significance today. *Expository Times.* 95: 105-109.

_____. (1993), Epilepsy. In: Metzger, B M. and Coogan, M D. (eds). *Oxford Companion to the Bible.* Oxford University Press, New York. pp 190-191.

_____. (1993). Exorcism. In: Metzger, B.M. and Coogan, M.D.(eds). *The Oxford Companion to the Bible.* Oxford University Press, New York. pp 216-217.

Hull, J.M. (1974). *Hellenistic Magic and the Synoptic Tradition*. SCM, London.

Hulse, E.V.(1975). The nature of biblical leprosy and the use of alternative medical terms in modern translations of the Bible. *Palestine Exploration Quarterly.* 107. 87-105.

Hurtado, L. (1989) *Mark. The New International Bible Commentary.* Hendrickson, Peabody, MA.

James, M R. (1924) *The Apocryphal New Testament*, Oxford University Press, Oxford.

Jeremias, J. (1960. *Infant Baptism in the First Four Centuries*. SCM, London. ET

Jilek-Aull, L. (1999). Morbus sacer in Africa: some religious aspects of epilepsy in traditional cultures. *Epilepsia* 40. 382-386.

Johnson, E S. (1979). Mark 8:22-26: The blind man from Bethsaida. *New Testament Studies.* 25. 370-383.

Jones, W.H.S. (1909). *Malaria and Greek History*, Manchester University Press, Manchester,

Kaplan, H. I. and Sadock, B. J. (1995). *Comprehensive Textbook of Psychiatry.* 6th edn. Williams and Wilkins, Baltimore.

Kaufmann, J. C. E. (1964a). Neuropathology in the Bible – II. *South African*

Medical Journal. 38. 788-789.

_____. (1964b). Neuropathology in the Bible – III. *South African Medical Journal.* 38: 805-808.

Kazmerski, C.R. (1992). Evangelist and leper: A socio-cultural study of Mark 1:40-45. *New Testament Studies* 38. 37-50.

Kee, Howard C. (1977). *Community of the New Age: Studies in Mark's Gospel.* SCM, London.

Kelber, W.H. (1983). *The Oral and the Written Gospel,* Fortress Press, Philadelphia..

Koester, H. (1990). *Ancient Christian Gospels: Their History and Development.* SCM, London.

Lane, W. L. (1974). *The Gospel of Mark (The New International Commentary on the New Testament).* Eerdmans, Grand Rapids.

Lasure, L.C., Mikulas, W.C. (1996). Biblical behaviour modification. *Behavioural Research and Therapy.* 34. 563-566.

Lendrum, F.C. (1952). The name 'leprosy'. *American Journal of Tropical Medicine and Hygeine.* 1. 999-1018.

Leuschner, J. (1963). Leprosy in the Bible: the diagnosis, epidemiology, treatment and prognosis. *Minnesota Medicine.* 46. 371-373.

Lightfoot, R.H. (1950). *The Gospel Message of St Mark.* Oxford University Press, Oxford.

Linnemann, E. (1992). *Is There a Synoptic Problem? Rethinking the Literary Dependence of the First Three Gospels.* ET. Baker, Grand Rapids.

Llewellyn-Jones, D. (1986). *Fundamentals of Obstetrics and Gynaecology.* Faber and Faber, London. Vol 2. pp 76-77.

Lloyd Davies, M. and Lloyd Davies, T.A. (1993). *The Bible: Medicine and Myth.* Silent Books, Cambridge. 2nd edn..

Mack, B. (1988), *A Myth of Innocence: Mark and Christian Origins.* Fortress, Philadelphia.

Mackay, D. M. (1973). The psychology of seeing. *Transactions of the Society of Ophthalmology.* 93. 391-405.

Malina, B.J. (1983). *The New Testament World.* SCM. London.

Maloney, M.D. (1980). Diagnosing hysterical conversion reactions in children. *Journal of Pediatrics.* 97. 1016-1020

Manson, T.W. (1962). The foundations of the synoptic tradition: the Gospel of Mark. In: Black, M. (ed). *Studies in the Gospels.* Fortress, Philadelphia. pp 28-45.

Marshall I.H. (ed). (1985). *New Testament Interpretation.* Paternoster Press, Exeter. 3rd edn.

Marshall, C. (1989). *Faith as a Theme in Mark's Gospel (SNTS Monograph 64).* CambridgeUniversity Press, Cambridge.

Martin, R P. (1972). *Mark: Evangelist and Theologian.* Paternoster Press, Exeter.

Massey, E.W. (1978). Leprosy, biblical opprobrium? *Southern Medical Journal* 71.1294-1295.

Matthews, W B. and Miller, H. (1979). *Diseases of the Nervous System.*

Blackwell, Oxford.

Mayer Gross, W., Slater, E. and Roth, M. (eds). (1960). *Clinical Psychiatry*, Cassell, London.

Mayou, R. (1991). Medically unexplained physical symptoms. *British Medical Journal*. 303. 534-535.

Meier, J.P. (1994) *A Marginal Jew: Rethinking the Historical Jesus*. Vol 2. *Mentor, Message and Miracles*. Doubleday, New York.

Menter, A and Barker, J.N.W.N (1991). Psoriasis in practice. *Lancet*. 338: 231-234.

Metzger, B.M. (1971). *A Textual Commentary on the Greek New Testament*. London, United Bible Societies.

_____. (1992). *The Text of the New Testament: Its Transmission, Corruption and Restoration*. Oxford University Press, Oxford.

Micklem, E.R. (1922). *Miracles and the New Psychology*. Oxford University, Oxford.

Moule, C.F.D. (ed). (1965). *Miracles: Cambridge Studies in their Philosophy and History*. Mowbrays, London.

Neirynck, F. (1985). Papyrus Egerton 2 and the healing of the leper. *Ephemerides Theologiae Lovanienses*. 61. 153-160.

Nichols, M.P., Dax, M. (1977). *Catharsis in Psychotherapy*. Gardner Press, New York.

Nicholson, F W. (1897). The saliva superstition in classical literature. *Harvard Studies in Classical Philology*. 8. 23-40.

Nineham, D.E. (1963). *St Mark (Pelican Gospel Commentaries)*. Penguin Books, Harmondsworth.

Nun, M. (1999). Ports of Galilee. *Biblical Archeology Review*. 25. (4). 18-31, 64.

O'Brien, M.D. (1998). Medically unexplained neurological symptoms. *British Medical Journal*. 316. 564-565.

Palmer, B. (Ed). (1986). *Medicine and the Bible,* Paternoster Press, Exeter.

Paul, J.R.(1955). *Poliomyelitis (WHO Monograph No 26)*, World Health Organisation, Geneva.

Pilch, J. (1981). Biblical leprosy and body symbolism. *Biblical Theology Bulletin*. 11: 119-133.

_____. (1988). Understanding biblical healing, *Biblical Theology Bulletin* 18: 60-66.

_____. (2000). *Healing in the New Testament: Insights from Medical and Mediterranean Anthropology*. Fortress Press, Philadelphia.

Pilowsky, I. (1997). *Abnormal Illness Behaviour*. Wiley, Chichester.

Porter, R. (ed). (1996). *The Cambridge Illustrated History of Medicine* Cambridge University Press, Cambridge.

Putnam, F.W. (1989). *Diagnosis and Treatment of Multiple Personality Disorder*. Guilford Press, New York

Ramsay, I.T. (1957). *Religious Language*, SCM, London.

Reiner, G.J. (1950). *History: Its Purpose and Method*. Allen and Unwin, London.

Richardson, A. (1941). *The Miracle Stories of the Gospels*. SPCK, London.

Robbins, V. K. (1973). The healing of blind Bartimaeus (Mark 10:46-52). *Journal of Biblical Literature*. 92. 225.

Rosner, F. (1975). Neurology in the Bible and Talmud. *Israeli Journal of Medical Science*. 11. 385-397).

Ross, C.A. (1989). *Multiple Personality Disorder: Diagnosis, Clinical Features and Treatment*. Wiley, New York.

Ross, J M. (1978). Epilepsy in the Bible. *Developmental Medicine and Child Neurology*. 20. 677-678

Roy, F.H. (1974). World blindness: definition, incidence and major treatable causes. *Annals of Ophthalmology*. 6. 1049.

Sanders, E.P. (1985), *Jesus and Judaism*. SCM, London.

_____. (1990). *Jewish Law from Jesus to the Mishnah*. SCM, London.

_____. (1993). *The Historical Figure of Jesus*. (Penguin Books, Harmondsworth)

Sanders, E.P. and Davies, M. (1989). *Studying the Synoptic Gospels*. SCM, London.

Sargant, W. (1957). *Battle for the Mind: A Physiology of Conversion and Brainwashing*. Heinmann, London.

_____. (1973). *The Mind Possessed*. Heinmann, London.

Sargant, W. and Slater, E. (1940). Acute war neuroses. *Lancet* ii. 1-2.

_____. (1963). *An Introduction to Physical Methods of Treatment in Psychiatry*. Livingstone, Edinburgh.

Sawyer, D. (1996). *Women and Religion in the First Christian Centuries*. Routledge & Kegan Paul, London.

Schweizer, E. (1971). *The Good News according to Mark*. SPCK, London. ET.

Shepherd, P.M. (1955). The Bible as a source book for physicians. *Glasgow Medical Journal*. 36. 348-375.

Short, A. Rendle, (1953). *The Bible and Modern Medicine*, Paternoster Press, London,

Sinclair, S. G. (1990). The healing of Bartimaeus and the gaps in Mark's messianic secret. *St Luke's Journal of Theology*. 303. 249-257.

Skinsnes, O.K. (1964). Leprosy in society - II The pattern of concept and reaction to leprosy in oriental antiquity. *Leprosy Review* 35: 106-122.

Smith, M. (1971). Prolegomena to a discussion of aretalogies, divine men, the gospels and Jesus. *Journal of Biblical Literature*. 90. 174-199.

_____. (1978). *Jesus the Magician*. Gollancz, London,

Stein, R.H. (1991). *Gospels and Tradition: Studies on Redaction Criticism of the Synoptic Gospels*. Baker, Grand Rapids.

Steinhauser, M. G. (1983). Part of a 'call story'. *Expository Times*. 94. 204-206.

Straudinger, H. (1981). *The Trustworthiness of the Gospels*, Handsel Press, Edinburgh.

Surgitharajah, R S. (1992). Men, trees and walking: a conjectural solution to Mark 8:24. *Expository Times*. 103. 172-174.

Taylor, V. (1955). *The Gospel according to St Mark (Macmillan New*

Testament Commentary), Macmillan, London, 6th edn.

_____. (1957). *The Formation of the Gospel Tradition.* Macmillan, London. 6th edn.

Thiede, C.P. and D'Ancona, M. (1996). *The Jesus Papyrus.* Weidenfeld and Nicolson, London.

Thiessen, G. (1983). *Miracle Stories of Early Christian Tradition.* T & T Clark, Edinburgh. ET.

_____. (1991) *The Gospels in Context: Social and Political History in the Synoptic Tradition.* Fortress Press, Minneapolis.

Thigpen, C and Cleckley, H. (1960). *The Three Faces of Eve*, Pan Books, London.

Tidball, D. (1983). *An Introduction to the Sociology of the New Testament.* Paternoster Press, Exeter.

Trocmé, E. (1975). *The Formation of the Gospel according to Mark.* Fortress Press, Philadelphia, ET.

Twelftree, G.H. (1985). *Christ Triumphant: Exorcism Then and Now.* Hodder and Stoughton, London.

_____. (1993). *Jesus the Exorcist: A Contribution to the Study of the Historical Jesus.* J.C.B. Mohr, Tübingen/Hendrickson, Peabody, MA.

_____. (1999). *Jesus the Miracle Worker: A Historical and Theological Study.* IVP, Downers Grove, IL.

Valvo, A. (1968). Les guerisons des aveugles de l'évangile. *Annales Oculistique (Paris).* 201. 1214-1222.

Van der Loos, H. (1965). *The Miracles of Jesus.* EJ Brill, Leiden.

Vaughan, D. and Astbury, T. (1977). *General Ophthalmology.* Lange, Los Altos, CA.

Vermes, G. (1973). *Jesus the Jew: A Historian's Reading of the Gospels.* Collins, London.

Von Senden, M. (1960). *The Perception of Space and Shape in the Congenitally Blind before and after Operation.* Methuen, London. ET.

Wenham, D. and Blomberg, C. (eds). (1986). *Gospel Perspectives 6: The Miracles of Jesus.* JSOT, Sheffield.

Wilkinson, J. (1967), The epileptic boy. *Expository Times.* 79. 39-42.

_____. (1980). *Health and Healing: Studies in New Testament Principles and Practice.* Handsel Press, Edinburgh.

Witherington, B. III. (1990). *The Christology of Jesus.* Fortress Press, Minneapolis.

Wright, N.T. (1992) *The New Testament and the People of God.* SPCK. London.

_____. (1996). *Jesus and the Victory of God.* SPCK, London.

Yahav, D. (1999). Diseases, contagions and medicine in the Bible. *Harefuah.* 136. 73-81.

Zias, J. , Mitchell, P. (1996). Psoriatic arthritis in a fifth-century Judean Desert monastery. *American Journal of Physical Anthropology.* 101. 491-502).

Zysk, K.G. (1985). *Religious Healing in the Veda.* American Philosophical Society, Philadelphia.

Standard reference texts used in this and succeeding chapters are:

Baltz, H. and Schneider, G. (1990-1993). *Exegetical Dictionary of the New Testament.* 3 Vols. Eerdmans, Grand Rapids, ET.

Bauer, W. (1979). *A Greek-English Lexicon of the New Testament and Other Early Christian Literature.* (Revised and augmented by Gingrich, F.W. and Danker, F.W.). Second edition. University of Chicago Press, Chicago. (referred to as Bauer).

Liddell, H.G.and Scott, R. (1996) *Greek-English Lexicon.* (Revised by Jones, H.S. and McKenzie, R.) Ninth edition with a revised supplement, 1996. Clarendon Press, Oxford. (referred to as Liddell and Scott).

Kittel, G. and Friedrich, G. (eds). (1964-1974). *Theological Dictionary of the New Testament.* (Translated by G. W. Bromiley). 10 Vols. Eerdmans, Grand Rapids.

Chapter 3: The Healing Ministry of Jesus: The Non-Markan Synoptic Traditions

Achtemeier, P.J. (1978). The Lukan perspective on the miracles of Jesus: a preliminary sketch. In: Talbert, C.H. (ed). *Perspectives on Luke-Acts.* T & T Clark, Edinburgh. pp 153-167.

Akenson, D.H. (2000). *Saint Saul: A Skeleton Key to the Historical Jesus* McGill-Queen's University Press, Montreal/Oxford University Press, New York.

Allen, W.C. (1912). *The Gospel according to St Matthew (International Critical Commentary).* T & T Clark, Edinburgh.

Aune, D.E. (ed). *Studies in New Testament and early Christian Literature: Essays in Honour of Allen P. Wikgren.* E J Brill, Leiden.

Bauckham, R. (ed). (1998) *The Gospel for all Christians: Rethinking the Gospel Audience.* Eerdmans, Grand Rapids.

Betz, H.D. (1968). Jesus as divine man. In: Trotter, F.T. (ed). *Jesus and the Historian: In Honour of E.C. Colwell.* Westminster, Philadelphia. pp 114-133.

Betz, O. (1972). The concept of the so-called 'divine man' in Mark's christology. In: Aune, D.E (ed). *Studies in New Testament and Early Christian Literature. Essays in Honour of A.P. Wikgren.* E.J. Brill, Leiden. pp 229-234.

Borenstein, D.G., Wiesel, S.W. (1989). *Low Back Pain: Medical Diagnosis and Comprehensive Management.* W.B. Saunders, Philadelphia.

Bornkamm, G. Barth, G. and Held, H.J. *Tradition and Interpretation in Matthew.* SCM, London. 2nd edn.

Bradford, D.S., Moe, J.H., Winter, R.B. (1982). Scoliosis and kyphosis. In: Rothman, R.H., Simeone, Fa. (eds). *The Spine.* W.B. Saunders, Philadelphia. pp 316-439.

Bultmann, R. (1963). *History of the Synoptic Tradition.* Blackwell, Oxford. ET.

Byrskog, S. (1994). *Jesus the Only Teacher, Didactic Authority and Transmission in Ancient Israel, Ancient Judaism and the Matthean Community.* Almqvist & Wicksell, Stockholm.

Cadbury, H.J. (1920). *The Style and Literary Method of Luke (Harvard Theological Studies No 6).* Harvard University Press, Cambridge, MA.

Caird, G.B. (1963). *Saint Luke (Pelican Gospel Commentaries).* Penguin Books, Harmondsworth.

Carrington, G.P. (1986). *The 'Divine Man': His Origin and Function in Hellenistic Popular Religion.* Peter Lang, New York.

Ceccarelli, G. (1993). Obstetrics and neonatology in the Bible. *Minerva Medicine.* 84. 565-570.

Comber, J.A. (1978). The verb therapeuō in Matthew's gospel. *Journal of Biblical Literature.* 97. 431-434.

Duling, D.C. (1978). The therapeutic Son of David: An element in Matthew's christological apologetic. *New Testament Studies.* 24:392-410.

Dumont, M. (1990). Gynecology and obstetrics in the Bible. *Journal of Gynecology, Obstetrics and the Biology of Reproduction.* 19. 1-7 and 145-153.

Elliott, J.K. (1978). The healing of the leper in the synoptic parallels. *Theologische Zeitschrift.* 34. 175-176.

Farrer, A. (1985). On dispensing with Q. In: Bellinzoni, A.J. (ed). *The Two-Source Hypothesis: A Critical Appraisal.* Mercer University Press, Macon, GA.

Fenton, J.C. (1963). *Saint Matthew (Pelican Gospel Commentaries).* Penguin Books, Harmondsworth.

Gelma, E. (1932). The transitory mutism of Zecharias: the relation of the condition to motor aphasia. *Paris Medicine.* 86. 237-241 (in French).

Goulder, M.D. (1974). *Midrash and Lection in Matthew.* SPCK, London.
_____. (1989), *Luke - A New Paradigm. (JSNTSS 20).* JSOT, Sheffield.

Harrell, D.E. Jr. (1975). *All Things are Possible: The Healing and Charismatic Revivals in Modern America.* Indiana University Press, Bloomington.

Harrington, D.J. (1991). *The Gospel of St Matthew (Sacra Pagina Vol 1).* Liturgical Press, Collegeville.

Havener, I. (1987). *The Sayings of Jesus: Good News Studies 19.* Glazier, Wilmington.

Heil, J.P. (1979). Significant aspects of the healing miraclers in Matthew. *Catholic Biblical Quarterly.* 41. 274-287.

Hemer, C.J. (1989). *The Book of Acts in the Setting of Hellenistic History (Wissenschaftliche Untersuchungen zum Neuen Testament: 49).* J.C.B. Mohr, Tübingen.

Hiers, R.H. (1974). Satan, demons and the kingdom of God. *Scottish Journal of Theology.* 27. 35-47
_____. (1985). 'Binding' and 'loosing': the Matthean authorizations (Matt 16:19; 18:18). *Journal of Biblical Literature.* 104. 233-250.

Hobart, W.K. (1892). *The Medical Language of St Luke.* Dublin University Press, Dublin.

Hull, J.M. (1974). *Hellenistic Magic and the Synoptic Tradition.* SCM, London.

Keck, L.E. and Martyn, J.L. (eds). *Studies in Luke-Acts.* SPCK, London.

Kidd, B., Mullee, M., Frank, A. (1988). Disease expression in ankylosing spondylitis in males and females. *Journal of Rheumatology* 15. 1407-1409.

Kingsbury, J.D. (1976). The title 'Son of David' in Matthew's gospel. *Journal of Biblical Literature.* 95. 591-602.

_____. (1991). *Conflict in Luke: Jesus, Authorities, Disciples.* Fortress Press, Minneapolis.

Kloppenborg, J.S.(1987). *The Formation of Q: Trajectories in Ancient Wisdom Collections.* Fortress, Philadelphia.

_____. (1988). *Q Parallels: Synopsis, Critical Notes and Concordance.* Polebridge Press, Sonoma, CA.

Koester, H. (1982). *Introduction to the New Testament. Vol 2: History and Literature of Early Christianity.* Walter de Gruyter, New York & Berlin .

_____. (1990). *Ancient Christian Gospels: Their History and Development.* SCM, London.

Linnemann, E. (1992). *Is There a Synoptic Problem? Rethinking the Literary Dependence of the First Three Gospels.* Baker, Grand Rapids.

Lloyd Davies, M. and Lloyd Davies, T.A. (1993). *The Bible: Medicine and Myth.* Silent Books, Cambridge. 3rd edn.

Lohse, E. (1981). *The Formation of the New Testament.* Abingdon, Nashville. ET.

M'Neile, A.H. (1915). *The Gospel according to Matthew.* Macmillan, London.

Meier, J..P. (1994). *A Marginal Jew: Rethinking the Historical Jesus. Vol 2.* Doubleday, New York.

Mack, B. (1993). *The Lost Gospel.* Collins San Francisco, San Francisco.

Marshall, I.H. (1978). *The Gospel of Luke (New International Greek Text Commentary).* Paternoster Press, Exeter.

_____. (1988). *Luke: Historian and Theologian.* Paternoster Press, Exeter. Third edn.

Metzger, B.M. (1958). Seventy or seventy-two disciples? *New Testament Studies.* 5. 299-306.

Meyer , B.F. (1979). *The Aims of Jesus.* SCM, London.

Moriarty, M. (1992). *The New Charismatics.* Zondervan, Grand Rapids.

Morris, L. (1992). *The Gospel according to Matthew.* Eerdmans, Grand Rapids.

Moule, C.F.D. (1959) *An Idiom Book of New Testament Greek.* Cambridge University Press, Cambridge. Second edn.

Parker, P. (1952). *The Gospel before Mark.* University of Chicago Press, Chicago.

Pilch, J.J. (1991). Sickness and healing in Luke-Acts. In: Neyrey, J.H. (ed). *The Social World of Luke-Acts.* Hendricksen, Peabody. MD. pp 181-209.

Pilowsky, I. (1997). *Abnormal Illness Behaviour.* Wiley, Chichester.

Plummer, A. (1915). *The Gospel according to St Luke (International Critical Commentary).* T & T Clark, Edinburgh. Fifth edn.

Reicke, B. (1986). *The Roots of the Synoptic Gospels.* Fortress, Philadelphia.

Robinson, J.A.T. (1976). *Redating the New Testament*. SCM, London.

Sanders, E.P. and Davies, M. (1989). *Studying the Synoptic Gospels*. SCM, London.

Schweizer, E. (1976). *The Good News according to Matthew*. SPCK, London. ET.

Short, A. Rendle. (1953). *The Bible and Modern Medicine*. Paternoster Press, London.

Siker, J.S. (1992). 'First to the gentiles': a literary analysis of Luke 4;16-30. *Journal of Biblical Literature*. 111. 73-90.

Streeter, B.H. (1930). *The Four Gospels: A Study of Origins*. Macmillan, London. Revised edn.

Stronstad, R. (1984). *The Charismatic Theology of St Luke*. Hendrickson, Peabody. MA.

Tannehill, R.C. (1986). *The Narrative Unity of Luke-Acts: A Literary Interpretation. Vol 1. The Gospel according to Luke*. Fortress Press, Philadelphia.

Thiede, C. and D'Ancona, M. (1996). *The Jesus Papyrus*. Weidenfeld and Nicolson, London

Turk, D.C. (1996). *Psychological Aspects of Pain*. Springhouse Press, Spring House, PA.

Turk, D.C. and Meichenbaum, D. (1994). A cognitive-behavioural approach to pain management. In: Wall, P.D. and Melzack, R. (eds). *A Textbook of Pain*. Churchill Livingstone, Edinburgh. 3rd edn. pp 1337-1348.

Turner, M. (1991). The Spirit and the power of Jesus' miracles in the Lucan conception. *Novum Testamentum*. 33. 124-152.

Turner, R.G. (1976). Hysterical blindness. In: Rose, F.C. (ed). *Medical Ophthalmology*. Chapman and Hall. London. pp 224-237.

Twelftree, G.H. (1985). *Christ Triumphant: Exorcism Then and Now*. Hodder and Stoughton, London.

_____. (1993) *Jesus the Exorcist: A Contribution to the Study of the Historical Jesus*. J.C.B.Mohr, Tübingen.

_____. (1999). *Jesus the Miracle Worker: A Historical and Theological Study*. IVP, Downers Grove, IL.

van der Linden, S. (1997). Ankylosing spondylitis. In: Kelley, W.N., Harris, E.D., Ruddy, S., Sledge, C.B. (eds). *Textbook of Rheumatology*. W.B. Saunders, Philadelphia. Fifth edn. p 978.

Wenham, J. (1991). *Redating Matthew, Mark and Luke: A Fresh Assault on the Synoptic Problem*. Hodder & Stoughton, London.

Wilkinson, J. (1977). The case of the bent woman in Luke 13:10-17. *Evangelical Quarterly*. 49. 195-205 = (1980) *Health and Healing: Studies in New Testament Principles and Practice*. Handsel Press, Edinburgh. pp 70-80.

Wright, N.T. (1996). *Jesus and the Victory of God*. SPCK, London.

Chapter 5: The Healing Ministry of Jesus: The Johannine Tradition

Barrett, C.K. (1978). *The Gospel according to St John: An Introduction with Commentary and Nortes on the Greek Text.* SPCK, London. Second edn.
_____. (1982). *Essays on John.* SPCK, London.

Beasley-Murray, G.R. (1987). *John (Word Biblical Commentary).* Word Books, Waco, Texas.

Bernard, J.H. (1928). *The Gospel according to St John (International Critical Commentary).* T & T Clark, Edinburgh..

Bligh, J. (1966). The man born blind. *Heythrop Journal.* 7. 129-144

Brodie, T.L. (1993). *The Quest for the Origin of John's Gospel.* Oxford University Press, New York.

Brown, R.E. (1965). The Qumran scrolls and the Johannine gospel and epistles. *New Testament Essays.* Paulist Press, New York.
_____. (1966, 1970), *The Gospel according to John (Anchor Bible).* 2 vols. Doubleday, New York.
_____. (1979). *The Community of the Beloved Disciple*, Paulist Press, New York.

Bruce, F.F. (1979). *Men and Movements in the Primitive Church.* Paternoster Press, Exeter.

Burge, G.M. (1987). *The Anointed Community: The Holy Spirit in the Johannine Tradition.* Eerdmans, Grand Rapids.

Carroll, K.L. (1957). The Fourth Gospel and the exclusion of Christians from the synagogue. *Bulletin of the John Rylands Library.* 40. 19-32.

Cassidy, R.J. (1992). *John's Gospel in New Perspective.* Orbis Books, Maryknoll.

Charlesworth, J.H. (ed). (1972). *John and Qumran.* Chapman, London

Dodd, C.H. (1953). *The Interpretation of the Fourth Gospel.* Cambridge University Press, Cambridge.
_____. (1963). *Historical Tradition in the Fourth Gospel.* Cambridge University Press, Cambridge.

Fortna, R.T. (1988).*The Fourth Gospel and its Predecessor.* T&T Clark, Edinburgh.

Fuller, R.H. (1963). *Interpreting the Miracles.* SCM, London. p 105.

Harvey, A.E. (1982). *Jesus and the Constraints of History.* SCM, London.

Horbury, W. (1982). The benediction of the *minim* and early Jewish-Christian controversy. *Journal of Theological Studies.* 33. 19-61

Hoskyns, E.C. and Davey, F.N. (1947). *The Fourth Gospel.* Faber and Faber, London. Second edn.

Latourelle, R. (1988). *The Miracles of Jesus and the Theology of Miracles.* Paulist Press, New York.

Lindars, B. (1971). *Behind the Fourth Gospel.* SPCK, London.
_____. (1972). *The Gospel of John (New Century Bible Commentary).* Marshall, Morgan & Scott, London.
_____. (1981). John and the synoptic gospels: a test case. *New Testament Studies.* 27. 287-294.

_____. (1992). Rebuking the spirit: A new analysis of the Lazarus story of John 11. *New Testament Studies*. 38. 89-104.

Martyn, J.L. (1979). *History and Theology in the Fourth Gospel*. Abingdon, Nashville. Rev. edn.

Martyn, L.J (1992). Pediatric ophthalmology. In: Behrman, R.E., Kliegman, R.M., Nelson, E.W., Vaughan III, V.C. (eds). *Nelson Textbook of Pediatrics*. 14th edn. pp 1578-1579.

Meeks, W. (1972). The man from heaven in Johannine sectarianism. *Journal of Biblical Literature*. 91. 44-72.

Meier, J.P. (1994). *A Marginal Jew: Rethinking the Historical Jesus.* Vol 2. Doubleday, New York. Vol 1.

Metzger, B.M. (1971). *A Textual Commentary on the New Testament*. United Bible Societies, New York.

Morris, L. (1969). *Studies in the Fourth Gospel*. Paternoster Press, Exeter.

Neirynck, F. (1977). John and the Synoptics. In: de Jonge, M. (ed). *L'Evangile de Jean: Sources, Rédaction, Théologie*. Louvain, Leuven University. pp 73-106.

_____. (1984), John 4. 46-54: Signs source and/or synoptic gospels. *Ephemerides Theologicae Lovaniensis*. 60. 367-375.

Richardson, A. (1941). *The Miracle Stories of the Gospels*. SPCK, London.

Robinson, J.A.T. (1985). *The Priority of John*. SCM, London.

Schnackenburg, R. (1968, 1980, 1982). *The Gospel according to St John*. 3 vols. Burns and Oates, London. ET

Scobie, C.H.H. (1982). Johannine geography. *Studies in Religion*. 11. 77-84.

Smalley, S.S. (1978). *John: Evangelist and Interpreter*. Paternoster Press, Exeter.

Thompson, M.M. (1988). *The Incarnate Word: Perspectives on Jesus in the Fourth Gospel*. Hendricksen, Peabody. MA.

Vaughan, D. Asbury, T. (1983). *General Ophthalmology*. Lange, Los Altos,

Vermes, G. (1983). *Jesus the Jew*. SCM, London. 2nd edn.

Wilkinson, J. (1966). A study of healing in the gospel according to John. *Scottish Journal of Theology*. 19. 442-461.

Wright, N.T. (1996). *Jesus and the Victory of God*. SPCK, London.

Chapter 6: Healing in the Early Church: The Witness of Acts

Adams, M.M. (1993). The role of miracles in the structure of Luke-Acts. In: Stump, E. and Flint, T.P. (eds). *Hermes and Athena: Biblical Exegesis and Philosophical Theology*. University of Notre Dame Press, Notre Dame IN. pp 235-272;

Barrett, C.K. (1994, 1999). *The Acts of the Apostles (International Critical Commentary)*. 2 vols..T & T Clark, Edinburgh.

Bruce, F.F. (1952). *The Acts of the Apostles: The Greek Text with Introduction and Commentary*. Tyndale Press, London. Second edn.

_____. (1988). *The Acts of the Apostles (New International Commentary*

on the New Testament). Eerdmans, Grand Rapids.

_____. (1990). *The Acts of the Apostles: Greek Text with Introduction and Commentary.* Eerdmans, Grand Rapids. Third edn.

Cadbury, H.J. (1933). The summaries in Acts. In: Cadbury, H.J. and Lake, K. (eds). *The Beginnings of Christianity.* Macmillan, London. Vol 5. pp 392-402.

Cansdale, G. (1970). *Animals of Bible Lands.* Paternoster Press, Exeter.

Case, S.J. (1946). *Christian Supernaturalism.* University of Chicago Press, Chicago.

Fitzmeyer, J.A. (1968). Jewish Christianity in Acts in the light of the Qumran scrolls. *Studies in Luke-Acts.* p 237.

Fletcher, R. (1997). *The Conversion of Europe from Paganism to Christianity: AD 371-1386.* Harper Collins, London.

Foakes-Jackson, F.J. (1931). *The Acts of the Apostles (Moffatt New Testament Commentaries).* Hodder and Stoughton, London.

Ford, J.M. (1988). The social and political implications of the miraculous in Acts. In: Elbert, P. (ed). *Faces of Renewal: Studies in Honor of Stanley M. Horton presented on his Seventieth Birthday.* Hendricksen. Peabody. MA. pp 137-160;

German, G.A. (1972). Psychiatry. In: Shaper, A.G., Kibukamasoke, J.W. and Hutt, M.S.R. (eds). *Medicine in a Tropical Environment.* British Medical Association, London. pp 329-347.

Guthrie, D. (1990). *New Testament Introduction.* Inter-Varsity Press, Leicester. Fourth edn.

Haenchen, E. (1968). The book of Acts as source material for the history of early Christianity. In: Keck, L.E. and Martyn, J.L. (eds). *Studies in Luke-Acts.* SPCK, London.

_____. (1971). *The Acts of the Apostles.* Blackwell, Oxford. ET.

Harnack, A. (1907). *Luke the Physician.* London, Williams and Norgate. ET.

Hemer, C.J. (1975). Euraquilo and Melita. *Journal of Theological Studies.* 26. 100-111.

_____. (1989). *The Book of Acts in the Setting of Hellenistic History.* J.C.B. Mohr, Tübingen.

Hengel, M. (1983). *Between Jesus and Paul.* SCM, London. ET.

Hennecke, E. and Schneemelcher, W. (1974). *New Testament Apocrypha.* SCM, London

Hobart, W.K. (1882). *The Medical Language of St Luke.* Dublin University Press, Dublin..

Hull, J.M. (1974. *Hellenistic Magic and the Synoptic Tradition.* SCM, London.

Jeremias, J. (1969) *Jerusalem in the Time of Jesus.* SCM, London. ET.

Kelly, W. (1914). *An Exposition of the Acts of the Apostles.* F.E. Race, London. Second edn.

Lampe, G.W.H. (1965). Miracles in the Acts of the Apostles. In: Moule, C.F.D. (ed). *Miracles: Cambridge Studies in their Philosophy and History.* Mowbray, London. pp 165-178

Lindars, B. (1968). Elijah, Elisha and the gospel miracles. In: Moule, C.F.D.

(ed). *Miracles: Cambridge Studies in their Philosophy and History.*
Mowbray, London. pp 63-79

Lloyd Davies, M., Loyd Davies, T.A. (1993). *The Bible: Medicine & Myth.*
Silent Books, Cambridge. Second edn.

Lüdemann, G. (1989). *Early Christianity according to the Tradition in Acts.*
Fortress Press, Minneapolis.

Madkour, M.M. (1996). Brucellosis. In: Weatherall, D.J., Leadingham, J.G.J.,
Warrell, D.A. (eds). *Oxford Textbook of Medicine.* Oxford University
Press, Oxford. pp 612-623.

Mayer Gross, W., Slater, E. and Roth, M. (1960). *Clinical Psychiatry.* Cassell,
London.

Menoud, P.H. (1954). Le plan des Actes des Apôtres. *New Testament Studies.*
1. 44-51.

Miller, R.J. (1988). Elijah, John and Jesus in the gospel of Luke. *New
Testament Studies.* 34. 611-622.

Pilch, J.J. (1991). Sickness and healing in Luke-Acts. In: Neyrey, J.H. (ed). *The
Social World of Luke-Acts.* Hendricksen, Peabody. MD. pp 181-209.

Robinson, J.M. (1988). (ed). *The Nag Hammadi Library in English.* Harper
Collins, San Francisco/E.J. Brill, Leiden. third edn.

Schweizer, E. (1981). *The Holy Spirit.* SCM, London.

Short, A. Rendle. (1953). *The Bible and Modern Medicine.* Paternoster Press,
London.

Skirrow, M.D. (1996). Enteropathogenic bacteria. *Oxford Textbook of
Medicine.* pp 550-560.

Smith, C.C. (1991). Peter, Saint. In: *St James Guide to Biography.* St James
Press, Chicago. pp 620-622.

Torrance, T.F. (1948). *The Doctrine of Grace in the Apostolic Fathers.* T&T
Clark, Edinburgh.

Trebilco, P. (1989). Paul and Silas - 'servants of the most high God'. *Journal
for the Study of the New Testament.* 36. 51-73.

Turner, M. (1991). The Spirit and the power of Jesus' miracles in the Lucan
conception. *Novum Testamentum.* 33. 124-152.

Twelftree, G. (1985). *Christ Triumphant: Exorcism Then and Now.* Hodder and
Stoughton, London.

van der Horst, P. (1989). Hellenistic parallels to Acts (Chapters 3 and 4).
Journal for the Study of the New Testament. 35. 37-46.

Wilkinson, J. (1980). *Health and Healing: Studies in New Testament Principles
and Practice.* Handsel Press, Edinburgh.

Witherington, B. (1998). *The Acts of the Apostles: A Socio-Rhetorical
Commentary.* Eerdmans, Grand Rapids.

Ziesler, J.A. (1979). The name of Jesus in the Acts of the Apostles. *Journal for
the Study of the New Testament.* 4. 28-41.

Chapter 7: Healing in the Early Church: The Witness of the New Testament Letters

Alexander, W.M. (1904). St Paul's infirmity. *Expository Times.* 15. 469-473 and 545-548.

Altschule, M.D. (1967). The two kinds of depression according to St Paul. *British Journal of Psychiatry.* 113. 779-780.

Anon (Annotation). (1978). Paul's blindness re-evaluated. *Journal of the American Medical Association.* 240. 98

Armerding, C. (1958). Is any among you afflicted? A study of James 5:13-20. *Bibliotheca Sacra.* 95. 195-201

Avalos, H. (1999). *Health Care and the Rise of Christianity.* Hendickson, Peabody, MA.

Baker, J.P. (1973). *Salvation and Wholeness: Biblical Perspectives of Healing.* Fountain Trust, Eastbourne

Balch, D. (1981). *Let Wives be Submissive: The Domestic Code in 1 Peter.* Scholars Press, Chico, CA.

Barrett, C.K. (1973). *The Second Epistle to the Corinthians (Black's NT Commentaries).* A & C Black, London. second edition.

_____. (1994). *A Critical and Exegetical Commentary on the Acts of the Apostles.* T&T Clark, Edinburgh.

Bear, D., Fedio, P. (1977). Quantitative analysis of interictal behaviour in temporal lobe epilepsy. *Archives of Neurology.* 34. 454-467.

Betz, H.D. (1979). *Galatians: A Commentary on Paul's Epistle to the Churches in Galatia.* Hermeneia, Philadelphia.

Bittlinger, A. (1974). *Gifts and Ministries: A Commentary on 1 Corinthians 12-14.* Hodder & Stoughton, London

Bornkamm, G. (1971). *Paul.* Hodder and Stoughton, London. ET.

Bowker, J.W. (1971). 'Merkabah' visions and the visions of Paul. *Journal of Semitic Studies.* 16. 157-173.

Brown, M.L. (1995). *Israel's Divine Healer.* Paternoster Press, Carlisle

Brown, R.E. (1980). Episkope and episkopos: the New Testament evidence. *Theological Studies.* 41. 322-339

Bruce, F.F. (1963). *The Epistle of Paul to the Romans.* Tyndale Press, London

_____. (1977). *Paul: Apostle of the Free Spirit.* Paternoster Press, Exeter

_____. (1982). *The Epistle of Paul to the Galatians (New International Greek Testament Commentary).* Paternoster Press, Exeter.

_____. (1990). *The Acts of the Apostles: Greek Text with Introduction and Commentary.* Eerdmans, Grand Rapids. third edn.

Bullock, J.D. (1978). The blindness of St Paul. *Ophthalmology* 85. 1044-1053.

_____. (1994), Was St Paul struck blind and converted by lightning? *Survey Ophthalmology.* 39. 151-160

Burkitt, F.C. (1924), *Christian Beginnings.* University of London Press, London.

C.C. Smith (1991) 'Paul', In: Schellinger, P.E. (ed). *St James Guide to Biography.* St James, Press, Chicago. pp 613-615.

Calvin, J. (1834=1539). *Commentary on the Epistle to the Romans.* Translated by F. Sibson, Seeley and Sons, London.

Church of England Review Group. (2000). *A Time to Heal: A Contribution towards the Ministry of Healing.* Church House, London.

Clarke, W.K.L. (1929). *New Testament Problems.* SPCK, London.

Cranfield, C.E.B. (1975, 1979). *Critical and Exegetical Commentary on the Epistle to the Romans (International Critical Commentary).* 2 vols. T&T Clark, Edinburgh.

_____. (1985). *Romans: A Shorter Commentary.* T&T Clark, Edinburgh.

Davids, P.H. (1982) *A Commentary on James (New International Greek Testament Commentary).* Eerdmans, Grand Rapids.

Dumeige, G. (1972). Le Christ médicin dans la litérature chrétienne des premiers siècles. *Rivisita di Archeologia Cristiana.* 47. 115-141.

Dunn, J.D.G. (1974). *Jesus and the Spirit.* SCM, London

_____. (1988). *Romans (Word Biblical Commentary).* 2 vols. Word Books, Waco, Texas.

Dupont, J. (1970). The conversion of Paul and its influence on his understanding of salvation by faith. In: Gasque, W.W. and Martin, R.P. (eds). *Apostolic History and the Gospel: Biblical and Historical Essays presented to F.F. Bruce.* Paternoster Press, Exeter. pp 176-194.

Elliott, J.H. (1981). *A Home for the Homeless: A Sociological Exegesis of 1 Peter, Its Situation and Strategy.* Fortress Press, Philadelphia

Fee, G.D. (1987). *The First Epistle to the Corinthians (New International Commentary on the New Testament).* Eerdmans, Grand Rapids.

Ferngren, G.B. (1992). Early Christianity as a religion of healing. *Bulletin of the History of Medicine.* 66. 1-15.

Flood, E. (1989). *All is Ours: Paul's Message to all Christians.* Fount Paperbacks, London.

Foot, D.R.P. (1967). *Divine Healing and the Scriptures.* Henry Walters, Eastbourne, U.K

Forbes, C. (1986). Comparison, self-praise and irony: Paul's boasting and the conventions of Hellenistic rhetoric. *New Testament Studies.* 32: 1-30.

Frend, W.H.C. (1996). *The Archaeology of Early Christianity: A History.* Geoffrey Chapman, London.

Fung, R.Y.K. (1988), *The Epistle to the Galatians (New International Commentary on the New Testament).* Eerdmans, Grand Rapids.

Gelder M, Gath D, Mayou R (eds). (1990). *The Oxford Textbook of Psychiatry.* Oxford University Press, Oxford.

Giles, K. (1989). *Patterns of Ministry among the First Christians.* Collins Dove, Melbourne.

Gobel, H. Isler, H. Hasenfrantz, H.P. (1995). Headache classification and the Bible: Was St Paul's thorn in the flesh migraine? *Cephalgia.* 15. 180-181.

Goppelt, L. (1993). *A Commentary on 1 Peter.* Eerdmans, Grand Rapids.

Greig, G.S. and Springer, K.N. (eds). (1993). *The Kingdom and the Power.* Regal Books, Ventura, CA

Greyson, B. (1993). Varieties of near death experience. *Psychiatry.* 56. 390-

399.

Gusmer, C.W. (1984). *And you Visted Me: A Sacramental Ministry to the Sick and the Dying.* Pueblo Publishing. New York.

Guthrie, D. (1990). *New Testament Introduction.* Apollos, Leicester. 4th edn.

Haenchen, E. (1971). *Acts of the Apostles.* Blackwell, Oxford.

Hamm, D. (1990). Paul's blindness and its healing: clues to symbolic intent (Acts 9, 22 and 26). *Biblica* 71. 63-72.

Harnack, A. (1904). *The Expansion of Christianity in the First Three Centuries.* Putnam's, New York. ET. Vol 1.

Harper, M. (1965). *As at the Beginning.* Hodder and Stoughton, London

Hawthorne, G.F. and Martin, R.P. (eds). (1993). *Dictionary of Paul and his Letters.* Inter-Varsity Press, Downers Grove, IL.

Hayden, D.R. (1981). Calling the elders to pray. *Bibliotheca Sacra.* 138. 258-266.

Hemer, C.J. (1980). Observations on Pauline chronology. In: Hager, D.J. and Harris, M.J. (eds). *Pauline Studies.* Paternoster Press, Exeter. pp 3-18.

_____. (1986). Medicine in the New Testament world. In: Palmer B (ed). *Medicine and the Bible,* Paternoster Press, Exeter. pp 78-80.

_____. (1986). *The Letters to the Seven Churches of Asia in their Local Setting.* Sheffield Academic Press (JSOT Press), Sheffield.

_____. (1990). *The Book of Acts in the Setting of Hellenistic History.* Eisenbrauns, Winona Lake.

Hennecke, E., Schneemelcher, W., Wilson, R.McL. (eds). (1965). *The New Testament Apocrypha.* Lutterworth, London. ET.

Hill, D. (1972). Prophecy and prophets in the Revelation of St John. *New Testament Studies.* 18. 405-406.

Hobart, W.K. (1882). *The Medical Language of St Luke.* Dublin University Press, Dublin.

Jennett, W.B. (1970). *Epilepsy after Non-missile Head Injuries.* Heinemann, London.

_____. (1982). Post-traumatic epilepsy. In: Laidlaw J and Richens A. (eds). *A Textbook of Epilepsy.* Churchill Livingstone, Edinburgh. second edn.

Jowett, R. (1979). *Dating Paul's Life.* SCM, London

Judge, E.A. (1968). Paul's boasting in relation to contemporary professional practice. *Australian Biblical Review.* 16. 37-50.

Käsemann, E. (1964). Ministry and community in the New Testament. In: *Essays on New Testament Themes.* SCM, London.

_____. (1980). *Commentary on Romans.* Eerdmans, Grand Rapids. ET.

Kelly, J.N.D. (1969). *A Commentary on the Epistles of Peter and Jude (Black's New Testament Commentaries).* A & C Black, London.

Kiddle, M. (1940). *The Revelation of St John (Moffat New Testament Commentary).* Hodder and Stoughton, London.

Kümmel, W.G. (1975). *Introduction to the New Testament.* ET. SCM, London.

Landsborough, D. (1987). St Paul and temporal lobe epilepsy. *Journal of Neurology, Neurosurgery and Psychiatry.* 50. 659-664.

Lane, W.L. (1991). *Hebrews. (Word Biblical Commentary)*. 2 vols. Word Books, Waco, Texas.

Levin, S. (1963). St Paul's sickness. *Medical Proceedings*. 9. 264-265.

Liwak, K.D. (1983). The use of quotations from Isaiah 52:13-53:12 in the New Testament. *Journal of the Evangelical Theological Society*. 26. 385-394.

Lloyd-Davies, M. and Lloyd-Davies, T.A. (1991). *The Bible: Medicine and Myth*. Silent Books. Cambridge. second edn.

Lüdemann, G. (1984). *Paul, Apostle to the Gentiles: Studies in Chronology*. SCM. London

_____. (1989). *Early Christianity according to the Traditions in Acts*. SCM, London.

Lydahl, E., Philipson, B T. (1984). Infrared radiation and cataract. *Acta Ophthalmologica,* 62. 961-975 and 976-992.

MacArthur Jr, J.F. (1992). *Charismatic Chaos*. Zondervan, Grand Rapids.

Manchester, P.T. and Manchester, P.T. Jr. (1972). The blindness of St Paul. *Archives of Ophthalmology*. 88. 316-321.

Manson-Bahr, Sir Philip H. (1960) *Manson's Tropical Diseases*. Cassell, London. 15th edn.

Marshall, P. (1983). A metaphor of social shame: ΘΡΙΑΜΒΕΥΕΙΝ in 2 Cor. 2:14. *Novum Testamentum*. 25. 302-317.

Martin, R.P. (1984). *The Spirit and the Congregation: Studies in 1 Corinthians 12-15*. Eerdmans, Grand Rapids

_____. (1986). *2 Corinthians (Word Biblical Commentary)*. Word Books, Waco, Texas.

_____. (1987). *James. (Word Biblical Commentary)*. Word Books, Waco, Texas.

Mayor, J.B. (1910). *The Epistle of St James*. Macmillan, London. 3rd edn.

McCrossan, T. J. (1982). *Bodily Healing and the Atonement*. Faith Library, Tulsa.

Norman R. (1987). Pathogenesis of temporal lobe epilepsy. In: Ounsted C. Lindsay J., Richards P. (eds). *Temporal Lobe Epilepsy, 1948-1986: A Biographical Study*. Clinics in Developmental Medicine No. 103. Blackwell, Oxford. p 101.

Nutton, V. (1985). Murders and miracles: Lay attitudes towards medicine in classical antiquity. In: Porter, R. (ed). *Patients and Practitioners: Lay Perceptions of Medicine in Pre-Industrial Society*. Cambridge University Press, Cambridge.

Ogg, G. (1968). *The Chronology of the Life of Paul*. Epworth, London.

Paton, D and Goldberg, M.F. (1976). *Management of Ocular Injuries*. W.B. Saunders, Philadelphia.

Pearson, B.A. (1973). *The Pneumatikos-Psychikos Terminology in 1 Corinthians*. Scholars Press, Missoula.

Plummer, A. (1915). *The Second Epistle of St Paul to the Corinthians (International Critical Commentary)*. T & T Clarke, Edinburgh.

Pryse-Phillips, W. and Murray, T.J. (1986). *Essential Neurology*. Elsevier, New York. third edn.

Ramsay, Sir W.M. (1893). *The Church in the Roman Empire*, Hodder & Stoughton, London.

_____. (1895). *The Cities and Bishoprics of Phrygia*. Clarendon Press, Oxford.

_____. (1899). *A Historical Commentary on the Epistle to the Galatians.* Hodder and Stoughton, London.

_____. (1904). *The Letters to the Seven Churches of Asia.* Hodder and Stoughton, London.

Ridderbos, H.N. (1975). *Paul: An Outline of his Theology*. Eerdmans, Grand Rapids.

Rieu, E.V. (1957). *The Acts of the Apostles*. Penguin, Harmondsworth.

Rutherford, W.J. (1935). Hippocratic allusion in the New Testament. *Glasgow Medical Journal.* 14. 71-74.

Schaefer, P. (1984). New Testament and Hekhalot literature: The journey into heaven in Paul and in Merkevah mysticism. *Journal of Jewish Studies.* 35. 19-35.

Schatzmann, S. (1986). *A Pauline Theology of Charismata*. Hendrickson, Peabody, MA

Schweizer, E. (1961). *Church Order in the New Testament*. SCM, London. ET.

Scobie, C.H.H. (1993). Local references in the letters to the seven churches. *New Testament Studies.* 39. 606-624.

Segal, A.F. (1990). *Paul the Convert: The Apostolate and Apostasy of Paul the Pharisee*. Yale University Press, New Haven.

Shogren, G.A. (1989). Will God heal us? *Evangelical Quarterly.* 61. 99-108.

Shorvon, S.D. (1984). The temporal aspects of prognosis in epilepsy. *Journal of Neurology, Neurosurgery and Psychiatry.* 47. 1157-1165.

Stanley, D.M. (1953). Paul's conversion in Acts: Why the three accounts? *Catholic Biblical Quarterly.* 315-338.

Sumney, J.L. (1990). *Identifying Paul's Opponents: The Question of Method in 2 Corinthians (JSNT Supplement No 40).* JSOT Press, Sheffield.

Tabor, J.D. (1986). *Things Unutterable: Paul's Ascent to Paradise in its Greco-Roman, Judaic and Early Christian Contexts.* University Press of America, Lanham, MD.

Talbot, C.H. (1987). *Reading Corinthians: A Literary and Theological Commentary on 1 and 2 Corinthians.* Crossroad, New York.

Tasker, R.V.G. (1956). *The General Epistle of James*. Tyndale Press, London.

Thomas, J.C. (1993). The devil, disease and deliverance: James 5:14-16. *Journal of Pentecostal Theology.* 2. 25-50.

Vaughan, D., Astbury, T., and Tabbara, K.F. (eds) (1989). *General Ophthalmology.* Appleton and Lange, Norwalk, Connecticut.

Vercelletto, P. (1994). St Paul's illness: ecstasy and ecstatic seizure (in French). *Revue Neurologique.* 150. 835-839.

Vermes. G. (1981). *The Dead Sea Scrolls: Qumran in Perspective.* Revised edn. Fortress Press, Philadelphia.

Vouga, F. (1984). *L'Épitre de s. Jacques (Commentaire du Nouveau Testament).* Labor et Fides. Geneva.

Warrington, K. (1993). Anointing with oil and healing. *European Pentecostal Theological Association Bulletin.* 12. 5-22.

Waxman, S. and Geschwind, N. (1975). The inter-ictal behaviour syndrome of temporal lobe epilepsy. *Archives of General Psychiatry.* 32. 1580-1586.

Wilkinson, J. (1971). Healing in the epistle of James. *Scottish Journal of Theology.* 24. 326-345.

_____. (1980). *Health and Healing: Studies in New Testament Principles and Practice.* Handsel Press, Edinburgh.

Wrede, W. (1907). *Paul.* P. Green, London. ET.

Wright, F.J. (1991). Healing: an interpretation of James 5:13-20. *Journal of the Christian Medical Fellowship.* 37 (1). 20-21.

Chapter 8: Drawing the Ends Together

Amundsen, D.W. (1982). Medicine and faith in early Christianity. *Bulletin of the History of Medicine.* 56. 326-350

_____. (1996). *Medicine, Society and Faith in the Ancient and Medieval Worlds.* Johns Hopkins University Press, Baltimore

Avalos, H. (1999). *Health Care and the Rise of Christianity.* Hendricksen, Peabody, MA.

Barrett-Lennard, R.J.S. (1994). *Christian Healing after the New Testament: Some Approaches to Illness in the Second, Third and Fourth Centuries.* University Press of America, Washington, DC.

Brown, C (1984). *Miracles and the Critical Mind.* Grand Rapids, Eerdmans.

Brown, P. (1971a). *The World of late Antiquity:AD 150-750.* Harcourt Brace, New York.

_____. (1971b). The rise and function of the holy man in late antiquity. *Journal of Roman Studies.* 61. 80-101.

Burkill, T.A. (1973). Miraculous healing in the gospels. *Central African Journal of Medicine.* 19. 99-100.

Case, S.J. (1923). The art of healing in early Christian times. *Journal of Religion.* 3. 238-255.

_____. (1929). *Experience with the Supernatural in Early Christian Times.* Century, New York.

_____. (1946). *The Origins of Christian Supernaturalism.* University of Chicago Press, Chicago.

Church of England Review Group, (2000). *A Time to Heal: A Contribution towards the Ministry of Healing.* Church House, London.

Crimlisk, H, Bhatra, K, Cope, H. et al. (1998). Slater revisited: 6 year follow up of patients with medically unexplained motor symptoms. *British Medical Journal.* 316. 582-586

Davies, S.L. (1995). *Jesus the Healer: Possession, Trance and the Origins of Christianity.* Continuum, New York/SCM, London.

Dunn, J.G.D. (1975). *Jesus and the Spirit.* SCM, London.

Dunn, J.G.D. and Twelftree, G.H. (1980). Demon possession and exorcism in the New Testament. *Churchman.* 94. 210-225.

Edelstein, E.J. and Edelstein, L (1975=1945). *Asclepius: A Collection and Interpretation of the Testimonies.* (Arno Press, New York). 2 Vols.

Edmunds, V., Scorer, C.G. (1979). *Some Thoughts on Faith Healing.* Tyndale Press, London. Third edn.

Ferngren, G.B. (1988). The organisation of the care of the sick in early Christianity. In: Schadewaldt, H and Leve, K-H. (eds). *Proceedings of the XXX International Conference of the History of Medicine.* Vicom KG, Dusseldorf. pp 192-198.

_____. (1992). Early Christianity as a religion of healing. *Bulletin of the History of Medicine.* 66. 1-15.

Frank, J.D. (1972). Common features of psychotherapy. *Australian and New Zealand Journal of Psychiatry.* 6. 34-40.

Funk, R.W. (1996). *Honest to Jesus: Jesus for a New Millennium.* Hodder & Stoughton, London.

Grudem, W. (1993). Should Christians expect miracles today? In: Greig, G.S. and Springer, K.N. (eds). *The Kingdom and the Power.* Regal Books, Ventura, CA.

Harnack, A. (1904). *The Expansion of Christianity in the First Three Centuries.* (translated and edited by James Moffatt). Putnam, New York. Vol 1.

Hopkins, K. (1998). Christian number and its implications. *Journal of Early Christian Studies.* 6. 161-267.

Howard, J Keir. (1991). In the eye of the beholder: an approach to the healings of Jesus. *Journeyings.* 4 (2): 7-13

_____. (1996). Is healing ever 'miraculous'? *Stimulus: The New Zealand Journal of Christian Thought and Practice.* 4(2). 7-13.

Lampe, G.W.H. (1965). Miracles in the Acts of the Apostles. In: Moule, C.F.D. (ed). *Miracles: Cambridge Studies in their Philosophy and History.* Mowbray, London.

McMullen, R. (1984). *Christianizing the Roman Empire.* Yale University Press, New Haven.

Meier, J. (1994), *A Marginal Jew: Rethinking the Historical Jesus. Vol 2 Mentor, Message and Miracles.* Doubleday, New York.

Micklem, E.R. (1922). *Miracles and the New Psychology.* Oxford University Press, Oxford

Numbers, R.L. and Amundsen, D.W. (eds). (1986). *Caring and Curing: Health and Medicine in the Western Religious Tradition.* Johns Hopkins University Press, Baltimore.

Nutton, V. (1984). From Galen to Alexander: Aspects of medicine and medical practice in late antiquity. In: Scarborough, J. (ed). *Symposium on Byzantine Medicine. Dumbarton Oaks Papers No 38.* Dumbarton Oaks, Washington DC.

_____. (1985). Murders and Miracles: Lay attitudes to medicine in classical antiquity. In: Porter, R. (ed). *Patients and Practitioners: Lay Perceptions of Medicine in Pre-Industrial Society.* Cambridge University Press, Cambridge.

O'Brien, M.D. (1998). Medically unexplained neurological symptoms. *British Medical Journal.* 316. 564-565.

Perkins, J. (1995). *The Suffering Self: Pain and Narrative Representation in the Early Christian Era.* Routledge, London.

Pilowsky, Issy. (1997). *Abnormal Illness Behaviour.* Wiley, Colchester.

Scorer, C.G. (1979). *Healing: Biblical, Medical and Pastoral..* Christian Medical Fellowship, London.

Sheils, W.J. (ed). (1982). *The Church and Healing.* Blackwell, Oxford.

Thiessen, G. (1983). *Miracle Stories in the Early Christian Tradition.* T & T Clark, Edinburgh.

Turner, G. (1991). Healing in church services. *Journal of the Christian Medical Fellowship.* 37(2). 7-9.

van der Meer, F. (1961). *Augustine the Bishop: The Life and Work of a Father of the Church.* Sheed and Ward, London. ET.

Wagner, C.P. (1988). *The Third Wave of the Holy Spirit.* Servant, Ann Arbor, MI

Warfield, B.B. (1918=1972). *Counterfeit Miracles.* Banner of Truth, London.

Waterson, A.P. (1957). Faith healing and faith healers. *Theology.* 60. 8-16.

Weatherhead, L. (1951). *Psychology, Religion and Healing.* Hodder and Stoughton, London.

White, J. (1992). *When the Spirit Comes with Power.* InterVarsity Press, Downers Grove, IL. Revised edn.

Willingale, A.E. (1968). Can we recognise a miracle? *Faith and Thought.* 97. 52-58.

Wimber, J. (1986). *Power Evangelism.* Hodder & Stoughton, London
_____. (1987). *Power Healing.* Hodder & Stoughton, London

Wright, N.T. (1996). *Jesus and the Victory of God.* SPCK, London.

INDEXES

BIBLICAL INDEX

Old Testament

GENERAL INDEX